D1450216

Sister Saints

Sister Saints

by

Vicky Burgess-Olson

Volume Five of the Series
Studies in Mormon History

James B. Allen, Editor

Brigham Young University Press

Library of Congress Cataloging in Publication Data

Burgess-Olson, Vicky, 1945–
  Sister saints.

  (Mormon history series)
  Includes bibliographical references.
  1. Mormons and Mormonism—Biography.   2. Women—
United States—Biography.   I. Title.
BX8693.B87   289.3'3   [B]   78-5080

ISBN 0-8425-1235-7

Brigham Young University Press, Provo, Utah 84602
  © 1978 by Brigham Young University Press. All rights reserved
Printed in the United States of America
5M 3/78 30806

Contents

Preface   vii

The Eliza Enigma: The Life and Legend of Eliza R. Snow   1
    Maureen Ursenbach Beecher
    Used by permission from *Dialogue* and the Charles Redd
    Center for Western Studies, Brigham Young University

Sarah Melissa Granger Kimball: The Liberal Shall Be Blessed   21
    Jill Mulvay Derr
    Used by permission of the Utah State Historical Society

Louisa Barnes Pratt: Missionary Wife, Missionary Mother,
    Missionary   43
    Ann Gardner Stone

Susa Young Gates: The Thirteenth Apostle   61
    Rebecca Foster Cornwall

Amy Brown Lyman: Raising the Quality of Life for All   95
    Loretta L. Hefner

Susanna Goudin Cardon: An Italian Convert to Mormonism   119
    Louise Degn

Lucinda Lee Dalton: A Tough Kind of Testimony   139
    Lavina Fielding Anderson

Jane Snyder Richards: The Blue-White Diamond   173
    Connie Duncan Cannon

Bathsheba Bigler Smith: Woman of Faith and Courage   201
    Barbara Fluckiger Watt

Aurelia Read Spencer Rogers: Humble Heroine   223
    Elizabeth Kohler Ritchie

The Two Miss Cooks: Pioneer Professionals for Utah's Schools   242
    Jill Mulvay Derr

Maud May Babcock: "Understand the Thought, Hold the Thought,
    Give the Thought"   261
    Ann Gardner Stone

Alice Louise Reynolds: A Woman's Woman   275
    Reba Keele

Stena Scorup: First Lady of Salina   289
    Vicky Burgess-Olson

Patty Bartlett Sessions: More Than a Midwife   303
    Susan Sessions Rugh

Dr. Ellen Brooke Ferguson: Nineteenth-Century Renaissance
    Woman   325
    Ann Gardner Stone

Dr. Romania Pratt Penrose: To Brave the World   341
    Christine Croft Waters
Dr. Ellis Reynolds Shipp: Pioneer Utah Physician   363
    Gail Farr Casterline
Dr. Martha Hughes Cannon: Doctor, Wife, Legislator, Exile   383
    Jean Bickmore White
Dr. Margaret Ann Freece: Entrepreneur of Southern Utah   399
    Vicky Burgess-Olson
Sarah Elizabeth Carmichael: Poetic Genius of Pioneer Utah   415
    Miriam Brinton Murphy
    Used by permission of the Utah State Historical Society
Louisa Lula Greene Richards: "Remember the Women of Zion"   433
    Carol Cornwall Madsen
Emmeline Blanche Woodward Wells: "I Have Risen Triumphant"   455
    Patricia Rasmussen Eaton-Gadsby and Judith Rasmussen
    Dushku
Augusta Joyce Crocheron: A Representative Woman   481
    Judith Rasmussen Dushku and Patricia Rasmussen Eaton-Gadsby

Preface

Sister Saints they were, bound together both by gender and baptismal covenants. But the resemblance ended there. They were people from all classes, as varied as we are today: doctors, lawyers, farmers, businesswomen, educators, administrators, novelists, poets, journalists, editors, and politicians. They were polygamous, monogamous, and single. Each contributed in her own way to nation, state (territory), community, church, and family. They were individuals with their own commitments, living in the past and heralding the future.

Popular history has long neglected the contribution of women to society. This is generally true of both ancient and modern history; it is generally true of world, American, and Utah history. Now, with the ever-increasing interest in the involvement of women in modern society, it is important that we understand their roles in the past.

Most theories of sex differences are based on the obvious biological differences between men and women, such as the function of women in reproduction and their continuing dominance in child rearing. Women are expected to be more patient, more gentle, more kind, and generally more self-effacing than men, largely because they have generally assumed a role in society that demands these characteristics. They are therefore also thought to be non-competitive, non-aggressive, non-self-assertive, and non-all the other traits that are supposed to be characteristic of the male. These assumptions would be put to a severe test if a sizable sample of women could be found who were, for whatever reason, freed in substantial measure from the traditional maternal role.[1] What would such independent women choose to do with their time?

Mormon women of the nineteenth and early twentieth centuries provide us with such a sample. The expanded roles enjoyed by large numbers of these women were in measure made possible by the institution of polygamy. Polygamy gave many women time and energy to spend outside the home, and these women in turn may have provided the stimulus for non-plural wives to take up pursuits other than fulltime child rearing.[2] Single women presented

vii

in this collection of essays also found opportunities for distinctive accomplishments.

Not only polygamy, but also other factors allowed these Mormon women to depart from more traditional roles. Most were frontier pioneers with towns and homes to build, food and clothing to produce, goods to sell, newspapers to publish, schools to administer, sick to heal, governments to run, and industries to found—women contributed skills and leadership in all these areas. Frequently Mormon men would be absent on extended evangelical missions for the church, thus leaving the entire responsibility for the daily life on the frontier with the women. Simple economics of the period demanded the expanded involvement of women.

Another important consideration concerning the variety of endeavors undertaken by Mormon women is the encouragement given them by the Mormon Church leadership. This can best be summed up in a statement by Brigham Young:

> ... We believe that women are useful not only to sweep houses, wash dishes, make beds and raise babies, but they should stand behind the counter, study law or physics or become good bookkeepers and be able to do the business in any counting house, and all this to enlarge their sphere of usefulness for the benefit of society at large. In following these things they but answer the design of their creation.

Because of these factors—polygamy, frontier demands, the absence of men, and encouragement of church leadership—Mormon women provide us with some excellent case studies. The facts of their lives, along with interpretation, are presented in the essays of this volume. Those facts tell how women, freed in part from excessive household duties, chose to live out their lives.

Historical Background

Some background on Mormonism in America and the origins of polygamy is needed in preparation for understanding the essays that follow.

Mormons are Americans in every sense of the word. Organized in New York in 1830, the church soon included New England Puritans, Midwestern Protestants, and the wealthy and poor alike of England, Scotland, Wales, Ireland, Scandinavia, Switzerland, Germany, France, and Italy.

Joseph Smith, the founder of the Mormon religion, attempted to organize a new and complex theological system that encompassed all of life and that emphasized reinterpreted Biblical values and practices. He governed his people with the help of revelations dealing with both mundane and cosmic matters: revelations ranged from those concerning the size, financing, and location of a hotel in Nauvoo to the United Order and the anthropomorphic nature of God. He taught that the heavens are inhabited by many gods and that every person can aspire to become a god. He proclaimed that his new church was the one true church of Jesus Christ in these "latter days."

Born in Sharon, Vermont, on December 23, 1805, Joseph Smith later moved with his parents and brothers and sisters to western New York, where as a youth he experienced his first visions. Western New York between 1800 and 1850 is aptly described as the *burned-over district* because of the frequency with which the fires of religious enthusiasm swept through the region. This area, says Whitney Cross, was settled by people of Yankee inheritance, people given to extraordinary religious beliefs and intense crusades for the perfection of the human race and the goal of millennial happiness.[3] Intense rivalry between sects caused strain on sincere people seeking to acquire a religious faith.

Poor and uneducated, the Smith family earned a living through farming and various forms of primitive entrepreneurship. Along with many other inhabitants of the area, they possessed a deep religious concern that sought an institutional outlet. This search led the Smiths, as it did many others in the area, to a search for new religious truth. Competing value systems and rapid economic expansion and mobility were some of the main causes of this seeking.

The followers of Joseph Smith, usually called Mormons (named after one of their books of scriptures called the Book of Mormon), saw themselves as a covenant people, divinely appointed to build the kingdom of God on the earth. This rapidly growing group stimulated hostility and was driven from New York to Ohio and then to Missouri. They continued to grow amid persecutions and sufferings and were, again, driven out of Missouri in the winter of 1838-39 to settle on the banks of the Mississippi River. Here they founded a city called Nauvoo, a city with an independent government located within the state of Illinois.

During this Nauvoo period Joseph Smith first began teaching polygamy (*celestial marriage*) to select followers. Evidence indicates that the concept and practice of this doctrine existed among the church leaders even earlier, perhaps shortly after the founding of the church. This plan, which Joseph Smith recounted having received from God in answer to a question about its practice in Old Testament times, is recorded in Mormon scripture (see the Doctrine and Covenants, Section 132).

Mormon political activity and independence, as well as charges of polygamy and lawless conduct, aroused intense opposition to the church in Illinois. In 1844, rioting broke out in Hancock County;

Joseph smith and his brother Hyrum were murdered. The Mormons fled from Illinois in 1846. The majority of the church members followed Brigham Young, a capable administrator and colonizer, who led the exodus to the Great Salt Lake Basin.

Until Joseph Smith's death in the summer of 1844, the practice of polygamy was limited to a few trusted leaders. Following Smith's death and the assumption of power by Brigham Young and his associates, the number of polygamous marriages increased considerably.

The Mormons felt they needed to move west to avoid further hostility; the vanguard of westward-moving Mormons reached the site of Salt Lake City between July 21 and 24, 1847, and, under the leadership of Brigham Young, began establishing a commonwealth. Salt Lake City became the central city of Mormon colonization of the West. A planned community from the outset, it was laid out by Brigham Young in accordance with a plat for the City of Zion drawn by Joseph Smith in 1833. Geographically, the Mormon kingdom included the vast expanse of land between the Sierra Nevadas and the Rocky Mountains.

The city charter of Salt Lake City almost duplicated the one that had been granted to the Mormons in their city of Nauvoo by the Illinois legislature. It made Nauvoo virtually an autonomous political unit, empowered to pass any law not in conflict with the state or federal constitutions and to maintain its own military and city court. Until its repeal, the Nauvoo Charter was a storm center of Illinois politics. In a different environment, the Salt Lake City charter occasioned no trouble.

With Salt Lake City as a base for arriving Mormon converts, incoming Mormons were sent out to open or strengthen new communities located the entire length of the Great Basin. Men and women began colonizing all the fertile valleys north and south of Salt Lake City wherever streams permitted irrigation. The Mormons practiced a planned economy of a type on a scale not frequently attempted, and it gave the area a culture differing from that of all other western territories, a mixture of the cultures of New England and the west.

During the second generation of Mormon history (1847-85), polygamy became a normal part of Utah social practice. Temporarily relieved from the fear of persecutions from the outside world, the Mormons practiced polygamy openly from the outset of their settlement in the Great Basin. Despite some opposition, polygamy was practiced under these conditions for more than a quarter of a century.

After Brigham Young's death in 1877, John Taylor, senior

apostle in the Council of the Twelve, became president of the Mormon Church. Taylor's administration was marked by outside opposition to polygamous marriage. United States public sentiment, primarily mobilized by the mainline Protestant clergy, was so opposed to polygamy that Congress passed a law in 1862 (Antibigamy Act) prohibiting polygamy. Twenty years later this law was supplemented by the Edmunds Law, and still later was strengthened by the Edmunds-Tucker Law, which defined polygamous living as *unlawful cohabitation* and which made it a misdemeanor.

Under these statutes vigorous prosecution, often referred to as *the Raid*, was carried on in Utah, Idaho, and Arizona, wherever polygamous families were found. Many polygamous husbands and plural wives had to go into hiding, which was often referred to as going on *the underground*. Men and women were fined, imprisoned, and sometimes even shot. Certain Mormon leaders were driven into exile, and a great deal of suffering was inflicted. In 1887 most of the church's property was seized by the federal government, and all who practiced polygamy were forbidden to vote. The Mormons fought back with every legal means possible. They challenged the antipolygamy laws as an infringement upon religious liberty as guaranteed by the United States Constitution, but in 1890 the United States Supreme Court reaffirmed the constitutionality of antipolygamy laws. Wilford Woodruff, who succeeded John Taylor as president of the church after Taylor died in exile, feared complete destruction of the church. Finally, he issued a public manifesto that read in part:

> *To Whom it may Concern: Inasmuch as laws have been enacted by the Congress forbidding plural marriages, which laws have been pronounced constitutional by the court of last resort, I hereby declare my intention to submit to those laws, and to use my influence with the members of the Church over which I preside, to have them do likewise.*

The general conference of the church in October 1890 sustained the manifesto and thus withdrew public sanction of further solemnization of polygamous marriages. This did not prevent the Mormons from holding polygamy as a sacred and valid principle, but the practice has ceased except in some splinter groups, no longer affiliated with the Mormon Church.

Polygamy is the one characteristic of the social organization of the Mormons that has received the greatest notoriety; even after the 1890 manifesto publicly declared polygamous marriages no longer sanctioned, Mormonism and polygamy have continued to be synonymous in the public image.

Contrary to public conception, it appears that Mormon society of the nineteenth century took a more progressive attitude toward women than did American society at large. The bad publicity Mormons received because of polygamy during this period prevented any serious coming to terms with the idea that the institution of polygamy, given the demands of frontier life, served as a liberating force for women. Plural wives (as they were called by the Mormons) frequently took advantage of the shared responsibilities, dividing wifely duties and directing their energies and personal talents not only to rearing families, but to developing the state of Utah and to a large extent to achieving an inevitable independence from men. The opportunity was there, and the women took it.

Available Sources

In the history of America and the west, Mormon women have contributed significantly. This fact is slowly being recognized by scholars who deal with original sources; few of these sources are available to the general population.

Available sources on the Mormon people are outstanding in their depth, breadth, and variety. Mormons are characterized as a record-keeping people. On the day the church was organized a church recorder was appointed, and from that time to the present twenty-six different people have served as church historians and recorders. Each of the church auxiliaries and organizations has kept minutes, and many have published newspapers and magazines. Synthesized accounts and documentary histories are plentiful.

Gathering the biographies of the early members of the church and preparing them for publication was undertaken around the turn of the century by Mormon historian Andrew Jensen. In addition, a mammoth multivolume scrapbook record of the day-by-day activities of this church was kept. This journal history of the church includes 1,300 well-indexed and microfilmed legal-size scrapbooks. All these materials, along with a vast and ever-expanding collection of personal records of individual church members (both published and unpublished) in the form of diaries, journals, autobiographies, letters, family histories, and tape-recorded interviews, are located in the library and archives of the Historical Department of the church in Salt Lake City. The total number of individual documents concerning both men and women exceeds one million. Also located in Salt Lake City is the Mormon Genealogical Society Library. Here records are available on many Mormon families, past and present, including their ancestors. This library is the largest genealogical library in the world.

Authors and Subjects

The experiences of the Mormon women found in these numerous sources, though regional and peculiar, have elements of universality. The largest group of these women is polygynous, though single women and women with a more traditional family situation are well represented. Some of the women's contributions were concrete, such as owning and publishing a newspaper or founding and running an industry. Others contributed a life of rich internal resources as indicated only by the original diaries and journals they left behind. Though most of the women discussed here are of the nineteenth century, some lived in the first half of the twentieth century. None of the title women in this volume is presently living. The most contemporary woman in this collection died in 1959.

Different types of sources were available on each woman, greatly affecting the way the authors have presented their lives. Different authors also approached similar sources in a diverse manner.

The essays highlight each woman's unique contributions to society, the effect of Mormonism on her, and sometimes her relationship with the other women here represented—for many of these women knew each other, worked and worshipped together, and often commented about each other in their diaries.

The authors themselves are exciting and accomplished people. Most are women and most are Mormons. The Mormon authors represent different commitments to their church, just as did their historical subjects. Some are well-known scholars in the field, and some are only now gaining the recognition they deserve.

About the Author

Vicky Burgess-Olson, author, compiler, and editor, a recent graduate of Northwestern University with a doctor of philosophy degree in Psychology and Family Therapy, is a Mormon mother of four children. Originally from Salina, Utah, she grew up helping her father on the family's cattle ranch. She graduated from Utah State University in 1967 with a bachelor's degree in political science and history and a master of science degree in psychology in 1968. She has taught at Lasell Junior College in Massachusetts, at the University of Maryland's European Division in Berlin, Germany, and at Brigham Young University, and has also been an instructor of Mormon Woman Studies at the LDS Institute of Religion at the University of Chicago.

Presently Dr. Burgess-Olson is serving as a district psychologist working with special education programs for Alpine School District in Utah. She also has a direct commission as a First Lieutenant in the United States Army Reserve Medical Service Corps.

While researching diaries and journals for her dissertation entitled *Family Structure and Dynamics in Early Utah Mormon Families, 1847-1885,* she became familiar with many of the subjects of this volume and decided to share this acquaintance with others. Through various contacts, these subjects were then assigned authors. The authors will be introduced more specifically preceding their essays.

Appreciation and Acknowledgments

Appreciation is deeply felt and expressed to the many people who made this book possible: to the authors of the essays themselves, who contributed their work, particularly to Ann Gardner Stone and Rebecca Jean Cornwall, who assisted in reading and editing many of the manuscripts; to the LDS Church Historical Department, which has the care of most of the primary sources used in preparing these essays; as always, to my companion, Eric Jay Olson, whose own projects were interrupted many times during the completion of this book; and to the women who are represented in these essays—for the lives they lived, for respecting themselves enough to record their failings and accomplishments, and for caring enough about future generations that we indeed have become enriched inheritors of these noble foremothers.

Eliza Roxcy Snow Smith Young 1804–1887

*Maureen Ursenbach Beecher came to
women's history by devious ways.
Educated at the University of Alberta,
Brigham Young University, and the
University of Utah in English and
comparative literature, she found
herself, following the completion of
her dissertation, accepting a job as
editor of the Historical Department of
The Church of Jesus Christ of
Latter-day Saints. Editing historical
manuscripts led her to a new interest
in the history of Mormonism and to
an awareness that the story of the
women of the church had remained
largely an untold tale.*

*Under the direction and assignment
of the church historian, she began her
research with perhaps the most
influential Mormon woman of the
nineteenth century, Eliza Roxcy Snow.
Canadian by birth, Dr. Beecher has
been an active member of the Mormon
Church all her life. She has served in
ward and stake and branch and
district capacities, and filled a
fulltime mission for the church in
Switzerland. She was recently
released from the Instructional
Development Committee of the church.
In 1974 she married Dale F.
Beecher. They are the parents of a
son and a daughter. They live in Salt
Lake City.*

Eliza R. Snow

Maureen Ursenbach Beecher

Poetess, prophetess, priestess, and *presidentess* are terms which her contemporaries applied with reverent awe to Eliza Roxcy Snow. This woman, this *captain of Utah's woman host,* commanded such respect among the Mormon women of Utah that they celebrated her birthday, whether or not she was among them; they took up a collection to pay her fare on a jaunt to the Holy Land; they turned out in numbers whenever and wherever she spoke on her many visits throughout the Great Basin kingdom; they listened to her, quoted her, obeyed her, and found in her "the president of the female portion of the human race."[1] She was a legend before half her effective life was done, and lived that legend for the rest of it. She was aware of her position, and both played upon it and was plagued by it: "Sisters," she told an audience, "I occupy an honorable position, but the great responsibility attending it prevents my feeling proud."[2]

It is not difficult to catalog the public accomplishments of Eliza R. Snow. There is hardly an auxiliary organization in The Church of Jesus Christ of Latter-day Saints which does not bear her imprint: the women's Relief Society, which she helped found and then directed through its formative stages; Mormon Church youth groups, initiated with her support as Retrenchment Associations; the children's Primary Association, carried by her from its birthplace in Farmington to nearly every settlement of the Mormon Church in the west. And there are her published works: nine volumes extant, plus another tome of separately published pieces. Those are tangible reminders. Less obvious are the events now slid into history: the 1876 centennial territorial fair; the women's commission store; courses in medicine for women; the Deseret Hospital; and a long-enduring tradition of thought about women's place in church and society. Her contemporaries, and ours, have assessed her as a great woman. But then, as she saw it herself, "true greatness" is merely "usefulness."

What is elusive about Eliza—enigmatic, if you will—is the woman herself, the person within, the interior source for the exterior strength. Or is it more appropriate, or accurate, to see her accomplishment in terms of the times and the needs of a band of Israel wandering their forty years—or was it forty months?—in the wilderness and then wresting from a desert Canaan their promised Zion? Whether the circumstances changed the woman or whether the woman altered the circumstances is a question to be left hanging while we dissect the life and the times into bits small enough for present scrutiny.

For that closer examination, let us take those four alliterative titles one by one: *poetess, prophetess, priestess, presidentess.* They are useful divisions of the areas of Eliza's activities; even more conveniently, they fit as chronological emphases in her life pattern. Each concern rises during its own period, reaches its zenith, and declines to a lesser but still significant level as the next rises. The cumulative effect is a piling up of interests and abilities, characteristics of the one woman of Mormondom recognized by the present Mormon laity and the historical community alike as the epitome of Latter-day Saint womanhood. The question, though, arises in this generation's assessment of those qualities. Therein lies the conflict of the life and the legend of Eliza R. Snow.

Her life began in Becket, a town nestled in the Berkshire hills of Massachusetts, in January 1804, but she was soon transplanted to the wild Ohio territory, then the Connecticut western reserve. The Snows and their Ohio neighbors brought New England with them: the same patriotic spirit which a generation earlier had inspired a revolution informed the attitudes of the Portage County society in which Eliza grew. Her family was loyal American, socially conscious (Oliver Snow, Eliza's father, was justice of the peace and county commissioner in Mantua, Ohio, where they lived), religious, educated (Oliver Snow had taught school back in Massachusetts, and did again for a term in Mantua), and intellectually liberal. They were also practical, industrious, and financially successful. Eliza grew from early childhood with a sense of family pride and a reflected awareness of personal worth.

School was easy for little girls with linguistic talents, and Eliza had these in superfluous amounts. Bored with writing simple prose accounts of Mediterranean geography or of the battle of Hastings, she would compose her homework assignments in verse, mimicking the patterns and themes of the poets she read with insatiable appetite. It is not difficult to see her as the pet of her teachers; her sisters who followed seem to have paled in comparison. None but her father seems to have filled her need for intellectual companionship until Lorenzo, her brother born when she was ten, who, like Eliza, was often "shut up with his book." The two developed a closeness that lasted until her death.

There seem to have been examples enough of poetry for Eliza to follow in her own attempts at versifying. Shakespeare was commonplace in the United States by this time, as was Milton. The romantic poets had not yet been discovered in America, but the styles and themes of the eighteenth-century Rationalists were available, and the renewed interest which that century felt in Greek and Roman classics had introduced the literate to the ancient myths and the epic forms. And every newspaper had its poetry column, filled with verses of all varieties.

It was to the local newspaper that Eliza sent her first public poem, an epic-styled celebration of the romantically poignant "Battle of Missolonghi."

> *Arise my infant muse, awake my lyre,*
> *To plaintive strains; but sing with cautious fear*
> *Lest thou profane . . .*

she writes, choosing a poetic mode a cut above that of the usual poetry column offerings. Gaining confidence, she continues:

> *. . . Ye favor'd daughters, ye*
> *Who nurs'd on blest Columbia's happy soil*
> *Where the pure flag of liberty shall wave*
> *Till virtue's laurels wither on your breasts:*[4]

The lines scan well, in the formal iambic pentameter of Shakespeare. And the diction is as high-flown as could be expected from a fledgling Milton. All told, this, and the similarly high-toned elegaic ode on the deaths of Adams and Jefferson that followed in the same newspaper two weeks later, demonstrate a literary sensitivity and a craftsmanship that augured well for a developing poet.[5] One would hope that the innovative, imaginative thrust would come to match the developing skill. A search through subsequent writings is disappointing. The two early odes, published in 1826 when Eliza was twenty-two, built in her a confidence that led not to greater imagination, but to a popularizing of her style into form and subject matter more in keeping with what her contemporaries were submitting to the local papers:

> *If there's a smile on nature's face*
> *It is the farmer's dwelling place*

she writes in a homey poem called "The Farmer's Wife." The strict four-foot pattern, rhymed in unerring couplets, winds down to a simplistic conclusion:

> *If you would make the best of life,*
> *Be (if you can) the farmer's wife.*[6]

One would like to imagine this as a sarcastic toying with both the genre and the society's simple mores—it would be about this time that Eliza received offers of marriage, probably from young men from neighboring farms. But, alas, the verses that follow leave us no recourse but to assume she had slipped easily, effortlessly, into the popular style of her times.

This is not to say the poetry is bad. On the contrary, some of it reads quite well, and the suggestion made in a later biographical sketch that Eliza sacrificed a promising literary career to cast her lot with the Mormons may not be far from wrong. Certainly the neighboring Cary sisters, Alice and Phoebe, wrote no better, and they, some twenty-five years behind Eliza, left their Ohio farm and moved to New York where they made an adequate living from their verses.

Eliza, however, had interests too diverse to devote her whole attention to poetry. Her life paced rapidly through the subsequent years from Mantua to Mormon Kirtland and on to Missouri in company with her adopted people. It was not until she found a period of relatively settled external circumstances, coupled with a disruptive emotional life, that the poetic gift reasserted itself with new promise. The place was Nauvoo, a seven-year stopover in the hegira of the Mormons, and the disruptive stimulus was the internal turmoil occasioned by her secret marriage to the prophet Joseph Smith, whom she later designated "the choice of my heart, the crown of my life."[7] That event proved the fulcrum on which her life balanced itself. Her diary entry for that day, June 29, 1842, reads: "This is a day of much interest to my feelings," and continues in a similar vein of ambiguous prose that ascends toward poetry as the emotion finds itself later "recalled in tranquility." Her next several poems in the diary deal with her Joseph, and by inference, with her secret polygynous relationship with him.[8]

Among the usual verses, many of which found themselves, with or without her permission, in the *Times and Seasons* and the *Millennial Star,* are some confessional poems that approach the poetic standards from which present critics judge. In her retirement, "Where there's nobody here but Eliza and I," she could loose the reins, give her mind its soul, and compose such lines as these "Saturday Evening Thoughts":

> My heart is fix'd—I know in whom I trust.
> 'Twas not for wealth—'twas not to gather heaps
> Of perishable things—'twas not to twine
> Around my brow a transitory wreath,
> A garland deck'd with gems of mortal praise,
> That I foresook the home of childhood: that
> I left the lap of ease . . .[9]

In these times, though, she felt a responsibility beyond art and beyond her own emotions. There were Saints to be cheered and doctrines to be taught. *Zion's poetess,* for so Joseph had named her, turned her talents to the cause. The confessional writings extant from her Illinois period are far overshadowed numerically by such works as the poems to the gentile *Quincy Whig* pleading for aid and succor for the persecuted people; the hymns of encouragement to the distressed, that "though deep'ning trials throng [their] way," the Saints of God should "press on, press on"; and the doctrinally exciting "O My Father," written in this period as "Invocation, or the Eternal Father and Mother."

Eliza wrote on almost to her death, 1,200 miles and forty-one years from Nauvoo. Her collected poetry tells, better than do many prose accounts, the history of a faith in the building and a nation in the making. In her verses can be found the whole sweep of the Mormon story. But as poetry it fails of greatness. Twentieth-century critics find it superficial, maudlin, trite, and unimaginative. As a poet, had she made no other contribution, Eliza might have been as obscure to us as Hannah Tapfield King is. But to her own contemporaries, Hannah King among them, she was muse, mentor, kindred in spirit. As Hannah King wrote to her:

> *My Spirit bends instinctively to thine:*
> *At thy feet I fain would sit and learn*
> *Like Paul of old before Gamaliel.*[10]

Zion's poetess to her literary disciples, as to the rest of her Mormon contemporaries, was building the reputation that would evolve into legend.

The poetic gifts and the prophetic gifts of Eliza R. Snow are so closely related that one finds them hard to separate. Nor, perhaps, should one try. The title *prophetess* had a meaning to Eliza's nineteenth-century contemporaries that evades us now, we who are in a church so strongly regimented that the prophetic calling is by custom restricted not only to males in general, but to a specific body of church leaders in particular. In a looser sense, however, one can see some prophetic functions beginning early in the life of Eliza R. Snow, growing as she finds and embraces the revelatory gospel, and reaching a peak of spirituality in that most unlikely of places, Winter Quarters, the Nebraska shanty town where the Mormons regrouped for their final push to Utah.

Let us backtrack to the first few years of Eliza's poetry publishing in search for her prophetic beginnings. In the February 14, 1829, issue of the Ravenna, Ohio, *Western Courier,* Eliza published a poem that in retrospect is a little disconcerting. It contains what could almost automatically be interpreted as a prophecy of the Mormon restoration of the Christian gospel. The poem, dealing with the universal question of the transcience of life, contains these hope-infusing stanzas:

> But lo! a shining Seraph comes!
>   Hark! 'tis the voice of sacred Truth;
> He smiles, and on his visage blooms,
>   Eternal youth.
>
> He speaks of things before untold,
>   Reveals what men nor angels knew,
> The secret pages now unfold
>   To human view.

So she wrote in Ohio in early 1829. Years after her acceptance of the Mormon gospel, Eliza altered the phrase *secret pages* to read *long seal'd pages,* to make more explicit the reference to the coming of the *Seraph,* the angel Moroni, with the partially sealed plates from which the Book of Mormon was translated. Even without Eliza's later tamperings, we are left with the quandary: could she have heard, fully a year before its publication, of the book and of its translator? Was she toying with a local rumor, carried, perhaps, by an itinerant preacher? Had she adopted the Campbellite hope of an angel coming to restore the true gospel? Or was there in her poetic imagination a kernel of true prophecy that prompted such a confident expression?

From the winter afternoon, sometime in 1830 or 1831, when Joseph Smith warmed himself in her father's friendly living room until her baptism into the new faith nearly five years later, Eliza struggled for direction. Her hesitation seems to have stemmed from a lack of spiritual confirmation. She yearned after the gifts of the spirit of which the New Testament spoke, and saw about her in the religions of the times, perhaps even somewhat in the new Mormon practices, either barren intellectualizing or, worse, sham perversions of the spiritual outpourings. Whatever led her to finally present herself for baptism at the hands of the Mormons, it was not the fiery pentacostal assurance she wanted. But that night, the night following her immersion into the waters of the new faith, began her new visionary life: she received a witness which she read as ultimate and divine confirmation.

I had retired to bed, and as I was reflecting on the wonderful events transpiring around me, I felt an indescribable, tangible sensation ... commencing at my head and

enveloping my person and passing off at my feet, producing inexpressible happiness.
Immediately following, I saw a beautiful candle with an unusual long, bright blaze
directly over my feet. I sought to know the interpretation, and received the following,
"The lamp of intelligence shall be lighted over your path." I was satisfied.[11]

The new faith led Eliza to Kirtland, Ohio, where, despite the
fact that she soon owned a house, she continued to live as govern-
ess in the home of the prophet Joseph Smith. Her descriptions of
the pentecostal manifestations accompanying the dedication of the
Kirtland Temple suggest a growing appetite for such outpourings
as the speaking in tongues that became a regular part of temple
worship—so much a part, in fact, that they had to be restricted to
the last hour of the day-long Thursday fast meetings. We have no
account of Eliza's participating then in this prophesying and praising in tongues, but it is fair to assume that she was growing in her
spiritual abilities, if only by intense observation.

From Kirtland—where Eliza was joined by her now-converted
parents, her sister, Leonora, and her brother, Lorenzo—the family
moved to the newly founded community of Adam-ondi-Ahman in
Missouri. The Snows traveled with, and settled near, the Huntington family, and undoubtedly in the move cemented the long-
enduring friendship between Zina Diantha Huntington and Eliza
R. Snow. Of Eliza's spiritual activity in the Missouri settlement
there is no record, but we are told that Zina was practiced then in
the gift of tongues,[12] and it is fair to assume that Eliza learned
that communication, too. Until their deaths in Utah, Zina and
Eliza practiced the prophetic speaking in and interpretation of
tongues throughout the church.

Expelled from Missouri, the two families, along with their co-
religionists, moved to Illinois, aided in the building of Nauvoo,
suffered the indignities of persecution, and in 1846 found themselves refugees crossing Iowa. Privation and sickness create strife,
even among the faithful, and Eliza details in her diary the bitterness that even she felt, she who had grown so emotionally strong
and independent. Bickerings would have, could have, multiplied
through the long winter of waiting for spring and the rest of the
journey west. But there was something stronger than mutual privation to weld these people together, and Eliza was in the forefront
of the practice. The women would gather in each other's tents for
what might normally have been elite and cruelly cutting gossip
sessions. But not so. Eliza records a series of gatherings:

Spent the aft[er]n[oon] with Lucy in com[pany] of Zina, Loisa and Emily. E[mily]
and myself spoke in the gift of tongues.[13]
And:

Sis[ter] Sess[ions], Kim[ball], Whit[ney] and myself spent the eve[ning] at Sarah Ann's—had a pow'rful time—deep things were brought forth which were not to be spoken.[14]

And:

. . . a time of blessing at Sis[ter] K[imball]'s. . . . Sis[ter] Sess[ions] and myself blest Helen. I spoke and she interpreted. I then blest the girls in a song, singing to each in rotation.[15]

Such gatherings were not infrequent throughout the winter, and by spring Eliza seems to emerge as the leader in the blessing meetings. Patty Sessions records on May 1, 1847:

Sylvia and I went to a meeting to Sister Leonards. None but females there. We had a good meeting. I presided. It was got up by E. R. Snow. They spoke in toungues; I interpreted. Some prophesied. It was a feast.[16]

The gatherings, interrupted by the trek west, began again in the Salt Lake Valley when Eliza would collect the women together in their rude homes in the Old Fort, and again the blessings and the prophesyings would occur.

What was the nature of the prophecies and blessings uttered in the strange languages? Were they really prophetic, or were they the overenthusiastic imaginings of a spiritually excited people? Who can know? In a retrospective tally of accounts we come up with what is most likely an unfair gauge: about half the prophesies uttered by Eliza were fulfilled, about half were not. People to whom she promised the blessing of seeing the Savior return during their lifetime, or the blessing of standing in the temple to be built in Missouri, have long since died. But Heber J. Grant testified to his childhood memory of the prophecy uttered in tongues by Eliza, translated by Zina Huntington, that he would become an apostle. He did.[17] And Mary Ann Chadwick Hull, having buried two children in two years, was promised by Eliza that she would have a daughter (she was pregnant at the time) who would grow to womanhood.[18] The child, born healthy, was indeed a girl, and lived to age twenty. Two other daughters, one named after Eliza, outlived their mother.

But there are other prophetic gifts not so easily judged. There are understandings and awarenesses that are a more important expression of prophecy than are any number of predictions. Eliza is credited in Mormon thought with such insights. The favorite example is the concept of a Heavenly Mother, first expressed as doctrine in her hymn, "O My Father." Mormon general authorities have differed on the source of the revelation. Joseph F. Smith com-

mented in 1895 that, since God does not reveal his mind to a
woman, Eliza was taught the doctrine by Joseph Smith;[19] Wilford
Woodruff, just two years earlier, pointed out the singular appropri-
ateness of the Lord's revealing such a profound doctrine through
one of his daughters.[20] The historical evidence available seems,
however inconclusively, to favor the former interpretation: Joseph
Smith had comforted Zina Huntington, Eliza's friend and con-
fidant, with the mother in heaven doctrine near the time of her
own mother's death, which occurred in 1839, six years before the
poem was first published. Zina would doubtless have confided
such a revelation to her friend.

Other doctrines, less acceptable to modern Mormonism, worked
themselves into Eliza's theology and found their way into her
speeches and poems. One such was the theory that sent the ten
tribes and the city of Enoch spinning off into outer space on de-
tached particles of the earth. "Thou, Earth, wast once a glorious
sphere," she wrote, consoling the globe for its loss.[21]

A study of the popular speculations of the times suggest that
Eliza was seldom, if ever, the originator of the doctrines she accepted into her theology: Parley P. Pratt for one had expressed the
Enoch spinoff idea in 1841; Eliza's poem is dated 1851. Eliza
adopted ideas from whatever source she trusted—Joseph Smith's
utterances would be received without question—and worked them
meticulously into a neatly-packaged theology with the ends tucked
in and the strings tied tight. So it was, for example, when she
published her composition reconciling the doctrine of literal resurrection of the body with the disconcerting evidences of decay and
the cycles of nature. She followed Heber C. Kimball's suggested
format: there are two parts to the body, one of which disintegrates
and returns to the earth, the other of which remains pure and un-
touched awaiting the resurrection. She expressed the concept so
well that her piece, first published in the *Woman's Exponent* in
1873, was reprinted in the *Millennial Star* in 1874 and again in the
Exponent in 1875. At that time Brigham Young—prophet, president
of the church, and Eliza's husband since before the Nauvoo
exodus—protested. A strict literalist, he was not for watering down
scripture with such equivocating, and proclaimed so in a biting
editorial in the next issue of the *Exponent*. Six months later, in the
Deseret News, a carefully-worded retraction written and signed by
Eliza R. Snow appeared in a tiny box on a back page.[22] A doctrine, especially someone else's doctrine, was hardly worth defying
the priesthood over. Still, one wonders what conversation passed
between Eliza and Brigham in the intervening six months as they
met each evening in the family prayer service in the Beehive

House.

But do such lapses indicate the absence of prophetic gifts? The testimony of her contemporaries would refute such denial. From St. George to Cache Valley they bore witness to her perceptive preaching, to her vast knowledge, and to her speaking in tongues— *Eve's tongue,* as she termed the Adamic language—in their meetings, where she uttered such blessings as they were sure were prophetic. Men and women alike attested to her spiritual calling. We are again left with the enigma. Did her gifts include that of prophecy? Was she a prophetess in the present sense of the word? The life, and the legend, are a hundred years away from us.

Because of her involvement in the practice of the Mormon temple endowment, Eliza R. Snow was called by the title *High Priestess.* As early as Nauvoo, where she was recorder in the temple, and later in the Salt Lake Endowment House, where she presided over the women's section, she performed the high ordinances for the faithful of her sex, often blessing them with a special blessing beyond the scope of the ceremonies themselves. Her equivalent in a modern Mormon temple would be the matron, who is by tradition the wife of the temple president.

It is understandable that Eliza's image would take on a special holiness in the eyes of the women of the church, that the aura of sacred mystery that surrounds the ordinances of the temple should somehow cling to Eliza. It did indeed become a part of the legend, an addition to the sanctity that already clothed her in the eyes of her contemporaries. Added to the gifts of the spirit that she was practicing, the temple calling was the official sanction, the title that justified the reverence which they would accord her.

Other functions that she performed, now generally practiced only by priesthood holders, were likewise in keeping with the title *priestess.* Blessing the sick, administering to those who requested it, and washing and anointing women about to be confined were frequent practices with her. Eliza was not the only woman to whom the sisters would appeal for these ministrations; often a community or group would have among its number some sister who seemed especially gifted for the purpose. But it was Eliza whose word gave the practice official sanction, who taught the proper forms, and who specified the qualifications of sisters who might minister.

That the practice was linked to Eliza's name is clear from a letter, dated 1901, in which a sister is questioning the quasiofficial suggestion that the women no longer administer to the sick. "Eliza R. Snow taught us how to do it," is the sense of the letter; "Should we not continue to follow her directions?"[23] An official statement is recorded in two circular letters, one of indeterminate date on stationery of the Relief Society, the other dated October 3, 1914, over the signatures of the First Presidency, Joseph F. Smith, president. Their intent is the same: women may indeed administer with consecrated oil, *confirming* rather than *sealing* the blessing, making no mention of authority. They may also continue the practice of washing and anointing women who are about to give birth.[24] In other words, the practice promoted by Eliza Snow, following the approval of Joseph Smith, continued well into this century, and perpetuated the name of Eliza R. Snow as priestess to the women of the church.

By 1855, or thereabouts, when Brigham Young called Eliza to facilitate the reorganizing of the Relief Societies in some of the Salt Lake Stake wards, she had already been defined by the women over whom she would preside in the roles to which we have paid note. Already *poetess, prophetess,* and *priestess,* she could well expect to bring to the function of *presidentess* the admiration and respect of the women, irrespective of whatever administrative skills she might possess.

Fortunately for Brigham Young and for the church, she did have the ability to preside. As a clerk to her father, who had been a public administrator during her Ohio youth, she would have learned something of matters of government. Later, when some Nauvoo women had decided in Sarah Kimball's sitting room to organize a women's benevolent society and needed a constitution, it was to Eliza they turned, evidence that her understanding of such matters was early recognized.

The Nauvoo Female Relief Society, organized not according to the constitution Eliza drew up, but rather organized under the priesthood direction of Joseph Smith, elected Eliza its secretary. Her minutes indicated a lively interest in the processes of government, and by the time Brigham Young had need of her abilities, she had learned about leadership. By 1867, when the ward Relief Societies in Utah demonstrated the need for an auxiliary direction, she was the logical head to the first general board. Her sense of stewardship led her throughout the existing church, organizing groups where there had been none, and strengthening and directing existing societies. Her message was always, "We will do as we are directed by the Priesthood,"[25] but when a priesthood leader seemed about to thwart one of the Relief Society projects, her response was that he should be reasoned with. She was confident of her programs and of her ability, and that of her sisters, to facilitate them.

Eliza R. Snow, "Sister Snow" to him, was a plural wife to Brigham Young, their marriage having taken place in Nauvoo early in

1846. Far from the adoration with which she honored Joseph was the respect with which she followed Brigham. *Followed,* I am persuaded, is the right word, for as independent as she seems in her activities in behalf of the women of the church, she restricted her jurisdiction to the stewardship assigned her by Brigham Young. This was not as constraining as it sounds: she and "President Young," as she always called him, saw eye to eye on most things. Most things, that is, remembering the incident of the paper on resurrection, and one homey little story about her having hidden away one of his daughter's silk sashes, deeming it inappropriate to the president's daughter in those times of needed retrenchment. Brigham made her give it back, but later, with Eliza's help, established the Retrenchment Society, with goals similar to Eliza's purpose in taking away the sash in the first place. They two, Eliza and Brigham, thought and worked together; only slight misunderstandings required discussion. Confirmation of each of the other's projects was almost *pro forma.* More a counselor than a wife, Eliza seems to have carried as much influence as Brigham Young's counselors in the First Presidency, at least in regard to women's activities.

In administering the affairs of the women—which included, as she defined them, responsibilities towards the children and young ladies, hence her involvement with Primary and Retrenchment associations—Eliza seems to have been a paragon of administrative skill and a dynamo of executive energy. She lacked but one quality, that same quality that inhibited her poetry and limited her doctrinal insight: she had little imagination and little creative spark. She was not an innovator. The story repeats itself in the history of every project with which her name is initially associated. It was Sarah Kimball, not Eliza, who sparked the founding of the Relief Society in Salt Lake City as she had in Nauvoo; it was when Louisa Greene came to Eliza with the proposal for a magazine that the *Woman's Exponent* was founded; and it was Aurelia Rogers who first expressed her idea of a Primary Association to Eliza. In each case, Eliza was not the originator, but an initial executor of the project; not the agent, but the catalyst. Once she adopted a suggestion, however, Eliza changed roles. Codifying the concept into an organizational format, she would travel from one end of a Mormon settlement to the other implementing it. In one remarkable jaunt to southern Utah in 1880–81 the seventy-six-year-old woman rode nearly two thousand miles by train and wagon to establish some thirty-five Primaries among the Saints there.

In one concern of high importance to the women of Utah, however, she was not the leader—she was supportive, yes, but only peripherally so. That concern was the movement for women's rights, which was as active then as it is now. The Mormon Church was officially on the side of the crusading women most of the time and on some of the issues. Suffrage for women had the official blessing of church leaders. The Utah territorial legislature gave the franchise to women early, and Eliza's name headed the list of those who addressed their thanks to acting governor Stephen Mann for signing the bill into law. But the following year, aside from encouraging the women to vote, Eliza predicted the women's passivity in the political arena:

Although invested with the right of suffrage, [she told a group in Ogden] we shall never have occasion to vote for lady legislators or for lady congressmen.[26]

One might wish we had reason in our time to trust her optimistic justification for the belief:

The kingdom of God, of which we are citizens [she explained], will never be deficient in a supply of good and wise men to fill governmental positions, and of brave men for warriors.[27]

With all the other responsibilities she carried, Eliza surely cannot be faulted for not adding the women's rights movement to her leadership load. The question is, however, less one of activity than one of doctrine.[28] She firmly believed that a woman's divinely appointed role bound her kindly but firmly to the home. The building of the kingdom, she admitted, required that some mothers make the sacrifice of leaving home to obtain medical training, or to be the telegraphers, sales clerks, bookkeepers, and typesetters that President Young needed. A woman's sphere, she affirmed, and with some justification even from our point of view, was nowhere so wide as in Utah among the Mormons, especially guaranteeing as Mormons did, the most important right of women: the right of wedlock. Plural marriage, polygamy, was her answer to the feminists who pled the cause of women in Utah.

The logic may seem elusive, but typically for Eliza, it could all be made to fit. Justifying the status quo, the subjection in which most women found themselves *vis-à-vis* their male counterparts, she referred to the foreparents of the human race and the original sin. Eve was the first to partake of the fruit, and so deserved her punishment:

She led in the transgression, and was plac'd
By Eloheim's unchangeable decree
In a subservient and a dependent sphere.[29]

And almost as though "whatever is, is right," Eliza accepted that judgment and built around it—with some doctrinal suggestions from such theologians as Orson Hyde and George Q. Cannon—a theology that she could make consistent with the rest of her beliefs. Where there is organization, she insisted, there must be gradation. Eve having been the first to sin, her daughters were placed in the secondary position. God ordained it, and Eliza would not protest:

We stand in a different position from the ladies of the world [she told an audience in 1871]; we have made a covenant with God, we understand his order, and know that order requires submission on the part of woman.[30]

But the *curse of Eve,* that her desire should be to her husband and that he should rule over her, was not to last forever. As Adam had found redemption from his sins, so also would Eve from hers. In that same 1871 discourse she explained how the curse would be lifted:

The Lord has placed the means in our hands, in the Gospel, whereby we can regain our lost position. But how? Can it be done by rising, as women are doing in the world, to clamor for our rights? No. ... It was through disobedience that woman came into her present position, and it is only by honoring God in all the institutions he has revealed to us, that we can come out from under that curse, regain the position originally occupied by Eve, and attain to a fulness of exaltation in the presence of God.[31]

According to Eliza the institution through which a woman could honor God and regain her lost equality with man was, ironically, plural marriage. Eve disobeyed, Eliza reasoned; her daughters must obey, but obey in righteousness. Righteous men are less numerous than are deserving women; hence, polygamy. The inconsistent intervening steps in the syllogism seem not to have disturbed Eliza in her reasoning. Her pattern allowed for so many goods: order; the growth of the kingdom through large families; equality among women (theoretically, at least); and peace with the brethren. The day when women would receive "the power of reigning and the right to reign"[32] was far off in reality, but near enough to put a rosy cast over the whole question and justify the status quo in which she found herself and her sisters, she assumed, to be quite fulfilled. Eliza, then, was not a feminist in the Elizabeth Cady Stanton mold any more than in the Gloria Steinem pattern. First things must come first, and in Eliza's view many concerns came before women's rights as the society at large interpreted them.

So in all her presiding she failed to lead out in what seems to some women today to have been the major issue. And in her definition of "What Is and What Is Not for Women" Eliza sold short her sex, by today's lights. And so in much of her poetry she let ease and usefulness and dedication to her cause outweigh the finer poetic crafts. So some of her prophecies were inspired more by millennial enthusiasm than by divine witness, and so her priestly functions have all but disappeared from Mormon practice. Those are only part of the whole, a whole which, when we draw back far enough to see Eliza in the broader social landscape, takes on an aspect larger than the sum of its parts.

For there is no equivocating over the position she held, or the influence she wielded over the Mormon women of her time. The five thousands who filled the tabernacle to hear her defense of polygamy, or the one whom she warmly embraced for her faithfulness to her calling—all these attested, on whatever grounds, to her leadership.

If she was not the potter whose firm hand shaped the infant faith of the new society, Eliza was certainly the kilnsman who fired the newly molded piece into a hard and solid form. And if the edges are chipping away under the pressures of this century's demands, that form still stands recognizably as she left it.

Notes

1. *Woman's Exponent* 9(1 April 1881): 165.

2. *Woman's Exponent* 4(15 August 1875): 42.

3. Orrin Harmon, "Historical Facts Appertaining to the Township of Mantua..., Portage Co., Ohio," manuscript handwritten, 1866, in the Western Reserve Historical Society, Cleveland, Ohio; see also *History of Portage County, Ohio* (Chicago, 1885), pp. 475-485, the chapter dealing with Mantua Township.

4. *Western Courier* (Ravenna, Ohio), 22 July 1836; see also *Weekday Religious Education* 1(March 1937): 6-7.

5. *Western Courier,* 5 August 1826.

6. Eliza R. Snow, Diary and Notebook, photocopy of holograph, Church Archives, Historical Department, The Church of Jesus Christ of Latter-day Saints, Salt Lake city, Utah, hereinafter cited as LDS Church Archives. The diary has been edited by the present writer and published as "Eliza R. Snow's Nauvoo Journal," *BYU Studies* 15 (Summer 1975): 391–416.

7. *Woman's Exponent* 15(1 August 1886): 37.

8. Eliza R. Snow, Diary and Notebook, 29 June 1842 ff.

9. *Ibid.,* 16 November 1842; see also Eliza R. Snow, *Poems, Religious, Historical, and Political,* 2 vols. (Liverpool, 1856, and Salt Lake City, 1877), 1:3–6.

10. Hannah Tapfield King, "Lines, Affectionately Addressed to Sister Eliza Snow," photocopy of manuscript, LDS Church Archives.

11. *Eliza R. Snow, An Immortal: Selected Writings of Eliza R. Snow* (Salt Lake City, Utah, 1957), p. 6.

12. Benjamin F. Johnson, " 'Aunt Zina' as I Have Known Her from Youth," manuscript handwritten, Zina D. H. Young Collection, in private possession.

13. Eliza R. Snow, Diary, 1 June 1846–16 August 1849, under date 2 June 1847, microfilm of holograph, LDS Church Archives.

14. *Ibid.,* 3 June 1847.

15. *Ibid.,* 6 June 1847.

16. Patty Sessions, Diary, 1 May 1847, holograph, LDS Church Archives.

17. Heber J. Grant in *Conference Report of The Church of Jesus Christ of Latter-day Saints,* April 1927, pp. 17–18.

18. "Sketch of the Life of Mary Ann Chadwick Hull," Library of Congress Diaries, microfilm of typescript, p. 4, LDS Church Archives.

19. Joseph F. Smith, "Discourses," *Deseret Evening News,* 9 February 1895. This discourse was delivered 20 January 1895.

20. Wilford Woodruff, "Discourse," *The Latter-day Saints' Millennial Star* 56 (9 April 1894): 229. The discourse was delivered 8 October 1893.

21. Eliza R. Snow, "Address to Earth," *Poems,* p. 153. The verse was first published in the *Deseret News,* 31 May 1851.

22. *Woman's Exponent* 2(1 December 1873): 99, and 4(1 September 1875): 54. Brigham Young's reprimand follows in 4(15 September 1875): 60. Eliza's retraction is in *Deseret News Weekly,* 5 April 1876.

23. Louisa Lula Greene Richards to Lorenzo Snow, 9 April 1901, LDS Church Archives.

24. James R. Clark, ed., *Messages of the First Presidency,* 5 vols. (Salt Lake City, 1970), 4:312–317.

25. Eliza R. Snow to [Willmirth] East, 23 April 1883, Eliza R. Snow Papers, LDS Church Archives.

26. *Deseret News,* 26 July 1871.

27. *Ibid.*

28. Eliza Snow's stand on the whole question of woman's rights is discussed more fully in Jill Mulvay's "Eliza R. Snow and the Woman Question," *BYU Studies* 16 (Winter 1976): 250–64.

29. Eliza R. Snow, "The New Year, 1852," *Deseret News,* 10 January 1852.

30. "Miss E. R. Snow's Address to the Female Relief Societies of Weber County," *Latter-day Saints' Millennial Star* 33 (12 September 1871): 578.

31. *Ibid.*

32. Eliza R. Snow, "Woman," *Poems,* 2:178.

Sarah Melissa Granger Kimball 1818–1900

Jill Mulvay Derr developed an interest in Mormon women's history through her work as a research historian for the Historical Department of The Church of Jesus Christ of Latter-day Saints. She is a native Utahn with a bachelor of arts degree in English from the University of Utah and a master of arts degree in teaching from Harvard University. Following her work at Harvard she taught in the Boston public schools for two years and then returned to Salt Lake City, where she began her present work. In 1977 she married C. Brooklyn Derr.

She has published in the Utah Historical Quarterly, BYU Studies, Exponent II, *and* Sunstone. *Her forthcoming publications include a book of edited selections from the journals and correspondence of nineteenth-century Mormon women in collaboration with Kenneth W. and Audrey M. Godfrey, an annotated collection of the poetry of Eliza R. Snow in collaboration with Maureen Ursenbach Beecher, and a centennial history of the Mormon Primary Association in collaboration with LaVern Watts Parmley.*

Sarah M. Kimball

Jill Mulvay Derr

Sarah Kimball settled on the wooden seat and sat as always arrow-straight, wisps of white hair straying from her tight topknot. This was 1883 and certainly not the first time Sarah had taken the train; she had made trips north of Salt Lake City for Relief Society matters, south to St. George for temple work, and west to California to visit her brother, Farley Granger. But this was to be a trip east, back east to Nauvoo and Kirtland, and to New York—almost a retracing of the route that had brought her to Utah years earlier[1]—thirty-two years earlier to be exact, in 1851. She had come to the Salt Lake Valley as a young mother with two sons; her husband Hiram had joined her later. Now three sons were grown; the youngest, twenty-nine-year-old Franklin D., was traveling with her. Hiram had been dead for twenty years.

Sarah's adopted daughter Elizabeth was likely at the depot, and perhaps Eliza R. Snow was there. Sarah and Eliza had been together in the first Female Relief Society at Nauvoo and had been close friends ever since. Now Eliza was general president of the Relief Society and Sarah was her secretary. Sarah need not worry about the record-keeping during her extended leave; there would be few conferences and little traveling for the Relief Society officers that summer. Certainly some Fifteenth Ward sisters were at the depot. Sarah had been their Relief Society president for twenty-five years, "longer than any president living," she boasted, and she would serve another fifteen. She was a judicious administrator who had always delegated responsibilities, so she could comfortably leave the hall, the granary, and the poor of the Fifteenth Ward, with the assurance that all would be cared for. Goodbyes and baggage were probably limited: Sarah Kimball was a woman careful with words and means.

A phrenologist once said that if Mrs. Kimball were "seated in a railway carriage with parties on one hand discussing fashions, and politics to be heard on the other, she would turn to the discussion of politics."[2] She may have rattled the way back to New York in political discussion with her son Frank who, unable to share his mother's allegiance to The Church of Jesus Christ of Latter-day Saints, shared her enthusiasm for local and national politics. In the 1870s Sarah had served as a member of the territorial committee of the People's Party, and she was a member of the constitutional convention that drew up Utah's unavailing petition for statehood in 1882. In 1891 she would head the Utah Woman Suffrage Association and travel to Washington, D.C., as Utah's delegate to the NWSA. Frank Kimball was later to manage the campaign of Utah's first state governor, Heber M. Wells, and then to run for several public offices on his own, always without success.

On the train in 1883 the Kimballs probably found extended time and ample subject matter for political caucusing. A series of attempts at more stringent antipolygamy legislation had resulted in passage of the Edmunds Law in 1882. Thousands of Mormons were already feeling the sting of disfranchisement, and within three years antiMormon abuses under the Edmunds Law would become so intolerable that Sarah Kimball would head a woman's committee petitioning Congress against outrages inflicted upon Utah women by federal deputies.

The conversation between mother and son was undoubtedly lively, but there must have been considerable space for reflection in that long stretch from Salt Lake City, Utah, to Phelps, New York. Sarah's thoughts probably moved with the train toward Phelps, toward family beginnings. With the dedication of the St. George Temple in 1877, Sarah had committed herself to searching her own lineage, and from the trip to Phelps would come the names and dates necessary to complete the temple work for her kindred dead.

Sixty-five-year-old Sarah Kimball, with her head full of family, church, and politics, is representative of her generation of Mormon women, a sisterhood eager to make their influence felt in a wide sphere. Whatever restrictions they may have felt from a priesthood-oriented church structure, Sarah and women like her found room within that system for a broad scope of activity and expression. From her New England roots to her fruitful years in Salt Lake City, Sarah Kimball evolved as a woman—shaped by but also shaping women's rights and responsibilities within the Mormon Church and the Utah community.

Sarah Melissa Granger was born December 29, 1818, in Phelps, Ontario County, New York—a small town midway in the near twenty miles between Palmyra and Seneca Falls, a fortuitously appropriate beginning for a woman so committed to the gospel restored by Joseph Smith and the principle of the equality of the sexes. She was one of eight children of Lydia Dibble and Oliver

Granger, and she grew up as part of an even larger extended family. Sarah's grandfather, Pierce Granger, had arrived in Phelps in 1789 with his brother Elihu. The two young men barely out of their teens had erected a small log house and prepared the land for planting, readying the tiny settlement to which their father and stepmother moved the following spring.[3]

Sarah never knew her great-grandmother Sarah Pierce for whom she was named, but well into her own old age she remembered her great-grandfather Elisha Granger "leaning upon his staff, bowed by the weight of many years." She always pictured him trying to lead sinners to repentance. His son Pierce was a licensed Methodist preacher. Under Pierce Granger's direction a schoolhouse had been built in Phelps, and Sunday classes gathered to hear sermons from Seneca Lake circuit preachers. Later Pierce had furnished the site and part of the materials for the first meetinghouse in Phelps.[4] His wife, Clarissa Trumbull Granger, was five years his senior. She married at age twenty-six and bore nine Granger children, the last just three years before her death in 1813. Oliver Granger, the second of seven sons, married Lydia Dibble the month following his mother's death.[5]

Young Sarah Melissa was part of the second generation of Grangers born in Phelps. Her family was prominent—her father Oliver served for some time as Ontario County sheriff—but they were restless, and late in the 1820s they began to scatter, some to faraway Michigan and others north a few miles to Sodus, Wayne County, New York. It was in Sodus that Oliver Granger was baptized into The Church of Jesus Christ of Latter-day Saints. Like his father, Oliver had been a licensed exhorter for the Methodist Church, and shortly after his baptism he was ordained a Mormon elder by Brigham Young and Joseph Young and he devoted his time to active missionary work. In 1833 he moved his family to Kirtland, Ohio, to gather with the Saints.[6]

Sarah was barely fifteen years old when the family arrived in Kirtland. By this time she, too, had doubtless been baptized a Latter-Day Saint, and what a city Kirtland was for an inquisitive young mind! The Saints were publishing their own newspaper, first the *Evening and Morning Star* and later the *Messenger and Advocate,* filled with explications of the doctrines and revelations of Joseph smith. Sarah was interested in what she read, and she discussed religion with her father. At his suggestion or upon her own request she attended the School of the Prophets, an irregular gathering where the priesthood-bearing elders studied the gospel and gospel-related topics. In later years she proudly reminded her sisters that she had attended the school, perhaps to underscore the importance she placed upon doctrinal study among Mormon women.[7]

Emmeline B. Wells, Mormon *Woman's Exponent* editor, remembered Sarah Kimball as a "deep religious thinker, and reasoner, and a student of the bible, Book of Mormon and other Latter-day Saint books of a similar kind." Sarah grew fond of the sermons and writings of Parley P. Pratt and Orson Pratt, apostle brothers whose works sometimes tended toward doctrinal intricacies and speculation. Wells further commented that Sarah was "an advanced thinker ... fond of diving into the unknown, or soaring upward to sublime heights. ... In her writings she was abstruse and inclined to be mystical, and yet she was so strong-minded, and well-balanced that she would never be the least likely to go beyond her depth."[8] Actually she saw little that was beyond her depth or the depth of her sisters.

"Does all knowledge come through the Spirit of the Lord?" seventy-five-year-old Sarah posed as a discussion question for her Relief Society sisters. "Our Sixth Sense, or the Sense of Spiritual Understanding," she titled an address she gave in 1895 in Washington, D.C., at the Triennial Council of Women, an address in which she portrayed women "received into communion with the Infinite Father and Mother" and "permitted to enter hallowed mansions to attend the school of the Prophets, and, by advancing steps to reach the school of the Gods, where they learn the processes by which worlds are organized ... the uses for which worlds are called into existence; the manner in which they are controlled, and the laws of progression by which all beings and animate things are perfected, and glorified in their respective spheres."[9] Some nineteenth-century women may have been content with the piety proffered them by religion, but in Kirtland Sarah had grasped an intellectual and spiritual challenge that excited her throughout her life.

For Sarah, Granger family memories would always center in Kirtland, where the Grangers lived for almost ten years. From there Oliver Granger set off on several missions for the church to Ohio and New York. There he served on the church's high council, and when Kirtland collapsed financially Joseph Smith designated Oliver his fiscal agent with responsibility for settling a substantial debt. Though Oliver attempted to move his family from Kirtland to Far West, Missouri, late in 1838, antiMormon mobs forced him back. For a year the Grangers joined the Saints in Nauvoo, but the Prophet Joseph sent them back to Ohio so Oliver could exchange remaining land there for land further west.[10]

Sarah's 1840 return to Kirtland was short-lived. Her twenty-first year had been spent in Nauvoo, where her intelligence and charm had attracted the attention of thirty-four-year-old Hiram S. Kimball, a prosperous non-Mormon merchant. Hiram and Sarah were married in Kirtland with her parents' blessing in September 1840, and the newlyweds made their home in Nauvoo. There Hiram was making handsome profits selling everything the growing city was buying: land, lumber, and bricks. His holdings in livestock, merchandise, and real estate made him one of the wealthiest and most prominent men in the city. He was as conspicuous in city politics as he was in business, and was well respected by the Mormon Church hierarchy, even though he was not a Latter-day Saint until 1843.[11]

Sarah M. Kimball became an affluent young matron whose home, often the site for social and religious gatherings of Mormon Church leaders and their wives, was remembered for its elegance long after the city of Nauvoo faded. Hiram's prosperity must have delighted his young bride, but she was at times frustrated that she as wife owned nothing. Later in her life she confessed that she had not wanted to ask her nonmember husband for funds to contribute to the church for the building of the Nauvoo Temple, so when she bore their first son, she asked Hiram if she owned half of the boy. When Hiram said yes, she inquired as to the boy's worth, posing $1,000 as a reasonable estimate, and Hiram agreed. Sarah declared she was contributing her half to the church. When Hiram related this conversation to Joseph Smith, the Prophet told Hiram that he had "the privilege of paying [the Church] $500 and retaining possession, or receiving $500 and giving possession." Mr. Kimball paid the church in land, but Mrs. Kimball maintained that the contribution was hers.[12]

It was in Nauvoo that Sarah Kimball developed the concern for Mormon women that would characterize her life. In 1842, when her seamstress offered to make shirts for Nauvoo Temple workers if Mrs. Kimball would provide the material, Sarah suggested that other women might similarly like to pool means and efforts. She then set about organizing a "Ladies Society." After their first gathering the group asked Eliza R. Snow to write their constitution, which was then submitted to Joseph Smith. He responded: "Tell the sisters their offering is accepted of the Lord, and He has something better for them than a written constitution." On March 17, 1842, Joseph Smith organized the Female Relief Society of Nauvoo, the name and officers being selected by the eighteen women present, and he explained that "the Church was never perfectly organized until the women were thus organized."[13]

Sarah Kimball attended that first meeting and the weekly meetings that continued in Nauvoo until just before Joseph Smith's martyrdom in 1844. By that time some 1,200 women were involved. These sisters shared their feelings about the restored gospel, sewed clothing for the poor and the temple workers, visited troubled and needy Saints, and at one point petitioned the governor of Illinois "for protection from illegal suits pending against the Prophet Joseph Smith."[14] Early meetings were frequently addressed by Joseph Smith; Sarah, later counseling Relief Societies in Utah, would quote him profusely regarding Relief Societies' obligation to improve property and conduct business and regarding woman's obligation to gain intelligence.

Sarah especially accepted one phrase as being prophetic: she heard the Prophet Joseph declare in 1842 that he was turning the key in behalf of woman "in the name of the Lord," and that knowledge and intelligence would flow down from that time henceforth. And in her lifetime she saw women given significant educational, economic, political, and religious opportunities and responsibilities. Sarah, by her own definition a "woman's rights woman," traced the suffrage movement itself to this "turning of the key," asserting that "the sure foundations of the suffrage cause were deeply and permanently laid on the 17th of March, 1842."[15] Just six months before her death in 1898, as Sarah addressed her sisters in the Fifteenth Ward Relief Society, she surveyed the property buying and building, silk manufacture, grain storage, cooperative mercantiles, publications, medical study, and political activity in which Mormon women had become involved, as well as the gains of American women generally, and "spoke of the breadth of meaning contained in the statement made by the Prophet Joseph Smith, 'I now turn the key for women.' "[16] For over fifty years that statement colored Sarah Kimball's perception of woman's changing sphere.

Hiram and Sarah Kimball did not leave Nauvoo with the main body of the Saints in 1846. Apparently Hiram's business interests kept him traveling in the East and required that he station his family in Nauvoo. Though a number of Saints remained in Illinois, Sarah was anxious to join her friends in the West. "O Sister Hyde," she wrote in 1848 to one close friend who had journeyed west as far as Council Bluffs, Iowa,

how I wish you could visit me during my husband's absence. I shall feel verry lonesome indeed. I sometimes flatter myself that I shall see you all next spring. Mr. K talks of haveing me take the children & mother & go on next spring & leave him to close his business & follow. I dont want to leave him but shall do as he thinks best.[17]

Ultimately this was the plan the Kimballs followed, but not until 1851. That spring business complications detained Hiram in New York City, and, according to Sarah, he by that time "had become financially much embarrassed." She with her two sons and widowed mother journeyed by wagon to the Salt Lake Valley, where she exchanged their traveling outfit for a small but comfortable home. Hiram Kimball arrived a year later, "financially ruined and broken in health."[18]

To support the family, Sarah began teaching school in Salt Lake City's Fourteenth Ward. Franklin D. was born in April 1854, and by June Sarah had resumed teaching, not, however, without opposition. Emmeline B. Wells indicated that Sarah taught "under very trying circumstances, and while thus engaged in teaching she became even more than ever convinced of the need of changed conditions for women engaged in work that came in competition with men, and determined to push the matter to the utmost." It is clear that Sarah was not rehired to teach in the ward school. When her private students became too numerous for her own sitting room, she asked her husband and sons to haul timber from the canyons and build her a schoolroom.[19]

By 1857 Hiram Kimball was again prospering in business. Fifteenth Ward records indicate that he was able to purchase more shares for building the ward storehouse than any other man in his ward.[20] Sarah's life became increasingly centered in ward activities when in February 1857 she was named president of the Fifteenth Ward Relief Society, a position she held until her death. At Brigham Young's suggestion ward Relief Societies had been reorganized in the early 1850s, but their activities were cut short by the Utah War and the subsequent move south in 1858; the local organizations were not fully revived until the end of 1867.

During that ten-year interim Sarah's life changed dramatically. Her mother, Lydia Dibble Granger, died after having lived with the Kimballs for twenty years. Hiram was killed in a steamship explosion while traveling to the Sandwich Islands as a missionary. Sarah adopted a young daughter, Elizabeth; and the two oldest Kimball sons married. When Brigham Young called upon bishops to reorganize Relief Societies in their wards, Sarah M. Kimball eagerly assumed her position. She was forty-nine years old, committed to service in The Church of Jesus Christ of Latter-day Saints, and dedicated to the burgeoning movement for woman's rights. The last thirty years of her life would be public rather than private years, during which time her work with the Fifteenth Ward Relief Society would make her realize the value of her own strong opinions and her administrative talents and would motivate

her to prod other women to likewise discover their personal resources and make their influence felt.

"Mrs. Sarah M. Kimball was essentially an organizer," wrote
Susa Young Gates in describing Relief Society beginnings in Utah.
And so she was. Almost immediately "Presidentess" Kimball drew
up a description of the duties of Relief Society officers, a listing
slightly revised by Eliza R. Snow and used by her as she carried
out her assignment from Brigham Young to organize Relief Societies throughout the territory. The organization included a presidentess, two counselors, a secretary, and a treasurer; a council of
teachers with a presidentess and a secretary, whose responsibility it
was to visit the sisters in the ward, caring for the needy and
collecting donations; a deaconess to prepare the meeting place;
messengers to run errands; superintendents of work to provide for
the handwork; a board of apprizers to assess donations; and a
commission merchantess to sell or exchange what the society received or made.[21]

In Salt Lake City's Fifteenth Ward that organization was quickly put to work with tremendous success. In reporting on the society's first year of activity, Sarah Kimball told President Brigham
Young and Eliza R. Snow that the poor, the sick, and the sorrowful had been looked after "so far as we had the means and power
to relieve and comfort them." "We soon found an increasing treasury fund which it became our duty to put to usury," Sarah proudly informed her superiors. That money was invested in a small lot
(2½ x 3 rods) on which the society planned to build a hall, the
first Relief Society hall in the church.[22] The laying of the cornerstone for this hall in November 1868 was no small occasion, at
least for Sarah Kimball, who was provided with a silver trowel
and mallet and an assembly of Fifteenth Ward men and women
with whom to share her vision of woman's work. Her speech was
carefully recorded:

> I appear before you on this interesting occasion on behalf of the Female Relief So-
> ciety to express thanks to the Almighty God that the wheels of progress have been
> permitted to run until they have brought us to a more extended field of useful labor
> for female minds and hands.
> With feelings of humility and gratitude I stand upon this consecrated rock, and
> contemplate the anticipated result of the completion of this unpretending edifice
> (which I will here call "Our Store"), the upper story of which will be dedicated to
> art and science; the lower story to commerce or trade. I view this as a stepping stone
> to similar enterprises on a grander scale.[23]

Sarah's vision was accurate: by 1888 Mormon Relief Societies
owned land and buildings valued at $95,000, and by the turn of

the century Relief Society halls had been constructed throughout Utah, Idaho, and Arizona and in Canada and Mexico.[24]

In 1895 when Anna Howard Shaw and Susan B. Anthony visited Utah, Sarah Kimball, then Utah Honorary Vice-president of the National American Woman's Suffrage Association, reminisced about reading Anthony's feminist articles in the *Revolution* in the 1860s. She explained that at that time she "would not have dared to say the bold, grand things that Miss Anthony said, . . . and as time rolled on we were very careful."[25] When the Fifteenth Ward hall was under construction in 1868–69, Mrs. Kimball encountered some opposition and attempted to negotiate with the brethren in the ward for the women's increased activities. "We know there is strong prejudice existing in the minds of many against female organizations, and we regret to acknowledge there is cause for this prejudice," she said, indicating that she did not subscribe to the feelings of the woman calling "for a place in the senate and all public offices and responsibilities, neglecting her first and highest duty, that of making home happy." In essence Mrs. Kimball promised that she and her sisters would assume only such powers as were delegated to them by the ward's priesthood leaders, but these powers the women must assume or be doomed with the "unprofitable servant." "In relation to the storehouse being erected," she added, "the echo has reached our ears that the society wished the brethren to do all the work, and for them to have credit of it. We do not know where the sound originated, but we wish to inform all present that it is entirely a mistake."[26]

In the years that followed the woolen cloth, carpet rags, spools of cotton, baby stockings, crewel and braid, dried fruits, valentines, buttons, shoes, and mocassins made by Fifteenth Ward members and sold on a commission basis by the sisters in their store helped pay for the building. These funds, combined with what the sisters collected in monthly donations, were extensive enough to furnish the hall; to purchase shares for the ward organ; to build a granary and stock it with grain; to contribute to funds for Perpetual Emigration, for the Salt Lake and Logan temples, and for the Deseret Hospital; to provide a carpet for the ward meetinghouse; and to purchase a knitting machine and to set up a tailoring establishment within the ward. Such contributions would have been typical of Relief Societies throughout the church in the 1870s and 1880s, who also provided food, clothing, and quilts for the poor and temple and burial garments for church members.[27] In addition, Fifteenth Ward sisters engaged in some less typical Relief Society activities: sending assistance to those who suffered in the Chicago fire, mailing the *Woman's Exponent* to English sisters too poor to subscribe, beginning a ward kindergarten and financing the teacher's professional training as well as paying tuition for poor children, founding a ward library, and sponsoring quarterly parties for the ward's widowed and aged. These were profitable servants putting their delegated powers to usury.

Remarkably complete minutes of Fifteenth Ward Relief Society meetings are extant for the years between 1867 and Sarah Kimball's death in 1898. They reveal something of her concerns and expertise as a leader. Sarah, "who had been both rich and poor, [who] had moved in all grades of society, had always seen much good and intelligence in woman." She was constantly striving to help her sisters exercise their minds. A few months after the hall was dedicated and the sisters were settling down to regular meetings, Sister Kimball said she "wished the sisters to come to the society meetings prepared to entertain each other with reading, speaking, or singing, and not spend all the time in work." This they did, and the society gathered to sew carpet rags and quilts while members took turns reading from the scriptures, from Parley P. Pratt's *Key to Theology,* and from some contemporary books and periodicals such as *Woman and Her Era* and the *Phrenological Journal.*[28]

Mrs. Kimball attempted to vary the curriculum, placing heavy stress on the study of physiology in 1872–73. She told her sisters that "human bodies were not forlorn, disagreeable objects, and should not be subjected to the causes that would make them such." Accordingly she preached dress reform, declaring that "tight lacing was a sin against humanity."[29] She did not limit her scope of concern to her own ward, but suggested the setting up of physiology classes among the Relief Society and Young Ladies MIA organizations throughout the church.

In 1881 the Fifteenth Ward Relief Society attempted to center weekly discussions on basic gospel principles, and Sarah became frustrated when attendance dropped off. On April 14, 1881, the secretary recorded:

Pres. S. M. Kimball said that we were eternal beings and that there was a germ within us that was eternal. Said the glory of God was His intelligence and that our glory hereafter was our intelligence. Said we came together to learn our responsibilities to ourselves, to God and to all the world. Said if these meetings were not interesting to the sisters we would return to work again.

They returned to work and for some time "the ever faithful basket of carpet rags was brought forth and distributed among the sisters." But not indefinitely—by 1884 the sisters were taking turns presiding and designating topics for discussion such as prayer, the

Constitution, the Atonement, and the Word of Wisdom (the Mormon Church's health law).[30]

Sarah Kimball later maintained this same emphasis on woman's education in her work with the Utah Woman Suffrage Association. As soon as she was elected in 1890, she suggested that each woman read over the United States Constitution six times and that county chapters take up the study of municipal government. "This would lead to our advancement and the enlargement of our capacities," she said. Fifteen hundred members of the UWSA participated in classes in civil government during 1890–91, forming mock legislative assemblies to help women understand the bill-passing process. Woman, said Mrs. Kimball, must "intelligently assert her selfhood in a manner that will enable her to labor more effectively for the general good of humanity."[31]

Convinced that each woman should have a sense of self, President Sarah Kimball delegated significant responsibilities to the Fifteenth Ward sisters, and did not intrude upon such assignments. Elizabeth Duncanson was president of the Relief Society's teachers quorum (or visiting committee) for almost as long as Sarah was Relief Society president. This committee held separate weekly meetings and kept separate minutes. Sarah was usually present, but did not take charge. When Brigham Young encouraged home manufacture among Latter-day Saint women, Sarah Kimball designated six women to oversee everything the ward sisters were producing, from feather brushes to temple clothing. She was interested in developing leadership skills in women other than herself, and her efficient administration in the Fifteenth Ward left her free to pursue other political and church activities.

And she served as a first-rate example of confident, capable womanhood. Emmeline B. Wells recalled that her ideas were independent and original and that "in public measures her plans were well-matured before she presented them, and therefore the more convincing." Wells added that Sarah's "decidedly positive manner" was construed by some as aggressive, but others appreciated her straightforwardness. When her Relief Society considered building a granary in 1876, Mrs. Kimball approached the ward bishopric and spelled out three alternatives. A brother had proffered space in one of his buildings; the Relief Society could sell stock subscriptions and purchase the vacant lot behind their store; or, if the ward would help in the construction of a fireproof granary and stock it with 350 bushels of wheat, Sarah would donate some of her own land in the ward for the site. A decision was not reached immediately, but Sarah's preparation raised the pertinent issues, and one of the brethren present noted that "he was always pleased with a plain statement of facts such as had been presented by Sister Kimball."[32]

Though Sarah Kimball indicated that she was somewhat reluctant to express her views on the equality of the sexes as early as did Susan B. Anthony, she apparently lost all hesitation as soon as it was clear that there was a place within the Latter-day Saint scheme for a woman's rights advocate. Sister Kimball was never one to go against the church's presiding males, but when the territorial legislature granted the right of suffrage to Utah women in 1870, Sarah affirmed "that she had waited patiently a long time and now that we were granted the right of suffrage, she would openly declare herself a woman's rights woman."[32] In the years that followed, Sarah's oft-expressed opinions on woman's equality gained her a reputation for being strong-minded. "She was a woman one liked to talk with even if one could not always coincide with her views, and one was pretty sure to learn something by conversation with her," recollected one associate. "Even if one was worsted in an argument, she was certainly well worth listening to, and excellent in debate."[34] Writing to the *Deseret News* editor to disagree with his comments about women's right to hold public office, admonishing Relief Society sisters to honor women as well as the brethren, petitioning the governor to appoint women as university regents, or telling younger women that maternity meant schooling the child in "social, moral, and political purity and majesty," Sarah Kimball "never hesitated in giving her opinion upon equality of the sexes." And no one who knew her doubted the strength of her convictions.

Although remembered by Utahns as the state's pioneer suffragist, Sarah M. Kimball waged her most ardent campaign for woman's rights during the 1870s and 1880s when Utah women were exercising their elective franchise. She geared her efforts at awakening women to their responsibilities and possibilities. The real struggle for suffrage came after 1887 when the Edmunds-Tucker Bill disfranchised Utah women. During the urgent campaign of the 1890s, aging Sarah Kimball was not as active in organizing local suffrage auxiliaries and communicating with national suffrage leaders as were younger proponents of woman's suffrage, most notably Emily S. Richards. But Sarah's endorsement of the goals and programs of the local movement was unwavering and her sanction, as one of the older generation and an established advocate of woman's advancement, undoubtedly helped to garner support for the cause.[35]

By choice, it seems, Mrs. Kimball refused to allow her involvement with public weal to usurp her vital concern for individual men and women. Perhaps it was this concern that kept her so occupied with her work in the Fifteenth Ward. Though she was active in territorial politics and suffrage activities and though she served with the general Relief Society presidency and board for almost twenty years, much of her life continued to center in her own ward, where as Relief Society president she was called upon to administer to the wants of the needy. The ward bishop, Robert T. Burton, praised her for her "heart full to overflowing with love and kindness to [her] fellow creatures," and Fifteenth Ward minutes reveal her as a leader sensitive to the personal problems of the brothers and sisters in the "ward family":

> Sister Kimball felt that Sister Ruth had a claim on us. Said she was a great sufferer in her feeling, and if we can comfort her in our prayers it would be a great blessing to her and us. Also spoke of Sister Ann. Said her case was to be [considered]. Said she was one of us. She did not know what was best to do for her. Also spoke of Father Andrews. Said he had grown old amongst us. She thought he had a claim on us as a ward. She thought the sisters had earned a blessing in what they do. She thought the people responded good in giving. She felt to say God bless the people, God bless the poor, God bless the society.[36]

And even when the sick and poor were cared for there were other needs to attend to. "This year I am happy in believing that the needy poor in our city are supplied with a reasonable abundance of fuel, food and raiment," Sarah wrote church leader John Taylor one Christmas. "But there are other hungers besides that for food," she continued, "and the question is, Shall we take cognisance to these other legitimate hungers and try to supply the requisite nutriment that we may have joy in witnessing the *best developments* of our home talents?" She was writing in regard to a young woman who hungered for "musical advantages," asking the church leader to help finance study for one who had unselfishly shared her musical talents with church members.[37]

Sarah showed an awareness of individual needs as women related to one another in groups. When she sensed that disagreements in Relief Society discussions were alienating some members, she pleaded with the sisters to recognize that "when we grow old we get very sensitive," reminding them that "we should govern our sensitiveness with judgment." She thought sisters "tried and wounded each other's feelings, but not knowingly," and should work to cultivate good feelings toward each other. It would seem the Relief Society sisters celebrated their successes in this area, since the secretary once proudly recorded: "The wool was picked without the merits or demerits of neighbors being discussed."[38]

Sarah Kimball celebrated her seventy-fifth birthday by sponsoring a special dinner for the widows and aged women in her ward. "The ladies came and went in carriages at her expense," the *Woman's Exponent* reported. Whenever personal support was needed, Sarah Kimball seemed willing to give it. She constantly admonished her sisters to pray for their leaders, be they men or women leading the church, the state, or the nation.

During 1897–98 Sarah attended her Relief Society meetings less frequently. Her health declined rapidly, and not infrequently the Relief Society officers met with Sarah in her home. At one of the last meetings she was able to get out to attend, plans for a new Relief Society hall were discussed, and President Sarah M. Kimball announced that "she desired to give the funeral sermon of our old hall." She reviewed the history of the hall and the Fifteenth Ward Relief Society, "and the work of progress intellectually as well as attending to the wants of the poor and needy."[39] She was proud of the society of sisters in her ward, a society that many said "prospered beyond any branch in Zion." In Salt Lake City's Fifteenth Ward she had seen in microcosm the effects of Joseph Smith's "turning of the key," and the subsequent "extended field of useful labor for female minds and hands."

Sarah Melissa Granger Kimball died December 1, 1898, on the eve of her eightieth birthday. "What an amount of interesting history you have helped to make," Mormon leader George Q. Cannon had scribbled to Sarah in her book of autographs in 1892. "Now you stand venerable in appearance, your head silvered, if not by age, at least by the trials you have endured, in an important station and as a representative woman among your sex."[40] Because her life encompassed a broad spectrum of Mormon women's concerns and activities—from family to theology, from commission stores to politics, from the needs of the poor in her ward to the rights of women—Sarah Kimball is representative of her generation of Mormon women. If she was exceptional it is not because her options were significantly different, but because her own strong-mindedness and charity made her exercise of those options exceptional, and often exemplary. "The liberal shall be blessed," she had told her sisters at one Relief Society meeting, and that statement seems a fitting tribute to her ideology and works.

Notes

1. See "Editorial Notes," *Woman's Exponent* 12 (1 July 1883):20; "Notes and News," *Woman's Exponent* 12 (15 August 1883):48.

2. Augusta Joyce Crocheron, *Representative Women of Deseret,* Salt Lake City: J. C. Graham and Co., 1884, p. 28. This collection of essays contains an autobiographical sketch by Sarah M. Kimball.

3. Helen Post Ridley, *When Phelps Was Young,* Phelps, New York: Echo, 1939, p. 106.

4. This meetinghouse was completed just a few years before the Methodist Genessee conference gathered there in July 1819. The stirrings of that conference prompted young Joseph Smith to his religious search in nearby Palmyra. See Milton V. Backman, Jr., "Awakenings in the Burned-over District: New Light on the Historical Setting of the First Vision," *BYU Studies* 9 (Spring 1969): 301-320.

5. Family group sheet for Pierce Granger, Genealogical Archives, The Church of Jesus Christ of Latter-day Saints, Salt Lake City, Utah.

6. Obituary for Oliver Granger, taken from the Journal History, 25 August 1843. The Journal History is a scrapbook collection of newspaper clippings and relevant diary and journal excerpts surveying the history of the Mormon Church. It is found in the archives, Historical Department of The Church of Jesus Christ of Latter-day Saints, Salt Lake City, Utah, hereinafter cited Church Archives.

7. See Fifteenth Ward, Riverside Stake, Relief Society Minutes 1874- 1894, v. 5, 11 April 1894, manuscript, Church Archives. All Relief Society minutes cited hereinafter came from the Fifteenth Ward, Riverside Stake manuscript collection, Church Archives. In direct quotes from these minutes spelling and punctuation have been standardized.

8. Emmeline B. Wells, "L.D.S. Women of the Past," *Woman's Exponent* 37 (June 1908): 2.

9. Sarah M. Kimball, "Our Sixth Sense, or the Sense of Spiritual Understanding," *Woman's Exponent* 23 (15 April 1895): 251.

10. Obituary for Oliver Granger, Journal History, 18 October 1840.

11. The exact date of Hiram's baptism is difficult to determine. He received a patriarchal blessing in December 1844, an ordinance usually reserved for church members. Patriarchal Blessings, vol. 9, 25 December 1844, manuscript, Church Archives.

12. Crocheron, *Women of Deseret,* pp. 25–26.

13. *Ibid.,* pp. 26–27.

14. B. H. Roberts, ed., *History of the Church,* by Joseph Smith, 6 vols., Salt Lake City: Deseret News Press, 1949, 5: 140–41.

15. *Woman Suffrage Leaflet* (Salt Lake City), January 1892, p. 3.

16. Relief Society Minutes 1874–1894, v. 5, 9 June 1898, manuscript.

17. Sarah M. Kimball to Marinda Hyde, 2 January 1848, holograph, Church Archives.

18. Crocheron, *Women of Deseret,* p. 27.

19. Emmeline B. Wells, "President Sarah M. Kimball," *Woman's Exponent* 27 (15 December 1898): 77; Sarah M. Kimball's remarks, "Weber Stake of Zion," *Woman's Exponent* 8 (1 June 1879): 6.

20. Fifteenth Ward, Riverside Stake, Historical Record 1849–1859, 15 May 1857, manuscript, Church Archives; see also Leonard J. Arrington, *Great Basin Kingdom,* Lincoln, Nebraska: University of Nebraska Press, Bison Books, 1968, p. 164.

21. Relief Society Minutes 1855–1873, v. 1, loose sheet titled, "Duty of Officers of F. R. Society Written by S M Kimball, revised by E R Snow," manuscript, Church Archives.

22. Report by Sarah M. Kimball to President Young and Sister Snow, loose sheet in Relief Society Minutes 1874–1894, v. 5.

23. Account of the laying of the cornerstone for the Fifteenth Ward Relief Society Hall, from *Woman's Exponent* 14 (15 June 1885): 14.

24. See "The Women of Utah Represented at the International Council of Women, Washington, D.C.," *Woman's Exponent* 16 (1 April 1888): 165; also *History of the Relief Society*, 1842–1966, Salt Lake City: The General Board of Relief Society, 1966, p. 104.

25. "Conference N.A.W.S.A. . . . May 13 and 14, 1895," *Woman's Exponent* 24 (15 August 1895): 62.

26. Report by Sarah Kimball to President Young and Sister Snow.

27. See Leonard J. Arrington, "The Economic Role of Pioneer Mormon Women," *Western Humanities Review* 9 (Spring 1955): 145–64.

28. Relief Society Minutes 1868–1873, v. 1, passim.

29. Minutes of Retrenchment Meeting, 12 February 1873, in *Woman's Exponent* 1 (1 March 1873): 146.

30. Relief Society Minutes 1874–1894, v. 5, 14 April 1881, September 1884.

31. Report of Utah W.S.A. at 1891 N.A.W.S.A. convention, in *Woman's Exponent* 19 (1 April 1891): 147.

32. Relief Society Minutes 1876, v. 6, 23 November 1876.

33. Relief Society Minutes 1868–1873, 19 February 1870.

34. Emmeline B. Wells, "L.D.S. Women of the Past," p. 2.

35. An assessment of the activities of Utah's suffrage leaders in the 1890s is "Woman Suffrage Reclaimed," from Beverly Beeton, "The Enfranchisement of Women in the United States, 1869–1896," Ph.D. dissertation, University of Utah, 1976.

36. Relief Society Minutes 1873–1883, v. 4, 7 March 1868.

37. Sarah M. Kimball to President John Taylor, 30 December 1879, holograph, John Taylor Correspondence, Church Archives.

38. Relief Society Minutes, 1874–1894, v. 5, 18 November 1887. Relief Society Minutes 1868–1873, v. 1, 28 May 1868.

39. Relief Society Minutes 1893–1899, v. 8, 1 September 1898.

40. George Q. Cannon to Mrs. Sarah M. Kimball, 21 September 1892, Sarah M. Kimball autograph book, 1850–1898, photocopy of manuscript, Church Archives.

Louisa Barnes Pratt 1802–1880

Ann Gardner Stone is descended from many of the well-known Mormon pioneers who colonized Arizona. With a master of arts degree in English from Arizona State University, she moved to Washington, D.C., where she taught English on a college level. Presently, she lives in Evanston, Illinois, with her husband, Dan Stone, and their two small sons. In her spare time she teaches college, writes, and does consulting work for various governmental agencies. She also conducts tours of famous architectural structures in Chicago.

Louisa B. Pratt

Ann Gardner Stone

It is more than the blood we share as great-great-grandmother and daughter that makes me feel close to Louisa Barnes Pratt. There is an affinity of thought, of feeling, and of emotions—many unexpressed—which draws me to her. Her journal, which she compiled from notes, diaries, and other journals in her fiftieth year, served as the major source of information for this article. It is candid; it is honest; it is subjective; and perhaps at times it suffers from retrospection and a dimming memory. What emerges is the portrait of a woman who is the product of her times, but also a woman who had the vision to see her potential as a person and to act upon it. She is universal, yet unique. She is human; she is real.

She was born November 10, 1802, to Willard and Dolly Stephens Barnes, farmers of some success. Louisa had a pleasant childhood, most of it spent on the family farm located in lower Canada, where she recalls a close and loving relationship within her family. Louisa was well-educated, often leaving home to attend better schools than those that were available locally. Her first job was as a school teacher, an occupation she returned to with joy numerous times during her life. At the age of twenty she apprenticed with a tailor and became an accomplished seamstress. A few years later she opened her own tailoring business, hired a girl to help her, and became a successful businesswoman. After a year she decided to advance her education, so she closed her shop and entered Preceptor's Female Academy in Connecticut.

Numerous attempts had previously been made by colleagues and friends to find Louisa a husband: she was, after all, well into her marriageable years. But Louisa declined all negotiations and gave as her excuse, "I was firmly resolved to never marry one of whom my parents did not approve, and began to feel that a life of single blessedness was my destiny."[1] But at the Academy she met the sister of the man she was to marry some four years later. After a tentative and uncertain courtship, Louisa married a seaman named Addison Pratt on April 3, 1831. She was twenty-nine years old.

The newlyweds set up housekeeping in Ripley, New York, where

Addison did intermittent farming but mostly sailed schooners on the Great Lakes and the Erie Canal; this sailing kept him away from home much of the time. Louisa settled in and tried to learn to be a farmer's wife, but she had some trouble doing it: "Now began my trials about housework. I had not for eight years done as much of that kind of labor, as to wash and iron my own clothes. This was in a country town where it was fashionable for good wives to do their own work, or at least oversee it. My husband was conceited enough to imagine his knowledge superior to mine in reference to some particular branches of housekeeping: such as making soap and sausages. Some terrible blunders were made! I trusted to his judgment till I found by sad experience he knew less than I did. I then went to a good neighbor for advice. She counselled me to assume the responsibility in my own person; and not to trust my husband. . . . I soon became a model housekeeper."[2]

In 1837, through the urgings of Louisa's sister and her brother-in-law, Caroline and Jonathan Crosby, the Pratts joined the Mormon Church. After some delays and hardships, Louisa and Addison and their four daughters arrived in Nauvoo, Illinois, to begin life with the Saints. They were there approximately one and a half years when Addison was called by the Prophet Joseph Smith to go on a mission to the South Pacific. He left in June, 1843. Louisa had conflicting feelings about this separation, but resigned herself to making a life for herself and her daughters in Nauvoo. She finished building the house her husband had started, overseeing the construction and even doing some of the work herself. "I was left in a small log house. I immediately set about building a framed house, buying the lumber on credit. By the time the building was completed I had won the reputation of being a punctual business woman. I was proud of my house, lived in it three winters, had to make a sacrifice of it when we left Nauvoo; never realizing but $15 in exchange for the house and 2 city lots."[3] Louisa also became a shrewd businesswoman as it became necessary for her to barter and trade for her family's existence. Her ability as a fine seamstress was invaluable to her as a means of support, and her considerable talent did not go unnoticed. She was hired to make suits for the Prophet Joseph Smith and his brother, Hyrum. The next year she set up a school in her home, and that brought in some extra money.

These were difficult years for Louisa; her children were sick much of the time, she had to scratch for every bit of food they ate, and she was separated from her husband and relatives. However, these trials seemed only to strengthen her and prepare her for the more difficult struggles ahead. She mentions time and again that it is only her reliance on God that saw her through these dreary years.

When the Prophet Joseph Smith was killed and Nauvoo's destiny seemed uncertain, Louisa felt as if her own life was falling apart. The Saints were making preparations to go west, and Louisa complained that not one of those responsible for sending her husband away had called to see if she needed help. The reply was, "Sister Pratt, they expect you to be smart enough to go yourself without help and even to assist others." This sounded like a challenge; Louisa thought, "Well, I will show them what I can do."[4] Nevertheless, she vacillated. Her inclination and desire was to return to her parents' home; she reasoned that Addison would be certain to find her there rather than in the uncharted wilderness. Finally she wrote to Brigham Young asking for guidance. Word came back from the new prophet by messenger: " 'Tell Sister Pratt to come on.' Upon this I nerved up my heart and put all my energies to the test to get ready, determined to follow the Church, come life or death."[5]

A little over two years later, Louisa, along with her four daughters, arrived in Salt Lake City, having survived some of the most extreme hardships of her life. Most of those two years were spent at Winter Quarters, where the girls and Louisa had lived in a 10' X 12' hovel dug out of the ground. In the meantime, Addison had returned from his mission and was residing in San Francisco, where he served as presiding elder over the Saints there. He had not heard from his family for over two years, and had no idea where they were or what had happened to them. When Addison was at last reunited with his family in Salt Lake City in the summer of 1848 after a five-year separation, Louisa said, "So much did we seem like strangers we scarcely knew what to say to each other,"[6] and in Addison's own account he said, "At Winter Quarters she, with the rest of the family, all but the youngest, suffered under severe fits of sickness, and the scurvy deprived her of her upper front teeth and when she spoke, her voice was unnatural, except that I could discover no change in her."[7]

Addison was not home long before there was talk of sending him back to the Pacific Islands on another mission. Louisa was anxious for him to receive his temple endowments (he hadn't done so before he left on his first mission because the Nauvoo Temple had not been completed). Work on the Salt Lake Temple had not begun, and so, in a special ceremony conducted by President Brigham Young and his counselors, Addison received his endowments on the top of Ensign Peak. This was small comfort to Louisa, because they were together only one year before Addison was called

to a second mission to the South Seas. At the April 1850 church
conference, Louisa received a call from President Brigham Young
to join her husband. Louisa regarded this as an bonafide mission
call, even though there is nothing in the official church records to
substantiate it. A blessing given her by Brigham Young, as recorded in her journal, seems to indicate the official nature of the call:

*He said I was called, set apart and ordained to go to the Islands of the sea to aid
my husband in teaching the people. That I should be honored by those with whom I
traveled, that all my wants should be supplied, that no evil should befall me on the
journey, that I should lack nothing, I should have power to rebuke the Destroyer from
my house, that he should not have power to remove any of my family; that I should
do a good work and return in peace; many other things, all of which he sealed upon
my head in the name of the Lord.*[8]

At the age of forty-eight, Louisa and her four daughters, along
with her sister and her brother-in-law, Caroline and Jonathan
Crosby, set out on the thousand-mile trek through unsettled lands
to San Francisco, and then boarded a ship for the 5,000-mile voyage that would take them to a land of strangers. Louisa did all
this so that she would no longer have to be both father and
mother to her children.

The Once in Tahiti, Louisa took her mission call seriously. She did a
great deal of preaching, particularly to the women and children.
She set up a school and tried to educate the natives in whatever
civilized ways she deemed best. But even while she was in Tahiti
she saw little of her husband—in fact, he was being held prisoner
by the French government when Louisa arrived in Tahiti in October, and she didn't see him until the following January. Once out
of jail, Addison spent much of his time preaching on the other islands, which left Louisa to her own resources again.

The entire Pratt family returned to the United States in 1852,
Louisa bringing with her a native boy who was the son of one of
the other missionaries and his native wife. (The boy lived with
Louisa until he was an adolescent, at which time he joined the
United States Army and became a famous Indian scout.) The
Pratt family took up residence in San Bernardino, California,
where Addison bought a house and two large lots.

The ensuing years saw Addison and Louisa separated more than
they were together. Addison received two more mission calls to the
Pacific Islands; he wasn't able to get passage until the second time
and then, once he arrived in Tahiti, the French refused to allow
him to preach there. When he returned to San Francisco in 1856
he was persuaded by his daughter, Francis, to stay with her and
her family the remainder of the year; he took a job as a typesetter

to help settle some of his mission debts. He returned to San Bernardino in 1857 and was surprised to learn that Louisa was planning to return to Utah to be with the main body of the Saints. Rumors abounded: there was talk of a threat by President Buchanan to send an army to march on Salt Lake City, and Louisa felt that she needed to be with the main phalanx of Mormons in that event. Addison disagreed, saying that he could not sanction a rebellion against a republican government, and he chose to return to San Francisco. Except for a brief period in 1862 or 1863, when Addison joined Louisa in Beaver, Utah, they never lived together again.

After selling her house, her lots, and her belongings for a quarter of their worth, Louisa once more made the difficult journey across the desert, staying for a time in Cedar City, Utah, and finally settling in Beaver. She was to live out the remainder of her life there.

During the following years the family experienced considerable turmoil, and Louisa was particularly troubled by the trials of Ellen, her eldest daughter. Ellen and her first husband were divorced, and during the year that followed, two of Ellen's three children died. Louisa's youngest daughter also lost two children during this same period. In 1871 Louisa decided to return to Canada for a visit with her family. At the age of seventy she took her first train trip across the country—alone. At every opportunity during the trip she preached Mormonism, particularly to her own family. She was also somewhat of a curiosity to her fellow travelers, and she was known as the lady from polygamous Utah. On her return, she stopped in Chicago just three days after the great fire.

Her last years were spent in Beaver, where she enjoyed the company of her grandchildren and her sister, Caroline Crosby. Louisa became a compulsive gardener, helped organize the first Relief Society in Beaver, worked against the passage of the Cullum Bill, and enjoyed good health until her rather sudden illness and death in 1880.

This brief biographical account merely silhouettes an active woman of the nineteenth century. In order to benefit from the rich texture of Louisa's life, it is vital to flesh out the silhouette, to breathe life into it, and then to understand the human Louisa.

Louisa was independent and self-reliant. She had considerable time to develop confidence in her abilities, particularly in her ability to care for her own needs, since she remained single until the age of twenty-nine. Even after her marriage, she had to rely on her own resources most of the time simply because Addison was absent so much. She recounts many instances of bartering for food or clothing or for building materials while she was living in Nauvoo, and because of her ingenuity and ability, the family never went hungry. Once, when she was trying to get lumber on credit, she said to the proprietor, "Tis true I'm a stranger, but you need not doubt a woman, as a general thing they are more punctual than men. . . ." She became adept at fixing up her homes, in making home improvements, and in doing much of the carpentry work herself. To furnish her home in San Bernardino she made bedsteads, cupboards, and a table, and she also built the outhouses, for which she received many compliments: "I often called to mind the many times I had fitted up places and left them for others to enjoy. I couldn't endure to live in a shabby manner, improvements I must make though I might not enjoy them one year."[9]

This same independence manifests itself in her attitude toward the Mormon Church and her place in it as a woman. She gives numerous accounts of women anointing and giving blessings to heal the sick, of women speaking in tongues, and of women prophesying—all duties usually performed only by men holding the priesthood. Her explanation is very matter of fact: in speaking of the Relief Society women she said, "Great good was done in relieving the wants of the poor, in visitation of the sick, in fasting and prayer for the unfortunate. When one of the members was sick it was, and still is our custom, to fast and pray for their recovery. To wash and anoint them, lay our hands upon them and rebuke the disease. This to the unbeliever in the restoration of the Priesthood might seem a daring thing for woman to assume a right to perform. But when the Savior said, 'These signs shall follow them that believe, in my name shall they cast out devils, etc.' he made no distinction of sexes."[10]

While she was still in Nauvoo, Louisa blessed her own daughters who had been exposed to smallpox and were suddenly developing a fever, because the elders were afraid to come: "The devil shall not have power thus to afflict me. I then laid hands on my child and rebuked the fever. . . . In a few days the fever was gone."[11] She says that from then on she realized what a determined will along with a firm trust in God could accomplish. Time and again throughout the journal, Louisa mentions women who performed healings and administered to the sick by the laying on of hands. This was usually done in the absence of priesthood holders, but not always.

The account of the blessing that was given in tongues to Louisa by the sisters is very interesting, not only because it was given in tongues but because it was prophetic as well (Louisa called it a prophetic song). Louisa was still living at Winter Quarters, weak from a debilitating illness that she had suffered all winter. She had almost decided to remain in Winter Quarters with the hope that Addison would meet her there and aid her in the journey into Salt Lake. One afternoon, while Louisa was attending a prayer meeting, the women laid their hands on Louisa and blessed her in a strange language. The blessing was given by Elizabeth Whitney,[12] who sang that Louisa should have health to enable her to go to "the valleys of the mountains," meet her companion there, and be joyful. Louisa was not reconciled to this prophecy because she still wanted Addison to meet her in Winter Quarters. However, she was cautioned by those who had heard the song to prepare for the journey and to accept what she had heard. When the prophet Brigham Young echoed this same decree, she said that suddenly everything became easy for her. She was given food, a team, clothing, and a wagon driver, and was able to sell those belongings which she felt had no value for the extra money that was needed to make the trip comfortable.[13]

Louisa gives countless examples of blessings and healings she participated in while she was on her mission. She had been given consecrated oil that had been blessed by Brigham Young before she left Salt Lake, and when the Island women learned that she had it, they brought their sick children to Louisa and requested that she anoint and bless them. This she did, and she says that according to the women's own faith cures were often effected. She was often aided in these blessings by her sister and her daughters.

Louisa never doubted her right to these spiritual manifestations, and continually exercised her faith by performing such ordinances. Perhaps this rather humorous entry, written during the first days of the journey across the plains, sums up her feelings about women's rights within the church: "The brethren met by themselves, organized, and chose a president without the aid or counsel of the women. This evening the sisters proposed to organize themselves into a distinct body, to prove to the men that we are competent to govern ourselves. If they set the example of separate interests, we must carry it out. . . . Last evening the ladies met to organize. Several resolutions were adopted: 1st. Resolved: that when the brethren call on us for prayers, get engaged in conversation and forget what they called us for, that the sisters retire to some convenient place, pray by themselves and go about their business. 2nd: If the men wish to hold control over the women, let them be on the alert. We believe in equal rights."[14] This is the only mention made of the "distinct" organization, so it is difficult to know if the wom-

en's resolutions were kept. Louisa had been appointed secretary for
the organization, and, as an official of the group, probably used
her influence to help the women maintain their resolve. Only the
bitter hardships that followed could have modified Louisa's determination.

These incidents present only one side of Louisa's character. The
conditions of Louisa's marriage and her relationship with Addison
were potent influences on her, and perhaps added the greatest
strain to the fabric of her life. Her statements about this relationship offer great insight into the interior Louisa, and perhaps into
the lives of other women within the church who had to contend
with long periods of separation from their husbands.

Her recollections of her courtship and the early years of their
marriage must certainly be colored by the experiences of her later
years, but even so, they provide a close and very interesting look
at her more intimate feelings. As she relates it, her attraction to
Addison from the very outset seemed to be one of approach-
avoidance. She writes as though she was destined to marry him,
whether they were suited for one another or not. She had been
enamored of him before they even met because of the romanticized stories of his sea adventures that were told her by Addison's
sister, Rebekah. When she finally did meet Addison she said, "To
say that I admired his appearance would not be speaking truth-
fully, but there seemed some kind of attraction, either from the
charms of the sisters, the high respect I had for the family, or because fate would have it thus. We became in some degree attracted to each other."[15] They courted for three years, and all the
while Louisa was plagued by doubts, particularly because of fears
she had that the life of a sailor may have injured Addison's character. Not until she convinced him to abandon sea-going did they
make definite plans for marriage. Louisa related the following
dream, which she seemed to feel decided her destiny:

*I saw in the air above me a great wild fowl soaring aloft; I reached forth my hands
to entice him to come near me, that I might take hold of him and perhaps tame him.
For a long time he kept out of my reach, but at last lowered himself down, and settled in my lap. As the wild bird alighted, I began smoothing his feathers with my
hand, when he turned and bit me. I beat him with great severity until he appeared
tame and perfectly harmless. I felt pleased with my conquest, awoke, and behold, it
was a dream! Well did I understand the meaning of that night's vision, and I knew
there was destiny entailed to me.*[16]

As in any marriage, there may have been basic personality conflicts to work out. Louisa was gregarious and social; she loved to
entertain, to have friends and family around. Addison seemed the

happiest when he was at sea or off in the woods hunting with his dog as his only companion. However, one of his mission companions said that if he were to choose someone to be isolated with it would be Addison, since Addison was the best company he'd ever been in. Addison resumed his sailing soon after the wedding, which caused renewed marital conflict, but it was the separations that made Louisa complain. Some of her complaints may have been unfounded, for Louisa seemed given to harboring animosity, or at least she found it difficult to forgive and forget. The following letter written by Addison to Louisa in May 1835 indicates a rather poignant need for Louisa to be both forgiving and forgetting:

While sailing the Lakes I see so much wickedness. I often am led to exclaim blest are they that live retired from busy scenes of an evil world. I often think that you know that I am exposed, I well know it must cost you unpleasant feelings, but pray for me, that my faith fail not. Yes I know that wickedness is lurking in every place, and that my little faith is not secure from it. It is unprofitable that you should be ignorant that I well know that there is at times a revengeful feeling lurking in your breast towards me for follies past before I ever saw you. The thought of it hangs like a heavy weight on my heart, were it for present scenes since I knew you, I could not blame you, but I now think it hard. But I forebear. If I have said anything to injure your feelings tis more than I intended. I said it for our good. Forgive if there is anything wrong. This one thing I would say if you have been as true to me as I to you, tis all I ask. . . .[17]

Those long separations may have given Louisa too much time to nurture previous resentments, and her memory may have only intensified these feelings.

Addison's second mission call seemed the hardest for Louisa to accept, especially coming only one short year after their reunion in Salt Lake City. Perhaps Addison's mission call followed too closely on the heels of Louisa's struggle across the plains. She told Mary Anne Young, one of Brigham Young's wives, "If I am left again, I shall choose another man."[18] She reached out for assurances of affection from Addison as well as assurances that her and her daughters' welfare would be secure. She said that she "ground down the rebellion" of her heart, determined to let her heart break rather than to murmur at her fate: "I expressed my willingness to have my husband go in some parting lines I wrote. 'Now I am fully reconciled to say adieu!' My daughter said, 'Oh Mother, it sounds too willing: do change it a little.' Accordingly I did, writing,'I must try to be resigned.' "[19] As she watched Addison prepare for the journey, her emotions gathered near the surface. An unkind word brought a torrent of tears. That first night without him was sleepless and lonely; she cried, prayed, and gave vent to

long pent-up anger. The next day one of the men in Addison's
company returned, saying they had been detained only a few miles
away because an ox had gone lame and he had come to get another one. Louisa was incredulous. Why hadn't Addison returned for
it himself? She wrote him a note saying, "Had you returned yesterday it would have given me greater joy than your presence did
after five year's absence!" Rather than sending the note, she was
seized with a sudden impulse to see Addison, so she saddled a
horse and rode the ten miles to his encampment. What followed
must have been a tender and reassuring reunion, for when she returned home she said she felt quite cheerful and "we felt more like
ourselves again."[20]

This incident indicates the range of emotions Louisa felt during
these early separations; it is also one of the few examples of affection and love expressed by the couple that she records, no matter
how understated it was. The flame was still there, but it was beginning to flicker. As the separations became more frequent and of
longer duration, Louisa's reactions began to numb, and she seemed
to stifle her emotions.

That tender farewell didn't sustain Louisa for long, and she felt
the rebellion growing again inside her. She said that she imagined
her trials were greater than any other woman's, and she felt that
Addison was glad to go away from home because she was no longer pleasing to him. Brigham Young must have been aware of her
feelings, because just prior to the April church conference Louisa
was visited by Brigham's wife, Mary Anne Young, who came to
inquire about Louisa's state of mind. Louisa was asked if she had
any desire to join her husband, and Louisa was torn. For a woman
of forty-eight, the long journey to the South Seas was not too appealing, but her life alone seemed intolerable, too. She received a
call to join Addison in the Pacific Islands at that April conference.

The ensuing years of separation are harder to explain. Perhaps
they grew too independent of each other during the early years
alone. Louisa remarked once after Addison returned to her home
in San Bernardino that he had been away so long that he no longer knew how to manage and provide for a family. She could do
everything proficiently, and there was probably cause for conflict
in that. On the occasion of their twenty-fifth wedding anniversary,
one of the few they celebrated together, she mused, "I reviewed
my wedded life and marvelled that I had been enabled to endure
so much; I thought of the covenant I then made at the altar; had
I fulfilled the promise to 'love, honor, and obey?' I had done what
I could. Why should we be required to make solemn promises
when it depends all on circumstances whether we can fulfill

them?"[21]

The reasons for Addison taking up residence in San Francisco when Louisa was living in San Bernardino, and later in Beaver, are hazy. Louisa never offered an explanation. Her daughter, Ellen, in a letter to a friend, explained that the reason her parents lived separately was because Addison had to pay the debt for his passage to the South Seas. But why couldn't he have done that in San Bernardino? Ellen said he also hated the cold climate of Utah and was not anxious to start a new lifestyle at his age. He did suffer from poor health—he had pleurisy and associated ailments that were greatly aggravated by cold weather. She wrote, "Mother has never seemed to feel at home since she left the Valley and she thinks she shall never be satisfied till she gets back. She tries everyway to encourage father about going there. Says she will uphold him to the last in any move he may see fit to make; but he thinks he cannot go; he likes the sea air, and wants to live where he can feel it; it makes him look so vigorous and youthful; he is scarcely the same man. Mother has better courage to live in a hard place. She has had a deeper experience and does not dread hardness so much."[22] The couple were living apart when Addison died. Louisa's journal reads, "To us all the world seemed lonely. But in our loss and loneliness, we were happy in the knowledge that his faith in the Gospel was strong to the last."[23] It seems a benign dissolution to the struggles of that marriage union, although those struggles took their toll.

In her loneliness Louisa was drawn closer to her daughters for companionship, and her love often reached the point of possessiveness. She continually implored her sons-in-law to take up residence near her so she could be with her daughters. And she never appeared to be pleased by her daughters' choices in mates, and may have been right about two of those marriages. Ellen, the eldest daughter, had a particularly stormy life—she married and divorced, married a man younger than her, divorced him, and remarried her first husband. Louisa's youngest daughter also had an unhappy marriage—at least Louisa reported it to be—and this added to Louisa's sorrows. How much and what kind of influence Louisa and Addison's unconventional relationship had on their daughters is difficult to say, but it's certain to have made some differences in their lives.

For the most part Louisa handled her problems stoically and alone. Her journal was perhaps her only pressure valve. She does say that once she asked Brigham Young what could be done about getting Addison to return to his family, and if he would write to Addison about it. She says that Brigham replied with an impatient tone of voice that hurt her feelings immensely, and she reports that she regretted having ever mentioned it to him. Louisa's natural tendency was to be with people, socializing and entertaining, and she mentions that this brought her some criticism. This was probably as difficult a part of her marriage situation as were any of the other burdens she bore—to be married yet single. This passage from her journal best sums up her dilemma: "There was something uncongenial to my natural disposition. My companion was always gone from home and I was required to maintain the character of a married woman. I felt it measurably unjust; but I endeavored faithfully to discharge my duty as father and mother both in one; and those who knew me best all praised me for raising my daughters in a manner to be respected and beloved. I had pleasant society, kind agreeable neighbors. With industry and good management I could keep my family above want. . . . Strong confidence in God enabled me to triumph in great measure over every calamity."[24]

The mellowing process worked on Louisa. Her later years make little mention of her domestic problems. She became involved in the lives of her daughters, drew constant enjoyment from her grandchildren, involved herself in travel, and became immersed in the fight for women's rights. The first Relief Society in Beaver, Utah, was organized in her home in 1873 (she was seventy-one), and she worked unceasingly for the poor and the sick. She became a gardener—almost to the point of obsession. It was as if the garden was a symbol of her own well-being—if it was flourishing, so was she; she felt strengthened and renewed by hoeing and cultivating it. In the summer of 1880 she wrote, "We need not complain— summer will soon be gone, too soon I fear, for late planted gardens like mine." She was to die a few months later at the age of seventy-eight. The last words written in her journal are indicative of the independent-thinking person she was: "What a mockery to call this nation free, when more than one-half her legal loyal citizens are denied the right of the ballot, the foundations of a government. Ah! But the Lord rules. 'He can cast down the mighty and exalt those of low degree.' Let the faithful women trust in Him. He will ere long adjust their cause, and help them to fulfill their destiny of Mormonism. May I live to see that day, and be a co-worker, aged as I am."[25]

It is difficult to comprehend the pressures Louisa endured. Not only were there the pressures of a difficult pioneer existence—the daily struggle for survival—but she was also faced with the psychological stresses evolving from a complex personal relationship with a man she loved but couldn't live with. Louisa has drawn for us her portrait in flesh and blood. We can sense her loneliness, her desires to "fit in," the drive to be independent. Here is no one-dimensional portrait of a "pioneer woman in bonnet and tattered shoes" stumbling through the wilderness. She was a woman struggling with emotions easy to understand—struggling to maintain her family and her husband, yet trying to maintain her integrity and uphold her beliefs of what was right and true for her. That she endured with such grace is hope for us all.

Notes

1. Pratt, Louisa Barnes. *Journal* (published as part of the lesson program of the Daughters of Utah Pioneers), p. 201.

2. *Ibid.,* p. 213.

3. Pratt, Louisa Barnes. "A Few Incidents," *Woman's Exponent,* 10(September 1, 1881):49.

4. Pratt Journal, p. 235.

5. *Ibid.,* p. 236.

6. *Ibid.,* p. 246.

7. Green, Doyle, "The Story of Addison Pratt and the Society Islands Mission," *The Improvement Era* (March, 1950), p. 230.

8. Pratt Journal, p. 252.

9. *Ibid.,* p. 301.

10. *Ibid.,* p. 380.

11. *Ibid.,* p. 233.

12. Elizabeth Whitney was well known for her gift of tongues. She received the gift of singing inspirationally at the first patriarchal blessing meeting presided over by Joseph Smith, Sr., and was promised by the Prophet Joseph Smith that this rare gift should never leave her if she was wise in the exercise of it. (*The Contributor,* 3 [Feb. 1882], 156–158.)

13. Pratt Journal, p. 243.

14. *Ibid.*

15. *Ibid.,* p. 207.

16. *Ibid.,* p. 210.

17. From a letter by Addison Pratt to Louisa B. Pratt, May 31, 1835, on microfilm in the Archives of The Church of Jesus Christ of Latter-day Saints.

18. Pratt Journal, p. 247.

19. *Ibid.,* p. 249.

20. *Ibid.,* p. 250.

21. *Ibid.,* p. 308.

22. Ellsworth, S. George, *Dear Ellen: Two Mormon Women and Their Letters*, Tanner Trust Fund: University of Utah Library, Salt Lake City (1974), p. 58.

23. Pratt Journal, p. 379.

24. *Ibid.*, p. 317.

25. *Ibid.*, p. 398.

Susa Young Gates 1856–1933

Rebecca Foster Cornwall was the second of sixteen children born to a Mormon military family that grew up virtually all over the country (and out of it). She studied literature and American culture at the University of Utah before teaching English and remedial reading in Murray, Utah, and Sacramento, California. She took four years out to have a family (two sons), to tend house, and to be a military wife, but broke under the pressure and returned to normal living as a Fellow of the Roland Rich Woolley Foundation, for which she assisted in writing a biography of Edwin D. Woolley and wrote numerous numerous papers on Mormon history. Now living in Salt Lake City with her husband, Kenyon Cornwall, she practices writing, chiefly theatre and book reviews, and has written short stories and a novel on her conversion from fundamentalism to Christianity (for which she has yet to find a publisher).

Susa Y. Gates

Rebecca Foster Cornwall

Before World War II Mormonism had a tradition of *grandes dames*—women who played visible roles in its development and who were looked upon by leaders and commonfolk alike with fondness, respect, perhaps a measure of fear, and tolerance for their eccentricities. One of the last of the tradition, and one of the most memorable, was "Aunt Susa"—Susa Amelia Young Gates, founder of the *Young Woman's Journal,* of the *Relief Society Magazine,* of modern Mormon genealogical research, of nighttime temple work, of domestic science in Utah's colleges, and of Brigham Young University's music department. In addition, she was influencer of a host of other church and public causes, both state and national.

Susa was the first and only woman to occupy an office—albeit a small one—in the Church Office Building on South Temple Street in Salt Lake City and this, plus her confidential relationship with Mormon Church authorities, helped to earn her an unofficial reputation as the thirteenth apostle. If the title embarrassed her, she didn't show it: "I was once jokingly referred to by one of the Church authorities as the Thirteenth Apostle. He told me that if he could just put breeches on me, he would put me in the quorum."[1]

Susa was a legend by the time she died in 1933, and many Utahns still remember her. My grandmother, Florence Thompson, was a ten-year-old in Scofield (a small town in the mining district of central Utah) when my great-grandparents took her to sacrament meeting (children seldom attended in those days) to hear Sister Gates from the general board in Salt Lake City. Grandma remembers a flaming red-haired lady—"How she could preach! I was thrilled." Actually, Susa's hair was auburn, but her spirited manner left a flaming impression on a little girl.[2]

Though she never officially became the thirteenth apostle, through her pen and personality she impressed her thinking upon Mormons of her day as few church leaders did. It will require an entire book to evaluate the nature as well as the scope of her influence, but one likely conclusion will be that her ideas, or those she championed, are everywhere in the cultural attitudes of present-day Mormons. To understand this influence, one will have to look beyond the public Susa Gates to Susa as a wife, neighbor, mother, and associate, for her greatest influence was personal; the influence of her writings and her public statements are but a followup to her personal impact.

She was the forty-first child of Brigham Young and the second daughter of Lucy Bigelow Young, who at age sixteen had married Brigham at Winter Quarters. Lucy, the daughter of Vermont converts, had sworn she would never be a polygamous wife, while her older sister Mary Jane was not averse to the institution. When an older man came courting them both, they went to a family friend, Brigham Young, to ask for advice. He responded by asking how they would feel about marrying himself. Lucy avoided Brigham for days afterward, afraid that he would press her for a decision. Later it was Mary Jane who

decided that it would be impossible for her to be happy as the plural wife of any man ... so she went to father, explained her feelings, and asked to be released from her vows. Her wish was readily granted with no bad feeling on either side ....[3]

Lucy stayed on to become one of Brigham's favorite wives. Along with Clara Decker, she was always Brigham's nurse during his illnesses. During his last winter in St. George he said to Susa, "Daughter, your mother never gave me a cross word in her life nor did she ever refuse to take my counsel."[4] From 1848 to 1870 Lucy was the seldom-mentioned but constant companion of Eliza Snow and Zina Huntington Young in their ministrations to the sick and in their efforts to establish the church auxiliaries. As a triumvirate they were sought after for special healings because their healings always worked. Lucy was said to have a special gift that she exercised in the St. George temple, where maimed and childless sisters were brought to her.[5]

The story of Susa's birth was told several times, each time differently. Aunt Zina was midwife on March 18, 1856, the year of the Mormon Reformation. The authorized version is that when Zina informed Lucy that the baby was a girl, Lucy exclaimed, "with great force, if not elegance, 'Shucks!' 'No,' said Zina, 'it isn't all shucks, it's wheat, and full weight too!'"[6] With this story, Susa wrote elsewhere, "you have a thumbnail sketch of my life ever since. Someone always either inside of me or outside of me, is usually saying 'shucks' after my hurried entrance most anywhere. And I am usually trying to convince my other self and the rest of the folks that 'it's all wheat and full weight at that.' Sometimes of course I don't care and let it go at 'shucks.'"[7]

Brigham refused to name the baby, telling Lucy that "the mother names the girls and I name the boys," and Susa obtained revenge on both manchild-loving parents by pretending to see angels when she was a toddler, and once by informing her mother that she had seven brothers yet in heaven.[8] When she was older her parents had a disagreement as to what her real name was; Brigham insisted she had been named Susan after his sister, while Lucy said the child had been named Suzanne after a post-partum nurse. Susa sided with her father, as always, but she was usually just called Suzie or Susa by her family and friends. In middle age, during a conversation with Susan B. Anthony, Susa mentioned that her legal name was Susan and that she had been considering changing her pen name to match. Mrs. Anthony advised her not to—Susa Young Gates had such a ring to it. So Susa remained Susa.[9]

While for the adults a great deal of planning went into the orderly process of domestic affairs in the Lion House, for the children the environment was carefree. The home was an institution with hired help; Susa's younger half-sister, Clarissa, once stated that she had never done "any cooking or kitchen work even down to setting a table" until her marriage.[11] President Young said many times that if he had it to do over again, he would give each of his wives a separate home, because his daughters grew up to be immature and frivolous. An elderly lady from Heber City claimed that President Young once stated from the pulpit, "Do as I say, not as my family do." And he mourned to his family that he was afraid he would go to heaven wifeless and childless.[12]

The effusion of wives was not a conscious influence on the children. Susa hardly knew many of them, and although she was taught to respect them all, "Some of them were queer and even sarcastic." Perhaps she was referring to Aunt Twiss (Naamah Carter Twiss Young), the kitchen manager who smuggled treats with her scoldings of the children. Susa's half-brother, Hon (Mahonri Moriancumer Young), drew a picture on the schoolroom blackboard of Aunt Twiss, the sour half of her face representing her manner before Brigham came into the dining room, the other half her manner after.[13]

Or she may have meant Harriet Elizabeth Campbell Cook, her first schoolteacher in the basement of the Lion House and "a tall grenidier [sic] sort of woman" whose "tongue was tipped with vitrol [sic]."[14] Harriet used to take pleasure in telling Lucy that the sickly, premature Susan would never live to maturity.

Others of the wives were more like aunts, although they never intervened to discipline. Clara Decker loaned books to Susa, and

Aunt Zina was her confidante into adulthood. Aunt Amelia Folsom was an idol about the time Susa was baptized; hence Susa's middle name was added at that time. Susa seems to have learned, in retrospect, much about human nature from the many wives, and she accepted them for what they were. She wrote of Harriet Cook, for instance, that in spite of the caustic facade, Harriet had a taste for symbolism and taught this appreciation of gospel ordinances to her students; Harriet "fought the fight and kept the faith and has gone to a glorious reward."[16] Perhaps Susa's attitudes simply reflected those of her mother. She thought that Aunt Emmeline Free, her father's favorite for many years, never had a testimony of the gospel as did some of the other wives, which explained why Emmeline undermined Brigham's counsel and often treated the other wives inconsiderately.[17]

This picture of life in the Lion House given in Susa's private recollections "for my children only" is of strong, individualistic women trying to get along in a household where there was potential for "constant bickering and hatred," but where "comparative love and harmony" prevailed because of a general commitment to Mormonism and to the family ethic of stoicism. In her public writings Susa unfortunately failed to show the realism—perhaps out of deference to the other wives' children—so that her generalized sentiments about life with her father are unconvincing and dull next to outsiders' vivid works.

Susa's father was not entirely satisfied with the children's early education under Harriet Cook. Later Karl Maeser, a European convert, became tutor to the Young children and to the children of a few other leaders, holding classes in a small schoolhouse across State Street from the Beehive House. Still later Susa attended classes sponsored by the University of Deseret, held at various times in the City Hall, the Thirteenth Ward assembly rooms, and the Council Hall. The university was more a high school than a college, and at age fourteen Susa was coeditor of the student literary journal, *Lanterns*. She took stenography lessons in her free time from David Evans, who considered her to be one of his star pupils, and she became proficient enough to be her father's clerk at conferences from northern to southern Utah and to record the dedicatory services of the St. George, Logan, and Salt Lake temples.[18]

Performers and lecturers often boarded at the Lion House during Salt Lake City engagements. Susa herself took dancing and music lessons, occasionally performing as a *danseuse* in the Salt Lake Theatre.[19] One of the local musicians was Charlotte Cobb (a daughter of Augusta Adams and Brigham Young), who gave Susa piano and singing lessons. The hapless Charlotte was tone-deaf (according to Susa)—as she played a melody, she would accompany it with a steady base chord that she varied only occasionally and with no apparent reference to the melody. Charlotte may have been the reason Susa was later willing to see her singer-daughter study in the East.[20] The entire Young family was fond of music and theatre. As a child Susa peeped into the parlor at her older half-sisters spooning with their beaus after a dance in the Social Hall, and like any child she longed to be old enough to go to the balls.

In the fall of 1870 Susa helped her older sister, seventeen-year-old Dora, run away with Marley Dunford and be married by a Methodist priest. No, they walked away, Susa later corrected herself, and Dora *had* been engaged to Marley for two years. Furthermore, seventeen was a respectable marrying age for Mormon girls of the period. But Lucy and Brigham considered Marley a drunkard and had forbidden Dora to see him. For her part in the tragedy, Susa was confined by her usually indulgent father to an upstairs room in the Lion House. Only when Aunt Zina intervened was Susa paroled three weeks later to Zina's daughter's home on the outskirts of the city. She remained there only a few days, for when Brigham took his annual tour of the southern settlements, he took along Lucy, Susa, and Mabel, the youngest daughter, to St. George, where he settled them in one of his two homes there.[21]

Although Susa kept a journal throughout her life, the only one now available to scholars is an account of this trip, and contains a page or two about a visit to Salt Lake City two years later. In 1870 she was an alert, appealing fourteen-year-old who was constantly playing the guitar and reading, who looked first for what kind of piano a town had, and who delighted in mirth. "Father beat us out to the water closet in Payson," she writes while stopped at Scipio, "and we beat him here." She describes herself as 5' 3", 115 pounds, with dark blue or grey eyes and light, "rather curly" brown hair, and adds, "I must confess my teeth are the only redeeming feature of my face." She notes that a man in the party said of her, "She has a winning way with her that you can't resist."[22]

To Susa and Mabel St. George was banishment. Resentment against their father was unthinkable, but they nonetheless resented the move. There wasn't even a social hall in St. George. Susa soon redeemed the town by organizing the Union Club, a social and self-improvement society of boys and girls, and she joined the St. George Home Dramatic Troupe.[23] The leading lady during the winter of 1871 was Elizabeth Claridge, nineteen-year-old superintendent of the telegraph office, who became Susa's intimate and lifelong friend.[24] In 1921 Susa described Elizabeth:

There is just one person in the world with whom association gives me satisfaction, rest and confidence, and that person is Elizabeth McCune ... I love Emma Lucy (her daughter) almost dearer than anything in the world but she is like myself a human dynamo, and after a while we tire each other. Eliz. has such a sweet passive spirit, and is so wise that I always feel gently rested in association with her, where ever we are.[25]

The brief diary kept during Susa's trip to Salt Lake in 1872 indicates that St. George had not been far enough banishment, that Hurricane or Kanab would have been better. At sixteen, she had become obsessed with boys—how they looked and danced and their deportment toward her—and in May she had a crush on several. In December she married Dr. Alma Dunford, a twenty-one-year-old St. George dentist and cousin of her run-away sister Dora's husband. Alma built her a modest, comfortable home on First North between Main and First West, a half-block west of the Pioneer Hotel.[26]

Two children later, in May 1877, Dunford left on a mission to England, reportedly to help him overcome his drinking and marriage problems.[27] With Leah and Bailey, four and two, Susa went to Bloomington, Idaho, to visit her husband's parents. She and the children had not been well, and she hoped that "the cooler climate in the neighborhood of Bear Lake" would be invigorating.[28]

Brigham Young died that autumn of 1877, and Susa forthwith filed for divorce from Alma Dunford. In March 1878 Dunford returned to St. George, had Susa jailed for a night, and eventually obtained custody of Leah. Susa was given temporary custody of the baby, who was to have choice of which parent to live with at age twelve. Dunford never forgave Susa for divorcing him while he was on his mission.[29]

The conclusion of one biographer, based on information from descendants, is that the marriage failed because of Dunford's frequent drinking and Susa's "psychological unpreparedness for the intimacies of married life."[30] Susa later admitted that she was totally ignorant about sex at the time of her marriage, and as a general board member she campaigned for early sex education in the home. There is surely the possibility of physical abuse by Dunford during his drinking bouts. We may never know what happened; Susa once wrote the story of this early marriage, but just before her death she ordered the manuscript burned.

None of the explanations quite suffice, for Dunford was trying hard to overcome his drinking problems, and divorce had much less social acceptance in 1878 than it does now. In later life Dunford was known by his family and friends as a kind, intelligent, public-spirited man who stopped drinking entirely before his death and who raised his second family to be faithful, abstaining Latter-day Saints. Leah honored him and never took the step of being sealed to her mother, although she had conflicts with her step-mother and the second family. Perhaps there were subtler person-ality differences between Susa and Dunford that intensified the more obvious problems.

Dunford's mission letters suggest that he was unsure of himself and was dependent on others for reassurance and esteem.[31] He was intense and sensitive. As for Susa, she had married at sixteen, a flighty girl, ignorant about herself and completely unprepared for the emotional as well as the physical give-and-take of marriage. During the next seven years she grew up—she became Susa, in-tense and sensitive like her husband, intimidatingly energetic, needing freedom and craving attention and admiration. They must have had a lonely marriage. Her decision to divorce Dunford must have been traumatic, perhaps made with the encouragement of her mother and aunts, but cause of the greatest sorrows of her life. She did not obtain a temple divorce until 1890. On her deathbed she said, "I hope I have not wronged Dr. Dunford," and "I could die happy if Leah was sealed to me."[32] Leah remained with Dun-ford until she was fifteen, after which age she became her mother's confidante and collaborator.

Within a few months after the divorce Susa and Mabel were at Brigham Young Academy in Provo, a school she had never heard of until Erastus Snow suggested she go there. Her mother had con-vinced Karl Maeser that Susa could teach music on the basis of lessons she had given in St. George. It was a year of youthfulness and freedom, including coed diversions and holiday excursions, meetings of the Polysophical Society, and late-night chats with roommates, which she recounted in a *Young Woman's Journal* ar-ticle.[33] More than fun, she had a rigorous schedule as founder of the music department. There had been a choir off and on at the Academy, but there was no piano. Susa bought one. Besides keep-ing up with her own studies, she prepared ten hours each week for twenty-two hours of music lessons and for several two-hour choir rehearsals. During this time her children were staying with Dun-ford's parents in Bear River.

What she later considered most valuable about her academy ex-perience was her association with the academy head, Karl Maeser, from whom she learned to appreciate the Book of Mormon and to study the gospel systematically. "Brother Maeser taught me to think out the answer of my problem. Aunt Zina and my mother

... taught me to pray for the solution, but Brother Maeser set my feet on the upward road of thorough self-development."[34] Just as significantly, Maeser was the first to urge Susa to seriously pursue a literary career.

The following year, 1879, Susa accompanied Aunt Zina to the Sandwich Islands. Before his death Brigham Young had proposed missionary lecture tours for his wives and for leading sisters of the church, and Zina was one of the few to go. Her two-inch-square notebook of the journey survives, giving glimpses of the excitement such an adventure must have been for her and her companion. During both crossings Zina spent most of the time sick in her "birth," but Susa was not troubled at all by seasickness. When Zina finally ventured on deck, they watched the "flying fish" and "in the evening the sparkling waves" and a "most beautiful sunset" in which "5 suns could be seen."[35]

About July 18, 1879, they arrived in Hawaii, to be greeted by President Harvey Cluff and his wife who, with Jacob F. Gates, were supervising the church plantation at Laie. Every other day a special meeting of the Relief Society was held, because the Saints were eager to hear Brigham Young's wife. Zina and Susa found the natives and the island charming; "the roaring of the sea is delightful"—"no doors locked here." They purchased an organ for the branch and each donated fifty dollars "for the good of the natives." Several nights they actually slept in "a native house," Brothers Cluff and Gates matting them a screen behind which to dress.

But Susa was charmed by more than just the natives. She had known Jacob Gates only slightly in St. George, perhaps because he was six years older and a quiet farmer not much involved in the social whirl. But on at least one occasion he had attended a presentation of the St. George Dramatic Association at which Susa's family was also present,[36] and perhaps he had seen Susa herself perform on later occasions. At any rate, he became indispensable at the Relief Society meetings; at least once President Cluff sent for him, presumably to translate. Then there were outings, including a pleasant ride by the sea when the mules kicked and broke the wagon tongue and the party had to wait for it to be mended, and arrived home very late—"a good night," Zina wrote. One day Jacob invited Susa to go hunting for ferns, and by the middle of August when Zina went on an outing "to the gulch," she wrote quite naturally of "Br and Sis Cluff" and "Jacob and Susa" going along. During the last week in Hawaii "Susa and J Gates went to the canyon," and then on September 1, Zina and Susa left for San Francisco, Zina again staying most of the days in her berth with

"Sue up in the saloon."[37]

Jacob and Susa must have done some serious talking during that trip to the canyon, for a few weeks after his return to Utah in 1880 they were married. He took her to St. George where their first child, Emma Lucy, was born; Jacob continued farming.

Jacob deserves to be studied. Like Susa, he was musical, playing five instruments mostly by ear.[38] A fellow missionary, Joseph F. Smith, knew him as "a man of sterling integrity, simple and domestic in his tastes, a wide reader, a keen observer . . ."[39] He was born to a Vermont family of "homely virtues," his father serving for thirty years as one of the Seven Presidents of Seventies. From these family descriptions and from his few published writings, it is apparent that he was a consummately practical man, blunt but kindly, full of humor and solid stability, and untainted by public ambition. "Not caring for public life," wrote Augusta Grant, wife of President Heber J. Grant and a close friend, "he has always been content to sit back and let his much appreciated and honored companion do the things which she enjoyed and which he did not care so much about."[40] A granddaughter said:

She was brilliant—wrote, read, gave lectures, and Grampie understood that. She was helping with the church and the gospel. Grampie understood her talents were very different than his; he saw that much more good could come from her doing these things than staying home and washing dishes.[41]

Descendants hasten to add that Susa would never have approved of "women's lib." And it is true that "Obedience to authority and reverence for the Priesthood (was) the foundation stone of her life."[42] "Her husband held the priesthood; he was her lord and master. His word was law. She always asked him before she did anything, and he always approved."[43] On one occasion, when she had her bags packed and was ready to leave for Provo to keep house for her ailing sister, Jacob did not approve. She unpacked her bags without a word and returned to her housework[44]—undoubtedly relieved. Susa herself said of Jacob, "He is my rock in mid ocean . . . his wisdom and confidence rest me infinitely."[45] Susa believed that marriages were made in heaven, and this one most assuredly was.

In 1882 Jacob moved his wife and daughter to Provo. Of the next four years almost nothing has been recorded. Three sons were born in Provo—Jacob Young, Karl Nahum, and Simpson Mark, who lived only a few months.[46] In recognition of her remarkable success in getting releases from all her father's descendants so that the church could assume control of the Brigham Young Academy, she was made one of its trustees.

In 1886 Jacob was called on another mission to Hawaii and decided to take his family with him, which then included four children—counting Bailey Dunford, who was then ten years old. As they were preparing to leave, Susa travelled to Bear Lake, Idaho, where Leah was living with her grandparents, the Dunfords. Susa had had almost no contact with Leah, who was then twelve or thirteen years old. Leah recalls that her mother took her aside and asked, "Dear, what have you been doing? Tell me about your life. Are you happy?" And Leah had replied that she had had a patriarchal blessing promising her that she would be a mother in Zion; she told her mother that she wanted more than anything to have a big family. It was probably a brief visit, as the Dunfords did not trust Susa.[46a]

The Gateses had written to Dunford asking permission to take Bailey Dunford to Hawaii with them, but they had received no answer. An indication of the bitterness between Susa and Dunford is his assumption that she would not give up Bailey without a legal struggle; when they came to Salt Lake en route to San Francisco, Dunford met them at the train depot with the sheriff and a summons. Susa mournfully but without dispute relinquished the child. The Provo newspaper reported that next morning, when Bailey was brought to see his mother off, "the parting was very affecting and the boy wept loud and bitterly and was eager to go with his mother."[47]

Although the next year Bailey would have the privilege of selecting the parent of custody, his mother was to be gone for four years, so he remained with Dunford. As a young man he studied architecture, worked as a salesman, and in 1895 went to Butte, Montana, looking for work. There he was killed with forty-eight others in a powder factory explosion. Susa did not attend the funeral with Leah and Dr. Dunford, and no comment about Bailey has been found in any of her papers.[48]

In Hawaii Jacob again superintended the church plantation, doing missionary work on the side and gaining "complete mastery of the tongue."[49] Susa wrote, kept house, and bore three more children. Little Lucy learned to dance and play the guitar, performing for Queen Kapiolani.[50] The tour was marred by the accidental deaths of Jacob and Karl, Jacob and Susa's two oldest sons.

Upon returning to Utah in 1889, the Gateses resettled in Provo, where they could have some land for raising animals and for planting a garden on which to train their boys. They purchased a house on Second East and First North, and in 1892 Jacob built the Gates Furniture Company on Main and University Avenue (later the Knight Building). The company was close enough that

Jacob could walk home for lunch and discipline Cecil and Hal, who were supposed to be hoeing in the backyard.[51]

While in Hawaii Susa had conceived the idea of a church magazine for girls. Upon her return to Utah she founded the *Young Woman's Journal* with the consent of Joseph F. Smith and Elmina Taylor, the girls' auxiliary president, but with little financial or active support from anyone. In the beginning its existence was precarious. For the first two years Susa's mother travelled throughout the territory at personal expense to create interest in the *Journal* and to sell subscriptions. During her eleven years' editorship Susa commuted almost daily from Provo to attend board meetings and conduct magazine business in Salt Lake City, and she travelled to many stake conferences to promote her magazine.[52]

During these years she was trustee of the state college in Logan as well as trustee of Brigham Young Academy; she became an influential force in county and state Republican politics; she promoted physiology classes as her father had done, until she became known as "the mother of physical education in Utah"; she helped Leah establish the domestic science department at BYA, teaching that and parents' classes; she served as Young Women's president in her own ward; she attended a summer school at Harvard University where she met and wooed Leah's future husband; she wrote two novels and many articles, poems, and short stories for church magazines and occasionally for national journals; she represented the YLMIA seven times at the National Council of Women, serving as chairman of its Press Committee for three years; and she was offered the secretariat of the National Council of Women if she would only impose on herself a moratorium to preaching the gospel. She refused.[53]

She also had five more children. How did she do it?

First, she was an expert in domestic science. "She was always thinking. Mother had a great capacity for work ... she never wasted a minute ... She'd come home and she'd have dinner on the table in no time ... She systematized everything."[54] Her policy was never to do anything that wasn't necessary. She did not approve of frills in housekeeping—interior decorating and fancy doilies and fashionable clothing—and was critical of women who frittered away their time on nonessentials.

Second, she had help. Sometimes she hired a local girl. And, perhaps having learned from her own childhood, she trained Emma Lucy early to assume many of the household duties. Before music, Lucy's training was "guided towards an acquisition of the knowledge of the art of home management." She was reared to "become a dutiful wife to the man who honors you by choosing you."[55] In Susa's "Notes for the Day's Work," August 19, 1895, is the reminder, "Go down cellar with Emma Lucy and show her how to clean it."[56] Lucy went east at age sixteen to study music, and over the next two decades became renowned in Europe as a coloratura soprano; she returned permanently to Utah in her middle age to marry Albert E. Bowen (later an apostle), never having children but rearing two of her widower-husband's sons.[57]

Of her thirteen children, Susa lost nine to divorce, prematurity, accident, or illness. Joseph Sterling, born in Hawaii, died at age five after the Gates had returned to Provo. Sarah Beulah, having lost an argument with her brother over who was to play villain in a childhood playlet, was shot to death with a gun which had presumably been emptied of bullets. Heber died the day he was born, and three-year-old Brigham died from dye poisoning off a candy wrapper. Of thirteen children, Susa raised only four to maturity: Emma Lucy, Brigham Cecil (who was always sickly), Hal (Harvey Harris), and Franklin Young.[58] Leah and Bailey, children of her former marriage, were reared by others.

These four children were an exceptionally creative bunch. Cecil became a prominent western composer, director of music at the LDS Academy, and producer of operas for the Lucy Gates Opera Company in Salt Lake City. Hal, who could not spell, hired a good secretary and became writer and editor of the *World Telegram* in New York City, and he later became author of many silent pictures in Hollywood. Franklin, who had his father's ability to play musical instruments by ear, studied electronics instead and pioneered voice acoustics in Utah, supervising the installation of sound systems in the temples and many public buildings and becoming an acoustics consultant in demand throughout the West.[58a]

The many tragedies in Susa's life, plus her father's attitudes, help to explain the high philosophic value she placed on domestic life. Major Pond, a booker of lecture tours such as that of Susa's friend, Madame Mountford of Lebanon, once approached her with an offer to go on tour. The family story is that her father cautioned her, "Daughter . . . you can go east on this tour and maybe become renowned, but if you wake up on the morning of the first resurrection and you have failed as a wife and a mother, you have failed in everything. But, if you fulfill these two obligations first, anything you can do over and above that will rebound to your glory."[59] If Brigham Young said this to Susa, however, it could not have been on the occasion of the proposed lecture tour, since he had died years before.

The years she spent in Provo were the most active of Susa's life. But the public and private rigors began to tell even on her. In about 1900 she wrote to Elmina Taylor:

Maybe I am getting selfish and narrow but home is such a sweet place and the children get more precious every day ... I believe I have been hard to get along with lately. I have tried hard not to be so but it was always difficult even as a child for me to work when scolded or driven and too I have been placed in peculiar relations with some of the (board members) ... I love them all God bless them but they do rasp me up so.[66]

Not long afterward, at age forty-five, Susa resigned from the *Journal,* but she continued to serve on Young Women's board committees.

The story of this part of Susa's life would not be complete without telling how she obtained her testimony—her conviction of the absolute truthfulness of Mormonism. "Not all at once, but gradually, as I grew older," she began to ask questions about the gospel—why there had to be creeds and forms such as baptism, what free agency meant, why women could not hold the priesthood—"these and other points bothered me." "Knowing my own peculiar bent of mind, I did not ask for a dream or any vision but I did pray to the Lord that he might show me the why and wherefore of every principle of the Gospel."[67] Susa's bent of mind dictated that she obtain a sure knowledge of Mormonism by studying all other forms and creeds until she had exhausted the world's supply of religious knowledge. At least she had to make an attempt to do this, believing all the while what her mother and Aunt Zina believed: they *"felt* religion ... above all, that is the only way any of us ever get a testimony—it is through the heart and soul, not through the mind and reason."[68]

When she was past forty, she spent "a year of lent and prayer" in an attempt to get a testimony. "I disciplined my taste, my desires, and my impulses, disciplining my appetite, my tongue, my acts, and how I prayed!" She read and studied Mormon and secular histories.

Then one day—about 15 years after father's death—it came to me while I was sweeping, one of the most humble chores women can do. I heard the voice of my father saying, "You know it is true! Never doubt it again!" And I never have! All other truths and facts and philosophies which came to my attention, and come today, I measure by one standard of truth: Does this or that idea or theory agree or does it conflict with the truths of the Gospel as taught in the ancient and modern scriptures—if it does it is mine! If it does not, I cast it out.[69]

Following her departure from the *Journal,* Susa concentrated on genealogical research into the Bigelow family. She began giving lectures on genealogy and began collecting statistics on the temple work she and her mother had done in St. George in 1877. Soon discovering that Mormon genealogical work was in a primitive state, she set about to personally rectify the situation, beginning by asking the St. George recorder to make his records plain so that the next generation could understand them.[70]

In late 1902 she accompanied Jacob and Emma Lucy to New York City during his one-year mission to the New England states— or rather, he accompanied her during her stint as chairman of the NCW Press Committee. Jacob was unhappy sitting in the mission office with only occasional opportunities to proselyte, but Susa enjoyed her work, visiting libraries and museums and hunting genealogical data in her spare time. Neither of them liked the city, however, and they came home as soon as they could arrange safe boarding for Lucy.[71]

Afterwards Jacob decided to settle in Salt Lake City, where he had been asked to translate the Book of Mormon into Hawaiian. The existing edition, the work of George Q. Cannon, was fifty years old; Jacob's edition was organized by chapter and verse, with references and a comprehensive index. The work required nearly a year.[72] Susa, meanwhile (they were now living on First West only a few blocks from the temple), was doing ordinance work and researching family lines. In 1904 Bishop Joseph Christensen asked her, "Sister Gates, why don't you go over to the genealogical library and hunt out names for the Young family?" At the library she found a few books (all gifts of Franklin D. Richards, a church authority), all in disarray. Magnanimously attributing the "dimunition [sic] of interest" in genealogy to the "scattering of leaders" during the polygamy persecutions of the 1880s and 1890s, she associated herself with the DUP (Daughters of Utah Pioneers) with the "distinct understanding that they would permit her to take up the cause of Temple work."[73] She was president of the DUP in 1904, founder of the Hall of Relics, and originator of the historical balls. It was Susa who first proposed the construction of a DUP museum, a project realized a half-century later.[74]

The next year Susa organized a weekly genealogical class in the Lion House that continued for ten years, along with other courses begun at Brigham Young University and the LDS Academy in 1908 and 1909. Soon outlying stakes were holding genealogical conventions and asking for teachers—first Susa, then lecturers recruited from among her first students. By now the DUP genealogical department had been invited to join the Genealogical Society of the church, on whose board Susa became a protagonist. When in 1911 she was also appointed to the Relief Society General Board, she tried to persuade the sisters to incorporate genealogy into the women's Guide Lessons. Two years later she succeeded. Some of the brethren saw this as a triumph: "The great Relief Society would take a hand in 'Provoking the Brethren to good works.' " Susa's motto was, "Provoke the brethren to good works, but don't provoke the brethren while doing so."[75]

The Women's Committee wrote the first genealogical lessons in the church. Susa and Elizabeth McCune visited or wrote to libraries throughout the country, looking for models for a genealogy library and looking for information on their own families. They established a card index of families for whom temple work had been done, a system which, under the direction of John A. Widtsoe, Leah's husband, was later extended to all the temples. Semiannual conventions, with workshops on research and recording, were held in Salt Lake City beginning in 1914. In 1918 Susa's *Surnames Book and Racial History* was published, the first genealogical treatise in Mormondom.[76]

The brethren were well-provoked by the time Susa was made editor of the new *Relief Society Magazine* in 1913 and correspondence secretary of the Relief Society a few months later. For some years the Relief Society had had only a monthly bulletin; now it was expanded to include the Guide Lessons and other brief articles and literary pieces. It was never the well-rounded magazine that the *Journal* had been, but its function was not the same. Here Susa developed her editorial style praised by Paul Cracroft, and for many years she had great freedom in her choice of subject and opinion.

It's a shame that Susa's genealogical and temple interests began before 1913, because in that year an event occurred that would have made her entrance into the field even more dramatic. She and Jacob travelled to Copenhagen for a conference of the International Council of Women, to which Susa was the sole United States delegate. Starting home, she became ill at Lake Geneva but after a blessing from Levi Edgar Young recuperated enough to go to London.

In London Francis M. Lyman was "dedicating her to the Lord," "Telling me I should not fear to die, for there was a great work for me in the spirit world ... Suddenly he stopped, and after pausing for about two minutes continued with these words, 'There has been a council held in heaven, and it has been decided you shall live to perform temple work, and you shall do a greater work than you have ever done before.' "[77]

For two years after her return to Utah she remained an invalid.

One day my mother asked if I would like to have Patriarch William White ad-

minister to me. I said, "I don't want him to come and dedicate me to the Lord, for I want to live." He came and stood at the foot of my bed, I cried out to him, "I don't want to die, I want to live—to live to do temple work!" He said, "Well, Sister, if you want to live to do temple work, you shall live."[78]

Soon after this, Bishop Keller visited the Gates home "to tell Mr. Gates that he had dreamed on repeated occasions that Mrs. Gates was to be fed some meat." Jacob bought a steak, extracted its juice by scraping it, and fed the juice to his vegetarian wife. By continuing this treatment Susa was in time able to go to the temple, where the workers promised her, "Aunt Susie, you shall live until you are wholly satisfied with life."[79]

Besides her editing and genealogical columns she wrote for two newspapers (by which she supported Franklin and his new wife on a mission to Hawaii), Susa's interests as a Relief Society board member included its visiting teaching and charity programs. The years just before 1920 were years in which the church began to modernize its welfare system. A major force in social services was the newer members of the Relief Society committees, some of whom had had professional social work training. Prominent among these was Amy Brown Lyman, Susa's business manager for the *Relief Society Magazine*.

Susa feared the popularizing in Utah of charitable institutions and the elaborate machinery of the modern case work methods. It was a system, she thought, in which professionals disbursed charity, demeaning recipients and givers alike by depriving them of personal contact and responsibility. "But there is strong sentiment on the other side," she complained; "the popular trend is in the other direction. Sister Lyman is invited to speak in Denver next week on the subject. The title of her paper is 'Permeating an Established Relief Agency with Case Work.' "[80]

When some members of the general board recommended the establishment of a home for the elderly and orphans, Susa protested. "We Latter-day Saints have no orphanages, alms houses, etc. We have always taken care of our poor, our aged and our orphans, as families and as neighbors, while the State has provided houses for the incorrigible youth as well as the mentally imbalanced."[81]

She recommended instead an insurance program for members of the church that would include life and funeral insurance, maternity insurance, hospital insurance, school insurance, and educational insurance to be administered by the auxiliary organizations. Seeking support for her views, she queried Mrs. Gilbert H. Grosvenor, a national leader in charitable causes. Mrs. Grosvenor advised a "judicious combination of the new 'Case Worker, Card Index

System' with your own direct method" while assuring Susa that modern case workers were getting away from the idea of institutions for the poor and unfortunate but that homes were needed for the feebleminded, insane, criminal, and those with tuberculosis. Charitable clearing houses did prevent duplication and facilitated research, suggested Mrs. Grosvenor, but Susa did not cite this statement in her letter.[82]

Susa was not permitted to read her letter to the general board, and was advised by several brethren to keep it quiet for a while.[83] But the differences between her and the younger board members extended to other matters. In April 1921 Emmeline B. Wells was released by President Grant, and Sister Clarissa S. Williams was appointed, along with a new board. Elizabeth McCune and Susa were retained at the suggestion of the First Presidency, but Elizabeth resigned the following month.[84]

For Susa, the most trying aspect of the shakeup was her loss of autonomy on the magazine. Amy Lyman was made director of both the editor and of a new business manager, and her salary was raised while Susa's and others' were left unchanged with the idea that "the honor of the position compensated for the lack of salary." Susa was instructed to submit all manuscripts and copies to either Sister Lyman or to the new president.[85]

Susa maintained good will toward the new president in her private letters to Elizabeth ("I don't think she has had much to do with this business") and toward the new policies ("the Presiding Bishopric are having weekly meetings with Sister Williams . . . and they have instructed all the Bishops to follow that example, so that you can see what a power for good this movement has inaugurated").[86] This was part of the discipline of Mormonism that Susa took to heart. But by October of 1921 she was also writing, "They dropped me cold out of the Guide work . . . Little by little the cords are loosening and little by little I care less and less."[87] Rather than waiting to be asked to resign, she wrote a letter of resignation, undated, which she delivered to President Heber J. Grant with instruction to use it as soon as it seemed wise. He was pleased, saying that he hoped the newer board members would "have sense enough to resign when they are wanted to."[88] Early in 1922 Susa was released.

Susa continued as a member of the Genealogical Committee of the church, began work on her *History of Women*, taught biography lessons to Salt Lake women, and continued to speak to conferences and stakes, but worked most intensively on her *Life Story of Brigham Young*. The book was written in collaboration with her daughter, Leah, who did the greater share of editing and polishing of Susa's rough reminiscences. With Jacob, Susa attended the temple daily, where "We have an occasional eruption of the usual volcano among the sisters ... but things quiet down very nicely in a short time, and we get along pretty well considering."[89]

Among Susa's fears was death. On her deathbed she had not resolved her unhappiness over her early divorce, over Leah not being sealed to her, and over Hal's inactivity in the church. After weeks of pain and lying bedridden, she died of cancer May 27, 1933, at the age of seventy-seven.

"Utah's most distinguished daughter" left a great body of mourners.[90] One coworker wrote, "All that is written of Mrs. Gates ... will be necessarily inadequate, it is only through the perspective of years that her achievements and dynamic power will be discernible."[91] "She had a faculty for far-sightedness with respect to the spiritual and intellectual needs of her sisters in the church," wrote President Heber J. Grant's daughter. "Having sensed the need, she lost no time in providing for it."[92] Probably the finest tribute was paid by a son-in-law:

I shall mourn because I shall miss the exhibitions of her kindness and loyalty, the hours of illuminating conversation which I have enjoyed with her in the past, the stimulation which came from contact with her inquiring, alert and informed mind ... I shall miss that scintillating wit with which her conversation sparkled, and the rich humor which saved her always from taking herself seriously. ...[93]

Whether on a railroad car with church leaders and their families heading for Vermont for the dedication of the Joseph Smith Memorial, or bound to San Francisco for a world genealogical convention, Susa was welcome company with her wit, her love of fun, and her good conversation.

It is not easy to characterize Susa Gates. A cowriter of the history of the YLMIA described her as:

a public-spirited woman ... having extraordinary initiative (and creative) power, traits inherited from her father. A vivid personality is combined in an energetic and somewhat complex character. She is engaging and brilliant in conversation, and possessed the repletion of sentiment which naturally accompanies an artistic temperament, this emotional nature being held in check by the saving grace of humor.[94]

She was praised for having meshed well her public and private schedules:

She is orderly and systematic in all her ways, and very practical ... an excellent cook, entertainer, devoted to husband and family. It is said of her that she is a human dynamo; growth, activity, development, progress—all these are the ruling force of a busy and conscientious life.[95]

She was "Aunt Susa" to many young church members who wrote

letters from their missions or their kitchens. They kindly ignored her when she sent them letters bemoaning the frivolous tendencies at Brigham Young University. She was so well-known, so widely praised, that some women seemed to resent her, and some perhaps rightfully pointed out that her domestic accomplishments had been overblown. She was the first to reject praise, sometimes offending the admirer. On the whole, she made few enemies, and then only among those as strong-willed and opinionated as herself. Because of this generated fear, I doubt that anyone disliked her in her presence.

Among her more irritating qualities was her impatience. Her neighbors knew her only by an occasional meeting on the sidewalk—"Hi, how are you, I'm so busy." A slow-moving store clerk would have discovered a less charming side to her nature. Colleagues found her abruptness annoying: "Mrs. Gates had a knack of sizing up a situation quickly, finding an answer, and accomplishing something before many persons were clear as to just what the issues really were."[97] Sometimes she acted on a decision before everyone was quite agreed upon it, giving the appearance of a bulldozer in motion, and sometimes she made up her mind on what she hoped was the evidence rather than on what turned out to be the evidence. She was an uneasy combination of vanity and supreme self-composure (she considered herself the best writer in Mormondom, probably an accurate assessment) and self-deprecation (often she herself was the object of her sharp wit), applying this ambivalence to others, such as "common folk" and domesticated women, for whom she had both sentimentalism and disdain.

In a woman of such bold and daring temperament, there are the inexplicable fears—of death, of the dark, of physical danger, of devils, and of evil. On a conference visit to Idaho, she refused to step inside a bishop's home when she learned there had been a murder in it a decade before. Not until she was assured that there had been other church leaders and years of priesthood peace in the home did she reluctantly enter.[98] Fifty years ago a researcher could assume these fears were merely part of a romantic nature that delighted in the melodramatic. We know now that the human mind, conscious and subconscious, is far more ingenious than that, dealing in symbols, relentless in logic. The suggestion is that she was not nearly as resolute and fearless a character as her public image indicated.

Her own generation and younger associates understood her more as she was. Now her public image is downright intimidating, and I suspect at times that she is being used to intimidate. It might be useful to examine her thinking on one topic—women's rights—as a way of getting inside the woman.

Nearly all of her expository works had to do with woman's role—in the home, in society, in the church, in heaven. But the only solid conclusion that can be drawn is that her writings contain many inconsistencies. If, as some researchers say, other Mormon women leaders said one thing and did another, Susa said two contradictory things and did still another.

The writings of her younger wifehood, published in the *Young Woman's Journal,* are fairly consistent. She pleaded for feminine self-reliance and moral strength, and for masculine respect for women's needs and differences:

In times past, women have ... done many improper things; and one of them is they often preferred men's opinions to their own and even yielded points of conscience for the sake of pleasing them, until, very naturally, they are looked upon by men as shallow, weak, and contemptible ... A course of self-reliance and self-assertion will restore our credit.[99]

To the brethren she said, "Each individual make-up has definite rights, and when these are recognized, many human ills will fold their tents like Arabs of classic verse, leaving the world better and vastly more comfortable."[100]

There was specificity as well as a measure of pepper in these early statements. If women are self-supporting, she said, they will be free to reject marriage proposals from unworthy young men. She was not a believer in the classification of the sexes—women being the refined, gentle sex and men being the bold, aggressive sex—although she admitted that might be the tendency. "If some men lean so far to the right that they are more affectionate, more gentle and more merciful than the average man, does it not follow that some women should be more stern, bold and aggressive than the average man?" There should be, in other words, respect for individuality; a woman had the right to "follow the bend of ... individual tastes and inclinations so far as circumstances permit, and as long as they (did) not carry (her) outside of the Ten Commandments."[101]

Susa was allowed to publish these things mostly because they were not radical in her day, but partly because she allowed conflicting opinions to be published in her own magazine and because she blended it all with respect for priesthood authority. "If you have married, don't make up your mind for a single thing of any importance without first talking the matter over with your husband ... learn to have perfect respect to the authority over you, whether it be parental or marital."[102] She certainly did not advo-

cate elimination of the sex roles; "the higher the culture, the greater will be the tendency to differentiate between the sexes."[103] This
tendency she seemed to see as a liberating trend by which women
would be freed from menial tasks to pursue professional and cultural interests.

By the twenties she was much more willing to stereotype the
sexes, putting much more emphasis on self-restraint by women—
not out of duty, but because it was their nature to cling and to
want protection. Perhaps this was a reaction to her well-educated,
aggressive, articulate young board colleagues whom she saw as
overstepping the balance of freedom and obedience. I suspect, too,
that for her the tension between personal ambition and belief in
an inspired, near-infallible priesthood was diminishing; she was
growing tired, less eager to defend woman's territory, more willing
to relinquish responsibilities to Jacob and needing to rationalize
this dependence.

Her *History of Women* begins with credit to the priesthood for
whatever progress Mormon women had made. In other societies
women had to fight for the privileges they obtained, but in the
church the privileges were volunteered—first by Joseph Smith,
when he established the Relief Society. By doing so he "unlocked
the ancient door" of domestic restriction and "opened the gate
beautiful" to a new future for the sisters. They would no longer be
bound by "the limitations of inherent tradition": in time they
would be entirely freed from domestic chores and would become
true homemakers and governesses in their homes. In the church
they would be permitted to fill missions and study the gospel systematically, and church history would be rewritten to include
prophetesses and the women's organizations.[104]

Both Joseph Smith and Brigham Young, Susa wrote, knew that
"a measure of public activity would deepen a woman's life courses
and broaden her social vision."

Women are the developers of embryolic life, and the moulders of all social group ex-
istence. This makes it imperative that man and woman should, in a measure, share
the burden and half the responsibility of living both private and public.[105]

Women should have a choice as to whether they stayed in the
home or went out into the marketplace; although they would initially lean toward the marketplace, Susa said, "the balance would
be struck."

When women find they are at liberty to do or not to do, to be or not to be, to fight
or to raise sheep, to plead before a bar, to cut off a leg, to swarm into the school
teachers' ranks or to make homes, they will gradually adjust themselves and choose
their own more glorious sphere of activity, willing to obey the laws of their own

being happily and justly. That is, they will, if they and their families will accept the Gospel of Jesus Christ and abide by its laws.[106]

That was the catch. Abiding by the laws of the gospel was the only insurance that women's freedom would work, for it assured that men would retain religious leadership. If men were not moral, feminine strength would destroy both sexes. Susa was convinced that exalting women—worshippng Mary and putting morals and religion in the hands of women—was the first step toward male debauchery. "I discovered by some historical research what the worship of a woman or women did to all the ancient nations, and I would have none of it."[107] "The official leadership of man is vital to the race—no more and no less than is the tender sympathetic mothering which makes life."[108]

[Woman's] creative home labor ranks side by side with her husband's priestly responsibilities. His in the outer courts, hers in the Holy of Holies ... He is the leader and she follows, not because she must but because she will. Whenever this order of living has been reversed in individual or in national life, the loss to woman and to society is far more tragic than the loss to man himself.[109]

In short, if women wanted their men to be moral, they had better expect to follow them, and if men wanted to lead, they had better take the lead in morals first. There was apparently no option of sharing the leadership.

Woman did not hold the priesthood "always and forever because she is the mother of children."[110] Furthermore, "No woman could safely carry the triple burden of wifehood, motherhood, and functioning in priesthoodly orders," either here or in the hereafter. This is a startling statement from a lady who was called the thirteenth apostle.[111]

Susa seems to be bending backwards to reconcile her feminism to her belief in the gospel. Sometimes her assumptions are discomfiting:

No normal woman cares to take the responsibility of deciding crucial points—either in domestic, spiritual or even civil life ... Women want men to decide, and then if the thing don't turn out first class ... she can say, "I told you so." Women do love to sidestep responsibility.[112]

Sometimes they sound vaguely topical:

Emma Smith was quite as dominant a character as Aunt Eliza and possessed splendid executive ability but she lacked the fundamental element of greatness—the power to subordinate her own will to the will of those who had the right to direct her and the wisdom to counsel her; in this Eliza R. Snow was supreme.[113]

All of her writing evidences a strong personal dilemma: strong ambition side by side with strong guilts. On the one hand she cries that "Women have all down through the ages thought little and worked much"[114] and then she cries:

Today's young women ... resent the attempted classification of housekeeping and homemaking as an art or science. They want occupations long filled by men as their only avenues through which to express independence of character and resource. There is an alarming tendency to consider the home and housework as neither beautiful nor worthy of women's consideration. Decadence among the nations first places women on a moral pedestal and then flings her out of her home to secure imagined liberty in public activity.[115]

Only segments of her *History of Women* were published, and the whole probably never will be,[115a] because the book is strongly didactic and is based on little solid historical research (except for the chapters on Mormon women). This is not the honest, personal Susa writing from the heart and from her personal experiences as well as from her head—this is a tired Susa writing from the head without the heady substance of information and personal response.

In a study of Susa's life and philosophy there are factual gaps that must be filled—her activities in St. George and Hawaii, her work in the NCW, her contributions to politics, her work as a college regent. Then there are the more sensitive questions—questions about her life with Alma Dunford; her relationship with her children, especially Leah, Bailey, and Hal; the unspoken agreements in her partnership with Jacob; the intimate conflicts of a dynamic personality that are only hinted at in her essays but that are inadvertently revealed in her fiction.[116]

Is Susa worth further study? Yes, if only to preserve family pride and traditions. But history has even more important functions. Susa was creative, perceptive, unusually receptive to nuances in Mormon culture, and unusually vocal about her perceptions. Her home life is of as much interest as is her public life, for there too she perpetuated patterns of communication and interaction that she learned in childhood and that she perceived in adulthood as the correct way to do things.

It may be that in Susa's life lies the key to many perplexing questions about our own attitudes and how they developed. In all her writings, for instance, she has little positive to say about Emma Smith. She grew up hearing her father castigate Emma, but she seems to have identified with the Prophet's wife and feared that she herself would fall into the damning patterns of rebellion. On the excuse that "my profound admiration for the many fine traits of her character might lead me to praise where I should keep silent," she made sometimes cruel and misinformed references to Emma Smith.[117]

There is her attitude toward birth control. For Susa no legitimate method of birth control existed, not even continence. To the
"young women [single and married] who are coming into office
here and elsewhere with this new R.S. movement" she took it
upon herself to ask three questions: "Do you keep the word of wisdom? Do you play cards? Do you encourage by word or example
this birth control movement?"[118] A regular feature in the *Relief Society Magazine* was a column, "Unusual Mothers," invariably a ros-
ter of women who had had sixteen or more children, the greatest
praise going to those who had lost the greatest number of infants.

Other themes in her life and writings need to be explored.
Though she spent a lifetime in intellectual pursuits, she distrusted
intellectualism in herself and in others. After she reached middle
age, she was especially vehement in decrying the emphasis on
worldly education that led Zion's children from the truth. Though
she courted the "Gentiles," already in the second generation the
feeling of kinship with New England society had been lost and
Susa approached it as an outsider, defensive before ever meeting
it, always a bit surprised when it turned out to be humane.
Though privately she held a realistic assessment of the pioneers (at
least the female pioneers), she did not bequeath this to her public,
giving them instead a one-sided picture of their predecessors as human beings—although for her day her depictions were quite realistic.

Undoubtedly the major theme of her life will be her willingness
to jump in and begin the impossible. No one can avoid a profound respect for her energy, self-discipline, far-sightedness, and
the regard she showed us by refusing to leave the undone undone.
Her work was accomplished under great personal tensions, suggesting great personal courage. We owe her as much as we do almost
any leader in our history, and yet she has been mostly forgotten.
Why? Because she was a woman? Because the flaws in her life are
frightening? Or because, through all her protests, she deprecated
hers and other women's contributions and impressed this attitude
all too well on subsequent generations?

Notes

1. Susa Young Gates, notes on her testimony, typescript, Susa Amelia Young Gates collection, Utah State Historical Society.

2. Autobiography of Florence Elizabeth Johnson Thompson, typescript in possession of the author, December 1974, p. 1. I have been unable to verify any visit to Susa to the Scofield or Sunnyside or Winter Quarters wards in those ward and branch records.

3. Susa Young Gates and Leah Dunford Widtsoe, *The Life Story of Brigham Young*, New York: Macmillan, 1930, p. 342; M. R. Werner, *Brigham Young*, New York: Harcourt, Brace and Co., 1925, p. 337.

4. Gates, "My Recollections," typescript, Utah State Historical Society Collection (hereafter cited as *USHS*).

5. "Sketch of the Labors of Sister Lucy B. Young in the Temples," *Young Woman's Journal* 4:299 (April 1893).

6. Gates, "The Editor Presumes to Talk About Herself," *Young Woman's Journal* 7:200–203 (January 1896).

7. Gates, "My Recollections," crossed-out lines.

8. *Ibid.*

9. Gates, "The Editor Presumes."

10. Besides *The Life Story of Brigham Young* and "My Recollections," see "Family Life Among the Mormons," *North American Review* (March 1890), by a "Daughter of Brigham Young."

11. Gene A. Sessions, ed., *Mormon Democrat: The Religious and Political Memoirs of James Henry Moyle*, Salt Lake City: Historical Department of The Church of Jesus Christ of Latter-day Saints, 1975, p. 74.

12. Gates, "My Recollections."

13. *Ibid.*

14. *Ibid.*

15. *Ibid.*

16. *Ibid.*

17. *Ibid.*

18. Jas. T. Jakeman, *Album "Daughters of the Utah Pioneers and Their Mothers,"* n.p.: Western Publishing Co., Inc., n.d. but probably 1916, p. 29.

19. *Ibid.,* p. 30.

20. Gates, "My Recollections."

21. *Ibid,;* "Life Items of Susa Y. Gates, USHS Collection, typescript.

22. Typed transcript of the journal made by Mrs. Gates, USHS Collection. In preface to the transcript she wrote, "This little book has been out of my possession for years; and recently it has returned to me. What a glimpse these pages give of my girlish ideals and hopes. But thank God I was preserved from sin."

23. Jakeman, p. 30.

24. Gates, *Memorial to Elizabeth Claridge McCune,* Salt Lake City, 1924, p. 16.

25. Letters from Mrs. Gates to Elizabeth McCune, August 30, 1921, in Susa Amelia Young Gates Collection of the Archives of The Church of Jesus Christ of Latter-day Saints, now on microfilm.

26. According to descendants, Alma was a cousin of Marley Dunford. This could not be verified, as the marriage date was from Family Group Records of the Genealogical Society of the LDS Church; Kate B. Carter, *Heart Throbs of the West* Salt Lake City: Daughters of the Utah Pioneers, 1944, 5:346-7.

27. Journal History of the Historical Department, LDS Church, May 30, 1877.

28. Letter from Brigham Young to Mrs. Susy Dunford, August 13, 1877, Brigham Young Letter Book #14, LDS Church Archives, pp. 144–146.

29. R. Paul Cracroft, *Susa Young Gates: Her Life and Her Work,* master's thesis, University of Utah, 1959, pp. 8–9. Cracroft's thesis includes a comprehensive survey and criticism of Mrs. Gates' literary works, but the first chapter is a brief biography based on extensive interviews with descendants.

30. *Ibid.*, p. 8.

31. *Millennial Star*, December 3, 1877, quoted in Journal History, November 23, 1877, p. 2, and *Deseret News*, March 6, 1878.

32. Cracroft, p. 38.

33. *Young Woman's Journal* 3:337.

34. Letter of Mrs. Gates in response to a Sunday School worker's inquiry as to what constitutes good teaching; typescript, Gates Collection, USHS.

35. Diary of Zina D. H. Young, 1879, typescript in the Zina D. H. Young Collection, LDS Church Archives.

36. Account Book of the St. George Dramatic Association, 1869-1871, miscellaneous "Utah" collection, Church Archives, microfilm. In April 1870 Brigham Young purchased season tickets in the amount of $32.47. In November 1870 J. Gates, probably Jacob's father, purchased a dollar's worth of tickets to a single performance.

37. Diary of Zina D. H. Young.

38. John Louis Coray, "Emma Lucy Gates Bowen, Soprano — Her Accomplishments in Opera and Concert," master's thesis, Brigham Young University, 1956, p. 4.

39. Andrew Jenson, comp., *LDS Biographical Encyclopedia*, Salt Lake City: western Epics, 1971, 2:625-6.

40. Tribute to Susa Young Gates, *Relief Society Magazine* 20:400(July 1933).

41. Telephone interview with Anne Widtsoe Wallace, April 2, 1974.

42. Jenson, 2:629.

43. Wallace.

44. *Ibid.*

45. Letter to Elizabeth McCune, August 30, 1921, Gates Collection in Church Archives.

46. Susa Y. Gates and Mabel Y. Sanford, "Young Genealogy," *Utah Genealogical and Historical Magazine* 11:132-3 (July 1920).

46a. Oral Interview of Leah Eudora Dunford Widtsoe by Hollis Scott, 1965, typewritten transcript in BYU Archives.

47. *Territorial Enquirer,* October 30, 1885.

48. Journal History, January 16, 17, and 25, 1895.

49. Jenson, 2:625.

50. Coray, p. 5.

51. Oral Interview with Franklin Young Gates, April 1, 1976, typescript in possession of author.

52. Susa Young Gates, *History of the Young Ladies' Mutual Improvement Association from November 1869 to June 1910,* Salt Lake City, 1911, p. 107.

53. Jakeman; Jenson, 2:628-9; Cracroft.

54. Franklin Gates, p. 18.

55. Coray, p. 6.

56. Leonard J. Arrington, "Women as a Force in the History of Utah," *Utah Historical Quarterly* 38:5 (Winter 1970).

57. Coray, p. 64.

58. Gates and Sanford, p. 133; Franklin Gates, p. 9.

58a. Frankin Gates, throughout.

59. Franklin Gates, p. 15-16.

66. Undated letter in Almina S. Taylor collection, typescript, Church Archives.

67. Gates, Notes on her testimony, Gates Collection, USHS. Typescript.

68. Letter to Sunday School worker, typescript, USHS.

69. Notes on her testimony. She has added and then crossed out, "Or lay it upon the altar of prayer till God reveals the truth to His Prophet at the head of His Church."

70. Series of letters between Mrs. Gates and James G. Bleak, recorder at the St. George Temple, one dated January 7, 1901, typescripts, General Correspondence, USHS Collection.

71. Coray, p. 23.

72. Franklin Gates, p. 3.

73. Gates, untitled history of genealogical work in Utah, eight-

page typescript in Relief Society papers of Gates Collection, Church Archives. Now unfortunately on microfilm.

74. Jakeman, p. 29.

75. History of genealogical work.

76. Letter to Elizabeth McCune, November 29, 1921; Minutes of the Board of Directors of the Genealogical Society, manuscript in Church Archives, July 20, 1909; *Utah Genealogical Magazine* 3:91 (1912).

77. "Susa Young Gates," *Utah Genealogical Magazine* 24:98–99 (July 1933).

78. *Ibid.*

79. *Ibid.;* Cracroft, p. 26.

80. Letter to Elizabeth McCune, November 19, 1919, Church Archives, typescript.

81. Open letter to the General Board, May 12, 1920, Church Archives, typescript.

82. Letter from Mrs. Gilbert H. Grosvenor, January 14, 1920, Gates Collection, Church Archives.

83. Letter to Eliz. McCune, November 19, 1919.

84. Letter to Eliz. McCune, May 6, 1921.

85. *Ibid.;* letter of April 20, 1921.

86. Letter of May 6, 1921, and January 5, 1922.

87. Letter of October 25, 1921.

88. Letter of May 6, 1921.

89. Letter of January 13, 1921.

90. "Susa Young Gates," editorial, *Deseret News,* May 27, 1933, p. 4.

91. "Susa Young Gates," *Relief Society Magazine* 20:400 (July 1933).

92. *Ibid.*

93. "Susa Young Gates," *Utah Genealogical Magazine* 24:101 (July 1933).

94. *History of YLMIA,* p. 126.

95. Jakeman, p. 215.

96. Interview with Anne Wallace.

97. Cracroft, p. 32.

98. "Dreams and Manifestations," in Woman's Suffrage Papers, Church Archives.

99. Skurlock, "Woman's Power," *Young Woman's Journal* 1:442 (1890). Susa may have asked another author to respond to Santiago's characterizations of men and women.

100. "Overwork," *Young Woman's Journal,* 1:475 (1890).

101. Skurlock, p. 445.

102. *Young Woman's Journal* 4:528.

103. "The Intellectual Advancement of Women," *Young Woman's Journal* 3:566 (1892).

104. "Opening the Gate Beautiful to Women," chapter of *History of Women,* typescript, USHS.

105. From "Women and their Sphere of Action," chapter of *The Life Story of Brigham Young,* typescript, USHS.

106. "Women in Professional and Business Life," *History of Women,* typescript.

107. "Notes on her testimony."

108. *Ibid.*

109. "Women in the LDS Church," *History of Women.*

110. "Notes on her testimony."

111. *Ibid.*

112. *Ibid.*

113. Gates, "My Recollections."

114. "Women in Professional and Business Life."

115. *Ibid.*

115a. She slipped in excerpts or ideas from her *History of Women* into just about everything she wrote, however. And occasionally she gave lectures specifically on Mormon women. See "Women of the 'Mormon' Church," by Susa Young Gates and Leah D. Widtsoe,: Deseret News Press, 1926, a pamphlet.

116. For a somewhat harsh estimation of Susa's literary accomplishments and a tentative probe of reasons for failure, see Rebecca Cornwall and Jean Robbins, "Why Did Susa Fail as a Novelist," *Exponent II* (March 1976), pp. 12–13.

117. Susa gives little credit to Emma Smith for the founding and development of the Relief Society. Her most cutting comment on Emma Smith was: "The women of Nauvoo looked up to Sister Emma with affection and reverence. Her refusal to accept the invitation of Pres. Brigham Young extended repeatedly to her and her family through her husband's cousin, G. A. Smith, and through the Presiding Bishop of the Church, Newell K. Whitney—to accompany the Saints in their flight into the wilderness—was repeated again and yet again, sometimes with scorn. She remained behind, bringing up her children in the spirit of repudiation of the Church itself and what fundamental work which her husband suffered and died to establish, giving her support to a reorganized broken branch of the organized church. She married again, a Major Biddamon, a rough river captain, and suffered as only such a brilliant woman could in enduring the humiliation of his liaisons with other women.

'The mills of the gods grind slow, but they grind exceeding fine.' The principle she would not accept in righteousness with her god-like husband she was obliged to endure in its most corrupt and debased form to the end of her life." This is part of the biographical sketch of early Mormon women, perhaps intended for part of the *History of Women*. See Box 1, folder 1, USHS Collection.

118. Letter to Elizabeth McCune, May 6, 1921. Apparently Susa was not permitted to publish this editorial, for I have been unable to find it in any issues of the *Relief Society Magazine*.

Amy Brown Lyman 1872–1959

Loretta L. Hefner is one of twenty archives fieldworkers who visit repositories throughout the United States and describe women's unpublished sources for a multivolume reference work on women's sources, funded by the National Endowment for the Humanities through the University of Minnesota Social Welfare Archives.

Trained as an archivist at the National Archives and American University, she was a recent employee of the LDS Church Historical Department. She has a master's degree in western American history from the University of Utah.

She was raised in California and became a member of The Church of Jesus Christ of Latter-day Saints after she moved to Utah. She is currently employed by the Society of American Archivists, headquartered at the University of Illinois at Chicago Circle.

Amy B. Lyman

Loretta L. Hefner

Amy Brown Lyman is among Mormondom's most outstanding women of the twentieth century and stands out as one of its most sincere and devoted humanitarians. During her lifetime she assisted many people individually and created and led institutions that work today to lessen human anxiety and the unfortunate conditions that affect all of society.

Amy Cassandra Brown was born to John Brown and Margaret Zimmerman on February 9, 1872, in Pleasant Grove, Utah. She was the twenty-third of John Brown's children, and was the child of the third wife of their polygamous family. Pleasant Grove was only thirteen years old and was inhabited by many

> ...*original Utah pioneers, members of the Mormon Battalion and of Zion's Camp. These persons had all lived in Nauvoo and had experienced the persecutions there and also the persecutions in Missouri. There were Indian War Veterans and western explorers.*[1]

The community also represented many nationalities; people from England, Scotland, Wales, Denmark, Ireland, and Germany had emigrated and made their homes there.[2]

This rural town was a cross section of many lifestyles and cultures, all bound together by Mormonism. Amy said of it:

> *There was no evidence of wealth in our community, nor were there any elegant homes, but we had high educational, moral, and spiritual standards. We had plain living but high thinking.*[3]

Among Amy's fondest memories were thoughts of Pleasant Grove; she said:

> *I have said many times and have written if I could go back to the beginning of my life and choose my birthplace, I would choose Pleasant Grove.*[4]

The value of education was evident in the community in which she lived. The local elementary school was the pride of community members and was rivalled in importance only by the church. All the children who could attend school did so, and in their later youth this education was augmented by social organizations: liter-

ary groups, music associations, dramatic performing clubs, and
church auxiliary groups. To further their high school education,
most of the young people were sent to Brigham Young Academy
in Provo, Utah, and a few were sent to the Deseret University in
Salt Lake City. One administrator of the Brigham Young Academy said that more students were sent to BYA from Pleasant
Grove than from any other community of its size. This suggests
the strong role of education in the area.[5]

In their lifestyle, attitudes, and background, the Brown family
was clearly a part of the community. Amy's father, a deeply religious man, was a Mormon pioneer who helped lead the Mississippi Mormons in their trek to Utah. He was the church leader
in Pleasant Grove for over twenty years, acting as bishop in the
community and, in addition to this, was the town's mayor for
many years. Amy described him as a clean, sturdy, just man who
was unusually well-read.

Amy's mother, Margaret Zimmerman Brown, was a Pennsylvania German born to prominent educators on the paternal side and
aristocratic nobility on the maternal side. Amy said of her mother:

> My mother was a partial invalid for a number of years due to childbirth com-
> plications, and during that time she directed the affairs of her household and in addi-
> tion helped solve the social and economic problems of many of her friends. She was
> forceful, dynamic, and efficient, yet she was tender and sympathetic. A strict dis-
> ciplinarian, she kept both her children and her house in order. Some might have
> thought that she dominated over the lives of her children and required too much of
> them, and probably this was the case, but she was so wise and farseeing, and her
> judgment was so good, that we had more confidence in her ideas than we had in our
> own, and usually were willing to accept any plan she had for us without much argu-
> ment. She was a woman's woman and always maintained that girls should have
> equal opportunities and privileges with boys.[6]

Amy was reared in a religious home where church attendance
was stressed, where family prayer was held, and where the family's
activities centered around the Mormon Church. Loyalty to church
leaders, industrious living, and church and community service
were central values taught in her home. Furthermore, her childhood was affected by her physical surroundings. The Brown family
lived in a simple, one-and-a-half-story adobe brick home that was
illuminated by candles and kerosene lamps. There was no running
water in the house; water was carried to the house from a well.
Stoves heated the rooms, bedding was composed of straw ticks
placed on bedsteads, and food was, for the most part, homegrown.
She said:

> We had milk and butter, a variety of fruit and vegetables, and enough meat for our

good. With a root cellar, we had potatoes and other root vegetables practically all winter, and our cellar shelves were filled with preserves, dried and canned fruits. We planted lettuce and radishes in relay—as one patch was being exhausted, another was coming on. Our meat consisted of chicken and pork which we raised ourselves.... [7]

During Amy's childhood, she observed a high mortality rate in both infants and new mothers. Diseases such as diphtheria, scarlet fever, smallpox, and puerperal fever [child-bed fever] took many lives. Amy recalled one incident:

During one siege of diphtheria, three of five children in a neighbor's family died. They passed out through a bedroom window in black, homemade coffins, and were placed in the bed of a farm wagon to be taken to the cemetery, where brief funeral services were to be held. In another family, five children out of eight were stricken with this terrible disease. The parents became so desperate and terrified that they set fire to their home; the home and everything in it was burned. [8]

But mostly country life meant hard work, plentiful food, and the freshness of nature. The bountiful life of Pleasant Grove combined with a good education taught Amy the importance of a good environment.

In Amy's later travels, she learned just how fortunate she had been to live in Pleasant Grove. There had been no slums, orphanages, prisons, or almshouses there. There was nothing like the scenes reported by William P. Letchworth that were representative of conditions in urban areas throughout the country. She wrote of some boys living in a laundry room of a poor house:

They were intermingled with the inmates of the wash-house, around the cauldrons where the dirty clothes were being boiled. Here was an insane woman raving and uttering wild gibberings, a half-crazy man was sardonically grinning, and an overgrown idiotic boy of malicious disposition was teasing, I might say torturing one of the little boys. There were several other adults of low types of humanity. The apartment ... overhead was used for a sleeping room, and the floor was being scrubbed at the same time by one of the not overcareful inmates; it was worn, and the dirty water came through the cracks in continuous droppings upon the heads of the little ones, who did not seem to regard it as a serious annoyance... [9]

The contrast was strong, and an alert Amy Brown reacted with sympathy, altruism, and insight into the causes of problems.

Amy left Pleasant Grove in the fall of 1888 to attend Brigham Young Academy. Her study at BYA seems to have been one of the grandest times in her life, as she described it, because of her insatiable desire for knowledge and the eager response of her instructors. [10] She enjoyed the intellectual stimulation and benefited from her association with costudents, some of whom remained lifelong friends. Men like Karl G. Maeser and George H. Brimhall and such friends as Alice Louise Reynolds and Dr. George W. Middleton made tremendous impressions on the young girl.

Amy's student life continued until 1890, when she graduated from the BYA Normal School, but she did not leave there immediately. Dr. Maeser requested that she take charge of the Primary Department, which was under his supervision.

For four years thereafter, Amy was involved in teaching at the BYA Training School. She recorded that she did enjoy those years, but there were times when her young heart wanted to participate in less serious activities. Being an instructor and boarding with the all-too-circumspect Dr. Maeser left her a little less than happy. Of such experiences she said:

> One great disappointment that I remember distinctly was when I was advised not to take part in a grand masquerade ball given in the Provo Theater by the society folk of the town. It was really the ball of the season, and all of my girlfriends dressed and masked for the occasion. I felt quite rebellious at being advised not to take part and argued the point with Brother Maeser. I told him that I had been held down all my life, and that I was tired of being a bishop's daughter and a church schoolteacher. I think I even shed a few tears about it. But I finally gave in, and sat in the front row of the dress circle—we called it bald-head row—with the older people, where I watched my friends enjoy all the fun that accompanies those masquerade balls.[11]

After four years at the BYA, Amy was offered a position in the Training School at the University of Utah but declined it because, in her estimation, she had spent enough time in that line of teaching. It was at this time that she entered the Salt Lake City school system. She taught elementary school there for two years.

In the summer of 1895, Amy accompanied Elder Francis Marion Lyman, president of the Quorum of the Twelve in the Mormon Church and the father of Richard R. Lyman, to the University of Michigan where Richard was to receive his bachelor's degree in civil engineering. She enjoyed the trip very much and also toured Chicago, New York, Boston, Washington, D.C., and several other cities.

Amy was now a young and impressive woman. A friend wrote of her:

> She was unusual as a girl ... The beauty of her hair and the exceptional loveliness of her brown eyes, typified the unusualness of her intellectual and spiritual qualities. Her charm as a girl made her attractive in all circles. She was the most popular young person I have ever known. Back of her joyousness in life and its unfolding was the character developed in her pioneer home ... Whatever she did, she sought to do well, and she succeeded.[12] Her school record displayed that she performed exceptionally well.[13]

A year after the trip to see Richard graduate, the two were married in the Salt Lake Temple by President Joseph F. Smith, after which Senator and Mrs. William H. King (Mrs. King was the groom's sister) hosted an elegant reception in their home.

Amy and Richard made their home near the University of Utah, where Richard was a professor of civil engineering; he remained on the faculty for twenty-six years.[14] Richard would later become the only civil engineer to work on three of the seven engineering wonders of the United States: the Chicago sewage disposal system, the Colorado River aqueduct, and the Grand Coulee Dam.[15] Furthermore, he developed the curriculum of the civil engineering department at the University of Utah and devised the street number system that is used throughout Utah today.

Since Amy and Richard lived so close to the university, Amy took courses in English and history, joined the Author's Club (where she found great intellectual stimulation), and read widely in history, philosophy, and American literature.[16]

Fifteen months after the Lyman marriage, there was an addition to the family: Wendell Brown Lyman, born December 8, 1897.[17] Four years after Wendell's birth, Professor Lyman had his school debts paid off and took a sabbatical leave in pursuit of his graduate degree. He had plans to go to Cornell to complete a Master of Civil Engineering and a Doctorate of Philosophy, but first there was a summer stop-off at the University of Chicago in Illinois while waiting to hear of Cornell's acceptance. This was to be a very important move for Amy Brown Lyman, because it was at the Illinois institution that she was introduced to social work, the discipline that would consume the rest of her life.

At the University of Chicago Amy met many famous and noteworthy people, among them President William Rainey Harper, the famous president of that institution; John D. Rockefeller; Professor Richard G. Moulton, author of *The Modern Reader's Bible;* Hamlin Garland, novelist and dramatist; and Dr. George E. Vincent, a major instructor in the newly developed field of social work. In 1943, Mrs. Lyman wrote of her Chicago days:

> It was at this time that I first became interested in social work and social problems. Dr. Vincent was such a popular teacher that largely out of curiosity and because so many were rushing into his classes I decided to take this course with him, but it proved very interesting and practical. And through a former Michigan classmate of my husband, who was then working in the Chicago Charities, I was invited to do volunteer social work in this agency. These experiences, together with the contracts I had with the Hull House, the famous social settlement established by Jane Addams, were all profitable and started me on my way as a social worker.[18]

In a KSL Radio interview, Mrs. Lyman was asked about her

beginnings in social work. She answered:

> The summer studies [at the University of Chicago], Hull House and other Chicago charities proved to be the most interesting college work I had yet taken up, and I had decided before the end of the quarter that no work could be more important and more satisfying than that of helping raise human life to its highest level.[19]

After the Lymans' summer in Chicago, they went on to Cornell University for two and a half years, where Richard earned his M.C.E. and Ph.D. Once more Amy found the intellectual environment most exhilarating. She came in contact with many notable people in all professions, and of her stay at Cornell she wrote:

> Life at a great American University, with all its extensive buildings, equipment and facilities, and with its thousands of students from many lands and locations is full of interest and rich in opportunity. Contact and association with brilliant and well-trained faculty members is in itself a liberal education.[20]

Another significant event that took place during the Lymans' stay in New York was the birth of their second child, Margaret, who is now the wife of Alexander Schreiner, famous Mormon Tabernacle organist.

In 1909 Amy, thirty-seven years old and mother of two children, found a new vehicle for her desires to participate in social work. In October of that year she was called to be on the general board of the Relief Society, the Mormon Church's women's education and service organization that had been in existence for almost one hundred and forty years.

Amy was shocked at receiving the call. She had never worked in the Relief Society prior to that time, but had served in the Young Women's Mutual Improvement Association, the church's auxiliary organization for teenage girls. When Amy was asked to serve, she said, "I shed tears of anxiety because of the responsibility such an appointment involved."[21] She was also concerned that it was an "old women's organization" and that she was too young for it. She said:

> I shall never forget my first attendance at Board meeting in the office of the Woman's Exponent in the Templeton building. As I timidly entered the room I faced what seemed to me the most imposing group of women I had ever seen at such close range. I was well acquainted with only a few of them.
>
> At the head of the table sat Bathsheba W. Smith, the President. On her right was her second counselor, Ida S. Dusenberry, educator and Brigham Young University professor. On her left sat the general secretary, Emmeline B. Wells, and next was the treasurer, Clarissa W. Williams. Then there was Julina L. Smith, wife of the President of the Church; Emma S. Woodruff, wife of the former president; Rebecca N. Nibley, wife of the Presiding Bishop; Sarah Jenne Cannon, wife of the first counselor in the First Presidency; Emily S. Richards, nationally known suffrage leader;

Annie Wells Cannon, author; Alice Merrill Horne, artist; Elizabeth S. Wilcox, student of literature and a fluent public speaker; Priscilla P. Jennings, widow of the wealthy former mayor of Salt Lake City, who, with the poise of a queen, had entertained in her elegant home presidents of the United States, senators, and other men of national repute; Julia P. M. Farnsworth, Phoebe Y. Beatie, Carrie S. Thomas, and Susan Grant—experienced and able public speakers.[22]

Even though Amy seemed timid about being in the presence of such accomplished women, it did not take long for her talents to become evident. Her first term of office on the general board was from 1911 to 1913, during which time she served as assistant general secretary, and from 1913 to 1928, when she served as general secretary. During this period of time, Amy standardized local ward units' minutebooks, reconstructed central financing affairs, and developed a new central office procedure. She employed bookkeepers, typists, and accountants, thereby increasing the efficiency of the office. In 1914, Amy was named the assistant business manager of the *Relief Society Magazine,* a new publication replacing the *Woman's Exponent.* Later, Amy became the editor of the new publication.[23] These responsibilities with the *Relief Society Magazine* continued for twenty-eight years, and she later said, "I have lived and been interested in the publication; it is a dearly-loved child to me."[24]

These years were full years for the general secretary. She benefited a great deal from working with noble, capable women in the association. She also had the opportunity of meeting some of the country's most progressive social activists and humanitarians:

Among the visitors were Madame Mountford, famous lecturer on the Orient and Jerusalem; Lady Aberdeen, of Great Britain, president of the International Council of Women, former presidents of the International Council of Women of the United States, and one of the founders of these two organizations.

Four other presidents of the Council, all close friends of the Relief Society, visited the office: Dr. Kale Waller Barrett; Mrs. Philip Morse Moors; Dr. Valeria H. Parker, and Lena Madesein Phillips.

Among other distinguished visitors were Jane Addams, famous social settlement worker and founder of Hull House; Carrie Chapman Catt, great suffrage leader, successor to Susan B. Anthony and one of the finest public speakers that America has produced; Grace Abbott, chief of the Children's Bureau; Dr. Edward T. Devine and Gertrude Vaile, noted social workers; Rebecca West, English author; Charlotte Perkins Gillman, famous sociologist, brilliant lecturer and author, niece of Henry Ward Beecher.[25]

Amy became close friends with several prominent women on the general board, especially Emmeline B. Wells. This dynamic woman was the editor of the *Woman's Exponent,* fifth general president of the Relief Society, women's rights worker, delegate to the Women's Congress, and a strong political activist. Amy became dear friends with "Aunt Em," as everyone called her, and many letters passed between them over the years.

Relief Society gave Amy further opportunity to practice social work and family welfare. In Amy's opinion, Relief Society was created to efficiently administer assistance to the needy. In the fall of 1917, she was one of five women sent to Denver by the Relief Society for training in welfare work under the direction of the Red Cross and the University of Colorado. This was a significant step toward her role as a social worker. The Denver school was one of the most esteemed institutions for social work training in the country. There the students were introduced to the literature and problems, were introduced to the profession, and were given practical experience. Upon their return home, these five women became the best social workers in Utah.[26]

In 1918, Amy shared her expertise with organizations that emphasized social welfare reform, and she took many active leadership roles. On the local level, she was trustee and vice-president of the community clinic, organizer of the Municipal Department of Health and Charity, chairman of the Family Consultation Committee of the Red Cross, and vice-president of the State Welfare Commission. On the national level, she actively participated in the Colorado Conference of Social Work, American Child Hygiene Association, Home Services Institute, National Conference of Social Workers, National Conference of Charities and Correction, National Tuberculosis Association, and the American Association for Mental Deficiency.[27]

It was not only through her community and state offices that Amy improved social welfare facilities, but it was in her Relief Society office as well. In 1919 the Relief Society Service Department was established to coordinate services within the stakes and wards of the Mormon Church.

> It was a center for Latter-day Saints [Mormons], transients, and non-residents in need; as a clearing department for the Latter-day Saint families, as an employment bureau for women and girls; as a training center for Relief Society officers desiring to improve their methods of family welfare work; and as the official child-placing agency of the Church.[28]

It is not surprising that the general board named Amy Brown Lyman to be the first director of the department.

In 1920, under Amy's direction, Brigham Young University first offered courses in family welfare work. Delegates from the wards and stakes took coursework at BYU, and thereafter classes were taught to Relief Society members in the communities. The total number of Relief Society workers reached 4,155. In these courses, social work procedure and theory was taught, and insights to family welfare were discussed. Relief Society lessons were also developed to incorporate social work principles and humanitarian concerns. Amy and her associates taught courses at the LDS Hospital in Salt Lake City from 1923 to 1940.

Storehouses for clothing and supplies were established to benefit needy people:

> Relief Society women made great contributions in the interest of suffering humanity. They cooperated with the Red Cross and other agencies in producing clothing, including knitted articles, in preparing surgical dressings, producing and conserving food, and in caring for the sick, distressed and needy.[29]

Three other programs were developed at this time because of Amy's concerns. These projects are discussed in her autobiography, *In Retrospect,* but she does not mention her significant role.

There were at that time many malnourished children in the area, and in 1924 the Relief Society took decisive action:

> Through the generosity of individual donors, malnourished children were sent to the country and cared for in hospitable homes for at least two weeks' period for each child. In the five summers, 269 children were given the opportunity.[30]

Another program made specific efforts to increase milk in children's diets.

Another concern Amy had as director of the Social Services Department was care for the feebleminded. On January 6, 1923, Amy wrote to a dear friend and social worker, Miss Florence Hutsinpillar:

> Since I saw you last, I have had some interesting experiences in connection with the feeble-minded and insane. Dr. Hyde, the superintendent of our mental hospital, who passed away recently, was a splendid psychologist as well as a medical man, and with the professor of psychology at the University of Utah, he was very much interested in studying his patients and treating them as scientifically as possible. He persuaded me to go down to the institution quite often to talk to patients they considered incurable with a view of helping to untangle their difficulties and straighten out some of their ideas. It has all been very interesting to me.

One Salt Lake City woman who was a Relief Society ward president recalled that Amy took the Salt Lake City ward Relief Society presidents to Provo and American Fork each year in a rented bus. She instructed them to bring a notebook and pencil because she would lecture on the trip down and back from the State Mental Hospital in Provo and the School for Retarded Children in American Fork. Mrs. Lyman also counseled the women to write their legislators, urging them to be more conscious of the two facilities and of the people who need their care.[32]

The other program on which Amy spent much effort involved maternity care. She had a deep concern for the health and well-being of infants and new mothers. She had witnessed the death of many infants during her childhood. She had seen six new mothers die from puerperal fever, a disease that was transmitted by common midwives. One of these young mothers was her own sister. Furthermore, the invalidism of Amy's mother was a result of child-birth complications.[33]

In the fall of 1922, Mrs. Jeanette A. Hyde, a national Republican committeewoman from Utah, asked Amy if her name could be placed in nomination as a candidate to the Utah State Legislature. This was a sudden and unexpected request, since Amy had no experience in politics, but through Mrs. Hyde's coaxing, Amy consented.[34] Though unprepared and lacking in political background, she made her issue the untapped humanitarian leadership women could provide. She said:

> I called attention to the fact that since leadership is always scarce and since the supply had been increased by the emancipation of women, we should look among women's groups for new leaders, especially in certain fields; that women are a great asset to any humanitarian cause because they have a special and different viewpoint, which is based on their experience as mothers and homemakers; that their ability as directors and administrators is often apparent when they are left widows and therefore are required to manage their own business and family affairs; that they are especially needed in legislative bodies where the laws are made, because of their special knowledge of human needs and humanistic rights. I held that men, who must provide for their families and for the development of communities, are naturally and necessarily interested in lands, mines, flocks, herds, property ownership and rights, and property protection, while women are inclined to think more about education, health, recreation, morals and character; also, that most of the legislation of the late years had behind it the influence of mothers of the nation, and therefore legislative bodies should not be made up entirely of men; that there should be enough women to foster and secure the necessary humanitarian social action.[35]

Amy won the election and took her place in the House of Representatives, where she was appointed chairman of the public health committee and a member of the labor and appropriations committees.

While Amy served in the legislature, she took an active part. She introduced an old age annuities bill for educators at the Utah State Agricultural College and the University of Utah. She was particularly pleased with the passage of a bill allowing Utah to adopt the provisions of the federal Sheppard-Tower Act, which supported federal-state cooperation in improving maternity care. Amy's career in the legislature was brief, but many applauded the passage of the Sheppard-Tower Act, which Utah's own United

States senator, William H. King, filibustered against.[36]

One of the groups that supported and worked for the federal provision was the Relief Society, and at the adoption of the law a maternity care program was established in its organization.

Most local Relief Societies carried out the recommendation of the General Board that each Society equip maternity chests with the necessary accessories, utensils and articles for the mother and new baby, including ready-to-use bundles and layettes.[38]

These were busy years for Amy; she had general secretary duties, edited the *Relief Society Magazine,* directed the Social Services Department of the Relief Society, taught courses throughout the area, had numerous community positions, attended conventions and seminars to keep well-versed in her discipline, and served as a legislator. In addition to this, her husband had just been asked to serve as a member of the Mormon Church's Council of the Twelve. Due to all these obligations, one of Amy's friends once wrote to her, "I hope you won't come home a broken down nervous wreck. I know just how hard you work and how you are, but you should relax a little. . . ."[38]

Amy's exhaustive efforts during this time did not go unnoticed. Joseph F. Smith, president of the Mormon Church, wrote to Richard R. Lyman,

As for our dear Amy, I am proud of her fidelity, energy and intelligence in the performance of her Relief Society duties, and I could love her as one of my own daughters. She is well-entitled to the promise and hope of a distinguished future.[39]

Her own coworkers who served in the Relief Society also gave her praise and reinforcement. Susa Young Gates once wrote a short, encouraging message when Amy was very busy and tired. She said:

God bless you and He will . . . Go on—there is great work awaiting you. Be brave—and be patient, all will be well with you and yours.[40]

Her beloved President Clarissa S. Williams made some remarks after Amy had given her report to the Relief Society General Board. The record reads:

President Williams paid tribute to the general secretary, Mrs. Amy Brown Lyman, for her untiring efforts in the cause of social service in the Relief Society. She stated that since 1917, Mrs. Lyman has spared no pains nor energy in the interest of improving the social work of the Relief Society and in introducing modern scientific methods throughout the organization. Through lack of understanding, this task has been difficult, but the time has now come when the untiring work of Mrs. Lyman is appreciated.[41]

Amy received many awards in recognition of her labors. The general board of the Relief Society established the Amy Brown Lyman Scholarship Fund. She received the Brigham Young University Distinguished Alumnus Award as well, presented as "an expression of esteem for meritorious achievements which have brought honor and distinction to her Alma Mater and inspiration to her alumni."[42] A further honor came when she was asked to submit information to be listed in *Who's Who in America* and *Who's Who Among American Women.*

In October of 1928 Amy, then fifty-six, was called to be first counselor to newly selected president of the Relief Society, Louise Y. Robinson. As counselor, her primary duty was to continue supervising social welfare institutes and preparing the *Handbook* for the Relief Society, a very necessary ready reference for all Relief Society workers.

She continued all of her social welfare concerns, seminars, and conferences. She was also obligated to increase her activities in the National Council of Women, an organization with which she had been involved for many years and which now elected her to national office. Amy attended her first session with Emmeline B. Wells in 1911 as a delegate from the Relief Society, and she also attended several subsequent sessions. In 1925, she was honored by her election to the Council's executive committee. She served as recording secretary from 1925 to 1927, as auditor from 1927 to 1929, and as third vice-president from 1929 to 1934. Through the National Council of Women, Amy also served as a delegate to the International Council of Women—requiring her to travel to Switzerland, Yugoslavia, and Scotland. Amy enjoyed this very much and found a great deal of satisfaction in traveling and meeting so many well-known people.

This was a traumatic period of her life. In 1924 her daughter-in-law died most unexpectedly one day, leaving an eight-month-old girl in her crib. This was a deep tragedy to all the family, but Amy did not hesitate in taking the infant and rearing her in her home.[43]

Two years later, Amy went to the Mayo Clinic in Minnesota to have a kidney removed, an operation which resulted in a long convalescence.[44] Richard was to have an operation for bleeding ulcers, but for some unknown reason the operation was not performed. Their ill health was kept in strictest confidence.[45]

A third crisis occurred in 1933 when son Wendell Brown Lyman died tragically in the Lyman home at the age of thirty-six.[46]

With such unfortunate setbacks, it is understandable that the busy, emotionally taxed Relief Society counselor and social worker welcomed a stay abroad.[47]

From 1936 to 1938, Amy presided over women's organizations in Europe, where her husband had been appointed mission president for the Mormon Church. Now her work included not only the Relief Society, but the Primary Association (the children's organization) and the YWMIA (the young women's auxiliary). Amy recorded in her autobiography how special this position was to her:

> Our mission was a joy and satisfaction and inspiration throughout. In the first place, every hour of every day there was the constant realization of our special calling and assignment which was foremost in mind; and being far from home and from all local affairs and former personal problems we were free to devote ourselves wholly to missionary work.[48]

After two years the Lymans returned, and shortly thereafter the Relief Society was reorganized. On January 1, 1940, with the end of Louise Y. Robinson's leadership, Amy Brown Lyman was selected as the new leader by Heber J. Grant, president of the Mormon Church. Amy accepted the position out of love for the organization, but was modest and unassuming. In no existing records nor in the opinion of her friends, relatives, and coworkers had she ever let ambition negatively affect her work. It appears to have been a character trait of Amy's never to think of personal gain or honors but to think only of doing her best in the position in which she was asked to serve.

During her administration, the membership and influence of the women's organization continued to grow as the Social Service Department expanded to serve more people and more needs. Cooperative effort was also given to the newly developed Church Welfare Program, a program established to aid victims of World War I, the Great Depression, and World War II.

While Amy made many accomplishments between 1940 and 1945, two were major. The first was the transferring of the women's wheat in storage to the General Welfare Program. The wheat program was developed during Brigham Young's time to be a security to the women of the church and for their own profit. It was the interest on the stored wheat that financed the maternity care program Amy had worked so hard for.

A second major project was the centennial celebration of the Relief Society, which was under full-scale preparation when the war started. This precipitated the third grand undertaking of the women's organization—assistance in the war effort. The Relief Society contributed sewing, knitting, and nursing care; sponsored Red Cross first aid courses; relieved labor shortages; prepared food; supported savings bonds; and developed special lessons and articles relating to wartime problems.[49] Sister Belle Spafford, successor to Amy as general president, made the following observations of those years:

> Her administration has covered a momentous and unusually trying period in the history of the Relief Society. Almost immediately upon taking over her duties as president, Sister Lyman, with the aid of her capable Board, enthusiastically initiated plans for an appropriate observance of the Relief Society centennial, two years away, including completion of the membership campaign which had been launched in 1938 for the purpose of enlisting 100,000 members by 1940. Straight thinking, sound judgment, familiarity with the history of the Society and appreciation for the past, as well as a clear, certain hopeful outlook upon the future, coupled with a fine understanding of the purposes of the Society and its meaning in the lives of Latter-day Saint women were needed to direct plans and activities for this important event. Possessing all these qualifications, President Lyman was ideally suited to preside at this time, and was heavily drawn upon.
>
> Due to the engagement of the United States in war, December 1941, all centennial plans did not mature; some were cancelled and consummation of others delayed. These, together with the graceful acceptance of the situation by Relief Society women and their ready adjustment to conditions [were] are pronounced evidence of President Lyman's leadership strength.
>
> Not only did the war affect the centennial observance, it also brought about modifications in the regular Relief Society program. In accordance with recommendations of the First Presidency, whose counsel President Lyman profoundly respect [ed] and implicitly obey [ed], the program was greatly simplified and the recommended restrictions strictly observed. Moreover, her understanding of what is basic in the Society, her analytical mind and good judgment enabled her to meet difficult problems and guide the Society through perilous and discouraging war years with outstanding success. In spite of the greatness of handicaps, high standards were maintained in regular Relief Society work, effective cooperation was given the Church Welfare Plan, a vast amount of work was accomplished, and progressive action taken ... Relief Society activities during the administration of Amy Brown Lyman reflect the genius of her leadership.[50]

Among all the responsibilities that came with serving as the general president of the Relief Society, a tragic event occurred. Amy's husband, Elder Richard R. Lyman, was excommunicated from the Mormon Church on November 12, 1943. This was a blow worse than death to an unwavering member of the Mormon Church; however, Amy continued to serve as Relief Society general president. She performed all of her duties with the same expertise and efficiency that she had been known for in earlier years.[51]

But the following year was very difficult for Amy, and her health was declining. She was unable to give her all to the program that had been the object and vehicle of her concerns and energies.[52] The Relief Society General Board minutes bear out that she did preside at the meetings but relied more and more on the work of her counselor, Belle S. Spafford, and the general secretary, Vera White Pohlman. On September 12, 1944, in a letter to the First Presidency of the Mormon Church, Amy asked to be released. The following April 4, 1945, Amy Brown Lyman received her release. The letter read:

Dear Sister Lyman:

This will acknowledge your letter of September 12, 1944, in which you stated your desire to be released as President of the National Women's Relief Society of The Church of Jesus Christ of Latter-day Saints.

According to your request, we wish to first congratulate you upon the long devoted and faithful service that you have been privileged to render to Latter-day Saint women by virtue of your connection over the many years with the General Board of the Relief Society. You have brought to your work in the organization a training and ability of high order which have come to you over the years. Many, many thousands of our sisters have been the beneficiaries of your labor and wisdom that you have brought to it out of that training, ability and experiences. You have had a great career, rich in achievement. . . .

Faithfully yours,

Heber J. Grant
J. Reuben Clark
David O. McKay

The First Presidency

She ended her career in the general Relief Society nobly, but the past president had goals and hopes for the organization that reached long into the future. Sometime prior to Amy's release, she prepared a statement on "Visions of the Future for the Relief Society." Among all of her speeches, articles, and notebooks, there is no more complete statement of the things that concerned Amy than this; unfortunately, it is available only in outline form. She listed the following concerns:

1. Maternity death rate is too high.
2. Infant and child death rates are too high.
3. Too much malnutrition among children.
4. Too much juvenile delinquency.
5. Great need should be segregated [sic] and placed where feeble-minded can be happy and free, where they can be taught to their fullest capacities. . . .
6. Immigration problems need to be resolved. . . .
7. Many suffer from lack of employment.
8. There are inadequate provisions for the aged.

She went on to say, "The aim of the Relief Society should be and is to raise family life to its highest level . . . The organization should work for the abolishment of poverty, sickness and crime."

She closed by saying, "Looking on in the far distant future—we will probably find that the ultimate aim ... will be to make social welfare unnecessary."[54]

Amy's last fifteen years were as active as were the seventy-three that had preceded them. She continued to be her kind, concerned self. When neighbors, ward members, and friends called on her, she was sincerely interested in their welfare and activities.[55] She rejoined the Author's Club, taught the literature lessons in her home ward Relief Society, paid visits to the general board, and participated in the Daughters of Utah Pioneers.

Amy maintained to the very end her keen interest in local, national and world affairs, and any conversation with her was usually led from the trivial into these channels.

At the age of seventy-five, she wrote a beautiful biography of her friend of fifty years, Alice Louise Reynolds. Vera White Pohlman says:

> This warm and delightful life story was a shining example of Mrs. Lyman's ability as a writer, her fidelity to fact, her diligent and careful research, and her analytical insight.[56]

Many banquets, luncheons, and speaking engagements were held in honor of Amy. The Conference of Social Work awarded her an Honorary Life Membership Award for her outstanding contribution in the field of social welfare. Her popularity as a public speaker continued until the day of her death, with subsequent commitments still listed in her appointment book.[57] How pleased she must have felt at age eighty to know that all the years of case work, organizing, and administrative decisions were respected by her professional peers.

Amy Brown Lyman's influence runs much deeper than the institutions she fostered. She has helped innumerable people and has established a legacy of service, mercy, and mature living.

Her life, values, and concerns are something from which contemporary Mormon women can take great strength. She was a renaissance woman; a woman who was well-read, educated, and who had a remarkable ability to synthesize her experiences, academic studies, and principles of the gospel of Jesus Christ. Philosophy, theology, political science, history, psychology, literature, and many of the sciences fascinated her, and one cannot help but want to take the spectator's chair in her kitchen on those Sunday mornings when Dr. George W. Middleton or other friends entered and pursued discussions with Amy and Richard.

To Amy Mormonism was a gate—not a fence—to the rest of the world. She was secure in her convictions, and from them she moved outward in her experiences.

There is a sense of realism that surrounds her. She was not naive about the plight of many people; she was well aware of poverty, unemployment, long-term illness, emotional instability, delinquency, and divorce. With her clear perceptions, she never gave in to thoughts of fatality, thinking that nothing could be remedied or that bad situations would right themselves. Instead, she tenaciously worked with people and programs to solve their problems.

Amy was a dynamic leader who kept an optimistic outlook despite the tragic situations that her profession required her to deal with. She was confident in her belief that individuals could learn, grow, and adjust, yet in her counseling and leadership she never spoke in platitudes. Her remarks to groups and assemblies were positive but never shallow.

When Amy died on December 5, 1959, in her daughter's home, where she had been convalescing from a fall, the life of one of Utah's most prominent women came to a close. In reviewing the course of her life, Amy's unselfishness and concern for others becomes profoundly evident. Despite personal tragedies, family responsibilities, and her ponderous work load, Amy Brown Lyman helped innumerable people, established charitable institutions that still exist today, and left a legacy of service and mercy. Indeed, Amy Brown Lyman epitomizes the watchword of the Relief Society she loved so well—Charity Never Faileth.

Notes

1. Amy Brown Lyman, *In Retrospect* (Salt Lake City: General Board of the Relief Society, 1945) p. 1–2.

2. Manuscript Census of the United States, 1870. Located at the Genealogical Department of the Church of Jesus Christ of Latter-day Saints in Salt Lake City. Film number 553.111.

3. Lyman, *op. cit.,* p. 4.

4. Speech, Amy Brown Lyman Papers, Harold B. Lee Library, Brigham Young University.

5. Lyman, *op. cit.,* p. 4.

6. Lyman, *op. cit.,* p. 7.

7. *ibid.,* p. 11

8. Lyman, *op. cit.,* p. 13.

9. Robert Bremner, p. 49.

10. Oral interview with Margaret Lyman Schreiner, June 5, 1975. Notes in the possession of Loretta L. Hefner.

11. Lyman, *op. cit.,* p. 21.

12. Alice Louise Reynolds, "Tribute to Amy Brown Lyman," *Improvement Era* (September 1932) quoted by Vera White Pohlman, *In Memoriam,* (Salt Lake City: Vera White Pohlman, 1960), p. 21.

13. Church Education Records. LDS Church Archives.

14. University of Utah, *University of Utah Annual Catalogue.* Mr. Lyman was made an assistant professor in 1897, an associate professor in 1899, and a full professor in 1901.

15. Pohlman, *op. cit.,* p. 8.

16. Oral interview with Margaret Lyman Schreiner, June 5, 1975.

17. *The Deseret News,* May 15, 1933, p. 15.

18. Transcript of KSL Radio Interview, no date. Amy Brown Lyman Papers. Harold B. Lee Library, Brigham Young University.

19. Lyman, *op. cit.,* p. 33.

20. *ibid.*, p. 35.

21. *ibid.*, pp. 36–37.

22. *ibid.*, p. 38.

23. General Board Minutes of the Relief Society, June 23, 1922. LDS Church Archives.

24. Lyman, *op. cit.*, p. 54.

25. *ibid.*, p. 45.

26. Heber R. Taylor, "How Social Work Came to Utah," unpublished research paper located at the Social Work Library, University of Utah.

27. General Board Minutes, 1915–1940.

28. General Board of the Relief Society, *History of the Relief Society 1842–1966.* (Salt Lake City: The General Board of the Relief Society, 1966), p. 92.

29. Lyman, p. 67.

30. *ibid.*, pp. 67–68.

31. Letter to Florence Hutsinpillar, January 6, 1923. Amy Brown Lyman Papers, Harold B. Lee Library.

32. Oral interview with Fanny Mulder, October 12, 1975. Tapes in the possession of Loretta L. Hefner.

33. Oral interview with Amy K. Lyman Engar, July 3, 1975. Tapes in the possession of Loretta L. Hefner.

34. Letter to Florence Hutsinpillar, *op. cit.*

35. Lyman, p. 82–3.

36. Letter from Grace Abbott, January 19, 1927. Amy Brown Lyman Papers, Lee Library, BYU.

37. General Board of the Relief Society, *op. cit.*, p. 70.

38. Letter from E. R. Nibley, November 23, 1917. Amy Brown Lyman Papers, Lee Library, BYU.

39. Letter from Joseph F. Smith to Richard R. Lyman, December 26, 1917, Richard R. Lyman Papers, LDS Church Archives.

40. Letter from Susa Young Gates, April 4, 1916. Amy Brown

Lyman Papers, Lee Library, BYU.

41. General Board Minutes, July 21, 1925.

42. Pohlman, p. 19.

43. Lyman, p. 124.

44. Amy K. L. Engar interview, July 3, 1975.

45. Letter to Dr. W. F. Braasch, M.D., December 4, 1928, and January 8, 1929. Amy K. Lyman Engar Papers, Lee Library, BYU.

46. Amy K. Lyman Engar interview.

47. *The Deseret News,* May 15, 1933, p. 15.

48. Oral interview with Dr. T. Edgar Lyon, June 13, 1975.

49. Lyman, pp. 156–157.

50. Belle S. Spafford, "Amy Brown Lyman," *Relief Society Magazine,* Volume 32, no. 5, May, 1945, pp. 269–270.

51. General Board Minutes, 1943–1945.

52. Oral history with Belle S. Spafford, interviewed by Jill Mulvay, December 8, 1975. In the possession of the LDS Church chives.

53. General Board Minutes, April 4, 1945.

54. "Vision of the Future of the Relief Society," Notes, Amy Brown Lyman Papers, Lee Library, BYU.

55. Oral interview with Edna Schulz, October 19, 1975. Tape in the possession of Loretta L. Hefner.

56. Pohlman, p. 18.

57. *ibid.,* p. 19.

Susanna Goudin Cardon (woman seated in middle of front row) 1833–1920

*The subject of this essay, Susanna
Goudin Cardon, was so involved with
her environment that she almost
appears as a minor character. The
reader comes away knowing more
about the Vaudois (the handcart
company leaders) or about the Cardon
family than about Susanna. This is
due to the lack of more personal
information that is available that was
written by Susanna herself. However,
people are products of the times and
the circumstances they lived in, and to
understand this is to understand much
of their lives.*

*The facts of the life of Susanna
Goudin Cardon stand in a well-
crafted essay by Louise Degn,
currently a Salt Lake City journalist,
formerly a journalist in Chicago. She
served a mission for the Mormon
Church in the Australia Brisbane
Mission. She graduated from Utah
State University with a bachelor of
arts degree and from Northwestern
University with a master of science
degree in journalism.*

Susanna G. Cardon

Louise Degn

Susanna Goudin was only fifteen when a royal monarch, living hundreds of miles from her home, issued a proclamation that would determine the course of her life and the lives of a handful of transplanted French families who had taken refuge in the remote Alpine Mountains.

The occasion was February 17, 1848. On that day, the King of Sardinia granted religious and civil and political rights to a group of people known as *the Vaudois* or the *Waldenses,* a close-knit group of people who for centuries had resisted encroachment by the outside world on their independent religious way of life.

To understand Susanna Goudin Cardon, one must understand the Vaudois. Though they lived in the northern Alps of Italy, the Vaudois originated in France, near Lyons. Their unique and heretical religious beliefs caused hatred among outsiders, and through the centuries the Vaudois were forced to seek safety in the high, isolated, almost desolate mountain tops of the Piedmont Valleys in Italy.

They retained their French names, although their language became a mixture of French and Italian, a cultural phenomenon that only reinforced their isolation. They refused to intermarry with the Catholic Italians for religious reasons, and, as with many northern Italians, retained their tall, blond physical characteristics. Both Susanna Cardon and her husband, Paul, were tall, had blue eyes, and had a fair complexion.

The Vaudois claimed an unbroken succession of pastors back to the original Apostles of Christ, making them the oldest Christian community in the world. They were hated and persecuted by Popes and by monarchs for their refusal to bow to the power of Rome. Generations of Vaudois were savagely martyred and their communities were pillaged because of their tenacious resolve to live the purity of the gospel as they understood it.

Their lives were simple and pure. Families participated in Bible reading and parents taught their children the ways of the faith during daily religious devotion in the home.

One incident in particular dramatizes the value that the Vaudois placed on the Bible and the intolerance they were forced to endure because of that faith:

In 1555 a vendor named Hector Bartholomew had come into the Piedmont Valleys selling Bibles. Among the Vaudois he found ready sale for the book ... But he also encountered bitter Catholic enemies among those who believed that possession of a Bible would keep the people from going to Mass. Bartholomew replied that Mass then was an idolatry. He was thrown into a dungeon in Pignerol and later burned at the stake as were thousands of Vaudois who defended their faith.[1]

Of necessity, the Vaudois lived spartan lives. The Piedmont Valleys were rugged, narrow, and steep—barely wide enough to cultivate food or to graze a few animals. The mountain sides of the area rose thousands of feet within a short distance, and many pathways were too narrow for even a donkey to pass. Every spot of arable ground was used for miniature farms and vineyards; meat was scarce. Homes were made of stone and were barely heated in the winter. This was how the Vaudois lived—among persecution and prejudice and amid a forbidding landscape—when in February 1848 the King of Sardinia granted them the right to worship as their conscience demanded.

The very next year the Mormon Apostle Lorenzo Snow was called to organize a mission to Italy. Snow was in England when the call came; he wrote in his autobiography:

As I contemplate the condition of Italy, with deep solicitude to know the mind of the Spirit as to where I should commence my labors, I found that all was dark in Sicily, and hostile laws would exclude our efforts. No opening appeared in the cities of Italy; but the history of the Waldenses attracted my attention.

Amid the ages of darkness and cruelty, they had stood immovable almost as the wave-beaten rock in the stormy ocean.

A few narrow valleys, which in some places are only a bow's shot in breadth, are all that now remain in their possession except the mountains by which they are engirdled. But a period of deep calm has at length arrived, and since the storm of persecutions swept over Europe, they have received many privileges from the Sardinian government. Thus the way was opened only a short period before the appointment of this mission, and no other portion of Italy is governed by such favorable laws.[2]

Arriving in Genoa, Italy, on July 1, 1850, he sent Elders Joseph Toronto (a native of Sicily) and T. B. H. Stenhouse to the Vaudois people in the Piedmont Valleys. Three weeks later he wrote to the European Mission president, Franklin D. Richards:

Now, with a heart full of gratitude, I find an opening presented in the valleys of Piedmont, when all other parts of Italy are closed against our efforts. I believe that the Lord has there hidden up a people amid the Alpine mountains, and it is the voice of the Spirit that I shall commence something of importance in that part of this dark nation.[3]

A few days later Snow himself arrived in LaTour in the valley of Lucerne:

I felt assured that the Lord had directed us to a branch of the house of Israel, and I was rejoiced to behold many circumstances that reminded me of those with whom I had been associated in the valleys of the West.[4]

On September 19, Snow led the other elders in organizing the first branch of the Mormon Church in Italy. The first and only converts to the gospel in Italy during the nineteenth century were the Vaudois people—families with names like Cardon, Goudin, Malan, Stalle, Beus, and Chatelaine. Missionary work lasted only twelve years, until 1862, when Italy was closed to proselyting because of persecution. By then, however, nearly all the Vaudois convert families had left for Utah. (Years later, Susanna's son, Louis Samuel Cardon, would try to open the work in Italy as president of the Swiss Mission from 1898 to 1901. But again, the mission had to be closed after a short time.)

The first baptized convert in the new Italian church was John Daniel Malan, baptized on October 27, 1850, "opening a door which no man can shut," as Lorenzo Snow expressed it. Another elder recorded: "Sweet to them all were the soft sounds of the Italian tongue as Elder Snow repeated the ceremony and performed the ordinance of baptism."[5]

Thus it was that the religious climate among the Vaudois changed dramatically in the mid-nineteenth century, a change which opened the way for Susanna Goudin to embrace a new religion and change the course of her life unalterably.

Susanna Goudin Cardon was born July 30, 1833, at Prarustin, Piedmont, Italy. She was the seventh child born to Barthelemi and Martha Cardon Goudin. At the time of her birth, however, only three children—two sisters and a brother—were living. Her early life was one of struggle and difficult circumstances. As her granddaughter, Rebecca Cardon Hickman Peterson, later described:

When she was five years old, her father died and left the family to struggle and scrape for their livelihood. At this very young age she had to work and help support herself. She had to pick up potatoes, glean and get sticks ready for the vineyard, as that was one of their sources of making a living. When she was about nine years old, she had to leave home to get work and to support herself. She did this by picking leaves from the mulberry trees to feed the silkworms. She earned ten cents per day doing this. When she was twelve years old, she learned to reel silk and earned twenty cents per day. She continued in this work until she left Italy to come to Utah.[6]

Years later her skill as a silk worker would become a great resource to the Mormon pioneers as they struggled to establish a
home-based sericulture industry in Utah.

Susanna was the last one of her family to join the church, since
she was not living at home when the rest of her family was converted. She was baptized by George Dennis Keaton on August 18,
1853, at age twenty, and was confirmed by Jabez Woodward in
Piedmont, Italy.

Even though her family were all members of the Mormon
Church, it did not bring unity to their home. In fact, two years
later Susanna would be emigrating to Utah—alone. Her family
would be left behind, embittered toward the faith she now embraced.

The Vaudois emigration came in response to an 1853 epistle in
which the church leaders urged all Saints to come to Utah. Because of the persecution of Mormons many Vaudois Saints were
forced to pull up roots and leave everything behind. Unable to sell
their homes and farms, they simply had to abandon them without
recompense.

The first group of Saints to leave the Piedmont Valleys left on
February 7, 1854; it included the family of Susanna's future in-
laws, the Philippe Cardon family, and the man who would one
day be her husband, Paul Cardon, who was only a boy of thirteen
at the time. The group traveled to Liverpool, England, where they
boarded ship and sailed to New Orleans, then up the Mississippi
and Missouri rivers by steamer to Kansas City, Missouri. They
then traveled by ox teams to Salt Lake City, arriving October 28,
1854, making a journey that lasted eight and a half months.

By the next year, Susanna was also preparing to leave home and
her close family to make the same pilgrimage other Vaudois Mormons had made before her. Her route was different, but the hardships were the same.

The group Susanna traveled with included her relative Pierre
Stalle, which meant she was not traveling entirely on her own but
instead had some family member to watch over her and care for
her if the need arose. They left Piedmont in 1855, traveling first to
Turin by carriage, then on to Suza by railway. From there they
boarded a large coach that was set on sleds and was drawn by sixteen government mules that carried them over the snowy and icy
Mt. Cenis to Loundsbury. From there it was by coach to Lyons,
France, where they caught the train to Paris and Calais. From
Calais they took a steamer to London, then traveled by rail the final leg to Liverpool.

In Liverpool, these twenty-seven Vaudois were joined by four hundred and thirty-seven Mormons from Denmark, Norway, and Sweden and forty-two from Great Britain. They set sail for America on December 12, 1855, in the ship *John J. Boyd* for the three-month journey to New York City, where they landed March 15, 1856.

A letter written by C. R. Savage and published in the *Millennial Star*, Vol. 18, page 209, describes the journey:

The Saints were, by the sound of the trumpet, called to prayer mornings and evenings. Meetings were also frequently held in the Danish, English and Italian languages. . . . The weather got worse after crossing the Banks, so much so that they were driven into the Gulf Stream three times and many of our sailors were frost bitten. Our captain got superstitious on account of the long passage, and ordered that there should be no singing on board; the mate said that all ships that had preachers on board were all sure of a bad passage; however, the Lord heard our prayers and in His own good time we arrived at our destination. On the evening of February 5, we were safely at anchor having been 66 days out from Liverpool. . . our water supply was almost exhausted, we had [on] arrival only about one day's water on board.[7]

From New York City the emigrants boarded a train to St. Louis, where the company stayed for two or three months, after which it traveled up the Missouri River to Florence, Nebraska, where they stayed two or three months more.

Florence, Nebraska, was a regrouping site for the westward Mormon trail. The very year in which the Vaudois group arrived there (1856), the church leaders decided to begin transporting its emigrants across the plains by handcart rather than by animal-drawn wagons. The handcarts served four or five people, could carry about one hundred pounds of provisions, and were pulled by the emigrants themselves. Susanna, the Vaudois, and the other European Saints would be a part of the very first handcart company ever organized by the church, a company under the direction of Edmund Ellsworth.

In Florence, while she and the others waited for the start of the handcart journey, Susanna met and fell in love with a young Englishman who lived there. We do not know his name or much about him except that Susanna loved him dearly; the problem, however, was that he was not a Mormon and would not become one. Several months later, when the handcart company was finally ready to pull out of Florence, Susanna had to make the difficult decision—to stay with him or to leave for the West. After much troubled thought and prayer, Susanna decided to stay with the Mormons, who included her Vaudois people. She left behind the man she loved, but not without regrets. Her feeling of loss would trouble her for some time and would make her own decision to marry one year later a very difficult one.

While in Florence, Susanna also worked for a shopkeeper by the name of Samuel Lee. She helped in his home and also in his orchard picking fruit. The Lees were good to Susanna, and when it came time for her to leave, they gave her a new dress and a bonnet to take with her. They also included with their gifts a soft feather tick, but the tick was considered a luxury for a journey over the plains and had to be left behind, as did many other things. Susanna had brought clothes enough to last for some time, but the leader of the handcart company required everyone to travel light and ordered everyone to cast aside extra articles of clothing. This was difficult for people who had already left so much behind and who owned only those few things they now possessed.

The order to dispose of many of their belongings, unfortunately, caused some bad feelings, often dividing along national prejudices. The French Mormons felt they were being mistreated by the captain of the group, and when he reportedly allowed some of the English girls to wear some of the clothes the French had just discarded, "Susanna and some of the French Saints felt so bad that they decided to pile their things that they could not take with them ... and burn them rather than see them taken and used by others who did not need them."[8]

Such tension and anger are to be expected, no doubt, given the conditions of hardship and scarcity. Captain Ellsworth had to be extremely tough and firm in order to lead a large, diverse, and very inexperienced group of people across the frontier. His actions were interpreted many ways, depending solely on the point of view of those affected.

Despite all the troubles and hardships the Saints, diverse as they were, managed to set off from Florence and move across the plains. One very interesting coincidence about Susanna's journey is the fact that the person who was to become her husband's second wife, Madelaine Beus, rode most of the way across the plains in Susanna's handcart. She was a young two-year-old child at the time. How strange it is to think that these two people, twenty-one years apart in age, would one day be married to the same man and share one another's lives.

By September 1856, the Ellsworth handcart company reached Willow Springs outside Salt Lake City. On the morning of September 26, Brigham Young and other dignitaries rode out to meet them, presenting them gifts of Utah-grown melons. They then formed a procession and paraded into the city, where the residents greeted the tired pioneers with cheers and pomp:

The line of march was scarcely taken up before it began to be met by man, woman, children, and foot horses, and in wagons, thronging out to see and welcome the first handcart companies. The numbers rapidly increased until the living tide lined and thronged South Temple Street.

The procession reached the Public Square about sunset, where the Lancers, bands, and carriages were formed into a line facing the handcarts and after a few remarks by Pres. Young, accompanied by his blessing, the spectators, and escorts retired and the companies pitched their tents. . . .[9]

They had come fourteen hundred miles across the plains in nine months.

Now, at age twenty-three, Susanna began a new life in a new country with a new religion. If the persecutions in Italy had been severe, if the migration to Utah had been exhausting, then these experiences only prepared her for the difficult life of pioneering a new land.

The first winter in Utah was sparse. Fortunately, though, another Vaudois family—the Philippe Cardons—provided them with some aid. The Cardons had emigrated two years earlier in the first company to leave the Piedmont Valleys and had settled in Ogden. When the Cardons learned a group of fellow Vaudois had arrived in the Salt Lake Valley, they set out immediately to aid the new immigrants. Paul and Phillip, two of the Cardon sons, went to Salt Lake City and brought Stalles and Susanna back to Bingham's Fort in north Ogden. There they assisted the newcomers in building a crude dugout to live in during the first winter.

The winter was very severe and at times the Cardons had to go and dig them out of the snow as they would be completely covered. Margaret Stalle Baker writes, "While in Ogden, they were snowed in their dug out, without matches or a clock. They did not even get out of bed as they could not tell the time or make a fire. Paul Cardon came and dug us out."[10]

Later that year, Susanna went to live with the Cardons in their home, and it was then that Paul Cardon and Susanna became well acquainted—so well acquainted, in fact, that Paul proposed marriage to Susanna. He was sixteen and she was twenty-three; they were already first cousins by blood—her mother, Marthe Cardon Goudin, and his father, Philippe Cardon, were brother and sister. If that wasn't enough, Susanna had another problem—her remaining affection for the young Englishman in Florence, Nebraska. She still remembered him with great fondness, and her feelings were torn. But the practicalities of living needed to be faced immediately. She was alone in a new land, and she had no way to support herself on her own.

At this time she was very much in love with the young Englishman but because she was alone and was influenced by Father Cardon, she married him [Paul]. She grieved over this for a year. In fact, until she went to the Endowment house. She wept bitterly when she went there. Brigham Young, seeing her, sensed her trouble and told her to go through and all would be well with her. And this was literally fulfilled, as when they were old I have seldom seen a more devoted couple.[11]

They were married March 16, 1857, and in their life together they bore six sons and five daughters.

"Father Cardon," Susanna's father-in-law, is an interesting figure in this period of Mormon history. He must have been a forceful man to persuade Susanna to marry his son. He, his wife, and his children (except for his oldest daughter, Annette) were the second family to join the church in Italy—an act, in itself, which demonstrates forthrightness and decisiveness. Their conversion took place in the early 1850s, probably in 1851 or 1852. This is how it happened:

One night Philippe had a dream—he saw two messengers who had a book for him. The next day, while building a chimney for a neighbor, he felt compelled to quit in the middle and return home, where he told his surprised wife, "I can see two strangers coming up the mountains bringing us a message concerning the gospel. I must dress in my best clothes and go down to welcome them." That night, the men stayed up all night learning as much as they could about the new truths which the missionaries brought. Lorenzo Snow said they learned as much from the faithful Vaudois as they did from them.[12]

Such was the family into which Susanna married. Susanna and Paul had been married only a few months when they faced a crisis that threatened the entire Mormon community. The federal government, under order from President James Buchanan, had mobilized an army of several thousand men to march to Utah to quell the "Mormon rebellion." It was alleged that the Utah Territory was being ruled by Brigham Young in a theocratic dictatorship in defiance of United States law. The troops, under the command of Colonel (later General) Albert Sidney Johnston, left Fort Leavenworth, Kansas, on July 18, 1857.

In response to this march by the federal troops, the Mormons mobilized the Nauvoo Legion, a force of 3,000 men, under General Daniel H. Wells. Approximately 1,100 of these men were dispatched to Echo Canyon east of Salt Lake City to form an eastern defense.[13] Paul Cardon was along the legionnaires called to serve in the Echo Canyon unit. He spent the fall and winter of 1857 there building fortifications against the Johnston Army.

By the time spring came, the government and the church had
essentially worked out a compromise to allow the army to come
into the valley peacefully. The church, however, was determined
to dramatize the Mormon resolve to resist any government persecution, in whatever form it might come. It also wanted to be
prepared to exodus in case the government did not live up to its
pledge.

Therefore, on March 18, 1858, the decision was made to move
south. Every Mormon family in northern Utah would leave their
home and farm and exodus to the south, ready to flee into the
deserts if the army attacked.[14]

Leaving her husband behind, Susanna joined the march south,
walking the entire way to Spanish Fork, some one hundred miles.
In her arms she carried their first baby, Philip, who was only a
few months old at the time. Paul stayed behind in Ogden as part
of a small contingent of men who were given the assignment to
burn every mark of civilization in Weber County if the army
broke its promise and attacked.

From March through May of 1858, 30,000 Mormons abandoned
their homes in this manner. The evacuation was so complete that
when Johnston's Army finally did march into Salt Lake Valley on
June 26, they were psychologically devastated by the deathly silence that hung over the once-busy settlement. The Mormons had
so impressed their point on the government, and consequently the
army was so careful in observing its pledge of nonviolence, that
within four days, on June 30, the church announced that everyone
could return home. This Susanna did in August.

After the return, Susanna and Paul made their living farming in
Ogden. Even though the danger from the army had subsided, life
could not be free from outside threat:

*The Indians gave them considerable trouble. At one time an Indian came and wanted
her to go away with him. She refused to do so and he took her eldest son Philip and
threw him on his horse, thinking she would follow. She pulled him off twice but
could not get him away. The men were all in the fields some distance away, so her
mother-in-law got up on the house and whistled for them. The men heard her and
came running to see what the trouble was. When the Indian saw that his purpose
was defeated, he left the child and went to a neighboring house and threw their
things all out of doors in his anger.*[15]

In 1859, Paul, his older brother Phillip, and their father moved
north to Logan to aid in colonizing the northern Cache Valley,
where only a few families had gone to live by then. By the next
spring (1860), Paul's family, which now consisted of Susanna and
two children, joined them.

The Cardon family today is recognized as one of the founding families of Logan City in Cache Valley, and to this day many of their descendants remain prominent citizens of the area. Such honors, as they may come through the years, however, are meaningless to the founders themselves when they begin to struggle to eke out an existence in a new place. Immediately the task is simply to survive.

During the first spring the Cardons were in Cache Valley as a family (1860) they planted forty bushels of wheat. After grasshoppers ravaged the fields, however, only seven bushels were left for harvest. Just enough was saved to make bread which, when supplemented with water and greens, barely sustained them through famine.

Despite the bleak conditions, the Cardons somehow survived the first year and gradually, month upon month, they built a permanent life in their new home. Because they were part of the original settlement in Cache Valley, their various activities are often recorded by the history books as among the first in the area. Paul Cardon helped build the first home in Logan; it was made of logs. Paul was the first treasurer of Logan City and was also its first policeman. He became a first lieutenant in the cavalry that defended the settlement against Indians. He was in charge of the Temple Mill in Logan Canyon that supplied lumber for the temple construction; and he helped survey and build the road through Logan Canyon that connected the Cache and Bear Lake valleys. The Cardon family planted the first mulberry trees in Cache Valley; the trees prospered and later were used in the home-industry silk movement in Utah.

The Cardons lived in a log house until about 1870, when Paul built the first house of any size to be erected in Logan. This adobe home served a dual purpose as a family residence for the Cardons and also as a hotel and rooming house for travelers. The church had asked Paul Cardon to build this home, known as the Cache Valley House, at a cost of $5,000 so that people traveling to Logan to attend the Mormon Temple would have a suitable place to stay. Others also took overnight lodging there, which later proved a boon for the Mormons when the government began its crackdown on polygamy. As Paul and Susanna's granddaughter later recalled:

They were instructed to listen through the thin partitioned wall to the plans of the United States deputies who were trying to track down and punish polygamy offenders. Many plans were revealed this way and many Saints were warned in time to save them from being caught.

My father has told that many times he went out the back door of a home, after warning the Saints, just as the deputies came in the front. They continued to do this work for ten years and when the deputies became suspicious of my Grandfather, he went into the Northwest to work on the railroad, taking part of the older family with him. His wives were left to run this house, and they did not feel able to continue to do so alone, so it was sold.[16]

As this account indicates, Paul Cardon took a second wife, Madelaine Beus, on December 19, 1870. She had been the young two-year-old baby who had ridden across the plains in Susanna's handcart fourteen years earlier. For one who has never lived around polygamy, the institution must seem peculiar indeed; however, many families were very happy. According to one granddaughter, it appears the Cardons were one of those fortunate families:

I remember visiting them in their Benson Ward home and many times while I was still a small child. It was always a thrill. . . . I remember that Grandmother Cardon and Auntie Cardon always lived in the same house, each having their own side and their own furniture and personal belongings. We always went into Auntie's side of the house to visit for a little while when we were visiting Benson Ward. The two wives and families never seemed to have any trouble and I have never learned of any quarrels or strife in their home. They loved and respected each other and I was a big girl before I knew for sure, which were my father's own brothers and sisters instead of half brothers and sisters.[17]

Paul's trouble with the law over polygamy forced him to leave Logan for about five years, first going to Montana in 1886 and then to Oregon in 1888. He worked on the railroads in both places, but there still wasn't enough money to support his family; to secure that money, the Cache Valley House had to be sold.

While living in Logan, Susanna became an important figure in the drive to establish one of Utah's infant home-based industries. As early as the 1850s, church leaders were encouraging private individuals to raise and weave their own silk. This drive was part of the overall economic policy of Brigham Young, who counseled Mormons to "produce what you consume." One of President Young's counselors, John Taylor, propounded this theme in a speech in the Salt Lake Tabernacle on January 17, 1858:

Import silk worms and mulberry trees and you will find that this is as good a country and climate in which to raise silk as any on the face of the earth. Do some understand this? Yes, there are persons here from the Eastern States who have raised silk worms and manufacturers from the old country. Why, then, do we not have silk? Because no man takes steps to organize certain elements into silk. All this was told you in the beginning, and why did not men understand?[18]

By 1859 a local woman, Mrs. Nancy Barrows, had made a dress from silk that she had raised herself; it was the first homegrown silk dress in the territory. Brigham Young himself set the pace for the silk projects by planting a patch of mulberry trees and erecting a cocoonery for the silkworms behind his Eagle Gate home.

The wholesale push for the home silk industry, however, did not begin until June 15, 1875, when the Deseret Silk Association was organized with Zina D. Young, one of Brigham Young's wives, as president.

In conjunction with Eliza R. Snow, another of Young's wives and president of the church Relief Society, silk-raising projects were set up in every one of the approximately 150 local Relief Societies throughout the territory. In an article in the *Woman's Exponent* magazine on March 15, 1875, the women of Utah were advised:

Shall we wait for one another? Can we afford to wait in the consumption of food, of clothing, of life's necessities? Let each branch and each member of a branch remember that all are herself in all respects a non-producer. . . .

It is now time that those who propose interesting themselves in silk culture, commencing this season, should be making calculations for a start.[19]

During the following months, leaders of the Relief Society traveled extensively throughout the territory to promote their campaign. By the end of the year, Zina Young delivered an optimistic report at the association's first annual meeting, held June 15, 1876, as reported in the *Woman's Exponent* on August 1, 1876:

Samples of silk were taken from Utah, by Elder Paul Schettler, to France and Italy and by competent judges there were pronounced of the best quality. It now requires quantity before machinery can be made practicable, meantime, stockings, sewing-silk, floss and etc., can be manufactured for home use.[20]

Teaching inexperienced women how to make silk, however, was a difficult task, since the production of silk is an extremely specialized skill requiring a great deal of talent and practice due to the delicate way in which the worms manufacture the thread. Each silkworm spins a cocoon about the size of a peanut; this "peanut" is actually a continuous thread 1,000 to 1,300 yards long. Reeling the silk from the cocoons is a delicate process; it was this skill in which Susanna Cardon excelled and which had to be taught to hundreds of women in the territory. Susanna had been reeling silk since she was a girl of twelve in Italy; she and her husband had continued this tradition in their new home in Logan. Paul had sent to France for mulberry trees on which the silkworms feed, and he later purchased eggs for the silkworms. He had made a reel and Susanna had reeled silk from the cocoons.

Susanna was expert at making a twisted reel, which was much

preferred to a flat silk. Her work was of such high quality that Susanna was called by Brigham Young to Salt Lake City soon after the first annual Silk Association meeting in 1876 to teach others how to do the same work. There she joined other women who also knew the silk arts from the old country, and they began teaching a core group of women who would then return to their various homes and teach yet others. President Young was especially impressed with Susanna's skill:

As he watched her work he thought she must have some trick in handling the silk threads. So she put her hands in his and took it through the process giving it a quick flip and putting it on the reel, thus showing that it was all in knowing how to handle it. The silk she wove was of a very high grade and was as good as any from Italy.[21]

While Susanna was in Salt Lake City on the silk mission, which lasted three months, she left eight children behind at home, including a one-year-old baby. Paul's other wife, Madelaine, however, remained at home to care for the family.

Susanna's work in the silk movement was voluntary labor, without pay, as was the custom on church missions. Two years after her service in Salt Lake City, Susanna continued to teach her silk skills to the local women:

In 1878, the Relief Society of Logan decided to try and raise their own silk and Mrs. Cardon furnished eggs of the worm and taught classes of young women to care for the worms and reel the silk. This was done without pay, but as service to her Church and community.

Mrs. Cardon's silk was of a very high quality and she received medals for the excellence of her silk from New Jersey, California, Chicago, and St. Louis.

Mrs. Cardon gave over two rooms for the silk industry and kept at this work for about 15 years, when it was found to be no longer practical and was discontinued.[22]

Giving such dedicated voluntary service was a natural thing for Susanna to do when one considers her attitude towards life. As her granddaughter describes her:

She loved the people and they likewise loved her. Her faith in the promises of the Lord was great.

When her children were sick, she would always call on the Elders to administer to them. When she was unable to get the Elders, she would pray for them herself, as she was alone many times. She obeyed all of the principles of the gospel which she had embraced. Her charity and integrity were known everywhere she went. The Lord blessed her with inspiration and dreams which were a great guide to her. My mother, her daughter-in-law, asked her how she could have raised a large family so well, without any education or advantages of any kind, and she said she had raised them on her knees.

My mother was told that she was a wonderful mother-in-law. She was a kind

*and loving mother full of patience and long suffering and would rather suffer herself,
anytime, than to cause others to do so. Always praising and never interfering in any
way. She was a good neighbor. She took pleasure in doing good for others.*

*She was a loving wife. I have been told that she took pride and pleasure in the
appearance of her husband and children. They were always clean and well-clothed.
She, herself, was always neat and clean and well-dressed even in old age. She was
very talented with her hands and did many beautiful things in the line of sewing,
weaving, knitting, and crocheting.*[23]

In 1892, the Cardon family moved to Benson Ward, a small
community just northwest of Logan, where they purchased a large
farm and lived for twenty years. While there, Susanna was a
teacher, then a counselor, in the Relief Society organization, and
Paul was a counselor in the bishopric. During this time Paul also
went on a mission to Italy to gather genealogical records for the
church. Paul and Susanna's third son, Louis Samuel, was the
Swiss Mission president, and was in charge of Italy. Paul left Italy
in 1899 and returned home with Louis in March 1901.

In 1913 the Cardons moved back to Logan to be near their children and to do work in the temple. Two years later, on February
12, 1915, Paul Cardon died at age seventy-five. After his death,
Susanna spent the rest of her years living with her daughters until
her own death on December 8, 1920.

*She died at the home of her daughter Mrs. Sarah A. Turner at the age of 87
years. The following was taken from the* Logan Republican, *December 11, 1920:
"She was a splendid neighbor, a loving wife and mother and took pleasure in doing
good to others, always having in mind the happiness and welfare of others. Few persons, if any, have ever been more loved and revered than was Susanna Cardon. Her
faith in God and his glorious work was indeed sublime, and she radiated the spirit of
love to such a wonderful degree as to impress all who ever associated with her. She
goes to a well-earned reward, a realization of a well-spent and beautiful life, filled
with service and satisfaction."*

*Her funeral was held December 11, 1920, in the Stake Tabernacle. The large as-
sembly hall was filled with relatives and friends to honor one whom they dearly loved
and revered. At the time of her death she had sixty grand children and 45 great-
grand children to bless her memory. She is buried in the Logan City Cemetery and
her grave overlooks the beautiful valley which she helped to settle and build.*[24]

Susanna Goudin Cardon was the mother of eleven children:

	Born	Died
Philip Cardon	29 Jan 1858	10 Sep 1863
Martha Mary Cardon Merrill	7 Dec 1859	30 Apr 1961
Susette Cardon Ricks	23 Jun 1861	2 Jan 1919
Sarah Ann Cardon Turner	30 Nov 1862	16 Jan 1960
Louisa Cardon	14 Aug 1864	2 Oct 1868

John Paul Cardon	19 Nov 1866	3 Nov 1955
Louis Samuel Cardon	23 Jun 1869	14 Dec 1930
Lucy Cardon Merrill	28 Feb 1871	27 Nov 1951
Joseph Emanuel Cardon	28 Oct 1872	19 Jul 1956
Moses Goudin Cardon	16 Jun 1875	27 Aug 1965
Ezra Bartholome Cardon	26 May 1878	10 Mar 1902

Four of her children—Philip, Susette, Louisa, and Ezra—preceded her in death.

Notes

1. Adams, Ella Vida Cardon and Smith, Blondel Cardon Porter, *Philippe Cardon—Pioneer Father 1801-1889,* typescript manuscript in possession of the Mormon Church Archives, Salt Lake City, Utah, p. 1.

2. Bennett, Archibald F., "The Vaudois Revisited", *The Improvement Era,* January 1948, p. 14.

3. *Ibid.,* p. 14.

4. *Ibid.,* p. 14.

5. Adams, p. 4.

6. Peterson, Rebecca Cardon Hickman, *Susanna Goudin Cardon,* typescript family history in possession of Church Archives, Salt Lake City, Utah p. 5.

7. *Ibid.,* p. 8.

8. Peterson, p. 9.

9. Rich, p. 4.

10. Peterson, p. 10.

11. *Ibid.,* p. 11.

12. Adams, p. 2.

13. Arrington, Leonard J., *Great Basin Kingdom,* Harvard University Press, 1958, p. 171.

14. *Ibid.,* pp. 182-194.

15. Peterson, p. 11.

16. *Ibid.,* p. 13.

17. *Ibid.,* p. 16.

18. Potter, Margaret Schow, *The History of Sericulture in Utah,* thesis, Oregon Stage College, August 1949, p. 5.

19. *Ibid.,* p. 17.

20. *Ibid.,* p. 28.

21. Peterson, p. 14.

22. Carter, Kate B., *Heart Throbs of the West,* vol. 3. Daughters of Utah Pioneers, Salt Lake City, Utah, 1947, p. 131.

23. Peterson, p. 15.

24. *Ibid.,* p. 16.

This thought-provoking essay about a complicated woman, Lucinda Lee Dalton, is by Lavina Fielding Anderson, an associate editor of The Ensign *(the adult magazine of The Church of Jesus Christ of Latter-day Saints). She received her doctor of philosophy degree in American literature from the University of Washington in 1975. She married Paul Anderson in 1977. Mormon history, and especially the history of Mormon women, is her absorbing hobby.*

Lucinda L. Dalton

Lavina Fielding Anderson

A good way to meet Lucinda Lee Dalton is through one of her poems, a feminist statement of power and passion, irony and even bitterness, yet, paradoxically, of faith:

> *Woman is the first to know sorrow and pain,*
>   *Last to be paid for her labor,*
> *First in self-sacrifice, last to obtain*
>   *Justice, or even a favor.*
>
> *First to greet lovingly man at his birth,*
>   *Last to forsake him when dying,*
> *First to make sunshine around his hearth,*
>   *Last to lose heart and cease trying.*
>
> *Last at the cross of her crucified Lord,*
>   *First to behold him when risen,*
> *First, to proclaim him to life restored,*
>   *Bursting from death's gloomy prison.*
>
> *First to seek knowledge, the God-like prize,*
>   *Last to gain credit for knowing,*
> *First to call children a gift from the skies,*
>   *Last to enjoy their bestowing.*
>
> *First to fall under the censure of God,*
>   *Last to receive a full pardon,*
> *First to kiss meekly the chastening rod,*
>   *Thrust from her beautiful garden.*
>
> *First to be sold for the wages of sin,*
>   *Last to be sought and forgiven,*
> *First in the scorn of her dear brother, man,*
>   *Last in the kingdom of heaven.*
>
> *So, a day cometh, a glorious day,*
>   *Early perfection restoring—*
> *Sin and its burdens shall be swept away,*
>   *And love flow like rivers outpouring.*
>
> *Then woman, who loves e'en thro sorrow and shame,*

> *The crown of a queen will be wearing,*
> *And love, freed from lust, a divinely pure flame,*
> *Shall save our sad earth from despairing.*

> *That latter-day work is already begun,*
> *The good from the evil to sever,*
> *The Word has gone forth that when all is done,*
> *The last shall be first, forever.*

> "Woman," *Woman's Exponent,* 21
> (15 January 1893):107

This poem contains the four great passions that weave the fabric of Lucinda's life. Most obvious is her strong sense of the injustice done to women, and as an inseparable second, how worthy women are of honor. Equally powerful is her sense that the issue of women's rights was a theological issue as well as a political one; women's ultimate redemption and compensation for the wrongs of mortality will be part of the purification of the earth itself. The fourth characteristic is simply that Lucinda Lee Dalton is an eloquent and polished poet, clear and forceful in her expression. She is not merely angry, merely sorrowful, merely hopeful; she is all three at the same time, her emotions controlled and channeled by her ironic edge and her poetic form.

And the poem, possibly her strongest, is an excellent introduction to the woman, still a mystery fifty years after her death. Her talent, her clear mind, her great personal strength, and her unflinching faith make her acquaintance valuable.

In surveying Lucinda's writings, we sense that her feelings about being a woman are inseparably connected with her feelings about men—and those feelings were generally not good. She was born in Alabama in 1847 to John Percival Lee and Eliza Foscue. Two years later, they joined The Church of Jesus Christ of Latter-day Saints in Texas, crossed the plains in 1850, went to help colonize San Bernardino, California, in 1851, and after seven years left to settle in Beaver, Utah, in the winter of 1857-58.[1] John P. Lee was a great influence on his daughter. Oldest of thirteen children, Lucinda was intelligent and thirsty for knowledge, recalling with gratitude that her father "at the close of his days' work patiently taught us, while yet too young to attend the common schools." (Autobiography, p. 3.) At the age of twelve she helped him teach school; four years later she was a teacher herself, a profession she dearly loved and followed for the rest of her life.

Lucinda says little else of her father in her unpublished autobiographical sketch, but later he was to take a new wife, a practice that was socially accepted and respected in the Mormon view that countenanced plural marriages; however, his action—possibly because of his manner or because of the timing—deeply hurt Lucinda's mother and alienated his children.

Lucinda mentions two more men who influenced her youth. One was her first teacher in Utah. "O bless him!" she exclaims. With compassion upon "my ravenous hunger for knowledge, [he] gave to me instruction many a noontide hour when other children played and other men went home to dinner." It was "this beloved tutor and friend" she had to leave when she began teaching school. (Autobiography, p. 5.)

The second man, likewise a teacher, was someone she humbly approached, asking "if in his opinion, I was sufficiently advanced in mathematics to study algebra with profit." This "gentleman teacher" replied that "it would be wasted time for me to ever study it, because I already had more learning than was necessary for a good housekeeper, wife, and mother which was a woman's only proper place on earth." Then she adds something significant: "It is but justice to him and myself to say that he has since warmly commended my efforts at self culture and the good I have done as a teacher." (Autobiography, p. 8.) Lucinda's sense of justice never deserted her; she would not lie, even by omission, and we learn to trust her unsparing honesty.

Lucinda, then, entered adolescence with some sense that being a woman meant being limited, and she remembers that she had always "longed to be a boy, because boys were so highly privileged and so free." (Autobiography, p. 7.) She envied their liberty, their mobility, and the encouragement that they received to seek education, but wryly attributes this envy to "my youth and 'blissful ignorance,' " and chastises men in one of the most scathing passages in her autobiography: "Not for all their boasted 'supremacy,' 'superiority,' and extensive advantages would I have women come down to their low moral level. Intellectual acquirements, fame, power, wealth, and even their self-conceit added, are as feathers in the scale against moral purity." (Autobiography, p. 8.)

She wrote this autobiography in 1876 for Emmeline B. Wells, then editor of the *Woman's Exponent*, "rising in the night" to do it. (Autobiography, p. 25.) She was at that time twenty-nine years old, living in Beaver, the fourth wife of Charles Wakeman Dalton, without doubt the man who was most significant both for good and for ill in her life. They had been married for eight years, Lucinda had borne six children and lost two. Her sixteen-year-old sister Emma had also married Charles five years earlier and had divorced him only the year before; Lucinda herself was to apply to

President John Taylor for a cancellation of sealing in 1884, eight years in the future and barely a year after Charles' death. This cancellation President Taylor granted in 1887.

Because of these facts, we might be tempted to interpret Lucinda's scorn of men as the result of a disappointing marriage, one in which she had expected too much, or expected the wrong things. Lucinda's marriage *was* a disappointment, but for spiritual reasons rather than romantic ones. We misread Lucinda completely if we do not take her deep faith and strong desire to obey the Lord into consideration as one of her most enduring motivations. She recounts, in her autobiography, several accounts of answered prayers, including one heart-rending story about the illness of a much-loved little brother. Feeling, in all humility, that she was entitled to claim the Lord's promise that he would grant the prayers of the righteous, the sixteen-year-old Lucinda "fasted and prayed with intense fervor that the little one's life might be spared." Indeed, she seemed to have halted the illness, but he did not improve. He simply lingered, suffering, and she felt "like I had lifted some heavy weight just to the edge of a place of rest, but lacked the one ounce of power necessary to deposit it thereon. Coming at one time suddenly into the room, I saw my mother wring her hands and cry in anguish: 'Why oh why must my innocent baby suffer so much; If it is God's will to take him away, oh, let his cruel sufferings end!' "

Lucinda says, "My heart smote me guiltily. Perhaps, thought I, it is God's will to take him—perhaps my shortsighted wishes stand between the beloved and his rest. I hastened away and with streaming eyes fell upon my knees crying 'Thy will, O Lord; not mine, be done!' As soon as I was calm enough to reenter the sick room I did so and was struck to the heart by the change in the precious one's face; and that same evening he died." (Autobiography, pp. 14-15.)

It was characteristic of Lucinda's faith that she could effect a great work and accept a hard answer. It stood her in good stead later. She tells this story purposefully as prelude to "the greatest spiritual manifestation ever vouchsafed to me," her decision to marry Charles. (Autobiography, p. 15.) She explains, indirectly, why her need of a special manifestation was so great: "I had seen in the married state so much that was disagreeable and humiliating to woman, that I was firmly resolved to remain single." She could support herself and provide for her old age. She knew she wanted children but expected to care for neglected motherless children in the community and also to influence children through her teaching.

Obviously, she could not be driven to marriage by economic necessity or because of personal restlessness with her situation. Instead it was her faith in the principles of Mormon theology that brought her to the altar. As her conviction that its teachings were true deepened, she was unable to avoid the stark fact that "in the highest glory of heaven, none are single." This was in full keeping with the Mormon doctrine that marriage, when performed and "sealed" by the proper authority, is an eternal as well as a temporal union and that the family unit can endure and increase throughout the eternities, the woman and man sharing power, kingdom, and glory together. Lucinda resolutely contemplated the idea of being "handmaiden to some sanctified woman" (the fate she felt was reserved for the righteous but unwed), since she "had been told in express terms by some blind leaders of the blind, that the Kingdom here, and hereafter belonged only to man; and that woman enjoyed its gifts and blessings only in sufficient degree to make her man's efficient servant; and that looked to me not worth striving for." The doctrine of celestial marriage—or eternal union as one of the blessings of salvation—, however, remained "worse than gall and wormwood to me, for in my pride of heart, I had determined to win my soul's salvation alone, . . . forgetting that the best and bravest of us are only too happy to be acknowledged coworkers with Christ." (Autobiography, pp. 16-17.)

Then she met Charles Wakeman Dalton. She was about twenty and he, nineteen years older, was only two years younger than her father. He had married his first wife a month before Lucinda was born and had married twice more by the time Lucinda's family came to Utah. She mentions no objection to his age or to his other marriages, and apparently objected to him only because he was male—for when he proposed, "I resented the thought, and told him that the man who thought I should be a meek, obedient, unobtrusive servant was very sadly wrong." He was apparently intimidated by neither frankness nor intelligence, for he overcame her objections by reasoning, an approach that communicated respect for both Lucinda's mind and her free agency. By pointing out that Christ had served all of mankind and thus exalted the position of servant, Charles was able to draw the analogy with marriage: by benefitting from Christ's service, we are his debtors. So a husband and wife, in need of mutual service, both have obligations, not just the wife. And no obligation which bound one did not also bind the other.

Lucinda exulted: "This was new light on a difficult problem. This was speaking from reason and common sense instead of vaguely hinting at some foggy superstition about man's being cre-

ated first and *consequently* best, noblest, and suprem-*est*. These were
arguments at once indisputable and satisfactory." (Autobiography,
p. 18.)

As this new concept penetrated Lucinda's mind, love also began
to touch her heart, but fear followed. She remembered the unhappy marriages made by wiser women than she, and felt the salvation of her soul in jeopardy. "For time alone, as the people of
the world marry, I could not and would not, because I considered
that in a woman's case, the burdens and trials of matrimony far
exceed its benefits and blessings. Only for the sake of its expected
joys in eternity, could I endure its trials through time; but that
cherished 'free agency' which gives a woman the choice with
which of her fellow beings she will undertake to find eternal happiness, began to look far more like a burden and a snare than a
privilege or a blessing." She applied the energies of her mind to
the problem, and took her questions to the Lord: "I thought and
dreamed about it," she records. "I fasted and prayed about it; I
grew pale and hollow-eyed over it but found no conclusion. I was
at last willing to love a man, but dared not assume the responsibility of becoming his wife." The only answer she got to her prayers was one which drastically humbled her pride:

*In very despair—and in deep humiliation because I was impressed so to do—I called
on him to pray with me on the subject. I knew he was startled by the demand, and
felt it like assuming a great responsibility but he hesitated only long enough to learn
that there was no shadow of trifling in me. He knelt down first, and I placed myself
beside him and laid one of my hands on one of his; and as I did so, I felt a thrill
through every fibre of my being and I know he felt the same. I was utterly crushed
under the knowledge that within a few minutes a question would be settled which
would shape and determine my destiny forever, and cowardly I dreaded to meet the decision. The prayer was short, simple and unassuming, but direct, earnest, and sincere;
and at every word uttered, a huge stone of my mountain load of doubt and fear rolled
from my heart. My stony pride and bitter humility were alike softened; a peace sweet-
er than joy took possession of my soul; I felt that we were in the presence of the
hosts of heaven; and a direct incontrovertible testimony was given me that it was the
will of God and not my will that I should accept this man for my yokefellow. He
knew as well as I what the decision was; and in awe-struck solemn silence, we left
the spot. To this day it is to both of us a most precious and solemn recollection, and
is never mentioned between us except with deepest reverence."* (Autobiography, pp.
19-20.)

They were wed in the Endowment House October 3, 1868, and
it should have been the beginning to an idyllic Mormon love story, not the prelude to a cancellation of sealing several years later.
Lucinda was teaching, and was loved by her pupils and respected
by the community. She also apparently participated in the meager

cultural life of Beaver by singing in the choir, partially satisfying "the master passion of my soul," her craving for music. (Autobiography, p. 5.) Lucinda was also a mother, little Charles having been born in 1869 or 1870. Her experience with this baby shows again her sensitivity and her faith. Six years after Charles' birth and four after his death, she records:

Early in my married life, one day my mother was sitting with me in my own house, and I was embroidering a delicate muslin robe for my expected child. After much pleasant conversation, she inquired half playfully, how I felt doing such pretty work for a child of my own. A most natural and innocent question, but, my mother thought, most direful in its effect; for, throwing down the work and bursting into hysterical weeping I wailed: "Oh! Mother, I feel like I were sewing on a shroud." She was alarmed for my safety, and urged the necessity of selfcontrol, and begged to know if she had said anything wrong. When I was sufficiently recovered, I explained. For months a haunting dread had hung like a great black cloud over me, that my child would die in infancy. I had tried to smile at it; I had refused it admittance to my thoughts; I had fought it like a deadly foe and barred the doors of my soul against it; but still it lay in wait, and my mother's unexpected question suddenly flung wide all those barred doors and gave the enemy full possession. Lying, as I may say, a bound and helpless captive at the feet of my foe, I confessed my secret grief. As in duty bound, even had she not fully believed it, my mother argued that I had mistaken nervousness for presentiment and assured me that by the time I had borne half a dozen children I should be able to discriminate better. I sobbed forth "I wish you were right, Mother, but my child will live six months or a year or possibly two years, but not longer."

Great was my surprise and delight when, instead of the puny, wailing little skeleton I had expected, my child was a great, lusty boy who seemed the very impression of good health, high spirits, and precocious intellect. Nothing ever seemed to hurt him, and in the pride of my heart I laughed my former fears to scorn. I told my mother she was right and I was tempted to give up my belief in presentiments entirely. But in his fifteenth month, I found myself compelled to wean him; and it was with a sinking heart that I took him from the breast and began the old warfare anew. He pined from that day *and in spite of all care, all weeping and praying,* he died in my arms on the second anniversary of his birthday, *and we buried him in the embroidered dress I had once called a shroud. A strange and sad experience, truly, and my mother lives to testify to its truth; but the warning which was once my torture and foe, is now my comfort and friend, because it assures me that it was not my ignorance of the laws of life and health which deprived the world of so noble a soul, but the will of God.* (Autobiography, pp. 21-23.)

Lucinda was to mourn this loss with elegaic poems for years; but even in so bitter an event, she was able to find sweetness and strength. It was still far in the future as she moved tranquilly through the opening months of 1870 with her beloved child and loving husband, but within a few months, her happiness was clouded. Ironically, those who had most power to hurt her were those closest. Her father took another wife in 1870, even though the price was the breach of his marriage with Lucinda's mother, the woman who had married him at fifteen and followed him faithfully into a new church and through three different states before they found their home in Beaver. Apparently the rupture was a painful one, for about the same time, Lucinda's sixteen-year-old sister Emma left the family home and came to live with her.

A year later, in April 1871, the ward teachers (representatives of the local presiding church authority who routinely visited a given number of homes monthly) were sent to make peace between Charles and his father-in-law. It was apparently an important case, for, in the ward clerk's uncertain orthography, "Bishop Ashworth Ashworth [sic] spoke at some length On the difficulty Existing Between John P Lee & Chas W. Dolton. Three Of the Brethren were Appointed to visit These Brethren." The trio returned to say that they "could not make any Reconciliation with them."[2]

The minutes do not specify the cause of the quarrel, but it may have been an event that occurred only six months later—Emma's marriage to Charles. Apparently they had been engaged for some time, possibly without the estranged father's permission. Before that fall wedding on October 16, 1871, in the Endowment House, the loss that Lucinda had been prepared for by premonition had occurred and the summer serenity was shattered by the death of her little son, an unimaginable strain on the devoted mother, still recovering from the birth of her daughter Belle on June 1.

Apparently Emma shared her sister's home after marrying Charles; relationships between the sisters seem unmarred by jealousy or competition, for Lucinda always speaks of Emma tenderly and affectionately. But the marriage itself was evidently a mistake for the seventeen-year-old girl and the forty-five-year-old man. They had no children and Emma seems to have refused domesticity.

We know little of the family during Emma's four years with them. A daughter Rosette was born to Lucinda probably in 1874, but apparently died within months. On February 18, 1875, Lucinda's third child, a son named Clifford, was born. Apparently Emma had reached the end of her optimism and patience the same year, for on September 12, she sent a cryptic letter to Brigham Young:

Sir, I was married to Charles Wakeman Dalton, in the house of endowments, on the ninth day of October, 1871.

For reasons, which Pres. Murdock has kindly informed me, you do not require me to state, I now desire a divorce.

By giving this matter your earliest convenience, you will confer an eternal obliga-

tion.

Yours respectfully
E. Lee Dalton

A clerk has noted on that letter that blank forms were sent to Bishop Murdock on September 15. However, two weeks later, the Beaver Literary Institute was organized for "persons of good moral character" under the auspices of that same John Murdock, and on October 4, Emma Dalton was there, nominated to serve on a committee to propose a list of officers. Between then and Christmas, she presented an essay, edited the first number of the *Literary Star,* helped plan the Christmas party, appeared on a spelling team, and gave a recitation. However, this flurry of activity faded suddenly, for the minutes of January 17, 1876, include the report of a delegation sent to find out why "Mrs. Emma Dalton was absenting herself from meeting with the Institute at regular meetings." Emma told them "that it is no intention on her part to relinquish her membership in the Institution and considering herself an honorary member, therefore [illegible] to excuse to offer and furthermore was not aware that she was violating any of the rules, or by-laws, or that an absentee was required to furnish an excuse in case of being absent a specified time."[3]

Despite these excuses, Emma never reappears in the minutes and apparently left Charles, Beaver, and the church, having decided, in Lucinda's sorrowful words, that "Mormonism was iniquity, and its followers hypocrites." According to Lucinda, she went to work for the Rio Grande and Denver Railroad in Little Rock, Arkansas.

In Lucinda's obituary, Emma is listed as "Mrs. Emma Sutherland of San Francisco." She had married Jabez Gridley Sutherland under her maiden name sometime between 1893 and 1897. Judge Sutherland, a widower, was a prominent gentile in Salt Lake City, some thirty years older than his bride, who was then in her late forties. He died in Berkeley "after a lingering attack of paralysis" at the age of seventy-seven, only a few years after their marriage.[4]

We know very litttle of what happened during those four years when Emma, Lucinda, and Charles struggled to make the marriage work and eventually abandoned the effort. It was during those four years, however, that Lucinda began writing for the *Woman's Exponent,* a lively paper devoted to matters feminine and feminist, first edited by Louisa Lula Greene Richards with a circulation that never rose above a thousand, although readership may have been that high. It was only five months old when Lucinda saw her work in print for the first time on November 1, 1872.

This initial essay was, pointedly enough, a criticism of fathers in a concrete and vernacular style that shows a keen mind and a satirical eye at work: "Oh, yes, I know the boys are wild, that they use bad language and cultivate bad habits, and, as you say, 'Make themselves a great nuisance; but, my friend, I don't think the boys deserve quite so much blame as they get. . . . When I heard a father complain that 'outside influences' was too strong for him, and it was almost more than he could do to keep his boys under any restraint whatever, I could not help wondering if 'inside influence' were what they should be." ("A Plea for the Boys," *Woman's Exponent* 1[November 1, 1872] 86.)

It would be mere wishful thinking to make her articles replace Lucinda's missing journals and letters. She was a woman with a deeply developed sense of privacy, and these articles are very public. But even if we cannot read them autobiographically, they are extremely valuable in showing us her attitudes on certain issues. A common theme was mourning the death of little Charles. She describes his baby beauty and bewitching ways, but finds comfort in his immunity from the world's guiles and snares:

> *I fear not worldly [sic] pride may win thee now,*
> *Nor guilt betray, nor flames or guilt devour; . . .*
> *God's will is wiser than our frail desires,*
> *His mercy tenderer than our purest love;*
> *And I can yield to this since He requires,*
> *And name thee now, "My waiting saint above."*

("A Mother's Resignation, *Woman's Exponent,* 1 [November 15, 1872] 90.)

The same issue also contains an article condemning intemperance. Charles drank, both before and during their marriage, and this essay may contain a hint of her feelings about his weakness. One trenchant paragraph slashes: "Do you degrade yourselves 'below' the brutes by disregarding Nature's laws in your own homes, and seeking only your own sensual gratification, persistently closing your eyes to the fact that thus you perpetuate and foster a low tone of morals, and send abroad into the world, exaggerated types of your own depravity, to carry their pestilential presence and shameful deeds everywhere?" ("Where Social Reform Must Originate," *Woman's Exponent,* 1 [November 15, 1872] 91.)

Her opening essay in 1873 was unabashedly feminist. She advocated exercise for girls—not only skating, swimming, and ball, but even shooting. She does not rely only on the relatively safe argument that exercise means better health. Instead she argues the psychological necessity for recreation as well as work and the desirability of a more self-confident generation of women. In passing, she thwacks such "foolish and groundless customs ... as the deep prejudice against whistling" and sketches a sarcastic portrait of the nineteenth century miss "laced up in corsets, with smelling bottle at nose, giving little plaintive screams if she should spy a mouse." ("Exercise for Girls," *Woman's Exponent*, 2 [January 31, 1873] 131.)

She returns to one of her favorite themes, prayer, for her next essay, a thoughtful and reverent article that differs in tone from the polemics she had written heretofore. From a few paragraphs we can see that her faith was maturing as she successfully assimilated her sorrows and learned to trust the Lord despite her pain:

That very frame of mind which is necessary to produce true prayer, is in many cases the answer to prayer—the starting point from which we may accomplish the good we desire. In His wisdom God so ordained it that many prayers should thus answer themselves. ...

To cultivate this prayerful resigned state of mind is the very best preparation against adversity, for we can believe our seeming misfortunes to be blessings in disguise, and generally prove them such. And prayer is an armor fitted to all wearers.
("Prayer," *Woman's Exponent*, 1 [February 15, 1873] 143.)

She also mentions the great shield prayer can provide for the innocent maiden who may not see beneath the roses. That she herself had formed the habit of prayer early is attested to in her autobiography where she states: "I do not recollect ever attending a ball or place of amusement without asking God to keep me from all ill or unbecoming thoughts, words or deeds, and from accidents or harm of any kind. During the entertainment I often recalled the prayer and I can truly say that my prayers were answered. Few young girls ever met with fewer little mortifying mishaps, or moved amid giddy pleasures with less danger of becoming enamored of them." (Autobiography, p. 13.)

She returns to the theme of temperance in her next essay, printed on March 1, 1873, but now discusses more than alcohol. One particularly vivid passage described the effects of lust: "Love, that heavenly radiance which ... lifts the weakest of mortals to a level with the angels ... is a name sorely misapplied. Alas, that it should be so! but many, by giving unrestrained liberty to all the emotions which it awakens in their peculiar natures, and pursuing the object with headlong speed, miss it altogether and grasp, instead—passion; that adder to sting the heart that warms it." ("Moral Temperance," *Woman's Exponent*, 1 [March 1, 1873] 151.)

Lucinda's own life seems to have been free from illicit sexual passion, and even from its temptations:

Even while polite attentions from gentlemen were in themselves pleasant, I always felt a sort of guilt in accepting for my personality what I knew was rendered merely to abstract youth and beauty; and much disgust at the thought that my quick intellect, my honest heart, my high aspirations, all the sterling worth that was really of myself, were never considered in this glittering realm of pleasure to which I was beckoned. What girl that ever paused to think that she was caressed [in] society merely for her youth and freshness, things not in the least due to herself, and which advancing time will soon take from her, and that then she will surely be forsaken by this same society through no fault of her own, could ever become enamored of its fleeting pleasure and hollow praise?

I never was. Although the metrical movements of the dance in time to the rhythm of sweet music were very pleasant, I could grow tired as of any other kind of exercise, but I have seen girls who professed never to tire of dancing. I have often looked on while the beautiful girls, radiant of youth and happiness, with their devoted partners whirled through the dreamy waltz or sprightly cotillion, and mused on the possibility of one of these lovely and carefree maidens, become a woman and perhaps wife of one of these same adoring youths, wearing out not only her youth but her very life, drudging from morning till night to keep his house in order, and from night till morning with his ailing baby, only be looked on by him as an inferior being, designed by nature to serve him. . . . I wondered how any man could have the effrontery to ask, or any woman the supineness to lay down the scepter and crown of girlhood to assume the yoke and burden of wifehood. My prayer was then as now, that the time may come speedily when women will know and hold themselves at their true worth; when their eyes will be opened to the degradation of wasting their spotless lives on worth-. less and depraved men; when by the depth of their contempt for men who lead unholy lives, and by the firmness of their resolution and the dignity of their self-respect, they shall compel men to come up to their standard of morality and with them seek something still better, or be outcast from the Eden of woman's association. (Autobiography, pp. 9-11.)

Possibly Lucinda's mistrust of men generally immunized her against sexual temptation, and she saw with sorrow and compassion those whose uncontrolled love became passion. She may have seen its effects in the marriages in her own family—possibly that of her father, or possibly that of her blooming sister, barely out of childhood, to Charles, who was already the father of twenty-five children.

Two months later appears "To Ernest," a love poem addressed to "my own." She remembers a "sweet night" when they wandered out, hand in hand, and:

> *. . . lowly bowed before th'Eternal throne*
> *(But one in spirit, though two hands were joined) . . .*
>
> *You plead for guidance for our troubled souls—*
> *O'er our coming lives a Father's kindly care,*
> *And that when dread temptation darkly rolls,*

> *Our steadfast faith might keep our purpose fair.*
> *The pure petition fell like summer rain*
> *Upon the thirsty fields when parched and gray;*
> *And doubts and fears that on my soul had lain*
> *Like cliffs of terror, melted soft away. . . .*

> *Our souls were mingled then for evermore,*
> *Like twin rills meeting in the mighty sea;*
> *And still as one we'll seek the shining shore*
> *Of that fair life we call Eternity.*

("To Ernest," *Woman's Exponent*, 1
[15 May, 1873] 186.)

The details of that last stanza—the shared prayer that reassured
her about her choice of a marriage partner—make it clear that she
is recalling her own courtship with Charles. Why she chooses the
name of Ernest we do not know, but six years later she gives that
name to her last child.

It is somehow not surprising, though, that she writes about the
happiness of shared bliss in the past tense and nostalgically. She
had known before her wedding that marriage would be hard,
something to be endured in this life "only for the sake of its expected joys in eternity." (Autobiography, p. 19.) The same tone is
reflected in her next published poem, addressed to a new bride.
The lovely and thoughtful young woman seems to see the "care
and   pain, . . . sorrow, . . . bitter   bereavement,   black   de-
ceit, . . . anxiety" and failed hopes of matrimony that await her,
yet she does not falter, for she also sees "the joy in duty nobly
done" and in bending her heart "to heaven's will/Though it de-
crees thee good or ill." Lucinda, after painting this future of tribulation stoically endured, describes the ceremony itself in a near-
dirge:

> *The hour is spent—thy girlhood's knell*
> *Is tolled, as by a passing bell.*
> *Thy bridegroom comes, with joyous eye,*
> *To lead thee to thy destiny.*
> *With smile half sad but wholly sweet,*
> *Thou turnest thy heart's lord to greet.*

("A Bride," *Woman's Exponent*,
2 [August 15, 1873] 42.)

This is hardly a glad celebration of matrimony. The woman's wisdom and acceptance of suffering contrast with the groom's blithe—
and blind?—happiness, but it reflects Lucinda's own unswerving
faith in the essential nobility of womanhood.

Perhaps it is only coincidence that the very same issue contains
one of the most scathing exposes of male insensitivity that she was
ever to write for publication. Deliberately gossipy, she addresses
the reader with a cordial confidentiality suitable for raking the
male sex over the coals: "You are a young matron whose girlhood,
with its peculiar tastes and feelings, stands so near you that you
could almost touch the hem of its garments; you think your husband about perfection; you have one baby old enough to toddle
about . . . and in your family lives an aunt whom you greatly respect." (If this is indeed autobiographical, it is Lucinda's only
published reference to Charles' other wives, all of whom were at
that time living in Beaver.)

She continues, "Your husband is absent on business much of the
time, and you have to be both master and mistress about home;
cut your own wood, water your own garden and do your own
marketing—when you have anything to market with—but as you
pride yourself on your cheerfulness and independence, you do not
even sigh over all this."

This model little wife decides to forego the pleasure of celebrating a July holiday with the rest of the town even though a married friend would willingly take her, her little daughter would enjoy the cool trees, and she would like a pleasant holiday herself.
The deciding factor is that "Charles . . . might feel a little sad to
think you could really enjoy such an excursion without him; or he
might return during your absence to find only an empty house,
and in his loneliness, he might think you ungrateful for all his toil
and care."

Then Charles reappears on the night before the outing. The loving wife circumspectly waits until he has been fed and had a
good night's sleep to tell him the news. He decides that it's too
late to arrange for a buggy, but proposes instead "a little home
holiday and a cozy dinner together."

*The darling fellow! you are so happy to think a day passed quietly at home could be
a holiday to him, that you are a thousand times glad you had not made any arrangement to go abroad. Full of happy thoughts you set about dressing Rosebud while
Charles goes on his errand. Presently he returns laden with parcels, and overlooking
Baby, who runs to meet him looking like a little white bird, he tells you hurriedly
that "Brown and them" encountered him over in town, and nothing would do but that
he must go out with them to see what the pic-nic-ers were doing. He explains that
he had no idea of such a thing when he left the house, but that they were good fel-
lows and he didn't wish to offend them.*

*All your boasted "independence" could not keep your countenance from falling, and
as your husband is neither blind nor a fool, he asks compunctiously, "Would you like
to go too?" "No," you answer softly, winking very hard to keep back the tears while*

he says in a relieved sort of way, and with the air of one who has done his whole duty, "I didn't think you would, since there are to be only men in the carriage, and I am only an invited party; but you and Aunty can make yourselves comfortable here and have your little dinner together all the same as if I was with you." Then with hasty adieux your adorable Charles hastens away to his bachelor friends and a day among the rocks.

No longer able to conceal your tears, you throw yourself face downward on your bed, grieved to the heart, not for the loss of a day's pleasure, but for the bitterness of the discovery, that all your delicate consideration was unheeded, and because the slight and loneliness you would not risk putting upon him, he would lay upon you ten times magnified.

The anger and hurt of this description comes from the very heart, but by the next and concluding paragraph, the wife regains control with a wry extravagance: she rises, bathes her face, spurns the parcels of groceries, gives the baby to Aunty, and sits down to write a hot letter to the *Exponent*, "hoping in [her] secret soul that 'he' will read it and be very indignant, thus proving that his conscience pricks him." That consolation isn't worth counting on, though, and the young wife turns to a more sure consolation, her certainty that "scores of wives ... will exclaim—'Isn't that the truth?' 'Just the way they do!' and applaud your fixed resolution to learn a lesson from this experience, and, where you can in the future, take care of yourself." ("The Way They Do," *Woman's Exponent*, 2 [August 15, 1873] 46.) Were those tears, those crushed hopes, the wounded tenderness Lucinda's? And even more poignantly, did she, in moments of betrayal, feel sustained by the sympathetic sorority of women who also knew the hard necessity of emotional independence?

Two weeks later in an essay written in the middle of the previous month, Lucinda is blasting again at the nineteenth century's equivalent of male supremists who demand belief without the courtesy of offering proof. After a half-dozen trenchant examples, she gives her crowning illustration:

You women sympathize with the Woman's Rights movement and honestly believe that the mothers of men and women have as deep an interest in their present and future welfare as the fathers, and, therefore, would be, if as well educated, quite as capable of properly shaping their destinies. But you learn with wonder and awe that "Woman never was and never will be capable of understanding political economy nor of acquiring a man's education." Having the testimony of all sacred and profane history that women have been chief rulers, high priests, counselors, commanders and warriors, you suppose, in your innocence, that you are to receive some new light on the subject, but instead of that, your informant looks the picture of injured innocence, that you even imagine that statement needed confirmation. Surely you do not doubt his veracity?

Now what I want to know is just this: Am I obliged to swallow all these nauseous doses of wisdom and call them "good" for me, or may I speak my mind, and say "If you can give me a reason sufficient to convince my judgment, then I will accept your views, if I shall consider myself at liberty to esteem my own opinion as highly as yours."

Then she issues her own manifesto:

If, in order to be womanly and keep my "sphere," I must do the former, then let spheres take care of themselves for I've no use for them. I do not feel like "giving proof" of woman's inferiority by any such complaint course. Every person, within whose soul the least spark of reason exists, has a right to cultivate that reason and give it satisfaction before adopting any principle or opinion; and because my head may be weaker than yours and my judgment less reliable, is no reason I should not cultivate and improve them. And when you give me your views on any given subject and withhold the support of these views, you defraud me of an opportunity to cultivate my judgment and arrive at a just conclusion for myself." ("Assertion is Not Proof," *Woman's Exponent*, 2 [1 September 1873] 54.)

We do not know who these men are, but we are not necessarily justified in numbering Charles among them. If the picnic episode really records an incident of their domestic life, he may have been insensitive to her tender feelings as wife, but there is no evidence that he ever considered her intellectually inferior. In her autobiography, after a particularly scornful passage about men who consider themselves superior, she adds:

I am not so unjust as to make no exceptions to all the sweeping assertions I have been making. I know all women are not good and true, nor all men tyrannical and unjust. I could mention the names of several men pledged heart and soul to the Latter day work of woman's emancipation from her long bondage; and one at least of my acquaintance is a far more ferocious antagonist of woman's slavery than I. From him I received the first antidotic draught to cure my misanthropy and disgust of life. He it was who first showed me wherein Religion is not leagued with woman's oppressors; who first assured me with a man's lips that a woman has as good a right to her individuality and her free agency on the earth as her brother-man. So you see, my dear friend, that for his sake, did I never know another liberal minded, large hearted man, I could not, and would [not] wish to condemn the whole race. I shall give honor where honor is due and while waiting for the good time coming when all men—and women—shall be free and equal, put in my feeble oar wherever I can in her service. (Autobiography, p. 12.)

A later paragraph makes it clear that this man is her husband. Lucinda wrote voluminously for the rest of that year and through 1874. Only five months passed in those two years without a contribution to the *Exponent*, usually one but not infrequently two, in every number. She recommends singing to babies, defends women's suffrage, denounces the Frelinghuysen Bill which would have admitted Utah to the Union at the price of permanently disenfranchising its women, contrasts the economic and legal inequality of gentile women with Mormon women, points out the advantages of Relief Society for every Mormon woman, vehemently denounced "interference" from busybody neighbors during first pregnancies, writes occasional verse, writes a rousing feminist song called "Woman Arise!" and writes a tender comparison between her sleeping baby daughter and the dead baby Charles.

Personal philosophy giving us another view of her marriage seems to appear in a poetic exchange between her and "Queery," who demands somewhat rhetorically, "Is it a crime for woman to love?" meaning, "How aggressively may a woman pursue a man?" Lucinda answers that forwardness is not sin but is usually stupid, since "man is perverseness within, / And values not things lightly won." She is not just offering a nineteenth-century version of fascinating womanhood, however. The concluding stanza gives the reason why love should always be kept in check:

> No passion should break our control,
>   No love supersede love of God—
> This anchor made fast to the soul
>   Will save from the angriest flood.
>   ("Is it a Crime for Woman to Love?"
>   Woman's Exponent, 3 [15 December 1874] 110.)

"Queery" responds the next month, hinting that Lucinda's answer was jaundiced by her mistrust of her own husband. Loyally, Lucinda counters, defending Charles, and—what is more significant—explaining the wryly practical need for womanly self-restraint: one rarely meets a man so ideal he won't take advantage of a woman. She continues, expressing concern for women married to the type of man she fears and mistrusts, one who through misunderstanding or a desire for power will betray a woman through her own love:

> Who think that God made her a slave to man's will;
>   If not, HE will make her so yet,
> Who will win her affections with cunningest skill
>   And lead her to lifelong regret,
> I wish her to learn to be wary and wise
>   That by such she may never be won,
> That poor, sightless Love may be furnished with eyes
>   And never cool judgment outrun.
>   ("Addendum," Woman's Exponent,
>   3 [February 1875] 138.)

It is ironic that this is Lucinda's last contribution for almost a year. Perhaps, considering the subject, it is even significant. She wrote her answer to "Queery"'s romantic argument January 23,

1875. Less than a month later, Clifford was born. Lucinda writes nothing during the entire spring and summer. In September, Emma applied for her divorce, obviously as the result of her own deteriorating marriage. She is gone soon after January 1876. Lucinda is, at that time, pregnant with Guy, who is born April 24, 1876. Apparently her babies keep her busy, for we see only four poems: two seasonal offerings, one mother's outpoured hopes and fears for her children, and one jibe at men who worry about what their own "true sphere" will be if women begin working.

Charles, by this time, is in financial difficulties and his health is failing as well. By 1878, Lucinda and Charles are in St. George, returning to Beaver after a three year's stay. On April 1, 1878, the *Exponent* published her "Questionings," a poem of poignant power lamenting the bitter lot of women.

Addressing the "sweet woman-child, that nestles near my heart," the mother expresses "pity" for the "woman's destiny" of her baby. That destiny she says, is:

> *An endless round of weakness, toil, and pain,*
> *Of deep humiliations, longings vain,*
> *And blind outreachings for the light above. . . .*
> *Self-sacrifice we drain as nectar cup;*
> *For others only we are taught to live.*

But worst is that "our brother creatures . . ./say the gentle Master them has sent/ To bid us come no nearer to His throne." Men say that they may petition the Master directly for the bread of life; women can receive it only from men. Men may love and serve the Savior directly; women must "love and serve and follow" men. The Master rewards men with "honors, kingdoms, crowns and lives divine," while "we may have naught; our very lives be theirs, / And even you, they'd tell me, are not mine." With a sure dramatic sense, the poet-mother asks her daughter:

> *Oh, darling! you have lately seen His face*
> *And in His presence felt no diffidence;*
> *Oh, tell! ere you forget or my heart break,*
> *If now you are forever banished thence?*
> *If after we have worn his crown of thorns*
> *And borne, like Him, the cross, with bleeding feet,*
> *To touch our outstretched hands He e'er will scorn,*
> *Or send, not bring, the balm of healing sweet?*

The baby's "slow, rapt smile" and "beatific look" comfort her with their affirming answer ("Questionings," *Woman's Exponent*, 6 [April 1, 1878], 161.) The anguish, the anger, the longing, and the hope are none the less poignant for the highly dramatic form of their presentation. The beginning tone of near-defeat and despair rising to anger, then turning to supplication, and finally becoming radiant faith is triumphant. This poem drew a prompt response from "Query"—possibly the same "Queery"—in the next possible issue advising Lucinda to "breathe no thought of doubt in thy babe's ears / . . . Too soon hard lessons she will have to learn." ("To Lu Dalton," Answer to 'Questionings' in *Exponent* of April 1st, *Woman's Exponent*, 6 [1 May 1878] 177.)

Since she also hinted broadly that an unhappy marriage could be cured if the wife would change her selfish attitudes, Lucinda quite properly saw in it a personal attack against her own marriage and responded, not by defending herself from charges of selfishness, but by defending her husband from charges of oppressiveness:

> *Not his the tongue a scornful word to fling,*
> *To wound a sister soul and rankle there;*
> *Not his the heart to whisper I am king*
> *And she my subject now and evermore;*
> *Not he says haughtily This child is mine,*
> *But tenderly and proudly It is ours;*
> *And deems the marriage vow a pledge divine*
> *Of mutual bonds, and equal joys and powers.*
> ("To Query, and All My Dear Sisters in Zion,"
> *Woman's Exponent*, 6 [May 15, 1878] 185.)

The next four years see scanty contributions, although Lucinda's carefully reasoned defenses of polygamy and Mormon principles in 1882 are important. Then Charles died on July 18, 1883, in Beaver, and Lucinda mourns him and supplicates his departed spirit for some sign of continued love a year later:

> *A year and a day—a year and a day!*
> *I linger and hearken; one whisper I pray:*
> *No matter how lightly your footstep may fall*
> *I'll hear it; I'll answer your faintest call;*
> *My famishing soul in your presence could gain*
> *The courage to labor and struggle again.*
> *My heart is aweary. No longer delay!*
> *I've waited and listened a year and a day."*
> ("Invocation," *Woman's Exponent*,
> 13 [August 15, 1884] 41.)

After scattered poems and essays during the next four years, she
wrote another expression of grieving widowhood:

> My eager hands, that fain would clasp
> His own in fond and fervent grasp,
> With patient labor strive to still
> The trembling pains that through them thrill.
>
> My paling lips that fain would press
> Upon his brow a pure caress,
> May only breathe his name so low
> That none but God can hear or know.
>
> ("Sundered," *Woman's Exponent*,
> 17 [September 15, 1888] 57.)

These public expressions of love for her husband—certainly with
the ring of sincerity—are a continuing counterpoint to the private
tragedy she was experiencing. That first lament, "Invocation," was
written only a month before she began the steps that would lead
to the cancellation of her marriage sealing, and "Sundered" was
penned eighteen months after she was eternally sundered from a
man for whom she obviously felt unquenched love.

What, then, explains her action? Certainly we do not have full
access to all the facts, but we need to remember her unwavering
testimony—for ironically, it was her understanding of the gospel,
accurate or not, that led her into eternal separation from Charles.

On August 24, 1884, she wrote to David Henry Cannon, president of the St. George Temple and the St. George Stake. His
uncle, John Taylor, was then president of the church:

*It is with reluctance almost amounting to shame that I come to you this time for
counsel, because it is on the subject of marriage, and my husband has been gone
scarcely thirteen months. I was always true to him in thought, word and deed during
his lifetime, and I laid his body in the grave dreaming naught else than that I should
be his only in time and in eternity, though I knew he had many imperfections. But
now the brethren say he was unworthy, (though I know not who appointed them to
judge him,) they urge that I stand in a very insecure position, and that for my children's sake, as well as my own, I ought to marry again.*

One of these judges was a suitor. She does not say whether his
attentions annoy her; with her fine sense of justice she describes
him only as being "beyond doubt, a faithful Latter Day Saint,
above reproach in his daily walk and conversation" and already
married with a wife and children.

The insecurity Lucinda feels is not economic or social, but spiritual. She confesses: "I have indulged in thoughts of being more to
my deceased husband than wives usually are; of assisting him with
my faithfulness and my favor in the sight of God, to recover any

ground he may have lost, to expiate any offenses. Is this vain
dreaming or could it be done?"

Possibly her suitor and the other "judges" had seized on this
dream of "atoning" for another's sins, a mission reserved for the
Savior, and stressed the implied pride as a sign of her spiritual
"insecurity." It seems uncharacteristic of Lucinda to have discussed
this dream openly, however, since it would have entailed discussing the faults for which she was "atoning" and she was obviously reluctant to refer even to Charles' lapses from strict sobri-
ety, evidently a matter of common knowledge in Beaver.

In any case, the argument that has the most weight with Lucinda is not that her dream of redeeming Charles is vain but that
by remaining married to him she will forfeit her claim to her children:

*Here is the thought that appalls me. My feelings as a mother are far keener and
deeper than my feelings as a wife. I am the mother of six children; four still living,
and two gone before; and I would not forfeit my claim to them as their mother, for
the sake of the best man in God's kingdom. And whatever these four may do, I know
those two to be spotless in the sight of God, and that they will act under his own
perfect counsel; therefore, if I could but know what course they will take, it would
decide my own. If they would choose to wait for their father to retrive [sic] mistakes
and come up to their standpoint, then by all means, so would I; but if they thought
best to press on toward perfection, waiting for none, I should be anxious to do the
same, though it looks to me like a selfish decision. But since I cannot know this
now, I feel too weak and ignorant to decide so great a matter for myself and so many
others, alone.*

Her request to President Cannon, with whom she has taken counsel before, is rooted firmly in her faith:

*God come to you, knowing you to be a sincere friend to my deceased husband, as well
as to myself; and because there is not in Beaver any one to whom I can go with the
same confidence that I would get disinterested, impartial, unprejudiced advice. As I
said before, I feel almost ashamed of even asking counsel on this matter so soon; but I
am pressed for a decision, and I dare not rely on my own unaided judgment. Dear
Brother Cannon, pray for me fervently; pray in the Temple, where your prayers will
surely be heard, and if need be, take counsel for me; and then write to me and advise
me what course to take.*

Her faith in the prayers of this righteous man and her faith that
the temple is a house of revelation is clearly exercised in her willingness to abide by his decision. She adds revealingly in the last
paragraph:

*God knows I would not wrong the dead; I only wish to know what is right. I do not
even desire to be married, for I naturally prefer a single life; but I do fervently desire
to serve the Lord with all my might, mind and strength, and am willing to do all*

that can be required of me in righteousness; and I know that God will not require more than this, and to him I commend myself and all that are dear to me. Amen.[5]

President Cannon wrote back, giving her what she calls "hard" counsel. Even though we do not have his letter, he obviously advised her to write to the president of the church and lay the case before him. Lucinda protests:

It almost seems more than my soul's salvation is worth, to make a written accusation or complaint against Brother Charles, and then be so coldhearted and relentless as to ask somebody to sign it. I am by no means sure that I can get my own consent to do that, although, as you say, I ought to know him better than anyone else. I have grown so accustomed to befriending, consoling, and sustaining him, that it would be hard to recognize myself if doing the opposite. Pray God pity him as I do.[6]

However, his counsel apparently prevailed, at least in part, for she wrote to President Taylor, heard nothing, and sent an anxious letter on November 24, inquiring after the previous letters.[7] Her usually exquisite penmanship is rough, she misspells two words, and has gone back to put in others. If ever a letter breathed agitation, this one mutely does. Her worry must have increased as again she received acknowledgment of receipt but no reply from President Taylor. He was suffering the antipolygamy persecution that would drive him as a polygamist to the Underground within a few months and she did not hear from him until March 17, 1887, two and a half years later. They must have been anguished years, but we know little of how she spent them. She continued teaching school.[8] Although she is a widow and the sole support of her children, she is listed in Relief Society records as having contributed two bushels of wheat for storage in 1885, that first year of her patient wait.[9] The Beaver Sunday School minute books for 1886-94 list Lucinda as both a student with one hundred percent attendance in a class where no teacher is mentioned, and as a teacher for at least two classes; she also appears on the list of choir members.[10]

But we have no indication of what Lucinda was thinking during the nearly three years before President Taylor was able to respond to her request. There may have been other correspondence between them, for when President Taylor wrote on March 17, 1887, he did not address it to Lucinda's home in Beaver but to Inverury (outside Richfield) where she was visiting. He apologized for not having answered her sooner and then said:

After considering your case and giving it such examination as has been possible under the circumstances, I have decided that if you desire the dissolution of your marriage for eternity with your deceased husband, Charles Wakeman Dalton, it should be granted to you. From all that I can learn concerning his life, in addition to what you yourself have written to me, I consider your future unsafe in his hands.

If you should decide to have the marriage for eternity dissolved, you will please give me the date when and the place where you were married to him, and I will have the entry made upon the record to the effect that the marriage is dissolved. When this is done you will be at liberty to contract a new alliance for time and eternity, and of course will take your children with you.[11]

It is worth noting that President Taylor does not tell her what to do. With a delicacy that honors her free agency he gives her the choice, his opinion, and the projected results, thereby assuring her that he has made a separate inquiry as well as considering her own report. The last sentence is ambiguous to a modern reader; was he promising her that she could have her children regardless of her marital status, or was he promising her children if she remarried? Lucinda clearly interpreted his instructions as a guarantee of her children. She sent him the information he requested, then pled poignantly for even more explicit reassurance. She wrote on April 2:

I realize solemnly the magnitude of the step you advise me to take, and my whole soul goes out in prayer to my Heavenly Father that His hand may lead me and his spirit guide me into all righteousness, and preserve me from all evil.

I read in the Book of Covenants that whomsoever you bless God will bless, and whosesoever sins you remit on earth they shall be remitted in the Heavens; therefore I beseech you, in the exercise of your rightful authority, to pronounce me pure and blameless in this thing, and bestow upon me by the holy spirit of promise the blessings of the Elect; that I may press forward in the battle of Life strengthened by the assurance that I am justified in the sight of God.[12]

President Taylor, responding to this whole-souled pleading, replied immediately, informing her that her sealing had been annulled. He reassures, "This will make you free to contract such an alliance as may be agreeable to you, for time and for eternity; and on taking this step you may rest assured, from all that I can learn of your former husband's conduct, you are free from all blame and condemnation, and stand acquitted before the Lord. It is not right that you should remain connected and bound up with that man for eternity, and for this you have been released, and are fully justified in the step you have taken."[13]

With this bleak comfort, Lucinda's marriage of almost nineteen years to "that man" came to an end. What do we know of him, the silent partner in this drama? The clues are pitifully sparse. We know that his father, Simon Cooker Dalton, gave him a heritage of sacrifice and courage. According to family history, Simon's wife left him when he joined the church, but undaunted, Simon took his two oldest sons, one of whom was Charles, and went to

Nauvoo where he remarried.[14] He crossed the plains in 1849. Charles, then twenty-three, either accompanied his father or followed him closely, even though he is not listed in the company, since his own oldest son was born "on the banks of the Sweetwater" in Wyoming on August 26, 1849, to Juliaetta E. Bowen, his first wife.

Charles is listed as a resident of Centerville on the roll of those called on May 19, 1855, to help found Fort Limhi and colonize the Salmon River Mission. John Murdock, the bishop and later stake president in Beaver, joined the company on May 15, 1856.[15] Possibly the friendship between the two men was a motivating factor in Charles' eventual settlement in Beaver. Juanita Brooks lists Charles among those called to colonize the Iron Mission December 2, 1850, "all of whom," she comments tantalizingly, "would be involved with [John D. Lee] in the blackest deed of Utah history"— the Mountain Meadows massacre.[16]

Charles was, by Lucinda's testimony, a loving husband and father to the end of his life, and was also a good provider. However, only Juliaetta, his first wife, was willing to retain her title for eternity. His third wife, Sarah Jane Lee, daughter of John D. Lee, and Lucinda's sister Emma divorced him while he was still alive. Lucinda and Elizabeth Allred, his second wife, cancelled their sealings after his death, Elizabeth apparently to be sealed to her second husband, Calvin White Moore, whom she had married on July 26, 1887, four years after Charles' death and, coincidentally, only four months after Lucinda's own sealing was cancelled. (This cancellation was later revoked by President Heber J. Grant on February 26, 1931, fifteen years after her own death which would, in effect, leave her sealed to Charles again.)[17]

We cannot, of course, attribute what amounts to the failure of four marriages exclusively to Charles Dalton. We have reason from ward records to believe that his behavior may have once prompted ecclesiastical inquiry, and that people felt he did not deserve his wife and children. We do not know why he did not rebuild what had apparently been a good character. But perhaps, in all justice, we must share that burden of blame with Lucinda. She may have refused to let him repent. She was not a weak woman, and she must have been dismayed to the very depths of her soul that the man she had married with such a clear promise from the Lord had proven himself less than worthy. Possessed of few illusions about marriage in the first place—willing to marry "only because of its expected joys in eternity," as she says—she may have seen in both her husband and her father lights that failed, towers that crumbled, whited sepulchres full of the bones of her dead dreams. Responding out of that disillusion, she may have given up on Charles completely and pressed him so closely with her mistrust that he could never build his own self-respect again. She was strong enough to do whatever her faith required; as she interpreted the gospel, her faith required her to press Charles toward right- eousness in his lifetime and to separate herself from him after his death. Obviously she loved him during his life and grieved for him after his death. Her decision after his death was obviously agonizing for her. But once she had what she thought was a clear answer, she was inexorable. But did she review her de- cision during those thirty-eight years? Did her love for her children and the church sustain her through the times of loneliness and dis- couragement that must have come?

Even though our information about how she spent those years is scanty, we have one important piece of nonevidence: she died Lu- cinda *Dalton*, Charles' wife in name if not in fact. We do not know what happened to that wooing suitor in Beaver. Perhaps his ardor had cooled in the long interval between his first interest and her permission to remarry three years later. Perhaps the ordeal had been so trying that she could not face the prospect of another mar- riage. And perhaps the simple political facts of the persecution against polygamy dictated her continued single state.

She moved, probably in 1888, to Manti, and probably at the same time her mother also transferred her residence to that city so she could "work in the temple."[18] We know that Lucinda contin- ued to teach school and, at some point, taught for a few years in Ogden as well, then returned to Manti "where she spent her last days in working in the Temple and attending to Church duties."[19] She continued to write occasionally, and her poems and essays ap- pear in the *Exponent* and the *Young Women's Journal*.

She opened 1893 with the blazing manifesto in "Woman," the poem that begins this sketch of her life. In it we feel her pride in womanhood, her sense of outraged justice, and her unwavering faith that the Restoration includes the restoration of woman's eter- nal honor as well, ending with its exultant prophecy: "And the last shall be first, forever." That year was a banner year for Lu- cinda's feminism. "Woman, Arise!", a rousing, militant song, was published March 1, and later became part of a suffrage songbook. The next she authored a "Woman Suffrage Column" on the front page, demanding rhetorically: "Shall our sons be untainted with servitude and degradation if their mothers be not free, any better than they could be all white if we gave them African mothers?" ("Shall Utah Become a State without Woman Suffrage?" *Woman's Exponent,* 22 [1 April 1894] 113.)

Her contributions to the *Exponent* were not her only contributions to the suffrage movement. There are still minutes extant from a suffrage association in Beaver a few years after she left the town that she would certainly have participated in earlier.[20] Her sister Rose was appointed Utah vice-president of the Utah State Chapter of Women Voters, and Lucinda is listed among five women praised in Manti for making "education and promotion of equal suffrage part of their daily lives."[21]

She was a teacher in Manti North Ward's Sunday School for several years, and gradually, her family dwindled as death took one after another. Her mother died in March 1905, and the obituary contains a curious error: "Mr. Lee died in 1871."[23] In point of fact, John Percival Lee was still alive and would not die until April of 1907, almost exactly two years later. Given the vagaries of reporters and the ease with which numbers may be mistaken by a typositor, it would be foolish to put too much emphasis on this discrepancy, but we recall that 1871 was, in fact, the year when John P. Lee and Eliza Foscue Lee separated, bitterly and permanently. Perhaps for her that *was* his death date.

Only a brief notice marks the passing of Lucinda's father two years later in Thatcher, Arizona. "Father Lee," it says, "was a man of sterling good character. His funeral was conducted here . . . where many friends of the deceased turned out to show their respect to him."[24] The summer of 1912 five years later was one that wrung Lucinda's steadfast heart again. Her son Guy, by then the father of a four-year-old daughter, had suffered from tuberculosis for some time. That summer he decided to try the air in a canyon near Manti, but his health was more fragile than he had supposed. He died—even before they reached "the point of their intended destination." The obituary reports: "Mrs. Dalton relates that there was nothing she could do but to place the dead body of her husband in the buggy and drive down the canyon to their home. The spectacle was a pathetic one when friends first saw the grief-stricken woman managing the team and seeking to comfort the 4-year-old daughter, while the husband and father lay dead in the bottom of the buggy."[25]

Thus, only two children survived Lucinda, her oldest daughter, Belle, and her youngest son, Clifford. She died herself on November 24, 1925, seventy-eight years old. Her obituary records that her services were held on a Sunday in the North Ward chapel; her former bishop read some of her poems and commended "the good life and character of the deceased." The minutes list the names of two other speakers and add that the songs sung were "I Know that My Redeemer Lives" and "There Is A Green Hill Far Away."[26] We have no way of knowing if the songs were her own choice; it would be appropriate if they were, for every line breathes her own unflinching faith in the Savior. We also do not know what poems he selected, but "House of Life" would have been an exquisite choice. In this poem, written a quarter century before, the narrator describes herself as the mistress of a beautiful home, exquisitely built, carefully furnished, and lovingly given to her by "my Lord." Yet the sight of more splendid palaces dispelled her joy. Dissatisfied, she neglected her mansion. Dust collected on the windows, the lovely rooms went unaired and ungarlanded, cobwebs festooned corners, and "its beauty began to decay."

> A footstep draws near! my Lord—He is here!
>   He gazes in pain and amaze—
> "This wreck is the Temple for you I did rear,"
>   For shame I could not raise my eyes.
> "O, foolish one, what didst thou lack, but the will?
>   If these were too narrow for thee,
> More stately apartments to plan and to build?
>   Who loves not my gift, loves not me."
>
> He passed, and I dared not beseech Him to stay—
>   My opened eyes saw clearly now,
> How foolish and blind was my envy; straightway
>   I made with repentance a vow—
> To honor my gift, to fill it with light,
>   Embellish and keep it with care,
> That henceforth it be in my Lord's kingly sight
>   A dwelling place lovely and fair.
>
> When next His dear footsteps draw near to my door,
>   With gladness I'll usher Him in;
> No mildew or rust shall He see as before;—
>   To restore it at once I'll begin.
> I'll live my dear home for the Giver's sake,
>   Nor sigh if more stately ones be,
> For God, the dear Giver, can make no mistake;
>   He knows what is best for me.
>   ("House of Life," Woman's Exponent, 29
>   [October 15/November 1, 1900] 41.)

That last stanza represents reconciliation, not relaxation; peace, not mere patience. There is a wholeness and holiness about its acceptance that fairly radiates. Possibly it was in this mood—envy laid and dissatisfaction dissolved by joy—that she spent the next quarter century before her death.

She had cause for bitterness during those last years in Manti. She had thought marriage something to be endured during life for the sake of its blessings afterwards, and now she would not have those blessings. In this time of double bereavement, she must have clung to her children as the one great good that her marriage had produced—but death took half of those that remained after Charles' death. However, the quality of her previous life and the resolution of her character let us predict with safety that those years at the close were indeed years of peace and faith. If she had, at any point, been given the choice between suffering with eventual salvation, and shallow contentment with dulled sensibilities and a less-than-total achievement, she would have held out both hands to pain at once. She was that kind of woman.

Notes

1. Lucinda Lee Dalton, Autobiography of Mrs. L. L. Dalton, pp. 2, 5; microfilm of holograph, Historical Department of The Church of Jesus Christ of Latter-day Saints, hereafter cited as Church Archives; original in The Bancroft Library, University of California, Berkeley, quoted by permission of the director. Hereafter cited parenthetically in the text as Autobiography.

2. Historical Record, Beaver Second Ward, Beaver Stake, 1869-1877, p. 15, April 2, 1871.

3. Beaver Literary Institute Minutes, in YMMIA Minutes, Beaver Stake, 1880-1894; see entries October 11, 1875 - January 17, 1876, Church Archives.

4. Orson F. Whitney, "Jabez Gridley Sutherland," *History of Utah,* Salt Lake City; George Q. Cannon and Sons, 1904, IV: 529-32. We have one other mention of Emma. Ida Frances Hunt Udall, visiting in Beaver after an absence of eight years, has an entry dated August 30, 1888: We "visited and took supper with our dear old friend Sister [Eliza Foscue] Lee. How natural it seemed to be there. How many times dear Emma & I, in the happy days of yore had paced up and down those cool shaded pathways, or worked, read, talked and sang together in that pleasant sitting room. Since then Emma has realized [her] fondest hopes, and becoming a first class reporter has gone out in to the world to make her own way. She is getting splendid wages in a R.R. [railroad] office, but has backed out entirely from the church. Her mother shed tears in speaking of her, & wished that she were only in my position. An exile and wanderer, but with the love of the gospel in her heart." (Ida Frances Hunt Udall, Journal, August 30, 1888, pp. 135–36; Church Archives; used by permission of Maria S. Ellsworth.)

5. Lucinda Lee Dalton to D. H. Cannon, August 24, 1884, in the John Taylor correspondence, Church Archives.

6. Lucinda Lee Dalton to D. H. Cannon, September 8, 1884, in the John Taylor correspondence, Church Archives.

7. Lucinda Lee Dalton to John Taylor, November 24, 1884, in the John Taylor correspondence, Church Archives.

8. During Ida Hunt Udall's 1885 visit to Beaver, she records:
    "My dear friend Lou Dalton called to see us. She is the same
    good noble woman she always was. Is teaching school in the
    Beaver Central, to support her family of four children, being
    a widow now." Ida adds a scathing judgment on the local
    equivalent of the board of education: "Her salary is exceed-
    ingly low considering her ability as a teacher, but they have
    the same class of trustees in Beaver as of yore. They consider
    the *sex* and not the qualifications of the teacher." When Ida
    leaves town a few weeks later, she interrupts classes at Beaver
    Central long enough "to bid dear friend Lou Dalton
    goodbye. (Ida Frances Hunt Udall, Journal, pp. 133-36, 138,
    Church Archives. Quoted by permission of Maria S. El-
    lsworth.) An earlier entry, page six, records that Ida was at-
    tending Lucinda's school before her marriage to Charles; an
    autograph album, also in the Church Archives, mentions that
    Ida's seventeenth birthday (1875) was spent at "Mrs. Dalton's
    school during the day" and at the theatre that evening.

9. Relief Society Minutes, Beaver First and Second Ward, Bea-
    ver Stake, 1879-1886, p. 558, Church Archives.

10. Sunday School Minutes, Beaver First and Second Ward, Bea-
    ver Stake, 1886-1894, pp. 14-15, 32, 100, Church Archives.

11. John Taylor to Lucinda Lee Dalton, March 17, 1887, John
    Taylor letterbook, no. 14, p. 346, Church Archives.

12. Lucinda Lee Dalton to John Taylor, April 2, 1887, in the
    John Taylor correspondence, Church Archives.

13. John Taylor to Lucinda Lee Dalton, April 12, 1887, John
    Taylor letterbook, no. 14, p. 468.

14. Mark A. Dalton, *The John Dalton Book of Genealogy*, Long
    Beach, Cal.: The Dalton Family Organization, 1964, pp. 30,
    182.

15. W. W. Henderson, ed., "The Salmon River Mission: Extract
    from the Journal of L. W. Shurtleff," *Utah Historical Quarterly*
    5 (January 1932):4.

16. Juanita Brooks, *John Doyle Lee, Zealot, Pioneer Builder, Scapegoat*,
    Glendale, Cal.: The Arthur H. Clark Co., 1962, p. 185.

17. Family group sheets of Charles Wakeman Dalton, submitted
    by Catherine Ann Muir, Genealogy Library of The Church
    of Jesus Christ of Latter-day Saints.

18. "Early Utah Pioneer Dies at Home of Daughter," *Deseret Evening News,* March 10, 1920, section 2, page 2 (misnumbered page 2), col. 3.

19. Kate B. Carter, comp., *Heart Throbs of the West,* II, Salt Lake City: Daughters of the Utah Pioneers, 1946, 155.

20. Beaver Women's Suffrage Association Minutes, 1892-1895, Women's History Archives, Harold B. Lee Library, Brigham Young University, Provo.

21. Daughters of the Utah Pioneers, "Woman Suffrage in the West," Historical pamphlet, October 1943, pp. 300, 313.

22. Sunday School Minutes, Manti North Ward, Sanpete South Stake, 1901-1903, 1903-1905.

23. "Early Utah Pioneer Dies at Home of Daughter," *op. cit.*

24. "Death of John P. Lee," *Deseret Evening News,* May 11, 1907, p. 14, col. 4.

25. "Wife Returns with Husband's Dead Body," *Deseret Evening News,* July 10, 1912, p. 12, col. 7.

26. "Pioneer School Teacher is Buried at Manti," *Deseret News,* December 1, 1925, p. 4, col. 5; Historical Record, Manti North Ward, Sanpete South Stake, 1921-1925, November 28, 1925, p. 175.

Jane Snyder Richards 1832–1912

Connie Duncan Cannon is originally of Salt Lake City, Utah, where she received her bachelor of science degree in history from the University of Utah, graduating cum laude. Currently she lives in Denver, Colorado, as a homemaker with James E. Cannon. The couple have three small children. She is also involved in many organizations related to the Mormon Church, having been a staff member of the Exponent II, *a newspaper for Mormon women, and captain of the Boston Camp of the Daughters of the Utah Pioneers.*

Jane S. Richards

Connie Duncan Cannon

On a cold January day in 1840 a crowd of three hundred persons gathered near Lake LaPorte in LaPorte, Indiana, as a young Mormon elder chopped a hole in the foot-deep ice. Word had spread quickly that Robert Snyder intended to baptize his sixteen-year-old sister, Jane, who had been so ill during the past three weeks as to be on the verge of death. So mortified were the townsfolk that they had threatened to have Robert arrested. They stood confounded as Jane was carried down to the lake and immersed in the icy waters. To their amazement young Jane came out of the water and immediately stated in a firm voice, "I want to say to all you people who have come out to see me baptized, that I do it of my own free will and choice, and if you interfere with the man who has baptized me, God will interfere with you."[1] Elder Snyder was not arrested, and Jane, who did not suffer from the exposure, was miraculously healed.

The pluck demonstrated on the occasion of her baptism was very characteristic of Jane Snyder. Until the illness she had been immovable in her practical belief that baptism was not necessary for her. "What sins have I committed?" she asked. "Have I not always obeyed my parents?"[2] Thus, Jane had held back after most of her family was baptized.

Isaac and Lovisa Comstock Snyder were living in Pamelia, Jefferson County, New York, when Jane was born on January 31, 1823. She was number ten in a family of eleven children. It was in East Camden, Ontario, Canada, that the Snyder family first became acquainted with The Church of Jesus Christ of Latter-day Saints. Jane's brother, Robert, then twenty-three, was a consumptive and so ill that even the most skillful physicians had given him up for lost. They had tried everything then known and nothing seemed to help him.

Robert used to spend his time in his room in meditation, preparing for his death. His father was not a religious man, though one of great moral character. His mother was a Methodist but not especially susceptible to religious impressions. One day while studying the New Testament, Robert was struck with the idea of baptism by immersion, which the Methodists did not practice. He became convinced that this was the only proper method of baptism and began praying to the Lord on the question of who could properly perform this ordinance. One night during his prayers he heard the name "John E. Page" distinctly spoken. The next morning he began a quest to find this man. He asked the name of the local priest and checked into other religions in the area, but to no avail.

About three weeks later a messenger knocked at the door of the Snyder home to tell them that on the preceding day their daughter, Mrs. Sarah Snyder Jenne, who lived three miles away, had been baptized into the Mormon Church by two Mormon elders. The family felt great embarrassment and only reluctantly told Robert of the event while the messenger waited. His reaction was different from that of the rest of the family; his main concern was to ascertain the names of the elders. The messenger thought one of them was named Page, but he couldn't remember the first name. Robert related to his father the conviction he had received of the importance of baptism by immersion and of the voice he had heard which told him "John E. Page" was the man who should baptize him.

The elders were summoned by the family, and upon their arrival, Robert established that Elder Page was in fact the man he sought. He desired to be baptized right away. However, because of the severity of the weather, the family prevailed upon Robert to wait until spring. In the meantime, the elders administered to Robert with oil, and his health improved. In late April his baptism finally took place. The Snyders humored Robert in allowing the service to be held in their home, not because they had come to believe in the elder's message. Jane recorded the family's feelings: "Although we did not feel like coming forward and embracing this religion, we never thought lightly of it, or dared to say as to anything against it for we felt it was all the dealings of the Almighty God and that we must leave my brother in His hands. And seeing him still alive and enjoying partial health was very gratifying."[3]

Robert Snyder then went forth as a great missionary of the church, baptizing hundreds in the United States and Canada, including eventually every member of his family. All but Jane and two of her brothers had been baptized by 1839 when the family, in obedience to the counsels of the church leaders, sold their property at a sacrifice and began moving toward the great gathering of the Saints in Missouri. The trek was interrupted in LaPorte, Indiana, on account of the illness of Jane's little niece, Sarah Jane.

It was here that Jane (always frail, never weighing over one hundred pounds) became extremely ill, and no physician was able to offer relief. For three weeks she was confined to her bed and grew gradually weaker. Her brother was preaching in the nearby town of Belmont, and returned for a visit to find her in critical condition. Jane later related that:

When he returned and found me so ill, he felt very anxious and fasted and prayed for me. I knew that he had fasted absolutely without food or water for three or four days, and I was distressed that he should do so. He came into my room, and laying his face beside mine on the pillow, he said, "Oh sis, I wish you were baptized."

The next morning when I awoke from a troubled night's rest, I saw my brother in my room, and scarcely able to articulate, I told him to call mother. She came at once, but I was paralyzed and apparently dying. I could not speak nor move though I could understand everything and nod my head. My brother wept beside me and again said he wished I were baptized. Then he asked if he could administer oil and pray for me. I nodded my head and he prayed to the Lord that he might suffer affliction for me if need be and told him how dutiful and good I was, and [prayed] that my life... be spared [for] the family. While he was praying light came into my mind and I could see plain as if a book were open with it written in it... my need of baptism. If Christ, who was sinless needed to be baptized, should I hold myself as better than he?

At that moment all pain left me. The paralysis was gone, I was only weak. As my brother arose from his knees, I showed him my restored arm and hand and begged for baptism. He remonstrated for it was now mid-winter and ice would have to be broken and the exposure might be fatal. But death I was not afraid of... only I must be baptized![4]

Jane's strong will prevailed, and she was baptized.

Six months after Jane's baptism Elder Jehiel Savage, an old friend of the family, arrived to live with them while he was on his mission. Years before, when he had known the family in Canada, Elder Savage had jestingly told Jane he would someday bring her a husband. Sure enough, his missionary companion at this time, Franklin D. Richards, turned out to be the man. Though Jane with her vivacious personality had always had plenty of suitors, Elder Richards was the first to whom she felt reciprocally attracted.

The family set out for Nauvoo in the spring of 1841, taking Elder Richards along with them, because the Prophet Joseph Smith had recalled him due to his ill health. They settled for awhile at Job Creek in LaHarpe, Illinois, where Jane and Elder Richards were engaged about one year after their first meeting. It was another year, however, before they were married. Upon his return from another mission to Cincinnati with Phineas Young, Elder Richards and Jane Snyder were married on December 18, 1842, just three months after the death of her brother, Robert. Two days after the wedding, they moved into the home of Brother Philo T. Farnsworth.

On November 2, 1843, a baby daughter, Wealthy Lovisa, was born to the young couple. They visited Jane's father for the last time when the baby was six weeks old; the father passed away immediately following the visit. Shortly thereafter, Franklin's parents arrived in Nauvoo, ending a five-year separation from him. A two-story brick home was constructed, and both families moved in. In the spring of 1844, Franklin departed for a mission in England, which was shortened unexpectedly upon the martyrdom of the Prophet Joseph Smith. All missionaries were recalled to Nauvoo immediately, although it took Franklin until October 2 to get back to Illinois. During his absence Jane received no letters from Franklin, since the mail service to the Mormons was terminated during a period of intense persecution by the people of Illinois and Missouri.

While awaiting his return, Jane took her little baby, Wealthy, and attended the special conference held on August 8, 1844, where Brother Brigham Young stood transfigured before the congregation. Jane bent over just as Brigham Young was about to speak to pick up a toy Wealthy had dropped. Suddenly she recognized the voice of the Prophet Joseph Smith and was so startled that she dropped the toy back to the floor and looked up to behold the form and features of the martyred Prophet.

Jane wrote a little concerning the Prophet Joseph in her own hand. "The first time I ever saw Joseph Smith, I recognized him from a dream I had had. He had such an angelic countenance as I had never seen before. He was 37 years of age . . . ordinary in appearance . . . in dress and manner . . . a childlike appearance of innocence. His hair was light brown, blue eyes, and light complexion. His natural demeanor was quiet, his character and disposition was formed by his life work. He was kind and considerate, taking a personal interest in all his people, considering everyone his equal."[5]

By January, just three months after he returned from England, Franklin was asked to go on another mission to Michigan to gather donations for the building of the Nauvoo Temple. Jane was again lonely until his return in April. Time, effort, and thoughts were now centered on completion of the temple, which finally occurred in late 1845.

On January 23, 1846, Jane and Franklin were sealed for time and all eternity in the Nauvoo Temple by Apostle Heber C. Kimball. Eight days later they entered into plural marriage—a doctrine which they both accepted as divine; Franklin married Miss Elizabeth McFate.

The California historian, Hubert Howe Bancroft, after an interview with Jane in her later years, wrote the following in regards to her feelings about polygamy:

A few months previous to her marriage the idea of more than one wife was generally spoken of, though the practice of polygamy was of later growth. It was repugnant to her idea of virtue, and it was not until she saw Joseph Smith in a vision who told her in time all will be explained, that she was satisfied to abide by Mormon teachings, whatever they were. About eight months after her marriage, Elder Richards told her he felt he should like to have another wife. It was crushing at first, but she said that as he was an Elder, and if it was necessary to her salvation, she would let another share her pleasure.[6]

According to Bancroft's notes, Jane and Franklin discussed the matter somewhat. Jane made the point that if they could not live in this manner without quarreling, she would leave him. Franklin stated that if she had serious doubts as to her ability to be happy in a polygamous situation, he would not enter into it.

It was several years later when Franklin suggested a person as his second wife; Jane was very surprised at his choice. She knew Elizabeth McFate well, and had found her to be very amiable. When Elizabeth entered the family, Jane was recovering from a miscarriage and was quite ill. Elizabeth, though only seventeen, understood the needs of the household and set about to be of great service to Jane. Upon moving into the house Elizabeth said, "I don't know how we are going to get along, but I will try and not make you miserable." Jane said, "Don't call me Mrs. Richards; call me Jane. I won't quarrel whatever happens."[7] She lived upstairs and Jane lived downstairs, but they coordinated the household chores very well.

Elizabeth continued to be very considerate, as this little incident shows: One night Jane was suffering from severe pain in her face, and Elizabeth asked her if she could take "our Wealthy" (Jane's little daughter) upstairs for the night so she wouldn't disturb her mother. During the night Jane awoke her husband, who remained in the next room for fear of awakening her, and asked him to go upstairs to see if Wealthy was warmly covered. The next morning Elizabeth confided, "I took Wealthy last night for I didn't want you to feel I should want Franklin to stay with me when you were suffering so much."[8]

Jane told Mr. Bancroft that there was never a quarrelsome word or any irritability manifested in the family while she and Elizabeth were together. They apparently felt no jealous or evil feelings toward one another.

It was June 10, 1846, when the Richards sold their lovely two-story brick home for two yoke of half-broken cattle and an old wagon. Taking with them two cows, one trunk of clothing, bread stuffs, and one pound of tea given to Jane by a neighbor, they crossed the Mississippi River to join the rest of the saints, after having been driven from Illinois by threatening mobs. Shortly thereafter, on July 3, Franklin left his two wives and daughter to travel west with his family while he turned east to once again attempt his mission to England. Before leaving, Franklin called them together for family prayer. Jane was about to bear another child and was extremely feeble; she felt she would probably not be living when Franklin returned. It was a sad parting indeed.

On July 23, 1846, Jane gave birth to a baby boy, Isaac Phineas, who died almost immediately. A midwife had been summoned from five miles back to help Jane with the delivery; upon completion of her duties she inquired in a brusque manner, "Are you prepared to pay me?" "If it were to save my life," answered Jane in agony, "I could not give you any money, for I have none; but if you see anything you want, take it." The woman seized a beautiful woolen bedspread worth fifteen dollars. "I may as well take it, for you'll never live to see it,"[9] was her cold remark, as she left Jane desperately ill with her dead babe at her side. Because Jane could not bear the thought of burying the tiny body on the plains where it could be dug up and devoured by wolves and coyotes, they carried the little child with them until they reached Mt. Pisgah, Iowa, where he could be buried a little more decently.

Jane's only other child, little two-year-old Wealthy, had taken sick the day following her father's departure and was becoming weaker and weaker as the journey progressed toward the Missouri River. En route they passed a large potato field and Wealthy asked for a potato. It was one of the only things she had desired to eat for many weeks; when her Grandmother Snyder went to ask if she could buy one, the owner's answer was, "I wouldn't sell or give one of you damned Mormons a potato to save your lives." She then sent her dog after Mrs. Snyder. When Wealthy was told of the incident she said, "Never mind, mama, she's a wicked woman isn't she? We wouldn't do that by her, would we?"[10] Jane turned in her bed and fought the tears back as Grandmother Snyder tried to comfort little Wealthy in her disappointment.

As Jane's wagon came to a halt at Mt. Pisgah, several of the elders gathered around her wagon and rolled the curtains back. Evidently they felt that neither Jane nor Wealthy had much chance of living. The elders anointed them and prayed earnestly for their recovery. The baby boy was taken and buried. Brigham Young, hearing of Jane's condition, rode back some fifty miles to counsel with her. Upon seeing her circumstances he said that if he had realized them sooner, he would not have asked Franklin to go on his mission.

Two months after the death of her baby, Jane also faced the loss of her sweet little girl, not yet three years old, who passed away at Cutler Park on September 14, 1846. She lay in the wagon, unable to move, with the body of Wealthy beside her, childless and alone in her grief, since Franklin was so far away and uninformed about the loss of his children. "It shall be said of you that you have come up through much tribulation," was the remark made to her by President Brigham Young at this time.[11] Jane stated that this was her crowning affliction, and she only lived because she could not die.

During the journey Jane also had to care for her "sister-wife," Elizabeth, who was desperately ill from consumption, a hereditary disease that Franklin hadn't been aware of at the time he married her. Elizabeth was in the wagon just ahead of Jane, often screaming in her delirium. Just hours after Wealthy's death, Jane was carried up to the next wagon to comfort Elizabeth.

The two wives spent the winter of 1846-47 at Winter Quarters, where Jane gained enough strength to enable her to care for Elizabeth. She found that her provisions were nearly exhausted, because during her illness she had allowed people helping her to take provisions as payment for services rendered. Hence, little was left. In fact, there was only one nonessential item with which to barter for food—Franklin's violin. She finally traded it for a gallon of wine to sustain Elizabeth. Some days there was barely enough flour for one pancake.

In her writings, Jane described that winter as very harsh. Her skirts were almost constantly frozen stiff about her ankles and would rattle as she brushed against things; there was nothing to thaw them. Scurvy broke out in the camp and hundreds died from it. Elizabeth was becoming weaker and had to be lifted from her chair to her bed. Jane felt as if she could not face Elizabeth's death, partly because it left her alone and partly because she feared that others—perhaps even Franklin—might wonder if she had done everything possible to keep Elizabeth alive. These feelings notwithstanding, Jane knew her own conscience was clear on this matter. Elizabeth used to say to Jane, "Jenne, the Elder never would've married me if he had known I should have been so much trouble to you."[12] She finally passed away at Winter Quarters on March 29, 1847. Jane's loneliness was now complete.

In the spring of 1848, Franklin finally returned from England. On July 5 he and Jane joined the party of Willard Richards and proceeded to Salt Lake City. Jane was so ill during the whole of the journey that she was bedfast in a wagon box. She had to be carried in arms across raging streams. Franklin's Uncle Willard had been a physician in Boston prior to his joining the church and was very helpful to Jane en route as well as later. Their arrival on October 19, 1848, would seem a great relief, but Jane said of this:

> We were three and a half months making this journey (and I was sick during the entire journey) arriving . . . in a city of people, but not a house, except an old fort, which the Pioneers had made the year previous. I can't here undertake to describe the great sufferings and privation of food and cold, for want of a comfortable house, that we passed through after three months' sickness on the way. The next June my son, Franklin S., was born, when one week old we were drenched with rain, which caused me to be so ill that my life was despaired of. President Willard Richards came and administered to me, and blessed me and my little son; he said we should live, and from that moment I began to recover.[13]

Much later one of Jane's sons wrote that on the morning this third child was born Jane was so faint and hungry that she turned her face to the wall where no one could see and cried because she had "neither crust of bread nor an ounce of flour or meal with which to appease her hunger."[14] The rain she mentioned fell on her and her baby because the roof over their heads at that time was made of rushes and an earth covering and was not adequate protection against a major storm. The bed she was in was drenched, causing her to come down with a raging fever. Jane further describes her hardships in the valley:

> I also had another setback in which it seemed I must die and leave my little infant son. Brother Daniel Spencer came and said, "Sister Richards, you seem to be dying, we do not want you to leave us, we can't spare you. Shall I pray for you?" I answered, "I should be pleased to have you." He and my husband in tears prayed earnestly that the Lord would spare my life. I began to feel the heeling [sic] influence and power of God resting upon me. He said, "Sister Richards, you shall live, and I say unto you, arise and walk, and leave your sickness in this bed; it shall not come out of the bed with you," which I did, and sat in my rocking chair and walked about the room, and the happy feeling which I enjoyed is impossible for me to describe. From this time I gained my strength right along and had no more sickness.[15]

She must have shown the effects of the illness, however, because when her brother saw her after a long separation he exclaimed, "Lord, Jane, how you look! Your bones look picked!" Her husband also noticed and said, "My gracious, Jane, it would take two of you to make a shadow."[16]

Just prior to the birth of this son, Franklin was called to be a member of the church's Council of the Twelve, which meant he would be away from home even more than he had been up to this point. When baby Franklin was just six months old, his father left on another mission to England. Despite all this, he did find time, on October 13, 1849, to take two other wives, just six days before leaving. One was Jane's sister, Sarah, and the other was Charlotte Fox. Sarah's husband had deserted her, leaving her with five small children. Jane had given Sarah her house, taking a smaller one for herself, and eventually got Franklin to marry her as well, thinking they would be of much more assistance to her under these circumstances.

Jane had only four dresses, one of which was a calico wrapper and one a black silk dress that was so impractical under the circumstances that it could not even be used for barter. She was deeply ashamed of the poverty these dresses represented and didn't want them to be seen even by her own poor neighbors. The apostles and their families received no regular support from the church, as all funds were needed at this time to support the missionaries and to emigrate people to Utah. Nevertheless, the church would have agreed to help such a family as Franklin's while he was on his mission; but Jane was resourceful and desired to be self-supporting. She established a very good boarding house in her home and took in many important travelers, since there were no hotels in Salt Lake City at the time. Because of the refinement and culture with which she provided this service, it was worthwhile. She also saved straw and from it braided forty hats for men and boys, which she sold to immigrants for one dollar apiece. Thus she was able to purchase the essentials for her family and still pay her tithing. Though it appeared she had none to spare, she always managed to stretch what she had to feed the poor around her.

Little Franklin was two years old when the Council of the Twelve proposed that Franklin stay three more years in England because the mission was benefitting so from his experience. Brigham Young suggested to Jane that she leave her son and join Franklin in England to avoid lengthening their separation. She pointed out, however, that she had already buried two children and would like to stay around to raise her only remaining child, who needed her care far more than her husband did. President Young agreed, but obtained her permission to extend Franklin's mission. In the end, he returned after just one more year.

It was during this mission that the first child was born to one of the "other wives." This was the true test for Jane, as evidenced by the following historian's report of an interview with her:

She felt she could yield herself to everything but the children, but that she should feel like wringing the neck of any other child than hers, that should call him papa. That they were poor and could not see their way clear to provide for their own easily, what could they do with more? Before he entered into these other marriages, her mind was satisfied on every other point, but she still carried this one reservation. It was probably fortunate, she felt, that Franklin was away when the first one was born. She said her heart nearly failed her when it turned out to be a girl, as she was still very lonely for her daughter, Wealthy, and yearned to have her own baby girl. However, she dressed the baby and cared for it a lot, as well as for the mother. She said that for these children she has always felt an interest, though it was not at all the same feeling she had for her own flesh and blood.[17]

In August of 1852 Franklin returned to his family. On May 25, 1853, Jane had her wonderful patience and endurance rewarded—she gave birth to a little daughter, Josephine. Franklin took a fifth wife, Susan B. Peirson, on June 26, 1853. Then in March of 1854 he married Jane's niece, Laura Snyder. Of all these wives Jane once wrote, "They were all good women who entered marriage with good intent and tried to live just and honest lives in the sight of the Lord."[18]

June of that year found Franklin leaving again for Europe on another mission. He was still away on this mission on March 20, 1856, when Jane's widowed mother, Lovisa Comstock Snyder, died. Her final words as she was dying were: "You have never caused me any sorrow or trouble, but have been a comfort to me in every way, and I hope your children will be to you what you have been to me."[19] Her hope in this last statement was fulfilled. Jane's children were a great credit to her.

One incident that occurred upon Franklin's return from this mission in England illustrates some of the difficulties that occasionally arose in a plural situation. Mr. Richards brought several shawls and other presents back from his mission to his wives and told them to choose what each would like out of the things he had brought. Jane, being the original wife, was to have first choice. As usual she yielded that privilege, even though she saw immediately which of the things she would like. She said, "No, girls, you care more about these things than I do; take your choice and I will be satisfied with what is left." They were insulted by this implication that perhaps they were selfish while she was noble. All of them were upset and refused to choose. Jane went to her room and cried.

Franklin came to discuss it with her. Failing to perceive the real nature of the problem, he told her that she never cared for any of the presents he brought for her. She, in return, told him that he should get something unique for each wife and decide what gift went to what wife, suggesting that each would appreciate the thoughtfulness of the gift more if everyone else didn't have one exactly like it. Later, they all met again and Jane said, "Now, girls, I've suggested this, which I'm sure you will approve. And now he will distribute these according to his own discretion."[20] It's easy to understand why such vexations would occur occasionally. The wonder is that they seem to have occurred so seldom.

Mrs. John Taylor, who was considerably older than Jane, had advised her in a motherly way concerning how she should live in polygamy. She asked Jane how she was getting along.

"Not very well, I guess," was Jane's reply. "Why, what do people say about it?"

"I never heard a thing," said Mrs. Taylor. "And I think you have too much pride and grit to let anyone know of your domestic trials."[21]

Mrs. Taylor advised her that everything would work out as time went on and that she should have faith. She also advised her to make herself happy whether her husband was there or not—not to think about where he was or who he was with and that she would eventually outgrow all the troubles she felt originally. The only mention of such "troubles" in Jane's writings and in writings about her were the aforementioned feelings she had anticipated concerning offspring of the other wives and the shawl incident. To the reader a hundred years later, it would appear that Jane handled well the challenge of plural living.

She apparently viewed herself as successful enough at this to pass advice along to younger women. A neighbor once confided to Jane that she didn't think she would be able to accept it if her husband took another wife. Jane told her that there were not as many problems with polygamy in reality as there were in anticipation of it. She advised her not to worry about it. Later, the neighbor was back to say that her husband had taken another wife, and she was having trouble coping. Jane told her she felt it was a mistake to confide in other women—that her husband would come to resent it. She said she should not speak to others of her domestic trials or even admit that there were any. In faith, they would all clear up. The neighbor went home and took the advice. Many years later she thanked Jane for her wise counsel, and had apparently been fairly triumphant at living in plural marriage.

It seems that Franklin had worried about being able to support more wives when he was first called upon to take them. He asked Brigham Young how it would be possible. President Young's answer was, "When you had but one wife, the Lord provided even when you could not see the way. Why, then, will He not provide for you more?"[22] Of course Jane had been rather poorly provided for, though she never complained. She had been very sick, yet cared for delicate children, and had earned most of their livelihood by braiding straw hats and keeping boarders. When Franklin asked her how she felt about dividing her little estate with others she answered, "If I am able to divide your time with other wives when you are away nine weeks in ten, I can dispense with the money. That is the last and least of my troubles."[23] Probably for someone with her values, it would be far easier to share material things than to share a relationship that was already severely limited in available time for development. In the first fifteen years of their marriage, Franklin was away on missions ten years. In fact, he was away so much that she actually learned to live quite comfortably without him. Evidently when he was home, Jane would occasionally even forget to call him to dinner, she was so used to his being gone. She had followed Mrs. Taylor's advice well.

Of the counsel of Brigham Young, Franklin Richards took to wife all of the widows of his beloved uncle, Willard Richards. It was a custom in ancient Israel that the nearest kinsman would marry and care for the wives of a deceased relative. Willard Richards had contributed so much to the church and community that everyone wanted to see that his family was well cared for following his death in 1854. Therefore, on March 6, 1857, Franklin D. Richards married Mary Thompson, Nanny Longstroth, Susan Bayliss, and Rhode Harriet Foss. Jane's feelings on the matter were expressed in one of her autobiographical sketches: "I can here say that Uncle Willard acted like a father to me, in the sickness and death of my children, and I felt thankful that we could return any kindness to his family."[24]

A few years later (1862) when a law was passed by the United States Congress prohibiting polygamy, Jane wrote the following:

Now what sin is there against the government in this practice? It is simply religious persecution. The difference between right and wrong in the matter of a man's having wives is this: In bigamy a man sets aside his lawful wife and unbeknown to her marries another woman. And it is all done wickedly and from the basest motives. In polygamy, a man marries again as a sense of religious duty, consults with his wife, and with her consent, and perhaps with her recommendation, takes to himself another wife. His religion demands it and all three enter into polygamy with conviction of it being done in the sight of God . . . at his command. Perhaps all live in one house, at least the relation is openly acknowledged, and before God and man it is lawful and holy. At the time polygamy was revealed to us as a sacred duty, there was no law in the United States against it. The government had to make a law to incriminate us. Now there is an effort making and has been for a long time past to break up the families already formed in that way. What a sin it would be not only to deprive wives of what they consider their lawful husbands, but to also brand their children as illegitimate. Many of these children (are) now grown with families of their own. The government has no right to deprive our women and children of their husbands and fathers. And yet there hangs over our heads the threatened fine and imprisonment of all the men who lived with more than one wife.[25]

Another indication of her feelings concerning polygamy was reflected in this statement:

In glancing over a book written by an apostate, Mrs. Stenhouse, I am induced to say that she never could have received the spirit of the Gospel before entering into polygamy or she never could have talked as she does. Many of our people have had trials, but never enough to make them give up Mormonism. Some statements she made induce me to give these facts: President Young could counsel men to marry, but he never commanded it. He would not allow any marriage or engagement while on missions abroad, for he wished the women to see how matters looked in Utah for themselves, and not feel as though they were drawn into a net. And he wished the wives at home to be consulted (so) that they should know one another before entering into such an alliance . . . and that their full consent should thus be obtained. Otherwise, how could they know if they could love one another?[26]

Another son, Lorenzo Maeser, was born in Salt Lake City in 1857. At this time the Saints were growing increasingly uneasy about the United States Army contingent encamped at Fort Bridger. Throughout the winter of 1857 and 1858 the army had sent to Salt Lake City for supplies. The Saints satisfied their requests, but made wry comments about feeding the hand that would soon invade.

When spring came, most of the church members left Salt Lake City for Provo with little hope of returning to their homes. Jane wrote about this occurrence as follows:

I remember my husband moved his family south, and I remained with my little ones almost to the last. We had to take all the provisions we could take . . . 1500 bushels of wheat, flour, etc., and, in fact, leave as little as possible behind. If the army should take the city, we determined to burn our possessions. Even the sisters worked with a will while their husbands were busy elsewhere, boarding up all the windows to protect the glass, (in case) we were permitted to return, and to burn otherwise.

However, a compromise with President Brigham Young was effected and we were permitted to return to our homes after incurring all this unnecessary trouble, distress, and expense, which the journey of 50 miles to Provo had entailed.

When I had left my home I had swept it out and left it in order, removing all the ashes and litter which moving makes, though many left everything in confusion. But my home was too dear for me to do that. I did not shed a tear. But when I returned and knew it was my own again, it seemed like a palace and I cried like a child. I was away but six weeks. Many were gone, however, for six months.[27]

The last of Jane's children, Charles Comstock, was born following these troubles on September 16, 1859. She stated that, "I have
taught my children to read at home and however busy I have
been, have never neglected a half hour before their going to bed to
give to them."[28]

Franklin D. Richards fulfilled his last mission as president of the
European Mission from 1866 to 1868. Upon his return to the Salt
Lake Valley, the Council of the Twelve had decided to send lead-
ers of the church to outlying areas of the valley to direct the
people there. Franklin was sent to Ogden with his family on May
13, 1869, replacing Chauncey W. West, the presiding bishop in the
Ogden Stake, and Lorin Farr, who had been the stake president.
He was also appointed a probate judge for Weber County.

Jane said of this period:

*We took a rock house on Main Street, in the Second Ward, which we lived in for
two years. It seemed to be a very unhealthy house, as some of us were nearly all of
the time sick, and I was sick for nearly a year and a great portion of the time confined to my bed; I was so low for months that my life was despaired of, and many
times during this period, my husband and children stood round the bed in tears, as it
seemed to me that my time had come and I must leave them. Medicine and doctors
afforded me no relief. Very many times they would all lay their hands on me at once
and pray in turn, their father; Franklin, my son; Emily, his wife; Josephine, my
daughter; Lorenzo, twelve years old; and Charlie, ten, and prophesy that I would get
well; this afforded me the most comfort and added strength to my weak and feeble
body. I would here mention a kind brother by the name of Thomas Wallace, who
united his faith and prayers in my behalf, and would always promise me to live.*

*In addition to this, Sister Eliza R. Snow came and visited me and said I must live
for there was something for me to do. She said I was the poorest person in flesh that
she ever administered to, and I can here say that I was healed by the power of God,
and raised up to health and strength. Soon after this I was called upon by the Presiding Bishop, Lester J. Herrick, and the sisters of Ogden City, to preside over the
Relief Society of Ogden City.*

*This I attempted to decline, but their answer was, "The Lord has raised you from a
bed of sickness to do us good, and we want you to accept the office." After being en-
treated in this manner for weeks, I accepted the office with reluctance, feeling my inability to fill such a responsible position. I entered upon my duties with fear and
trembling and trusting in the Lord to aid me in this arduous duty, whose assistance I
fully realized. Having left my home many times, feeling weak and feeble, to attend
my meetings, I have been so blessed that I returned home feeling the strength of a
Samson. At the present time we have nineteen Relief Societies in Weber County. I
have been set apart with two counselors, Sister Hattie Brown and Sarah Herrick to
visit, counsel, and preside over them all.*[29]

The theme of the Relief Society during the first few years of
Jane's administration as president of the Ogden City Relief So-

ciety was "Look After The Youth of Zion." The Relief Society officers under Jane's direction became increasingly concerned with their youth and began to consider ways of affecting their lives. Franklin, presiding over the Weber Stake, and Jane cooperated in these efforts. In 1873 Franklin organized the young men into a semireligious literary society. During the years 1872 and 1873 Jane began meeting with the young women of Ogden to instruct and direct them. On May 1, 1873, she invited all the girls from Professor Louis F. Moench's School to a picnic and meeting at City Hall where they heard from such great women as Lucy Young, Josephine West, Delecta Balentine, Eveline Farley, and Sister Jane S. Richards herself. The Relief Society officers were delighted at the response of the girls. Eighty were in attendance at the meeting, and they voted unanimously to meet again the following week. A number of them joined the Relief Society at that time.

By the close of 1873, 125 girls had joined and were attending meetings on a regular basis. Later they were organized into a retrenchment society with officers of their own. The name was later changed to the Young Ladies Mutual Improvement Association; it was under the direction of the Relief Society until a stake board was formed on May 10, 1879. By this date 250 girls had joined the Relief Society. Jane was therefore a mother to all the girls in Ogden, and came to be affectionately called "Aunt Jane" by these young people.

Jane was called by President Brigham Young to preside over all of the Relief Societies of the Weber Stake in July 1877. She was the first Stake Relief Society president in the church. At that time no vote was taken on Jane's appointment, and no assistants or counselors were appointed. But at the appointed conference three months later on October 30, 1877, Eliza R. Snow made the motion that Jane preside over the Relief Society of the Weber Stake and fill the office of an elect lady. The motion was seconded, and the vote taken was unanimous. Jane was in a new position with no precedent to follow, and desiring guidance she chose Eliza R. Snow and Mary Isabella Horne as counselors. Their role seems to have been one of advising her, but not one of presiding over a stake in which they did not live.

Jane received much wise counsel from Brigham Young when she traveled in his party north to organize the Box Elder Stake just ten days before his death.

Jane accompanied her husband east and west on a number of journeys in 1880. In the east they saw relatives, visited early church sites, and identified the spot on the Missouri River where little Wealthy had been buried. During the trip west they called upon the historian, Hubert Howe Bancroft, in San Francisco, and were received with hospitality. His notes of the visit have been heavily relied upon in the preparation of this essay.

On December 21, 1883, Franklin and Jane felt the blow of the tragic death of another of their children. Lorenzo Maeser died as a result of a serious injury incurred in an accident while riding a spirited horse on July 4 of that same year. He had become very ill and finally passed away at the age of twenty-six.

Jane again went east with her husband in 1884 to Washington, D.C., where she made the acquaintance of Mrs. Belva A. Lockwood, Miss Susan B. Anthony, and other famous women, and through them exerted an influence favorable to Utah over members of Congress, which was then considering anti-Mormon legislation.

Upon her return from one of the trips east, Jane wrote the following:

I cannot travel any distance in the cars but what the mention of Utah in answer to the question as to my home brings down the most abusive comment on Mormonism . . . whether my connections with the people are known or not. I did not know until my recent visit East that we were so looked upon. But as I approached my destination in New York I found that in all probability my relatives would be mortified to have it known Mormons were to visit them. And so in making inquiries in regard to them, I refrained from letting that fact be known. And when I met them I felt satisfied that they felt it a disgrace. They told me afterwards that they felt sorry for me that I should be so deluded as to belong to that dreadful people, and were sympathetic in their commiseration of my conditions. When I left them they were satisfied of the happiness my religion gave me, and said that instead of pitying, they envy me.[30]

In October 1888, Jane was called to be first counselor to Zina D. H. Young in the presidency of the National Relief Societies of The Church of Jesus Christ of Latter-day Saints. In 1891 she went with Mrs. Sarah M. Kimball, Mrs. Emmeline B. Wells, and others to the National Council of Women, which was in session in Washington, D.C., and obtained membership and representation for herself and for her associates in that great organization. In 1892 she was appointed vice-president of the Utah Board of Lady Managers of the World's Fair, and early in 1893, having just returned from several months in Alaska with her family, she spent several weeks at the great Exposition with Josephine.

In the *Deseret Evening News* of February 7, 1894, was found an account of a surprise party given for Jane S. Richards on her seventy-first birthday. The reporting of the times was very interesting:

This time at least Sister Richards was truly surprized and disconcerted, though she soon regained her composure and proceeded in her usual courteous manner to welcome the invaders and make everyone feel at ease, a characteristic of hers to which she is admirably adapted.

Bishop McQuarrie said he truly appreciated Sister Richards in the ward over which he presided; had never known anyone who possessed so much energy and determination, with so much genious in searching out the poor and distressed, and so much skill and ability in supplying their wants as Sister Richards had exhibited in her labor of love in the ward; and now, he was happy to state, her refining influence was felt throughout the city, county, territory and beyond its borders. His good wishes and prayers were many and beautifully expressed.[31]

The last of the deep sorrows to beset Jane came with the passing of her husband in 1899. They had been married nearly sixty years, and Jane, in her grief, removed herself from public activity for a time. However, her spirits were later revived, and she accomplished a few more important tasks before her own death.

An article in *The Woman's Exponent* of June 1, 1900, recounted a speech given by Jane at General Relief Society Conference, in which she gave a powerful pitch for attendance at Relief Society: "You will be glad when you meet the Prophet Joseph, who organized this society, that you are among those who carried out his instructions."[32]

She was largely responsible for the erection of the Relief Society House in Ogden, which was dedicated July 19, 1902. She spearheaded the project in 1898 when, at a Relief Society Conference, she spoke of the time when the Prophet Joseph Smith had mentioned that sometime the sisters would have a house in which to meet. She was encouraged that she might live to see this event, since Brother D. H. Peery had donated a piece of land for this purpose.

In June of 1898 an officers' meeting was called, and Jane asked for the support of the wards. A month later they met again and reported the results of the presentations to the wards. Nineteen wards promised support, with various amounts to be donated immediately. The nickel fund (started in 1894) was also pushed with increasing vigor—the teachers went into the homes and encouraged members to contribute five cents per month toward the hall. By 1900 there was $190.50 in this fund.

At a conference on September 14, 1901, Jane called for a vote of all those who desired that work on the building should commence. The vote was unanimous, and work began the next week. It stopped during the winter months, but the building was completed that spring and was dedicated in July. *The Woman's Exponent* at the time praised her: "One cannot help feeling that the President, Jane Richards, in her 80th year had displayed unusual tact and executive ability in originating, planning, and carrying to successful issue, a Relief Society Hall for the sisters in Ogden City and the sisters of the Weber Stake of Zion."[33]

The dedication took place twenty-five years after Jane was appointed to preside over the sisters in the Weber Stake. The actual building site was one that had been formerly owned by the Third Ward, rather than the one donated by D. H. Peery, because it was more conveniently located on Grant Avenue between 21st and 22nd streets on the west side of Tabernacle Square in Ogden. The final cost was $5,000. This effort later encouraged the Relief Society to erect the central Relief Society Building, which now stands opposite the temple in Salt Lake City. The edifice was eventually sold to the Daughters of Utah Pioneers for one dollar; they set up a museum, which still stands.

Speaking at another Relief Society General Conference in 1904, Jane instructed the sisters to always visit the sick or those in need, rather than idly taking tea with the neighbors. She said that one should even miss her meetings, if necessary, to provide the merciful service of taking the sick or elderly out for a ride.

Jane Richards' talents were well known, and she acquired several more responsibilities as a result. She was a member of the Board of Directors of the Deseret Hospital, where she raised funds to maintain the hospital and encouraged the best care for all without discrimination as to race, creed, or wealth. She also did work in all the temples that were erected during her lifetime since the Kirtland Temple, attending the dedications of all of them except the Logan Temple. She was instrumental in raising much money throughout the Weber Stake for construction of these temples. In 1877 she was responsible for the dedication of a milliner's store, which retailed straw hats and bonnets manufactured in homes in Ogden. This industry, spearheaded by Jane, provided employment to many.

Six years to the day after the Relief Society Building was dedicated (July 19, 1908), the Weber Stake was divided and Jane S. Richards, after thirty-one years of service, was released as active president of the Relief Society due to failing health. She was unanimously sustained as honorary president of all of the Relief Societies of the three stakes in Weber County, which was a great honor to her. Near this time, Nellie Becraft spoke in honor of Jane:

We love you for your true worth and for what you have done; for that broad charity that your life has exemplified. To quote your own favorite creed, "We did not all have the same mother," and so failings have been overlooked and the friendly hand extended. No cry of distress has reached your ears in vain, the naked have been clothed; the hungry fed; the sick comforted; the dying soothed, and the dead prepared for their last long sleep. The whitening snow of winter and the scorching sun of summer have found you at your post of duty, until the Priesthood of the Lord have said, "It is enough." Your day of labor is past, twilight has come.[34]

Jane stayed with her daughter, Josephine R. West, until she finally passed away on November 17, 1913. The funeral was one of the largest ever held in the Ogden Tabernacle. Speakers included President Joseph F. Smith, President Charles W. Penrose, Apostle David O. McKay, President Emmeline B. Wells, Bishop Robert McQuarrie, Sister Ruthinda Moench, and President Francis M. Lyman.

Apostle David O. McKay said of Jane: "I am unable to speak to you as an intimate associate of Sister Jane S. Richards. I stand before you rather as one of her boys, who has been influenced by her noble teachings. Just as a child I remember her visit and that of her daughter, Sister West, to our Ward, and I shall hold, as long as my life lasts, I hope, the influence of that visit and meeting. It was said of the Savior: 'He went about doing good.' I cannot think of a more beautiful eulogy than is contained in those few words. And that is the tribute we pay to Sister Richards . . . she went about doing good."[35]

President Joseph F. Smith added that "she was a loving and obedient daughter, a faithful and affectionate wife, a fond and devoted mother, a true and loyal friend. A Latter-day Saint in all that the name implies, she has won the crown of eternal life laid up for the righteous and just."[36]

Her son, Charles Comstock, wrote an impressive speech about her, which he gave on one occasion to the Relief Society sisters:

Mother's trials and hardships increased her capacity for human sympathy and prepared her for the labor of love awaiting her, and which she cheerfully performed, in the Relief Society organizations and in other capacities. Patient in misfortune, sympathetic, generous and helpful to others in sorrow and distress, she bestowed blessings upon thousands less fortunate than herself, in whose hearts her memory is lovingly enshrined.

. . . And just one of my father's many tributes paid to her: He and I were visiting in the parlor when Mother appeared and seemed busy picking up and laying away in suitcases different articles that would be needed by them while she and father were away on a trip they were about to take. As she passed out of hearing he said to me: "Watch her, my son, she is just as faithful and attentive as an angel in heaven." And so he felt and appreciated her life, her services and her companionship.[37]

In looking over her life, it is evident that Jane S. Richards learned great lessons from her trials. Their overall effect was to mold her into a very powerful person. Through many sieges of illness she learned empathy for the suffering of others. Everyone who wrote of her mentioned her administrations to the sick. And, of course, this is one of the main objectives of the Relief Society in which she played such an important role.

The poverty she had known gave her great compassion for those she saw in similar circumstances later on. She never formed much attachment to the material wealth she was able to accumulate, but rather visited the Poor House regularly, helping those who were there. She also opened her home to the beggars and bedraggled travelers who seemed to appear regularly at her door, living as close to the railroad as she did. An incident related at her funeral illustrates her deep concern for the needy. She heard of a woman who had been put off the train in Ogden due to insufficient funds while traveling to meet her husband and children. Jane packed an appetizing lunch, raised the money needed for the woman's ticket home, and accompanied her to the railroad station, where the woman appreciatively went on her way. Indians often came by her house begging; even though they had stolen many of her cattle, she was always helpful to them, feeling that she had intruded on the land that they had originally used.

Maybe it was the death of her two beloved little children as well as the death of a grown son that helped her keep her perspectives so firmly entrenched on eternity rather than on life on this earth. Sharing her husband so totally with the church as well as with his polygamous wives, rather than embittering Jane, caused her to blossom into an independent, self-confident woman— the sort needed to administrate over large organizations such as the Relief Society and the YLMIA—the sort needed to complete projects such as a Relief Society Building or a fundraising campaign for a temple or hospital.

Modern women could take a lesson from the way this great woman turned trials and seeming injustices into great victories of character. Throughout, her most important and dominant trait was an everlasting and complete faith in the Lord.

Notes

1. E. B. Wells, *Life Sketch of Mrs. Jane Snyder Richards,* Richards Family Register, Church Historical Department, p. 3.

2. *Ibid.*, p. 2.

3. Mrs. F. D. Richards, *Reminiscences of Mrs. F. D. Richards,* Bancroft Library, University of California, San Francisco, 1880, p. 3.

4. *Ibid.*, pp. 6-7.

5. *Ibid.*, p. 11.

6. Hubert Howe Bancroft, *Inner Facts of Social Life in Utah,* Bancroft Library, University of California, Berkeley, 1888, p. 1.

7. *Ibid.*, p. 9.

8. *Ibid.*, p. 10.

9. Wells, p. 3.

10. *Ibid.*, p. 6.

11. Nellie Becraft, *Jane Snyder Richards,* September 10, 1908, Church Historical Department, p. 3.

12. Bancroft, p. 2.

13. Jane S. Richards, *Paper From the Jubilee Box,* March 31, 1881, Richards Family Register, Church Historical Department, p. 3.

14. Charles Comstock Richards, from a speech given to Relief Society, Richards Family Register, Church Historical Department, p. 4.

15. *Paper from the Jubilee Box,* pp. 3-4.

16. Jane S. Richards, from autobiographical material attached to the *Autobiography, Diaries, and Journals of Franklin D. Richards,* May 1844-December 1867, microfilm, Church Historical Department, p. 34.

17. Bancroft, p. 3.

18. Jane S. Richards, autobiographical material, p. 35.

19. Wells, p. 8.

20. Nancroft, pp. 6-7.

21.   *Ibid,*, p. 16.

22.   *Ibid.*, p. 13.

23.   *Ibid.*, p. 13.

24.   *Paper from the Jubilee Box,* p. 5.

25.   Jane S. Richards, Autobiographical Material, pp. 44-45.

26.   *Ibid.*, pp. 41-42.

27.   *Ibid.*, pp. 38-39.

28.   *Ibid.*, p. 41.

29.   *Paper From the Jubilee Box,* pp. 5-6.

30.   Jane S. Richards, autobiographical material, p. 46.

31.   R. E. Moench, "A Genuine Surprise," *Deseret Evening News,* February 8, 1894, p. 6.

32.   *Woman's Exponent,* June 1, 1900, vol. 29, p. 2.

33.   *Ibid.*, vol. 31, p. 13.

34.   Nellie Becraft, *Token of Esteem to Jane S. Richards,* September 10, 1908, Church Historical Department, pp. 1-2.

35.   Franklin L. West, Ph.D., *Life of Franklin D. Richards,* Deseret News Press, Salt Lake City, 1924, p. 263.

36.   *Ibid.*, pp. 266-268.

37.   Charles Comstock Richards, Speech, p. 4.

Bibliography

Bancroft, H. H. *The Inner Facts of Social Life in Utah.* Bancroft Library, University of California, Berkeley, 1888.

Becraft, Nellie. Jane Snyder Richards. September 10, 1908, Church Historical Office.

————, Token of Esteem to Jane S. Richards, September 10, 1908, Richards Family Register, Church Historical Department.

Cannon, Annie Wells. A Tribute. January 1913, Richards Family Register, Church Historical Department.

Carter, Kate B. *Heart Throbs of the West,* vol. 3. Daughters of Utah Pioneers, Utah Press, Salt Lake City, 1941.

Deseret News Microfilm, 1911, Church Historical Department.

Gates, Susan Young. *History of the Young Ladies Mutual Improvement Association.* Deseret News Press, 1911.

Ogden Relief Society History Book. Ogden Stake 1842-1908, Church Historical Department.

Relief Society Magazine, vol. 10, no. 3. March, 1923, Salt Lake City.

Richards, Charles Comstock. Copy of a speech given to Relief Society, Richards Family Register, Church Historical Department.

Richards, Mrs. Franklin D. Richards, Reminiscences of Mrs. F. D. Richards. Bancroft Library, University of California, San Francisco, 1880.

Richards, Jane S. Paper from the Jubilee Box. March 31, 1881, Richards Family Register, Church Historical Department.

Richards, Jane S., from autobiographical material attached to the Autobiography, Diaries, and Journals of Franklin D. Richards. May 1844-December 1967, microfilm, Church Historical Department.

Roberts, B. H. *A Comprehensive History of The Church of Jesus Christ of Latter-day Saints,* century I, vol. IV. Deseret News Press, Salt Lake City, 1930.

Tullidge, Edward W. *The Women of Mormondom.* Tullidge and Crandall, New York, 1877.

8: Jane S. Richards

Wells, E. B. *Life Sketch of Mrs. Jane Snyder Richards*. Richards Family Register, Church Historical Department.

West, Franklin L., Ph.D. *Life of Franklin D. Richards*. Deseret News Press, Salt Lake City, 1924.

Woman's Exponent, vol. 1-41, 1872-1914.

Bathsheba Bigler Smith 1822–1910

Barbara Fluckiger Watt was born in Afton, Wyoming. She returned from a proselyting mission for the Mormon Church to Northern California and received her bachelor of science degree in Secondary Education from Utah State University. After graduating, she worked as a home economist for Utah State University Extension Service. She and her husband, Ronald G. Watt, face the challenge of rearing their five children.

Bathsheba B. Smith

Barbara Fluckiger Watt

It may have been considered a long, hard journey to travel by wagon from West Virginia to Far West, Missouri, but to Bathsheba Bigler, a new convert to The Church of Jesus Christ of Latter-day Saints, it was an exciting adventure. The company would occasionally pass through towns and cities, travel over wide prairies, pass through dense forests, and camp in tents at night as they traveled to join the people of their own faith and religion. Bathsheba loved to sing, and her voice, as well as the voices of the other young people in the company, would be heard singing and laughing as they traveled or camped.

Arriving in Missouri, the Bigler family found the state preparing to wage war against the Mormons. The nearer they came to their destination, the more unfriendly the people became. Often they were stopped by large groups of men who asked them their intentions, threatening not to allow them to go on, but after debating among themselves, would let them pass with a statement to the effect, "As you are Virginians, we will let you go on, but we believe you will soon return for you will quickly become convinced of your folly."[1]

As they prepared to cross the Grand River in Missouri, they were joined by another company of Latter-day Saints from the east. How good it was to talk with people of their own faith! But it was decided to again go different routes and cross the river by different ferries, as this would enable them to cross in less time. The Bigler Company arrived safely in Far West, but the other company was not so lucky: they stopped at Haun's Mill and became involved with an armed mob; some were killed, others were wounded for life. Three nights after the Bigler Company's arrival at Far West, Bathsheba had her first experience with mob activity when she heard the shouts and savage yells of the mob and saw homes burned, property destroyed, and men killed and wounded. David Patten, one of the Twelve Apostles, was brought wounded into the house where she was sheltered, and there she saw him die. These experiences and many hardships to follow left an impression

on Bathsheba: even in her later life she would refer to "the
enemy," and one of her greatest fears was for the safety of her husband when he was gone from her in the duties of his calling as an
apostle of the church.

But the trials and hardships only served to strengthen the faith
and convictions of this sixteen-year-old girl. They gave her strength
to push on with her family and not turn back to the peaceful
memories of the three hundred-acre farm in West Virginia, where
she had ridden horseback, forded the mountain streams, laughed
with her friends, and attended the Presbyterian Church. Though
she never joined the Presbyterians, she had gone there often to listen to the eloquent sermons preached by the handsome, pious Mr.
Bristol. Her spiritual yearnings were never satisfied until she heard
the message of the gospel of Jesus Christ taught to her family by
the Mormon missionaries. She had been baptized a member of
The Church of Jesus Christ of Latter-day Saints on August 21,
1837.[2]

Leaving behind her home and her father, who would join them
later, she, with her mother, brother, two sisters, and their husbands, in company with an uncle and his family, had started their
journey west. She was happy when her father finally joined them
in the spring of 1838 in Quincy, Illinois, where the family went
when they were forced to leave Far West. The joy of this reunion
was short lived; her father, Mark Bigler, sickened and died soon
after his arrival.

It was about this time that Bathsheba Bigler again met George
A. Smith, a cousin of the Mormon Prophet Joseph Smith. He had
been one of the missionaries present at her baptism, and now he
was a frequent visitor in their home. He was a handsome young
man, soon to be made an apostle. Bathsheba easily fell in love
with him. He, too, was greatly impressed with her, for on February 21, 1838, he made a provisional arrangement with her that:

*with the blessings of the Almighty in preserving us, in three years from this time, we
will be married, or as soon thereafter as circumstances will permit.*[3]

True to this commitment, Bathsheba and George were married
on Sunday, July 25, 1841, just fourteen days after he had returned
from a mission to England, where he had been for a little over
two years.

Two days after their marriage, "carpet bag in hand," they headed for John Smith's home in Zarahemla, a small community
across the Mississippi River from Nauvoo, Illinois. Here Bathsheba
was introduced to George's parents, John and Clarissa Smith. It
was a time of rejoicing, and a fine wedding dinner was prepared

for the newlyweds. Father Smith gave a toast to their health and happiness and pronounced a blessing upon them. After living with the Smith family for about four weeks, George was able to rent a small log cabin and, with the happy anticipation of getting their own home, the newly married couple moved in. The roof leaked, the chimney smoked, and in general the house was uncomfortable, but with their few belongings and Bathsheba's inventive initiative, they made it as comfortable as possible. The first night they knelt on the floor by their bed and dedicated themselves to God for life, praying for His blessings to rest upon them and praying that prosperity might crown their labors. They thanked the Lord for his mercy in bringing them together after being so long separated.[4]

Next they bought an unfurnished log house. They hung a blanket at the window for want of glass and built a brick chimney, but found that it also smoked. However, it was home, and it belonged to them. Their stay here was short, for within the month they were moving again, this time to Nauvoo under the counsel of Joseph Smith. They rented for a while until Joseph Smith gave them a small lot with a log house on it. They fixed the cabin the best they could, but Bathsheba still thought it was the worst looking house they had yet lived in. It was a disappointment to Bathsheba; she longed for a beautiful home like the house in West Virginia which she had known as a young girl. She had acquired from her mother, who came from an aristocratic and well-to-do family in Maryland, the art of Southern hospitality, and she enjoyed entertaining her friends, but she was ashamed to have any of her acquaintances see her in such a place. It did, however, have the desirable qualities of a non-smoking chimney and a non-leaking roof. With all the spare time they could find, Bathsheba and George went to work and built a small frame house with four rooms, two below and two above. It was still unfinished when they moved their bed into one of the rooms and called it home. Twelve days later, on July 7, 1842, a son was born to them. John Smith, George's father, blessed the new baby and gave him the name of George Albert Smith, Jr.[5] With the house still unfinished and the baby only two months old, George left on a mission to the eastern United States. His goings and comings became a pattern in their lives as he fulfilled the assignments given him by Joseph Smith and later by Brigham Young. Bathsheba's letters to him through the years of his many absences from home reflect her great love for him and the need for his companionship and counsel. She wished that he could be with her all the time, but her faith in God and her strong convictions that what he was doing was the will of the Lord made it possible for her to bear these long absences.

With her husband gone and her house unfinished, Bathsheba went to work, determined to get the house finished before winter. She wanted the walls plastered and the floor laid, but could not obtain the lumber to do the work. Bathsheba felt she could do it herself if she had the lumber, even though she was not accustomed to such things. But George was gone only a few months; although winter set in early, he was able to finish the house. Then another call came for a mission to Boston and the surrounding area, and this time he did not return until the fall of 1843.

Bathsheba found this time very trying, as her small son was often sick, and she longed for her husband's aid and comfort. Her father-in-law, in trying to relieve her anxiety, would come almost every day to see her. She was always comforted by the blessings he gave to little George whenever he became very sick.

Married to the cousin and close friend of the Prophet Joseph Smith, Bathsheba was often invited to the Prophet's home. She enjoyed his wife Emma Smith's hospitality and the friendship of the other apostles' wives. She and her husband met many times with the Prophet Joseph Smith and others in a special room over Joseph's store. This room was dedicated for special meetings, and it was here that Joseph first introduced the temple ceremony called the endowment. Bathsheba and her husband received this blessing and also became sealed to one another as husband and wife for all eternity under the holy law of celestial marriage. Bathsheba became so proficient in the ceremony that when the Nauvoo Temple was completed she became an officiator, a position she also held in the Salt Lake and Logan temples as well as in the Endowment House. In her autobiography she said:

With my husband it was my privilege to meet with Brother Joseph and others who had received their endowments, and I heard the Prophet give instructions concerning plural marriage. He counseled the sisters present not to be troubled in consequence of this law that many would be called to live—that all would be right—and the result would be for their glory and exaltation.[6]

In her later life Bathsheba was called many times to testify that Joseph Smith had introduced both the endowment and plural marriage. At a Weber Stake priesthood reunion held June 12, 1903, in Ogden she stated: "The Endowments are given now the same as they were given in the Nauvoo Temple, as directed by Joseph Smith."[7] She also stated that Joseph Smith rather than Brigham Young revealed the law of plural marriage. She was called to Washington to be a witness in the Reed Smoot trial; at this time she was over eighty-two years of age and in feeble health, which made her unable to travel to Washington, D.C. She sent an affidavit to Washington stating that the endowment ceremonies were the same as when she had received them, under the direction of Joseph Smith, Jr.[8] She was asked at that time in letters to testify to the fact that the Prophet Joseph Smith had given the endowment and inaugurated plural marriage.[9]

After her experience of hearing Joseph Smith's instructions concerning plural marriage, she and George became thoroughly convinced that the doctrine of plurality of wives was from God, and Bathsheba felt that it was for her and her husband's exaltation that they obey this revelation, firmly believing that she "would participate with him in all his blessings, glory, and honor."[10] So like Sarah of old, she helped him select five wives within the year. They were Lucy Meserve, Zilpha Stark, Sarah Ann Libby, Sarah's sister, Hannah Maria Libby, and Nancy Clement, all honorable and virtuous young women who were proud to be the wives of George Albert Smith. Bathsheba said:

They all had their home with us, being proud of my husband and loving him very much, knowing him to be a man of God and believeing he would not love them less, because he loved me more. I had joy in having a testimony that what I had done was acceptable to my Father in Heaven.[11]

Bathsheba accepted her husband's other wives as sisters. She felt compassion for their sorrows and trials and shared with them the material things that she had, feeling responsible for their welfare in his absence. When discord arose among the wives while George was absent, it was Bathsheba, as the first wife, who was called upon as a mediator to establish harmony. She did not like playing this role, and at such times her letters contained longings such as "I hope I did right," or "Tell me if I did wrong," or "I will be glad when you return to handle the matter."

Sarah Ann and Hannah being sisters lived together. Sarah Ann became quite sick and Hannah took care of her. They were often together and sometimes did not join in the activities with the other wives. In crossing the plains they did their own cooking and washing and fed their teamsters while Bathsheba and Lucy did the cooking and washing for the rest of the families.

It was a lovely day in Nauvoo on June 15, 1844, when Bathsheba wrote to George telling him about the comfort she had in her home with the flower pots in the window and the new curtains that she had made and hung. She had cleaned house, baked a good dinner, and had apples stewing for a pie, preparing for company that evening. She was happy that little George looked so healthy after his long illness. He was now walking nicely, starting to talk, and laughing a lot. She had made a new dress for herself and pantlets for little George, who looked so cute in them. She told her husband about the garden she had planted and the potatoes and peas that would soon be ready. She would share these items with the "girls," as she called her husband's other wives. She was happy that the Prophet Joseph Smith and his companions were freed from arrest. Her whole letter depicted such peace and happiness and beauty in Nauvoo.[12] Yet less than two weeks later, the whole atmosphere had changed, especially for Bathsheba, as she wrote to George of the death of the Prophet Joseph Smith and his brother, Hyrum; both had been killed on June 27 by a painted mob at Carthage. She told of their bodies being brought home, and she told of such a day of mourning as was never seen by the Mormons. She said it pained her to even write of it. There seemed to be a great feeling of unrest in the city; she knew that the Council of the Twelve who were off on missions had been sent for, and so she expected that George would soon be home.[13]

George did return home, but not until the first of August. Two weeks later Bathsheba gave birth to a baby daughter, whom they named Bathsheba.[14] Excitement and unrest still prevailed until all of the Council of the Twelve had returned, when their leadership gave strength to the Saints and the turmoil abated.

It was good to have George home that year; he encouraged Bathsheba to take art lessons and also to sing in the choir. She loved attending the social events and especially the dances, but George would avoid the dancing if at all possible. She received a letter from Melissa (her younger sister) saying, "by report you have got your husband to dancing as well as myself (wicked wives ruling their husbands)."[15]

Now the plans and preparations for the completion of the Nauvoo Temple were put into action, and in spite of the persecution, rapid progress was made. The Female Relief Society members also did all they could to help with the temple's progress. Bathsheba had been eighteen years of age and the youngest of the group of eighteen charter members, but by 1844 the Relief Society's membership was over a thousand. Anxious to do their part that they might realize the promised blessings of the temple, the sisters one by one offered generously of their possessions and time.

Bathsheba proposed getting wool and furnishing the older ladies with yarn to knit socks for the workmen on the temple. With the persecution there was much need for compassionate service, and Bathsheba was willing to help with the others in the Female Relief Society; she spun thread which the sisters made into cloth for undergarments for the needy. When the temple was close to com-

pletion, thousands of people received their endowments and sealings.

After Joseph Smith's death, the leadership of the church was assumed by the Quorum of the Twelve, with Brigham Young as its
head. Brigham Young and the other apostles labored day and
night in the temple from December 10, 1845, until they left
Nauvoo in February, 1846, so that as many Saints as possible
might receive their endowments. Helping the men were many of
the leading sisters including Bathsheba.

Nauvoo was "one vast mechanic shop" that winter. Nearly every
family was engaged in making wagons for themselves or others.
Bathsheba's parlor was used as a shop in which wagons were
painted.

On February 9, 1846, in company with many others, George
took Bathsheba, their two small children, and other members of
his family and crossed the frozen Mississippi into Iowa. They left
their comfortable home and the accumulations of four years of labor, taking with them only such things as were necessary (clothing,
bedding, and provisions) and leaving all else to their enemies.
Bathsheba took a last look at the walls, the windows, the fireplace,
and the cupboard, watering for the last time the pretty flower pots
and setting them carefully on the floor away from the drafts that
would blow through her unheated house.

In her journal Bathsheba indicated how they traveled through
snow, wind, and rainstorms, how roads had to be built and rafts
constructed, how their poor animals had to drag on day after day
with scanty feed, and how the camps suffered from poverty, sickness, and death. It was a great comfort for her when they reached
Winter Quarters on the western bank of the Missouri River.
George was able to build four cabins and a dugout for his families,
since the winds had literally blown their tents into pieces. Here
the Saints could have their public and private meetings in peace,
could pray and sing the songs of Zion, and could rejoice that their
persecutors were far behind. Bathsheba felt that the Lord was with
them and that his power was manifested daily in their journey.
They had been preserved from savage Indians, wild beasts, winter's
cold blast, and the hot rays of the summer sun.[18] But every home
felt the sting of death. One wife, Nancy Clement, and her child
died. Bathsheba's mother, Susannah Ogden, also died, leaving an
empty spot in Bathsheba's heart; Susannah was a gentle woman,
with all the hospitable and generous qualities of the South. She
was an excellent housekeeper, and was adept and artistic with her
needle.[16] Bathsheba seems to have acquired many of these qualities

from her mother.

It was only a month later on April 14, 1847, that Bathsheba, after three days' labor, gave birth prematurely to a son they named John.[17] He lived only four hours. Bathsheba was sick for months afterwards, and never again bore children. George left Bathsheba in this weakened condition to go with Brigham Young in search of a place of settlement beyond the Rocky Mountains. Zilpha took care of Bathsheba, and the other wives came to see her, but she still felt lonesome. She would think about little John and wish that she could see his grave; when the children were quiet she would kneel down and pray for them and for her husband. During the evening the firelight would reflect off George's portrait and the portrait of her mother, and she would feel that she was not so alone as they looked so pleasantly out at her.[18]

In June a large body of the Saints left for the west, among them Father Smith's household and Bathsheba's sisters. Father Smith tried to get Bathsheba to go with his family, but she felt it was her duty to wait with George's other wives. Later she wondered if she should have gone; she thought this would be George's wish, and she did want to please him. [19]

As the warm weather in Winter Quarters began to produce early vegetables, the sick began to recover, but there was still anxiety for the pioneers who had gone west. In December a group of them returned, George among them. He told Bathsheba of their success in finding a place in the heart of the Rockies, and that about two thousand Mormons had already arrived in the valley of the Great Salt Lake. The Saints who could not go west by May 1848 were compelled by the government to leave Winter Quarters, recrossing into Iowa. According to Bathsheba, most of these were families of men who had gone with the Mormon Battalion and who were waiting for them to return.[20]

George moved his family into two cabins that he had purchased in Iowa, but before winter set in he built two more. The winter was extremely cold, but wood was plentiful, and Bathsheba used it freely. They had gathered a nice supply of wild plums, raspberries, and elderberries along with the wheat, Indian corn, buckwheat, and potatoes they had raised. The children had helped Bathsheba gather hickory nuts and walnuts, so they were better prepared for the cold months than they had been the previous winter.

George spent much of the time after his return from Salt Lake City counseling, comforting, and cheering the Saints in their camps. Bathsheba often went with him, savoring his companionship and giving comfort to the people herself. Not until late June 1849 was George able to obtain wagons and sufficient supplies to bring his family west; the expedition consisted of five wives, four children, and eight teamsters. There were three other wagons containing family possessions and several tons of freight for the building of their new city. Each wife had a wagon; Bathsheba worked hard to make her wagon comfortable and nice, even under these trying circumstances. The wagon cover was made of coarse Osnaburg cloth (a type of coarse heavy cloth) lined with blue drilling (cloth that was woven with three threads in a diagonal weave) and was high enough to allow an adult to stand erect in the wagon. Small eight-inch projections on each side of the top of the wagon box made the room inside of the wagon even larger. A frame was laid across the back part of the wagon and was corded as a bedstead; their heaviest articles could be put under the bed. They used a stepladder to ascend to the door, which was between the wheels in the wagon cover. On the opposite side was a window. Both could be opened and closed at pleasure. A homey touch was added inside by hanging a mirror, candlestick, and pin cushion. Four chairs made it possible for George, Bathsheba, and their two children to sit as they rode if they should choose. A carpet she had made covered the floor of their traveling house.[21] Pulling this unusual and somewhat cumbersome covered wagon was a fast-walking team of red oxen, Buck and Berry. Berry became crippled for a time after being bitten by a rattlesnake, and the whole camp shared Bathsheba's sympathy and concern for the animal. Fording a river almost brought disaster to their unwieldy outfit; it swayed and was almost swept downstream in the strong current. Bathsheba, watching from the shore with stoic good humor, said, "Behold Noah's Ark!"[22]

Near South Pass as they came in sight of some of the highest mountains in North America, they ran into a terrific snowstorm, indicating that winter was setting in. The day before the storm George had gone on foot searching for some stray cattle. He was some distance behind the company, and by the time he reached camp he was fatigued and ill. For thirty-six hours the storm raged and Bathsheba, caring for her sick husband, became discouraged. She recorded that it was a dismal time indeed as she listened to "the children cry, the oxen low, the cow bawl, the sheep bleat, the pig squeal, the duck quack, the chicken cheep, and we couldn't tell them why they had to suffer so much."[23]

After the storm the sun shone brightly on the glistening snow as the men shoveled through the fifteen-foot drifts so that the company could move on. What relief they felt when they were met by several men from Salt Lake City, including George's brother, John L. Smith, with additional ox teams to assist them into the valley.

On November 5, 1849, 105 days after they had left the Missouri
River, the company arrived in Salt Lake City with thankful
hearts, recognizing the Lord's blessings, as no deaths or serious accidents had occurred during that time. The Smith family went directly to the home of John Smith (George's father), where they received a warm greeting. Bathsheba's sister, Melissa Jane Lambson,
was also there, and invited them to her home for supper.

*O, how delightful it did seem to be once more in a comfortable room, with a blazing
fire on the hearth; where the mountain's rude blasts, or the desert's bleak winds could
not blow the smoke into our eyes, nor the sparks onto our clothes*[24]
wrote Bathsheba. They lived in their wagons for some time before
George was able to obtain a small log cabin and also two other
rooms which, with their wagons, made them a little more comfortable.

In the spring they planted eleven acres of wheat near the Jordan
River, only to have it destroyed when the river overflowed its
banks in the spring tide. They obtained land and planted again,
their labors yielding a light crop that proved sufficient for the
bread needs of the family that year. The walls of Bathsheba's
adobe house were up one story, and two fourteen-foot rooms and a
buttery were done when George was called to found a settlement
250 miles south in Little Salt Lake Valley (Parowan). Zilpha went
with him. Since her home was unfinished, Bathsheba and her two
children were invited to live with Father John Smith's family until
her home was completed. She accepted the invitation gratefully,
providing her share of food and helping with the housework to
earn their keep.

By the end of March the house was finished. It had a shingled
roof, walls nicely plastered with white clay, glass windows, two
fireplaces, and a bake oven. It was a dream come true: the wandering Bathsheba who had gone without what might be called a
home since she had left Nauvoo was finally settled. While moving
into the new home, Bathsheba and the children caught colds; the
doctor called the sickness scarlet fever, others called it the whooping cough, and still others called it the "Chin" cough. "Let it be
what it may," she wrote her husband, "it is bad enough." Fearing
that he would think that she could not do her part of the work after her illness, she continued:

*Now my dear, I do not want you to think I cannot work yet, so I believe I will tell
you what I have been doing this winter. I done nearly all Father's folks housework,
nine in the family most of the time, with the exception of washing, maid Father two
fine shirts, mother two dresses three caps ... maid her some pillar cases, maid John
two fine bosoms helped quilt two quilts wrote thirty odd blessings Recorded several.*

Father gave me about seven dollars and a half in money. I maid my Carpet, maid George a pair of pants and coat and siss some clothing, sued some for Melissa (two dollars and a half worth) maid me a nice hearthrug maid some nice soap, maid a cushion for my rocking chair sued some for myself also knit for the children since I have been here [referring to her new home into which she had just moved] I have maid my window curtains have three white ones in the best room ... maid my valances sued and fited down my Carpet maid some pillar cases and sheets quilled two Comforters ... maid me a dress and bonnet, Bathsheba an apron and various other things besides cooking washing mending milking churning feeding my cow pigs chickings and visiting the sick as well as the well.[25]

Getting settled in her new home and playing with her children was as much fun for Bathsheba as when she was a child playing with her dolls. She loved to make things for them and dress them in the outfits she had made. To make living expenses and furnish her home, Bathsheba took in a boarder who paid her five dollars a week in tithing office orders. She would share what she received with George's other wives, and if George sent supplies she would divide them. For example, she divided the wood Brother Baker brought with Hannah, and she shared the cheese with Lucy, because Hannah had just received some from the tithing office.[26]

In June 1851 one of the wives, Sarah Ann, died. Sarah had been extremely sick in the camp in Missouri, and the doctor had promised her only a short time to live. But the elders had blessed her and she had lived five years, during which time she had borne a son. Her death brought to light a conflict between Hannah and Bathsheba. Sarah and Hannah had lived together, and although Bathsheba felt Hannah's criticism, she still was concerned for her as expressed in a letter to George telling him of Sarah's death. She wrote, "What Hannah will do now I don't know ... I could take her home if she would be kind to me, but she will not."[27]

After the funeral Bathsheba and Hannah had an argument concerning Little John (Sarah's son), Hannah being afraid that Bathsheba would take the child away from her. This public incident upset Bathsheba so much that it made her ill, and writing of it to George she said:

... I was not very well and my mind was troubled knowing the feelings that existed in our family and Sarah just being dead and everybody looking on, one saying one thing and another thing for every mean thing that could be said had been said ... I will try to do the best I hope I can and if I do not rite I hope you will tell me how and I will try to do it as I always have.[28]

By August 1851 the difficulty between Bathsheba and Hannah seemed to have been solved somewhat, for in a letter to George she said:

I saw Hannah today at meeting, she was as friendly as I have seen her since you left. I hope she will continue to be friendly for I do hate to have anyone cross with me ... I [thank] you for your faith in me that I will try to do rite all the time is my study and prayer ... There is a great deal of predigdice against the first wife I think and I am glad of it for it will wisely make them be on their guard the more. We will grow better faster all is right I feel well.[29]

Bathsheba seems to have had a close relationship with Zilpha, writing often her hope that Zilpha was able to endure the hardships of this new settlement and that she would soon have a house. Zilpha also communicated with Bathsheba, sending the children gum or small packages when she had an opportunity.

After fulfilling his duties in Iron County, George was then called to preside over Utah County. He moved to Provo in August 1852, taking Lucy and Hannah with him. Bathsheba was the only wife left in Salt Lake City until 1857, when her husband married another wife, Susan Elizabeth West, and brought her home to live with Bathsheba. But Bathsheba did not feel lonely before Susan came to live with her because her sister, Melissa, lived just a short distance down the block, and Melissa's daughter, Julina, was often with them. Because Julina had no sisters of her own, Bathsheba filled her time entertaining Julina by making dolls for her and playing with her. Melissa's hands were full with several small children, and she was glad to have Bathsheba taking care of Julina. By the time Julina was seven years old, she lived almost exclusively with Bathsheba, although every day she went to see her mother.

When the United States Army came to Utah in 1857, Bathsheba again felt the pangs of fear that the enemy would destroy their peace. She watched her husband go off to the mountains to assist in conducting the campaign and finally to negotiate peace with the authorities of the invading army. One morning at about two o'clock, young George was also called to march to Echo Canyon, much against Bathsheba's wishes, since he was just recovering from an illness. She fitted him out the best she could, however, and bid him goodbye with her prayer and blessing. Word came from Brigham Young that all the women and children should prepare to move south. Men were given instructions to be prepared to burn the homes at a moment's notice, for rather than surrender their possessions to their enemy they would destroy the possessions themselves.

Bathsheba sadly packed trunks and boxes with the items she could not take with her. She felt again the way she had felt when she left her Nauvoo home ("Would she never see it again!"). On the last day of March 1858, after tidying the house and sweeping the floors, Bathsheba and her family and sister, Susan, with

George, Jr., left their home and headed south. Little Julina had gone with her own mother to Nephi. Bathsheba and her daughter stayed in Provo with Lucy and Hannah, and George and Susan went on to Parowan in Iron County. During this time Julina became so homesick for her beloved Aunt Bathsheba, with whom she had such a loving relationship, that it was thought best for her good to let her return. She stayed with Bathsheba until her marriage to Joseph F. Smith, later president of the Mormon Church.[30]

After peace was restored, Bathsheba and her family returned to their home in Salt Lake City. It was just about sundown as they entered the valley, and all was quiet. Every door and window was boarded up; smoke was coming from two or three of the chimneys, so she recognized that they were among the first to return. How different and desolate their home looked with weeds growing in place of flowers!

The large new home, also to be the Historian's Office, which had been in the process of building before the move south, could now be pushed to completion, and soon they were able to move into it. Bathsheba and Susan worked diligently making carpet, blankets, quilts, and comforters from wool they had obtained in Provo, and they spun and wove tablecloths, towels, and bed ticking from flax George had raised in Parowan. George even bought them a loom for weaving. Bathsheba worked hard to furnish her new home, but it was a challenge: the house contained twelve rooms, three halls, a cellar, and a wide front veranda on the north side. Bathsheba took in boarders to help provide the means for their task, and when the state legislature was in session, their house was full. This was a happy time for them all. The children took pleasure in having their friends come to visit with them, and almost every evening laughter and music would flow from their home. Young George played the flutina, flute, fife, and drum, and both children had good voices and liked to sing. When company came they would engage in singing, playing music, dancing, or reading good books. With her husband gone so much in his church callings, Bathsheba's children became the center of her life. She encouraged them in their studies and taught young Bathsheba and Julina to spin, weave, cook, sew, and knit. She would worry about them and plan for them. She loved to read to them in the evenings or to have young George play on the fiddle or other instrument to keep him from "going out with the boys."[31] She wanted her children to have a good education and to grow up in righteousness before the Lord.

It was in the summer of 1860 that George, Jr., accompanied his father in visiting the settlements in southern Utah. Shortly after their return young George received a mission call to teach Mormonism to the Mogui Indians with Jacob Hamblin; but before he had reached his destination, he was killed by Navajo Indians. There had always been a peaceful relationship between the Indians and the Mormon people, but a detachment of the United States Army had molested a Navajo village and had massacred about 250 old men, squaws, and children and had destroyed many head of sheep while the young men were on a hunt. George, Jr., and his companions who were traveling through the area were the first white men the Indians saw after this dreadful occurrence. Though his companions escaped, he did not.[32] His father, upon receiving the news, traveled from Provo to tell Bathsheba.

A few months after the death of young George, her daughter married Clarence Merrill. They lived only a year in Salt Lake City, and then moved to Fillmore. Bathsheba was now able to go with her husband on his travels. Many of these travels were done in company with President Brigham Young and his wife Amelia, as George was now a counselor to the president. Bathsheba enjoyed traveling to the settlements and visiting the Saints and being repeatedly met by bands of music and children bearing banners and flags and singing songs of welcome. George enjoyed having Bathsheba with him on these trips, since he suffered ill health. He had a lingering illness which seemed to stem from an accident in England when a lung had been punctured. Whenever he became overly tired or ill he would have complications. As her husband grew older, his condition became more severe.

If their journey took them to southern Utah, they would eventually find their way to Fillmore to see their grandchildren. If the grandchildren knew of their coming, they would run to meet them and be put in the traveling carriage by their grandmother who always said, "Hurrah!" by way of exclamation, since she considered "My Goodness!" or "Good Gracious!" as a mild form of swearing. Bathsheba was just as happy as her grandchildren were at these times and would make certain that she had her pretty flower-covered carpet sack in which there was sure to be gifts such as mittens, comforters, hoods, linsey (material for dresses), coats, and petticoats, all of Bathsheba's own making. To the grandchildren a visit from grandfather and grandmother was like an angels' visits.[33]

The last journey Bathsheba and George made together was to Provo, for he died about three weeks later. She loved him greatly, and her unselfish love is revealed in the words she wrote in her journal, after her husband's death.

He had a restless night, the following morning he walked into the front parlor twice.

The last time he sat down in his chair and expired in about five minutes after I could not think of my self I loved him more, he was now through all was quiet his head lay on against my bosom, good angels had come to receive his precious spirit perhaps our sons Prophets patriarchs saints beloved were there, but he was gone my light my Sun my life my joy my Lord yea almost my God but I must not morn but prepare myself to meet him but my hart sinks with in my bosom nearly.[34]

After his death Leila Merrill, a granddaughter, came to stay with Bathsheba to comfort her and to attend school. Bathsheba welcomed not only her own grandchildren into her home, but also welcomed the children of George's other wives. It was a treat to stay in the big, three-story home and ramble through its many rooms with carpet on every floor, including the halls and stairs. Many were spun and woven on the loom in beautiful color and design by Bathsheba's own hands.

At the age of eight Alice Merrill also went to stay with her grandmother and has given a detailed word picture of this home from which a few excerpts have been taken:

There were chairs and chairs; arm chairs, congress chairs, rocking chairs, great rustic porchchairs, children's chairs, carving chairs, dining chairs, bottomed chairs and kitchen chairs, painted red and among them the "money chair", named for its heaviness. All the arm chairs, rocking chairs and the congress chairs, everyone, were made inviting with a cushion, so that I, day after day went the round to find the most comfortable chair though ever remaining in doubt.

There were deep windows glassed with tiny panes, buff blinds with little hand painted scenes and on the bottom, a tassel. There were hangings of lace on gold cornices in the front parlor and bed rooms. The upper chamber windows were draped in muslin with fringe of hand made tassels. But I loved best, the drapes in the back parlor. From cornices of black and gold, white lace curtains draped over the top with green lambrequins, hung over the windows down to the floor and were drawn back with a heavy green cord and tassels.

A gas lamp stood on the great round center table and gas jets lighted the side walls. There were so many mirrors that I wondered if grandmother liked mirrors because she was so beautiful ... In the store room stood huge chests stuffed with wool comforters, quilts of unique patchwork and flower-strewn coverlids of grandmother's own design and handiwork ...

On the walls hung oil portraits of my grandparents and my great grandparents ...

Then there was the Historian Office itself, with quaint refined, gentle people writing in great books or pasting articles in scrapbooks ...

Best of all up stairs in the prayer-room there were two built-in cupboards stuffed with old magazines ... Here I browsed ... running to grandma for words with which I was unacquainted. She seemed never to tire of helping me.[35]

Bathsheba also had trunks neatly packed with many of her husband's mementoes, including his Sunday wig all curled and the green veil that shaded his eyes under southern Utah's glaring sun. She also had many other mementoes that her husband had brought back from his trips to Palestine, Greece, and Italy, including a flask of water from the Dead Sea and a number of tinted photographs. Bathsheba's book of drawings from her art class in Nauvoo and many items of her son's that were precious to her heart were also there.

Bathsheba continued her work in the church with the zeal and energy that characterized her more youthful days. She now divided her time between temple work and Relief Society work, becoming in 1888 a counselor to the general president of the Relief Society, Zina D. H. Young, which position she held until 1901, when she became general president of the Relief Society.

She encouraged the women of the church to be as self-sustaining as they could be, to raise as much of their own food as possible, to try and preserve their food, to card, spin, and weave, and to make their own clothing and to knit and embroider, and to otherwise enhance their surroundings, wherever they might be. In all this she set an example: she was noted for her punctuality and common sense talks and spent much of her time traveling through the territory in the cause and advancement of the Relief Society.

Bathsheba was among the group who organized the campaign for women's suffrage in Utah. Although she did not actively campaign for the movement or travel to Washington as did many of the younger women, she gave her support to the movement and let them use her name for its influence among the women. She said:

I hailed with joy the first gift of franchize to women and have never failed to use it nor to do anything in my power to secure and hold the right of equal suffrage in Utah.[36]

She built a small home in which she lived during the latter part of her life. She died at the age of eighty-eight in the home of her daughter, Bathsheba. Her funeral, attended by thousands, was held in the Tabernacle on Sunday, taking the place of the regular Sunday services.[37]

Thus Bathsheba completed what some may have considered a long, hard journey, but what to her had been an exciting adventure. It began in a lovely home in West Virginia, where, under her mother's guidance, she learned the art of Southern hospitality. She longed for a home where she could practice this art, thriving on her friendships with others and working hard to create a place of beauty where she would not be ashamed to invite her friends and where they would always feel welcome even in the trying circumstance of crossing the plains.

She lived through the Mormon expulsion from Missouri and the tragic events at Nauvoo, which experience became stamped indelibly on her character. She shared with her husband his apostolic callings and his missionary service. Her devotion to the church helped support her and give her courage, and although she saw and experienced many tragic events, instead of weakening her faith these daily trials seemed to strengthen her reliance upon the word of the Lord.

In her personal life she accepted and lived the Mormon doctrine of polygamy. And though there were times of stress and inner pangs of jealousy, deep concern, and loneliness, she took her part with her husband's other wives, sharing joys and sorrows and extending her love and support.

Notes

1. Bathsheba W. Smith Autobiography, p. 141, microfilm of holograph, Library-Archives of The Church of Jesus Christ of Latter-day Saints, hereafter referred to as LDS Church Archives.

2. *Ibid.*, p. 139.

3. George Albert Smith Journal, July 25, 1841, LDS Church Archives.

4. *Ibid.*, August 25, 1841.

5. Bathsheba W. Smith Autobiography, p. 148, microfilm of holograph, LDS Church Archives.

6. *Ibid.*, pp. 150-151.

7. "Journal History" June 12, 1903, pp. 4-5.

8. Affidavit Notarized by James Jack Notary Public — January 4, 1905. Bathsheba W. Smith Collection, LDS Church Archives.

9. Bathsheba W. Smith to Jacob T. Tanner, grandson of her brother, Jacob G. Bigler, Bathsheba W. Smith Collection, LDS Church Archives.

10. Bathsheba W. Smith Autobiography, p. 153, microfilm of holograph, LDS Church Archives.

11. *Ibid.*, p. 154.

12. Bathsheba Smith to George A. Smith, June 15, 1844, George A. Smith Collection, LDS Church Archives.

13. *Ibid.*, July 6, 1844.

14. Bathsheba W. Smith Autobiography, microfilm of holograph, LDS Church Archives.

15. Melissa Lambson to Bathsheba W. Smith, October 18, 1849, Bathsheba W. Smith Collection, LDS Church Archives.

16. Alice S. M. Horne memories, Bathsheba W. Smith Collection, LDS Church Archives.

17. Bathsheba W. Smith Autobiography, p. 159, LDS Church Archives.

18. Bathsheba W. Smith to George A. Smith, June 7, 1846,

George A. Smith Collection, LDS Church Archives.

19. *Ibid.*

20. Bathsheba W. Smith Autobiography, pp. 163-164, microfilm of holograph, LDS Archives.

21. *Ibid.*, p. 168.

22. Mary Isabella Horne, "Migration and Settlement of the Latter-day Saints," dictated memoir—microfilm of holograph, LDS Church Archives.

23. Bathsheba W. Smith Journal crossing the plains, October 3, 1849, microfilm of holograph, LDS Church Archives.

24. Bathsheba W. Smith Autobiography, p. 176, microfilm of holograph, LDS Church Archives.

25. Bathsheba W. Smith to George A. Smith, April 13, 1851, George A. Smith Collection, LDS Church Archives.

26. *Ibid.*, June 1, 1851.

27. *Ibid.*, June 12, 1851.

28. *Ibid.*, July 12, 1851.

29. *Ibid.*, August 1851.

30. Julina L. Smith memories attached to Bathsheba W. Smith Autobiography, LDS Church Archives.

31. Bathsheba W. Smith to George A. Smith, February 4, 1857, George A. Smith Collection, LDS Church Archives.

32. Bathsheba W. Smith Autobiography, pp. 187-188, microfilm of holograph, LDS Church Archives.

33. Alice Merrill Horne—"Child of the Frontier," typescript, LDS Church Archives.

34. Bathsheba W. Smith Autobiography, p. 40, typescript, LDS Church Archives.

35. Alice Merrill Horne—"School Days," typescript, LDS Church Archives.

36. Bathsheba W. Smith, "Reminiscences of Nauvoo," Bathsheba W. Smith Collection, LDS Church Archives.

37. "Journal History," September 24, 1910, p. 10; September 25, 1910.

Aurelia Read Spencer Rogers 1834–1922

*A homemaker residing in Ogden,
Utah, Elizabeth Kohler Ritchie is
married to Dee R. Ritchie and they
are the parents of eight children. An
active member of The Church of Jesus
Christ of Latter-day Saints, she is
currently president of her ward
Primary, having worked in this
organization for eighteen years.
Piano and vocal music are her special
interests, and she teaches several
music students. She attended Utah
State University and for several years
taught LDS high school seminary
students in Wyoming.*

Aurelia S. Rogers

Elizabeth Kohler Ritchie

A look at the lives of some of our heroines suggests that fame and acclaim were byproducts of their lives, not goals. Living was an effort to exist and to help others exist. Desire to please extended only to those in the immediate area and to God.

Aurelia Read Spencer Rogers is one of these heroines. She never planned for honor, yet she carried the idea in her heart, and finally spoke; it took root, and grew. The Primary organization of The Church of Jesus Christ of Latter-day Saints sprang from the concern of an ordinary pioneer woman for young boys. "Could there not be an organization for little boys wherein they could be taught everything good, and how to behave?"[1]

Aurelia Read Spencer Rogers, described by one biographer "as simple and as humble as a sparrow" (Ashton 1970, p. 5.), was born October 4, 1843, at Deep River, Connecticut, the third child of eight born to Orson and Catherine Curtis Spencer. Her father, a Baptist minister, was considered a highly educated man in those days, having earned two college degrees. Soon after Aurelia's birth the family moved to Middlefield, Massachusetts. Here Aurelia began school "at an early age." One day while playing she fell from a hay loft in the barn; for the rest of her life she suffered with a stomach ailment that she blamed on this incident.

In 1840 the family was visited in Middlefield by Daniel Spencer, Aurelia's uncle. He had accepted baptism into The Church of Jesus Christ of Latter-day Saints and came with the expressed intention of converting his minister brother. Many evenings were spent in discussion and prayer. On one such evening Catherine said to her husband, "Orson, you know this is true!"[2] He acknowledged that he did; a short time later the couple was baptized.

America's constitution makes provision for religious freedom, but it is not surprising that Orson Spencer fought his own knowledge of the truthfulness of this new faith. To accept meant baptism, and baptism meant giving up his livelihood. Mormonism promised the scorn and derision of old friends. It meant selling his property, including his library of choice books, and moving his family to the frontier. But once convinced that he was doing right, nothing could turn him from this purpose.

Aurelia's mother was from an affluent family. When she was baptized, her share of her father's estate was revoked. Some of her friends offered comfort and abundance if she would leave the Mormons and come home; her reply was, "No, if they will withhold from me the supplies they readily granted to my sisters and brothers, because I adhere to the Saints, let them. I would rather abide with the Church in poverty, even in the wilderness, without their aid, than go to my unbelieving father's house and have all that he possesses."[3] At the age of thirty-five, a short four years later, this valiant woman met her death in the severe cold as the Saints were driven from Nauvoo, Illinois.

The impact of Mormonism on Aurelia's life began that day her uncle visited. To conjecture what might have been her lifestyle had this event not occurred is fruitless. The fact remains that the course of her life and that of her posterity was unalterably changed.

After giving up a paid Baptist ministry and a salary which "kept his family comfortably," Orson Spencer by turns worked as a storekeeper, school teacher, missionary, newspaper editor, elected official, and college chancellor. They joined the Saints in Nauvoo where the Mormons prospered and the swamp was turned into a beautiful city.

While in Nauvoo Orson's parents lived with the family. Aurelia learned a habit at her grandmother's knee: it was common in those days for old people to smoke, and her grandmother would often ask Aurelia to light her pipe. In so doing Aurelia learned to smoke and came to enjoy it. This she innocently indulged in for several years. She writes, "There was a monitor within that told me it was wrong, and what it would lead to if persisted in; I should be, if I lived, an old lady smoker."[4] This thought so disgusted her that she broke the habit.

The peace and comfort of the Saints at Nauvoo was short-lived. After the murder of the Prophet Joseph Smith and his brother Hyrum, plans were made by the Mormons to move to a place where their enemies would not follow, a place undesirable to others. In the dead of winter the Mormons crossed the Mississippi River into Iowa. From Garden Grove to Mt. Pisgah to Council Bluffs, the Mormons moved slowly and painfully westward.

While the family was at Council Bluffs, Aurelia's father was called on a mission to England; it would be his task there to edit the *Millennial Star*, a Mormon periodical. He took his brood of seven motherless children across the Missouri River to Winter Quarters (Florence), Nebraska, where he put up a log cabin for them. James and Mary Bullock, friends whose cabin faced the Spencer dwelling, were asked to watch over the children in his absence. (Years later, after the death of her husband, Mary Bullock lived in polygamy as Orson Spencer's fifth wife.)

Orson Spencer left his children with what he thought was a good supply of provisions. Aurelia, thirteen, and her older sister, Ellen, only fourteen, took the parts of mother and father and cared for the four younger children. Because of the severity of that first winter, the supplies dwindled. Their horse, which was to be sold in the spring for supplies, died, and seven of the eight cows succumbed to cold and hunger. Many times the children were hungry and suffered from the cold. Aurelia sometimes went without supper so that her hunger would be great enough to make corn meal mush palatable the next day. The Bullocks lost two children with scurvy that first winter, but the Spencer children were spared.

Here at Winter Quarters Aurelia continued her education. Sister Louisa Pratt taught a school that the Spencer children attended. Jane Dudson, who lived across the street from the Spencers, gave Aurelia her first lessons in dressmaking, a skill valuable in later years. Not only did Aurelia sew clothing for her own family, but at times she helped support them by sewing for others.

Their father wrote to his little ones and sent them money. The letters arrived but never the money, although many times the letters were delivered in person. Seeing the plight of these young children did not soften the hearts of the money thieves; Aurelia wrote in her autobiography of her father's displeasure with his trusted friends who did not keep his trust. However, she left blanks where names would have broadcast the guilty.

The letters, however, contained encouragement, advice, and counsel. One such letter read in part:

Now my beloved children, love one another and strive to please each other and don't mind little offenses, but forgive and bear with each other's faults; pray often and be not angry nor contentious with anybody... When you are not well, fast and eat light food... Wash your bodies often in pure water, and comb your heads, that from the head to the feet you may be clean and healthy... Trust to the counsel of those who are set over you in the Lord. (Rogers 1898, p. 54-55.)

Another gave this advice:

Never yield to sin or do anything that you would be ashamed to ask God about or tell me of. Let no one entice you to do wrong, whoever it may be... Learn to trust in the Lord for all good things, and to be thankful for all favors.[6]

These admonitions came from a loving father who felt helpless thousands of miles away from his children. Often they were in answer to a plea for help from his older daughters in disciplining the younger children.

Wilford Woodruff visited the children and, upon seeing their dire circumstances, brought them provisions. He wrote their father a letter which said in part:

> When I considered what they had passed through, their young and tender ages, the share they had taken in the sufferings of the Saints, I regarded them not only a company of young pilgrims, but a company of young martyrs; and although in childhood, their faith, patience, forebearance and longsuffering and wisdom in the midst of all their trials, was such as would have done honor to a Saint of thirty years in the strength and power of his days, or been a crown of glory upon the grey hairs of him of riper years. A parent may well consider such a family of children a blessing from God.[7]

Brigham Young visited the family one day on business. "What would you say if I asked your father to remain another year in England?" was his question.

Ellen answered, "If it is thought best we would like it so, for we want to do for the best."[8]

President Young promised the Spencer children that he would personally see that they got to the Salt Lake Valley. When Orson Spencer returned to America at the end of three years, his family had emigrated to the Salt Lake Valley with Brigham Young's 1848 company. He had sent a letter of advice for the journey:

> Be cautious in regard to the hostile Indians, serpents, and dangerous roots and herbs, . . . Never forget or slight my counsel, for this is a commandment of God. I think I write to you according to the mind of God. I am not permitted to speak face to face, but I write unto you as a father with soberness and godly fear.[9]

In the valley the children had settled in a cabin built by their Uncle Daniel. That first winter Aurelia converted the one-room home into a veritable factory. She was very industrious and sewed clothes for the family and neighbors. She also braided attractive bracelets and necklaces out of horsehair; these she sold readily, bringing in a little money for the family. Ellen and Aurelia attended Hiram B. Clawson's writing school two nights a week.

Their second winter in the valley was made happy by the return of their father. Orson Spencer had married while in England and had brought his wife and a baby girl with him. He was appointed chancellor of the new University of Deseret and Aurelia became one of the first students. Wheat, potatoes, flour, building rock, and lumber were taken in for tuition. Being an educated man, Orson Spencer encouraged his children in their educational pursuits.

While on his mission his letters contained this counsel:

> Go to school as much as you can ... I want Catherone to learn to write ... I should like to have the girls and also Howard pay particular attention to arithmetic.[10]

Six months after her father's return from England, and against his wishes, Ellen married Hiram Clawson in polygamy. In 1851 Aurelia, at age seventeen, married Thomas Rogers. Their courtship must have started on the journey westward, where Thomas was a driver with the 1848 company. Aurelia and Thomas set up housekeeping in a two-room log cabin in Farmington, Utah.

Though her new life was secure compared to that she had led in Winter Quarters, it was not a life of plenty. Culinary water was carried from a stream down a small hill from her home. The roof was of willows, and on the dirt floor was a homemade carpet. Her vanity table was a dry goods box, held by pegs and covered with a cloth. In her kitchen she had four chairs, a table, and a cupboard. She cooked over a fireplace. Her one luxury was a set of china brought by her father from England. Her floor was scrubbed with sand, and when her broom wore out she used willows until a new one could be purchased. In spite of hardship and many seemingly insurmountable problems, Aurelia was "as happy as a bird."[11] She believed that "the Lord is pleased with lovely homes and when they are made beautiful with the workmanship of our own hands it is gratifying to behold or to reflect upon them."[12]

Because of her lifestyle and lasting contributions, Aurelia was capable of strong emotional expression. Her relationship with her husband is worth contemplating, for there is silence regarding it in her autobiography. True, she only recorded strong emotion twice: her anguish and despair at the death of a child and her intense feelings about the local boys and their need for help in learning to behave better. Yet, she lauds the virtues of her children and tells of the kindness of her brothers-in-law, while references to her husband are very brief and strictly factual.

Another gap in her writing is her attitude toward polygamy, for though she was meticulous in observing and mentioning the various laws of the church, she is silent on this one. Polygamy was all about Aurelia. Her father had four wives. Ellen and Catherine were plural wives; we know of Ellen's resignation toward her status, expressed in her letters to Ellen Pratt McGary. And we know that Aurelia had some religious social status, for Eliza R. Snow and Emmeline B. Wells paid her a visit that day when the idea of Primary was conceived, and she was honored by an appointment to attend the Woman's Suffrage Convention with all expenses paid. Ellen's husband, Hiram Clawson, was in the high echelons of the church. Catherine's husband was Brigham Young, Jr. Was Thomas' status equal to his wife's, and if so, why was he not called to live this higher law as were other men of position and respect? Or was he called?

A few months after moving to Farmington, Thomas and Aurelia bought a farm, and the next spring they built a sixteen by fourteen-foot frame house. Their first child, Orson, was born here. When he was six weeks old Aurelia became ill. She writes, "I had spells of the same sickness the rest of my life, causing poor health the greater part of my life."[13] Aurelia spent much time convalescing, with the attendant hours for thought and introspection, taking courage each time she seemed to be getting well again. At times she referred to her illnesses as "distressed spells," alluding to mental as well as physical distress. Perhaps there were times when these convalescing periods filled her need to be mothered and taken care of. Her sisters often cared for Aurelia during illnesses and brought comfort to her in time of sorrow.

My sisters, Ellen and Catherine, have acted the part of mother to me; they being better off as to this world's goods, have helped me to many needed comforts; and my brothers-in-law Hiram B. Clawson and Brigham Young Jr., have been just as kind, for I have had occasion to stay at their houses weeks at a time, when sick or troubled, mostly at their expense, and never heard a word of complaint. They were ever ready to get anything necessary to make me comfortable.[14]

Aurelia named children after her father, her father-in-law, her three sisters, and her two brothers.

During the summer of 1855 the grasshoppers robbed the Mormons of their crops, and Aurelia worked alongside her husband trying to save them. They dug ditches and drove the pests into the ditches covering them with dirt or water. There was much suffering from hunger. Flour was scarce. Aurelia took in sewing to help financially, and she also taught school in her home for two or three terms.

Aurelia liked teaching. As a child she had often gone to the woodshed and played at teaching school, using sticks of wood for scholars. She believed her "forte would be to teach children" if she had been educated for it. She became a great teacher, but did not teach in the public schools.

In 1858 Aurelia and her family left their home and traveled to Springville, Utah, seventy-five miles away. Johnston's Army (the Utah Expedition) was coming, and Brigham Young had counseled the saints:

Our duty to ourselves, to our families, requires us not to tamely submit to be driven and slain without an attempt to preserve ourselves.[15]

All persons were to flee from the cities. Guards were left to burn the homes and crops if necessary.

Five months later Aurelia and Thomas returned to their home. No life had been lost in the "Echo Canyon War." This time the Mormons would not have to move and homestead a new area.

Aurelia bore twelve children, seven of whom grew to adulthood, five of whom died in infancy. After Howard, her fourth child, died at fourteen months of age, Aurelia was ill all that winter and nearly died. She writes:

I had been so happy previous to this; the trials of poverty and sickness that we had passed through were nothing compared to this great sorrow that had overtaken me; and I mourned for my babe incessantly.[16]

Little Catherine died at three months of age of whooping cough. The following winter Aurelia was again very ill. In the spring she took three-year-old Lucy and went to visit her sister Ellen, who lived in Salt Lake City. While there Lucy became ill with measles and scarlet fever and Ellen's baby, Ivy, contracted the diseases. Ellen had already buried four children, and Aurelia blamed herself for bringing this trial to her loved ones. One night when Ivy was especially ill Aurelia prayed fervently that God would spare the lives of both girls, "but if either child was to be taken it might be mine." While anxiously wondering "if the Lord had indeed forsaken us, all at once a change came over me; everything seemed so lovely and beautiful, and I was as happy as could be for a few minutes."[17] Both children lived.

While still with Ellen, Aurelia gave birth to a premature child. Little Joseph lived only five hours. Two years later she lost another child, three-month-old William, who died of cholera. Of this sadness she wrote in her diary, "I almost lost faith. For once in my life I even doubted the existence of a Supreme Being." Then she remembered what her father had written in a letter: "Trust in God though he slay you." She repented of her lack of faith and began praying again.

I felt that perhaps all the people of God would have to pass through certain ordeals to prove whether they would trust in Him to the end.[18]

She gave birth to two more children, both of whom lived.

Aurelia was shown great love and devotion by her children. She wrote:

Although settled in life, and rearing a family of his own, Orson does not forget the love and duty he has ever shown his parents, but is still thoughtful of their comfort, and always ready to help them when necessary. My other children, both boys and girls, do all in their power to make their father and mother comfortable.[19]

At one time Loce (pronounced Lacy) and George hauled logs for a new room on her house; George worked to "raise means to furnish the room." Loce was once rewarded with two hundred dollars after returning a large sum of money he had found to its owner; he sent one hundred dollars to his parents. (Incidentally, of the other hundred dollars, sixty dollars went to his wife's parents, twenty dollars went to the church as a tithe, and he kept the remaining twenty dollars for his own use.)

In June of 1869 Aurelia bade farewell to her husband as he left on a mission to Europe. She had a two-month-old baby at the time. Sons Orson and Loce, at ages seventeen and fifteen, took over the farm work. Thomas returned home one year later, earlier than expected due to health problems associated with the climate.

In addition to her contributions to her own posterity, Aurelia also made an unforgettable contribution for good in the lives of many children. For it was from her timidly pronounced idea that the Primary organization of The Church of Jesus Christ of Latter-day Saints sprang. In the history of the Primary, written by Aurelia Rogers, she states:

I was always an earnest thinker, and naturally of a religious turn of mind. And for some time previous to the organization of the children I had reflected seriously upon the necessity of more strict discipline for our little boys. Many of them were allowed to be out late at night; and certainly some of the larger ones well deserved the undesirable name of 'hoodlum'.[20]

She called her age one of "carelessness in religion and morality":

Why should anything be allowed to come before the most sacred duty of parentage, that of looking after the spiritual welfare of the children? was the question which burdened my mind.[21]

She acknowledged that time was precious to a pioneer and was mostly given to making a living and to accomplishing daily activities of keeping a home.

The query then arose in my mind, could there not be an organization for little boys wherein they could be taught everything good, and how to behave?[22]

In 1878 Eliza R. Snow and Emmeline B. Wells of Salt Lake City came to Farmington to attend a Relief Society conference. After the meetings they stopped at Aurelia's home to visit. The topic soon turned to the "rough, careless ways of many young men and boys." Aurelia told them her concerns and her idea.[23]

Eliza R. Snow was impressed; she promised to present the idea

to John Taylor, the president of the Church, and others of the
Council of the Twelve. The brethren readily gave their approval.
Eliza Snow then wrote to Aurelia's bishop, John W. Hess, explaining the matter to him. He visited Aurelia and asked her to organize and preside over this new organization. Aurelia wrote:

> I felt willing, but very incompetent. From that time my mind was busy thinking
> how it was to be managed.[24]

In a public meeting on Sunday, August 11, 1878, Aurelia Read
Spencer Rogers' name was presented to the church members in
her ward area of Farmington as the leader of this new organization to be called the Primary. The members unanimously raised
their hands in approval. After the meeting hands were laid on Aurelia's head, and Bishop Hess gave her a blessing. Aurelia decided
that the meetings would not be complete without the girls. "Singing was necessary, it needed the voices of little girls as well as boys
to make it sound as well as it should."[25] She chose Louisa Haight
and Helen Miller as counselors. A visit was made by these women
to all the homes in the area to gather the names of the children of
suitable age and to explain the program to the parents. There
were 224 eligible children. The first Primary meeting held on August 25, 1878, was attended by 112 girls and 112 boys between the
ages of six and fourteen.

These early organizational days were a period of groping.

> While thinking over what was to be done for the best good of the children, I
> seemed to be carried away in the spirit, or at least I experienced a feeling of untold
> happiness which lasted three days and nights. During that time nothing could worry
> or irritate me; if my little ones were fretful, or the work went wrong, I had patience,
> could control in kindness, and manage my household affairs easily. This was a testi-
> mony to me that what was being done was from God.[26]

Soon after this she was "nearly overcome" by an opposite power.
She felt her extreme unworthiness and wrote:

> I was being humbled to the very earth; so much so, that whatever anyone said af-
> terward in my praise did not make me feel exalted, or lifted up in my own mind. I
> had been made to feel my entire dependence on God the Eternal Father.[27]

She later recorded,

> If anyone should ask me what I would desire above all other things, if I could
> have my wish; the answer would be without any hesitation, a fullness of the Spirit of
> God, for that includes everything my heart could desire.[28]

This new organization was much the same as it is today. The
children were taught obedience, honesty, faith in God, prayer,
punctuality, and good manners; they learned stories from the

scriptures; the girls were taught crafts and homemaking skills. Programs were presented during the year so that the parents could come and see what the children were learning. "We always endeavored," said Aurelia, "to impress the children with the fact that home is the place to begin to practice all good things."[29] Mothers reported they could see a change for the better in their children.

Shortly afterwards another Primary was started in the Eleventh Ward in Salt Lake City. Soon Primary associations became part of all the local ecclesiastical divisions or wards of the Mormon Church. It was a children's weekday auxiliary to the Sunday School and sacrament meeting that were held each Sunday. In 1880 Aurelia became president of the Primaries in the Davis Stake. In that same year the church authorities thought it best to have someone preside over all the Primaries of the church. Because Eliza R. Snow thought the new president should reside in Salt Lake City, Aurelia suggested Louie B. Felt. To be a leader of the central auxiliaries was a great honor in Mormondom, and some thought Aurelia should have been asked to assume this position. But,

I never had a moment's jealousy over anyone holding office; for no person will ever take my honors from me. I shall have all that I deserve.[30]

Later Aurelia was called to be a member of the Primary general board. She retired when age and ill health prevented further activity, but was retained as an honorary member until her death.

As she grew older Aurelia's contribution to the church and to the children was recognized. She was rewarded with love from many. The town held a program and celebration in her honor, and on this occasion a testimonial was given by a former Primary pupil. It read in part:

The joy that we realized in becoming acquainted with the Spirit of God, the simple but honest resolutions that entered our minds, cannot be too highly appreciated. I think that I speak for all faithful members of the Primary when I say that much of our happiness or prosperity, and ambition to become good and useful, is due to the valuable instructions and encouragement received in the Primary Association.[31]

In 1894 the Women's Suffrage Association of Davis County elected Aurelia as a delegate to the national convention to be held in Atlanta, Georgia, in 1895, and they raised the money for her expenses. The seven-week trip began with a three-and-one-half-day train trip east over much the same route she had traveled by covered wagon as a girl. At the convention she served on the committee of resolutions, and after the convention she attended the

Second Triennial Congress of the National Council of Women in Washington, D.C.

Again a biographer feels rather frustrated. The suffrage movement was very intense during this period of time, but Aurelia calls her position as a delegate to the convention an "honor," writing verbosely about the terrain, buildings, other meetings, celebrations attended, and so on, but recording very little of the convention.

She was once mistaken for Susan B. Anthony, and her analysis of this seems typical of her:

> *Miss Anthony is tall and thin, wears glasses and is not very handsome, so I thought I might look like her... but when she smiled, and began talking to the ladies, the expression of her face was lovely. And the next day at the convention, she walked with such grace, and presided with such dignity, that I felt quite honored with the possible resemblance.*[32]

Her succinct evaluation of the Atlanta sessions:

> *A spirit of kindness and good will prevailed. They were advocating the cause of humanity, and wanted the poor and suffering looked after.*[33]

Her contribution to the Congress in Washington was reported in part as follows:

> *The ladies from Utah had part of two evenings to deliver their speeches and read their papers ... I had the honor of offering the opening prayer ... "The Spirit of Reform Reduced to Practice," by Mrs. Lula Greene Richards, was a paper which I should have read, but it was omitted for want of time.*[34]

Her feelings on returning home were these:

> *I have heard of people going to Italy or Switzerland to take a view of the beautiful scenery, but our own mountain home furnishes much of interest to look at, if we could only find opportunities of visiting, and then appreciate the grandeur of nature near us.*[35]

Perhaps the shortness of her record on the political happenings of this trip speaks eloquently of Aurelia's desire to be known as the "Mother" of the Primary, not as a "political activist."

After being a widow for twenty-six years, Aurelia Rogers died on August 19, 1922, at eighty-seven years of age. She left behind a loving posterity and a lasting contribution to children — as one biographer put it, "a model life for every Primary girl to pattern after."[36] To the end she was thinking of others. She requested for her bier:

> *... just a few blossoms from my own garden. If anyone has any money to spend for flowers for me, it would make me happier to have it given to comfort someone in need.*[37]

Her passing came six days after the forty-fourth anniversary of the founding of the Primary. She was survived by seven children, twenty-nine grandchildren, forty-seven great-grandchildren, and seventy thousand Primary children.

Notes

1. Rogers, Aurelia S., *Life Sketches of Orson Spencer and Others, and History of Primary Work,* Geo. Q. Cannon and Sons Co., Salt Lake City, Utah, 1898, p. 207.

2. *Ibid.*, p. 16.

3. *Ibid.*, pp. 36-37.

4. *Ibid.*, p. 27.

5. *Ibid.*, pp. 54-55.

6. *Ibid.*, pp. 69-70.

7. *Ibid.*, pp. 103-104.

8. Ashton, Wendell J., *Theirs is the Kingdom, Aurelia Spencer Rogers, Primary Mother,* Bookcraft, Salt Lake City, Utah, 1945, p. 18.

9. Rogers, *Life Sketches,* p. 71.

10. *Ibid.*, pp. 55, 65, 73.

11. *Ibid.*, p. 126.

12. *Ibid.*, p. 229.

13. *Ibid.*, p. 128.

14. *Ibid.*, pp. 171-172.

15. Carter, Kate B., *Heart Throbs of the West,* Daughters of the Utah Pioneers, Salt Lake City, Utah, 1940, vol. 2, p. 407.

16. Rogers, *Life Sketches,* p. 163.

17. *Ibid.*, p. 170.

18. *Ibid.*, p. 180.
19. *Ibid.*, pp. 175-176.

20. *Ibid.*, p. 205.

21. *Ibid.*, p. 206.

22. *Ibid.*, p. 207.

23. *Ibid.*, p. 208.

24. *Ibid.*, p. 209.

25. *Ibid.*, p. 209.

26. *Ibid.*, p. 212.

27. *Ibid.*, p. 214.

28. *Ibid.*, p. 256.

29. *Ibid.*, pp. 215-216.

30. *Ibid.*, p. 223.

31. *Ibid.*, p. 262.

32. *Ibid.*, p. 304.

33. *Ibid.,* p. 305.

34. *Ibid.*, p. 316.

35. *Ibid.*, p. 251.

36. Barrett, Ivan L., *Heroines of the Church, Aurelia S. Rogers*M*Builder of Youth,* Brigham Young University, Provo, Utah, 1956, p. 67.

37. *Ibid.*, p. 68.

Bibliography

Ashton, Wendell J., *Theirs Is the Kingdom, Aurelia Spencer Rogers*м*Primary Mother*, Bookcraft, Salt Lake City, Utah, 1945.

Barrett, Ivan L., *Heroines of the Church, Aurelia S. Rogers*м*Builder of Youth*, Brigham Young University, Provo, Utah, 1956.

Carter, Kate B., *Heart Throbs of the West*, Daughters of the Utah Pioneers, Salt Lake City, Utah. 1940.

Carter, Kate B., *Our Pioneer Heritage*, Daughters of Utah Pioneers, Salt Lake City, Utah, 1970.

Carter, Kate B., *Treasures of Pioneer History*, Daughters of Utah Pioneers, Salt Lake City, Utah, 1952.

Clark, Amasa L., "A Tribute to Aurelia S. Rogers—Beloved Primary Founder" *Children's Friend*, Primary Association of The Church of Jesus Christ of Latter-day Saints, Salt Lake City, Utah, August, 1966.

Crocheron, Augusta Joyce, *Representative Women of Deseret*, J. C. Graham and Co., Salt Lake City, Utah, 1884.

Deseret News, Aurelia S. Rogers obituary, Deseret News Press, Salt Lake City, Utah, August 21, 1922.

Ellsworth, S. George, *Dear Ellen, Two Mormon Women and Their Letters*, University of Utah, Tanner Trust Fund, Salt Lake City, Utah, 1974.

Esshom, Frank, *Pioneers and Prominent Men of Utah*, Utah Pioneers Book Publishing Co., Salt Lake City, Utah, 1913.

Freeze, Lillie F., "Aurelia Spencer Rogers," *Children's Friend*, General Board of The Church of Jesus Christ of Latter-day Saints, Salt Lake City, Utah, November, 1922.

Irvine, Arnold, "Aurelia Rogers Credited With Idea for Church Primaries," Church News Section of *Deseret News*, Deseret News Press, Salt Lake City, Utah, December 28, 1963.

Jenson, Andrew, *Latter-Day Saint Biographical Encyclopedia*, Andrew Jenson History Co., Salt Lake City, Utah, 1901.

Morgan, Nicholas G., *Eliza R. Snow, An Immortal*, Nicholas G. Morgan Sr. Foundation, Salt Lake City, Utah, 1957.

Reading, Lucile C., "Shining Moments," *Children's Friend*, Primary

Association of The Church of Jesus Christ of Latter-day Saints, Salt Lake City, Utah, August, 1962.

Reading, Lucile C., "The Surprise Party," *Children's Friend*, Primary Association of The Church of Jesus Christ of Latter-day Saints, Salt Lake City, Utah, August, 1970.

Rogers, Aurelia S., *Life Sketches of Orson Spencer and Others, and History of Primary Work,* Geo. Q. Cannon and Sons Co., Salt Lake City, Utah, 1898.

Romney, Thomas C., "Representative Women of the church—Aurelia Spencer Rogers" *Instructor*, Deseret Sunday School Union of The Church of Jesus Christ of Latter-day Saints, Salt Lake City, Utah, March 1950.

Ida Ione Cook 1851–Death date unavailable

Mary E. Cook 1835–Death date unavailable

Jill Mulvay Derr, the author of this essay, was introduced preceding her essay on Sarah Melissa Granger Kimball.

Mary and Ida Cook

Jill Mulvay Derr

In the fall of 1870 some three hundred and fifty teachers opened schools in the Utah Territory. A few have been remembered in local histories, and one or two have been preserved in bronze. Midst the forgotten hundreds are Misses Mary and Ida Cook, highly trained and professional teachers whose impact on students and teachers was felt in Utah for almost three decades.

Less than a block of walking brought Mary Cook and her students from the Social Hall to Brigham Young's schoolhouse in October 1870. The two Salt Lake City teachers, Miss Cook and Mrs. Mildred E. Randall, had decided to combine their classes for an *exhibition,* a program of student recitations. The occasion caught the attention and commendation of *Deseret News* editor George Q. Cannon, who returned to the Social Hall a month later to see the pupils of Mary Cook and her sister Ida, this time taking with him Latter-day Saint Church President Brigham Young and two other church officials, George A. Smith and Albert Carrington.

"We remained while the classes were exercised in reading and in geography, and were much gratified at the manner in which the lessons were conducted," Cannon reported. Apparently he sensed that Utahns needed some introduction to the Cooks, since he explained that they had recently come from St. Louis, where Mary Cook had just "declined an advantageous offer of salary" to come to Salt Lake City. The sisters possessed what must have been impressive credentials to both Mormons and non-Mormons in the community, where district schools were sadly lacking qualified teachers: both were graduates of New York state normal schools. Cannon rightly predicted that it would not be long before their classes would contain all the scholars they could conveniently hold, and in the next few years hundreds of children found their way to the Social Hall school.[1]

At first imposing a graded system upon the irregularly schooled Utah children must have exasperated the cultured Cook sisters. "They found a sad mixture of [skills] among their pupils, some far advanced in one study and far behind in others, no order, no uniformity, no regular books, and they had quite a struggle to grade their school properly, the pupils rebelling against such an unheard of system," recalled a Social Hall scholar years later.[2] Confusion eventually gave way to order and uniformity, but not necessarily to boredom. Students familiar with the basic reading, spelling, arithmetic, and grammar that formed the core of the Cooks' curriculum found regular respite in dramatic and gymnastic exercises conducted on the stage of the old Social Hall.[3] And there were excursions, probably equally enlightening to the teacher-sisters who were new to Salt Lake City and to their young students. One spring the classes traveled north up City Creek Canyon, and the following spring they took a train excursion south to Draper. Ever ready to make these well-trained teachers a model to other teachers throughout the territory, the press constantly publicized and praised the Cooks' efforts. In reference to the Draper excursion, "Miss Ida Cook," the *News* was informed, "learned after getting on the last up train, that some of the excursionists were left behind and fearing that they might be children, actually got out at Sandy station and walked back to Draper, a distance of four miles, that she might remain with them all night."[4]

The *Deseret News,* published by the Mormon Church, seems surprisingly supportive of Mary and Ida Cook, considering the usual Mormon disdain for non-Mormon teachers. It should be noted, however, that Mary was apparently studying the Book of Mormon when she came to Utah, or at least began studying it shortly after her arrival. The two sisters were baptized members of The Church of Jesus Christ of Latter-day Saints early in 1871.[5]

By spring 1871 the expertise of the Cooks had been noted by University of Deseret chancellor Daniel H. Wells, who decided with the regency's permission to employ the Cooks at the university. At this time the University of Deseret (later renamed the University of Utah) offered two courses of study: collegiate and normal. An academic department served as a high school where students were primed for their college course work, and a primary department provided a model school where normal students could practice-teach. The Cooks were to be employed in connection with the academic and primary departments. University president John R. Park and Chancellor Wells made Mary Cook an offer: she clearly stated her terms, and Park arranged classes to meet her requirements.[6] In less than a month Mary E. Cook was named principal of the university's model graded school, Mrs. Randall's classes at the Brigham Young schoolhouse were incorporated as a grade in the school, and the model school itself was moved to the Social Hall.

Later that spring John Park ordered publication of the University of Deseret's third annual catalog for the school year 1871-72. Along with the instructors listed for the collegiate courses, Ida Cook was listed as an instructor in the academic department and Mary Cook was listed as principal of the primary department (or model school). But before the summer was out the regency asked Park to abandon his plans for a collegiate course. Karl G. Maeser, Dan Weggeland, and others who had been scheduled to teach college courses were excused, and Park himself was summoned by church authorities to leave on an education mission to visit schools in the eastern United States and in Europe. M. H. Hardy was to take charge of the model school and the academic department for the year that Park was away; Hardy soon resigned, and the responsibility fell to Mary and Ida Cook. The primary grades continued under Mary at the Social Hall, and Ida moved her academic classes to the Council House a block and a half from her older sister's school.

Feramorz Young, son of President Brigham Young and anxious thirteen-year-old candidate for the United States Naval Academy at Annapolis, studied under Ida Cook in the Council House during the winter of 1871-72. A small diary he kept during this period provides glimpses of his curriculum and his instructress. He used Colburn's arithmetic, Cornell's geography, Greene's grammar, Quachenbo's composition, Anderson's United States history, and Wilson's speller—the same books territorial superintendent Robert L. Campbell recommended in 1868 in an effort to get teachers to adopt uniform texts. At one point Feramorz lamented that he had "nearly lost spirit in school it being very dull," but a few days later he wrote proudly that he was "thoroughly established in the following lessons": history of the map and physical geography of North America, fractions, and extracts from the national fifth reader. Feramorz admired Ida's thoroughness and dedication, and when she was ill and her sister Mary took the class he simply commented that "Miss Cook is not well enough acquainted to teach us as Miss Ida does."[7]

The academic year closed in the spring of 1872 with the Cooks having run up a $1,643.10 deficit, due mostly to delinquent tuition fees; 662 students had been enrolled during the year, an indication that the Cooks had significant administrative responsibilities in supervising teaching assistants.[8] The next fall the university opened under the principalship of Mary Cook, but Dr. Park returned in November, and when spring term opened in February he again took charge. Park had been frustrated by the delay in setting up his collegiate course and was anxious to make the university an academic institution, less concerned for the time being with normal training and the model school. So even though during the 1872-73 school year the Cooks' school at the Social Hall was announced as part of the university, its students were never recorded in the official university books and it was not considered an integral part of the university.[9]

But the sisters and their scholars at the Social Hall had by this time gained an unimpeachable reputation for excellence, and the Social Hall school was well supported for the next five or six years. The school was large and continued to require numerous assistants, providing opportunities for normal training that became almost as significant as the actual training of the younger pupils. Emmeline B. Wells, Mormon *Woman's Exponent* editor, praised Mary Cook's system, which "prepared many young ladies well for practical work as teachers, giving several an opportunity to assist her, and thus having the benefit of her supervision and suggestions to fit them better for other spheres of labor."[10] The Cooks concerned themselves with other aspects of normal training in Salt Lake City, conducting normal classes for the teachers' association and making presentations at one- and two-week normal institutes held for teachers in the territory during the summers and early falls.[11]

Mary and Ida Cook did not continue long as a team, and their later lives in Utah are best illustrated in terms of their individual achievements. Mary Elizabeth Cook, an *apostle of education* as Utah historian Edward Tullidge would ordain her, was thirty-five years old when she arrived in Salt Lake City. Staid, quiet, and dependable, her poised temperament and able handling of the University of Deseret during the year of John Park's absence placed her in the public eye and won her the respect and confidence of citizen-parents and leaders. John Park hired Mary to work with him and John Morgan in recommending a program for grading territorial schools, and for some years she served on the executive committee for Salt Lake City's teachers' association. The model teacher in the minds of many individuals, not only did she teach a normal course for Sunday School teachers, but Latter-day Saint Relief Society women in Salt Lake City elected her vice-president and teacher of their physiological class that was held in the Social Hall.

In July 1874, just four years after the opening of her first school in Salt Lake City, the predominantly Mormon People's Party placed Mary Cook on their ticket as the nominee for Salt Lake County superintendent of common schools. Two days following the public announcement of the candidates on the tickets, a concerned

"Citizen" wrote to the editor of the *Salt Lake Daily Herald:* "Is Miss Cooke or any other lady eligible, under the laws of this Territory, to this office? The law creating the office of County Superintendent of Schools was approved Jan. 19th, 1886, and it is clearly manifested by that act that none other than male citizens were to be entitled to hold the office thus created." In fact the law referred to is stated in terms such as *his* office, *his* successor, *he* shall qualify. Taking this law into account and considering the 1859 law regarding territorial officers and jurors and the 1870 act granting the franchise to Utah women, the *Herald* concluded: "We think under the law, Miss Cooke—who is a very estimable lady, and we understand fully qualified to perform the duties of the office—is ineligible."[12] Without publicized debate or objection, it was generally conceded that Mary Cook was ineligible, and a party caucus withdrew her name from the ticket. One wonders if Emmeline B. Wells' 1878 *Exponent* article praising Mary Cook for her "untiring perseverance under the most unpropitious circumstances" reflects unforgotten disappointment with the People's Party decision.[13]

The professional setback did not affect Mary Cook's work at the Social Hall. The graded school—covering primary, intermediate, and grammar courses—was advertised as a preparatory school, one that would ready students for classwork at the university. Attesting that the school did just that, *Salt Lake Daily Herald* editor Edward Sloan commented in 1878 that from Mary Cook's school "the University of Deseret has probably secured as many scholars as from all others put together and satisfaction has been the result."[14] Few if any ward schools could offer such a comprehensive course, and almost none of the ward schools were graded. In 1874 inclusion of a high school department expanded the school into the Thirteenth Ward schoolrooms located nearby, where classes were offered in botany, mineralogy, Latin, German, algebra, and civil government.

For almost a decade the Social Hall school never opened or closed without the press observing the occasion with fitting encomiums; these little blurbs are really all that exist to suggest the quality of the school or Mary Cook's particular competence in certain areas. She had an expertise in elocution. On his first visit to the school George Q. Cannon had remarked on the "particular pains being taken" to impress upon students "the necessity of entering into the spirit of what they read, and of expressing it naturally and in tones adapted to convey the full force of the sentiment to the listener." At the close of the 1875 fall term, the students held an exhibition for their parents; "recitations, essays, select readings, Dialogues, songs and music composed the programme. All passed off successfully reflecting much credit upon the worthy principal and assistant teachers as well as the pupils."[15]

Appropriate to their location at Social Hall, Mary Cook's students frequently presented dialogues and dramas—"graded school theatricals," as they were sometimes termed in newspaper accounts. One well-reviewed program in 1876 consisted of songs, instrumental music, select readings, declamations, essays, and tableaux. Apparently the tableaux stole the show, especially the portrayal of "Girls of the Period," presenting a girl of 1776 spinning flax and looking happy and plump, and a girl of 1876 delicately reclining on a lounge with a novel in one hand and a poodle in the other.

Mary Cook's Social Hall school was of sufficient stature to secure as teachers some of the territory's most prominent women. In 1874 Eliza R. Snow, Zion's famed poetess and much-involved administrator of women's organizations among Latter-day Saints, joined Mary Cook's staff as a special instructor in composition and elocution. Dr. Ellen B. Ferguson, an accomplished linguist, an able instructor in both vocal and instrumental music, and eventually the first resident surgeon at the Deseret Hospital, teamed up with Mary Cook in 1877 as teacher of the senior scholars. That women of this caliber were willing to become involved with the Social Hall school reflects something of the high regard held for Mary Cook and her "model seminary."[16]

The school's popularity among church and community leaders is further manifested in an account of the closing exercises in June 1878. John Taylor, then president of the Latter-day Saint Council of the Twelve Apostles, gave an address congratulating Miss Cook on her success. Apostles Wilford Woodruff, Daniel H. Wells, and Joseph F. Smith were also present, and though these men may or may not have had children in the school, their presence certainly indicates their support of Mary Cook's professional endeavors.[17]

In the fall of 1877, correspondents from St. George, Utah, informed the *Deseret News* that their four school districts had been consolidated and that trustees Henry Eyring, Isaiah Cox, and A. R. Whitehead were preparing the basement of the tabernacle for the purpose of establishing a graded school there. "Miss Mary Cook, from your city, a lady thoroughly qualified and of no ordinary repute as a teacher, has been employed for the winter."[18] Mary Cook must have stayed but a few months in St. George and then returned the three hundred miles northward to Salt Lake City to finish out the year at the Social Hall. But she went back to St. George again the next fall, and the *St. George Union* carried an advertisement for her high school to be held in the basement of the tabernacle. Though Mary Cook's specialty was in primary grade work, it was probably easier to find local teachers qualified to teach the primary and intermediate grades than to find one qualified to teach high school.

Exactly what influence Mary Cook had on schools and students in St. George or exactly what her own response was to the small community is difficult to ascertain. She stayed only ten months. In one of few St. George reminiscences about Mary Cook a student recalled that she "was a good teacher for the times,"

but we little girls thought she favored the boys; especially one day when she kept her whole arithmetic class in during the entire noon hour, with the exception of Thomas P. Cottam, whom she dismissed with the remark: "Mr. Cottam, I think your head aches."[19]

When Mary Cook returned to Salt Lake City she continued teaching, although the press provides no telling glimpses of either "M.E. Cook's Graded School" or classes at the social Hall during this period. Local directories for the 1880s list Mary E. Cook, schoolteacher, residing in Salt Lake City at 323 East Third South with her mother, Sophia King Cook, whom she had brought to Salt Lake City in 1875. A younger invalid sister, Cornelia, also lived with Mary until Cornelia's death in 1885.[20]

In 1876 Eliza R. Snow invited Mary Cook to serve as first vice-president of the committee for the ladies' centennial territorial fair;[21] yet despite Edward Tullidge's assertion in his 1877 *Women of Mormondom* that Mary Cook was a "rising leader among the women of the church," Mary was never long in the foreground. In 1887 she was called to be general secretary of the Young Ladies' Mutual Improvement Association under president Elmina S. Taylor, but served only until the fall of 1891, when she left Utah to live in the east.[22]

If Mary Cook's star was setting during her last years in Utah, her sister's star was rising. Ida Ione Cook, "the gifted original thinker" known for her "somewhat erratic temperament and her scorn of male dominance," was barely twenty when she arrived in Salt Lake City with her older sister. That she was soon esteemed capable is apparent from John Park's willingness to employ her at the University of Deseret. Ida subsequently worked as an assistant but never as copartner at the Social Hall which, it would seem, was really Mary Cook's enterprise, Mary being fifteen years her sister's senior. Young Ida, restless for independence, did not continue at "M. E. Cook's Graded School." In September 1875 the *Woman's Exponent* announced that Ida Cook would open a high school in Logan, Utah, commenting: "She is a young lady of pleasing manners, possessing intelligence, culture and refinement and one infinitely calculated to carry an influence for improvement among the circle where she associates."[23]

Ida Cook's influence would be felt in Logan for the next twenty years. In the summer of 1876 she served as principal of a two-week Cache County normal institute that attempted to bring about some uniform method of teaching throughout the county. In August she returned briefly to Salt Lake City to work with the normal institute there, demonstrating the *word method* of teaching reading, a method that was probably similar to the current word recognition technique.[24] September saw Ida Cook's plans for a high school materialize. The Logan board of education employed her on the following terms: "Ninety dollars per month if the school makes it, if not Eighty dollars per month. In the event the school makes $100 per month or over, she is to receive one hundred dollars per month."[25] This salary indicates the board's high regard for the twenty-five-year-old professional, since starting salaries for teachers were as low as twenty-five dollars a month. By 1877 Ida Cook's high school (advanced third, fourth, and fifth readers) claimed 114 of the 456 students attending Logan schools.

Even greater successes for Ida Cook were in the offing. In August 1877, Feramorz Young's "Miss Ida" made the improbable leap from young female high school principal to superintendent of district schools for Cache County. With no hesitation she shouldered the responsibility and headed up a month-long normal school during the few weeks preceding the academic school year. Utah historian Orson F. Whitney, in referring to Miss Cook's election as superintendent, declared that she was "the first woman in Utah, perhaps in the entire West, to hold a position of that prominence."[26] There is some question as to how long Ida Cook served in that capacity; the laws regarding county superintendents had not been changed in the three years since Mary Cook's name had been quietly withdrawn from her party's ticket because of her sex, and apparently there were problems for the younger sister as well. Annie Wells Cannon, a local journalist who paid tribute to Ida Cook some years later, said that Ida Cook had been "elected to the office of school superintendent for Cache County, but owing to existing laws against women holding office was not allowed to act; the word male in the organic act prohibiting women as teachers from occupying positions of emolument and trust."[27] In 1880 Utah legislator Charles W. Penrose pled unsuccessfully for a bill to remove the political disabilities of women, arguing that "Cache County would have elected a lady to the office of County Superintendent of Schools, one who had proven to the people her ample qualifications for the post, but the law forbade it."[28]

If the Utah legislature was insensitive to the educational abilities of women like the Cooks, Brigham Young was not. A month before his death he had deeded to a board of trustees a tract of land in Logan to be used for the support of a new academic institution—Brigham Young College. Parties named in the deed of trust included Brigham Young, Jr., M.D. Hammond, and Ida Ione Cook. President Young had been anxious for the school to open in September 1877, but due to some financial difficulties the first term did not begin until September 9, 1878, when rooms were rented in Logan City Hall and Miss Ida Ione Cook took charge as the school's first principal. Her term as principal of the Brigham Young College would extend until she resigned the position in 1884.

Brigham Young had stipulated in deeding the land that in the college "all pupils shall be instructed in reading, penmanship, orthography, grammar, geography and mathematics . . . and the Old and New Testaments, Book of Mormon and Doctrine and Covenants shall be standard textbooks in the College . . . and further, no book shall be used that . . . in any manner advances ideas antagonistic to the principles of the Gospel."[29] In this regard Ida Cook seemed a promising choice as principal, her particular determination being that a student's knowledge of the Gospel should be manifest in his conduct. She told students:

All the doctrines of the faith which we have espoused tend to train our faculties and enable us to subject ourselves to the laws of God, but we sometimes act as if possession of the law was all that is required and do not measure our conduct by the law, hence we do not acquire the discipline and culture we so much desire.[30]

She required courteous conduct from her pupils. "We were taught to raise our hats to Apostles, Bishops, and officers of the various organizations, and always to women. Those who adopted [Miss Cook's] instructions are among the leaders in the communities where they reside," reminisced an old student years later.[31] The first year seventy-one students enrolled. The next year the number had increased to one hundred and ninety-eight, of whom forty-nine were in primary grades, giving older students the opportunity for normal training. Ellen Nash Parkinson remembered her "adored principal" Ida Cook as a teacher trainer:

She scared me at first because she demanded hard work, but we got along famously, though my schooling had been so irregular I had to take a very heavy course to catch up. When I had been there a year, she suggested my name as a teacher for the Franklin school. I felt utterly incapable but with her insistence and that of the trustees I went home to teach.[32]

Ida's influence on young people extended beyond the circle of her students. At the same time she served as principal of the college she was active in local Mormon Church organizations, being called to the Cache Valley Stake Young Ladies Mutual Improvement Association presidency as first counselor. She encouraged the YLMIA girls to use the money they raised at parties and entertainments to purchase books for their libraries, and Ida herself took charge of coordinating orders and supplying the books.

Her work even extended into adult education. In 1885 the Logan Temple Association organized a school to be conducted in the temple; appointed instructors delivered monthly hour-long lectures in theology, civil government, languages, history, domestic and political economy, and natural philosophy. For some time Ida served as a regular instructor, the only woman to do so during the school's fifteen-year history.[33]

Ida was not only well respected as a fine teacher and administrator, but she was personally well liked. George Thomas, later president of the University of Utah, became acquainted as a young man with Ida at a dance in Benson, Utah, to which she had been escorted by one of her students:

Her piercing black eyes, prominent nose, and outstanding personality impressed themselves upon me to such an extent that I shall never forget her. She asked that I be introduced to her, although I was a mere boy, and following the introduction I made bold to request a dance with her, which was graciously granted.[34]

In 1890 the territorial laws governing the election and responsibilities of county superintendents were changed, making any registered voter eligible for the office. In 1892 Ida became principal or general coordinator of the Logan schools. When she resigned after one year in the position, the school board refused to accept her resignation and instead elected her superintendent of the city schools at a salary of $1,500 per year—the highest salary ever offered a Logan teacher up to that time. She immediately set to work instigating the numerous reforms she considered necessary. Recognizing that month-long normal institutes could not adequately train teachers for the higher grade levels, Ida proposed to hire some competent lady teachers she knew in Chicago, and the school board agreed. With full support from the school board it seemed the government of Logan's schools was totally in Ida's hands. She set the rules and regulations, examined teachers for certification, and hired, assigned, and dismissed them. She fired one male teacher when he hugged and kissed against their wills young girls and a female teacher; she dismissed another teacher for frequenting saloons.[35]

The zealous Ida held the position of superintendent for one year. Maybe her high-powered changes disturbed the members of the school board and parents, and maybe her changes lessened their confidence in the woman whose eastern training and background must have seemed so alien to their own. Or perhaps Ida herself, having reached the pinnacle position for a schoolteacher in a small western city, did not find it satisfactorily stimulating, and so she prepared to move on. In any case, the year following her short term as superintendent found her in Salt Lake City, not teaching school but marketing patent medicines. By 1896 she was on her way to Denver, where she again became involved in education.[36]

The two Miss Cooks disappeared from Utah as inconspicuously as they had arrived twenty-five years earlier. Whether either or both married, or whether they spent the remainder of their lives together or apart, is not easily determined. They had ties in Denver where their brother had served for two terms as mayor, in St. Louis where they had spent some eight or ten years together previous to coming to Salt Lake, and in New York where they had been born, raised, and educated. Their destination is not so important as their midcareer departure and the comment that departure might make on late nineteenth-century life in Utah. Was there insufficient culture and sophistication for educated easterners? Did the well-established and homogeneous Mormon culture ostracize newcomers?

Heber J. Grant, financier and member of the Latter-day Saint Council of the Twelve Apostles, recorded in his diary that his 1889 visit with his former schoolteacher, Mary Cook, showed her to be "in very poor circumstances financially."[37] At that time she was one among a large and growing number of trained and professional teachers in Utah, and she, like other female teachers, was earning about half the salary of male teachers. What were the economic and social realities for a single career woman who neither by birth nor marriage could claim support from the priesthood and kinship network that influenced Salt Lake society?

Both Mary and Ida Cook made significant contributions during their stay in Utah. Their schools served as models, and their training in curriculum and methodology gave many new teachers exposure to normal training that they could not have had otherwise. Though the schools and students of these pioneer educators have long since faded from Utah, their lives as professional women will continue to instruct new generations.

Notes

1. "Academy," *Deseret News Weekly*, Salt Lake City, Utah, November 9, 1870.

2. Annie Wells Cannon, "Women in Education," *Woman's Exponent*, Salt Lake City, Utah, June 1, 1888.

3. In 1919 Heber J. Grant commented that the Cooks had "startled the community by introducing athletics" as part of primary school curriculum. "Leaves from Old Albums," *Deseret Evening News*, Salt Lake City, Utah, June 14, 1919. The fact is that the model school at the University of Deseret was offering gymnastics to its primary classes in the spring of 1870. See Levi Edgar Young, *Dr. John Rocky Park*, n.p., 1919, p. 22.

4. "The School Excursion," *Deseret News Weekly*, May 22, 1872.

5. Edward W. Tullidge, *The Women of Mormondom*, New York, 1877; reprint ed., Salt Lake City, 1973, p. 524; Certificate of Baptism for Mary and Ida Cook, manuscript, Early Utah Collection, Library-Archives, Historical Department of The Church of Jesus Christ of Latter-day Saints, Salt Lake City, Utah, hereafter cited as Church Library-Archives.

6. John R. Park diary, April 17, 1871, as quoted in Ralph V. Chamberlain, *The University of Utah: A History of Its First Hundred Years . . .* , Salt Lake City, 1960, p. 96.

7. Feramorz Young diary, January 2, 1872, to February 25, 1872, under dates January 24 and February 1 and 2, holograph, Church Library-Archives.

8. Chamberlain, *University of Utah*, p. 97; *Deseret News Weekly*, June 26, 1872.

9. Chamberlain, *University of Utah*, p. 102.

10. "Home Affairs," *Woman's Exponent*, July 1, 1878.

11. Robert L. Campbell to Editor, *Deseret News*, November 20, 1871, *Deseret News Weekly*, November 29, 1871.

12. "A Question," *Salt Lake Daily Herald*, June 15, 1874.

13. "Home Affairs," *Woman's Exponent*, September 1, 1878.

14. "Closing Exercises," *Salt Lake Daily Herald*, June 21, 1878.

15. "Academy," *Deseret News Weekly,* November 9, 1870; "Home Affairs," *Woman's Exponent,* November 15, 1875.

16. "Miss M. E. Cook's Graded School," *Woman's Exponent,* February 1, 1874; "A Model Seminary," *Deseret News Weekly,* November 14, 1877.

17. "Home Affairs," *Woman's Exponent,* July 1, 1878.

18. Cactus to Editors, *Deseret News,* December 9, 1877, *Deseret News Weekly,* December 19, 1877.

19. Josephine J. Mills on schools in Washington County, "The University of Utah and Other Schools of Early Days," Kate B. Carter, comp., *Heart Throbs of the West* 12 (1951): 40.

20. Robert W. Sloan, *Utah Gazetteer and Directory,* Salt Lake City, 1888, p. 110.

21. "Woman's Centennial Territorial Fair," *Woman's Exponent,* June 1, 1876.

22. Susa Young Gates, *History of Y.L.M.I.A.,* Salt Lake City, 1911, p. 89.

23. Untitled typescript dealing with Karl G. Maeser, John R. Park, and Ida Ione Cook, seven pages, p. 7, Susa Young Gates Collection, Box 17, Utah State Historical Society, Salt Lake City, Utah; "Home Affairs," *Woman's Exponent,* September 15, 1875.

24. Charles C. Shaw to Editor, *Deseret News,* July 22, 1876, *Deseret News Weekly,* August 9, 1876; "Normal Institute," *Deseret News Weekly,* August 16, 1876.

25. Joel E. Ricks, ed., *The History of a Valley: Cache Valley, Utah-Idaho,* Logan, Utah, 1956, p. 339.

26. Orson F. Whitney, *Brigham Young College, a History,* p. 8, pamphlet reprinted from *American University Magazine,* June 1896.

27. Cannon, "Women in Education."

28. "Speech of Hon. C. W. Penrose," *Woman's Exponent,* February 1, 1880.

29. *Prospectus of the Brigham Young College . . . for 1884-1885,* n.p., n.d., p. 6, pamphlet in Church Library-Archives.

30. Ida Ione Cook, "Discipline and Culture," *Contributor* 8 (May 1887): 277.

31. History of Nels August Nelson, p. 16, typescript in Church Library-Archives.

32. Ellen Elvira Nash Parkinson Journal, Kate B. Carter, comp., *Our Pioneer Heritage* 8 (1965): 206.

33. See Melvin A. Larkin, "The History of the L.D.S. Temple in Logan, Utah," master's thesis, Utah State Agricultural College, Logan, Utah, 1954, pp. 146-55; Cook, "Discipline and Culture," pp. 277-80.

34. "Latter-day Saint Schools," Kate B. Carter, comp., *Heart Throbs of the West* 11 (1950): 125-26.

35. Ricks, *Cache Valley*, p. 339.

36. R. L. Polk and Company, *Salt Lake City Directory*, Salt Lake City, 1896, p. 228. Heber J. Grant recollections in "Leaves from Old Albums."

37. Heber J. Grant diary, January 1, 1889, holograph, Church Archives.

Maud May Babcock 1867–1954

Ann Gardner Stone, the author of this essay, was introduced previously. She wrote two other essays for this collection.

Maud M. Babcock

Ann Gardner Stone

The scene is Salt Lake City, May 22, 1946; some three hundred people have gathered to praise and honor a stately lady of seventy-nine years. They are former students of Dr. Maud May Babcock, once head of the Department of Speech and Drama at the University of Utah and the "First Lady of Utah's Dramatic Arts." Dr. Babcock is composed, but obviously touched; she laughs when Utah Governor Herbert B. Maw exclaims that she was disappointed in him because he used the oratorical methods she taught him to become just a politician. The reminiscences continue—there are references to

... *her fondness for Chinese pug dogs, her cooking, her teaching, her health doctrines, her inability to finish a sentence, her redundant use of "straight down the line," her politics, and her dislike for the movies—"Why, look at Moroni Olson. If he hadn't gotten mixed up with that illegitimate art, motion pictures, right today he could still be teaching school at Ogden High."*[1]

The evening's program is evidence of the profound influence Maud May Babcock had on the lives of those she encountered during her eighty-seven years. She estimated that she had coached over eight hundred plays and thousands of students during her career. "This," she declared, "has become my reward. My years have brought me the devotion of my students. I still see them often. Many hundreds of them have stopped to call years later."[2]

The influence of a teacher on a student is an elusive thing, but there is an abundance of testimony from Maud's students about the strength of her teaching methods and the power of her personality. Lila Eccles Brimhall recalls, "She opened up for all of us a whole new world of culture. And we needed it; it was a young age, where everyone had been struggling for survival and existence. She dominated us so much that it took me a long time to dare to like anything without her approval."[3] Malcolm R. Meacham, actor, writer, and educator, personifies the type of student Maud produced. He worked in virtually all theatrical media—as an actor, writer, director, and producer—and he gave credit for his success to

Maud's farsighted techniques:

> To talk about Maud May Babcock is to talk about a legend. I do not really, in my own memory, know how to describe her. She was a woman of multiple aspects, of multiple personalities. I suppose you had to know her as long as I did to find out how multiple and complex she was. I'm not sure that I even know because the facets of her personality were such that I couldn't possibly have begun to understand them in the age that I knew her. Now that I am much older, I understand that she was much older than she seemed to be.... (She is) a personality who is so vivid and so alive that she cannot but be a part of my life.[4]

There was obviously more to Maud's teaching than classroom techniques.

Her professional standards were high and her classes were conducted in a very businesslike manner. It wasn't enough that her students recognize and select only literary pieces of high quality; she taught them to read their selections *with brains*. From this concept of reading with brains emerged her famous motto—"understand the thought, hold the thought, give the thought." According to Maud, great literature was to be heard, but only if the voice was that of an accomplished artist. A poem, a play, or a story could be reborn through the talents of an artist, and it was Maud's purpose to produce such artists in her classes.[5] Meacham recalled one of her unique methods:

> The important part of my studying with her was the study of "Hamlet." I went in, in my junior year, to read Hamlet. Subsequently I have played the role of Hamlet about five times now, but I do know where I got my start with the play, and that was from Miss B. ... In the little theatre downstairs where we did rehearsals, there was a stage which would hold four or five actors at a time. I had come back from Stanford for my junior year. I elected to take a course, for $35, studying with Miss B. I said I wanted to study Hamlet. She said, "We'll get at this presently." She noted that I had a complete Shakespeare with me. I sat on a chair on the stage. She sat in the auditorium. I was to receive an hour instruction each time we met during the quarter. It ended up two and a half hours later, and I was a little puzzled about this, wondering how I paid her for the extra time spent with her. She said, "I'm already paid; you've paid your fee." She asked me if I had a copy of the mercy speech. I said that I knew it, and I did have it in my book. She subsequently asked me to recite the mercy speech, and I began. I don't know what it was—at this late date in my life I can still say the mercy speech without acting it, it is so simple and beautiful, that it doesn't need acting. Well, at the next session, I started reading the mercy speech for Miss B. For one entire quarter I sat in that room an hour or an hour and a half each day and she would say, "No." All she ever did was say "No." I sat there on the edge of the stage, weeping my heart out; I screamed at her. Everything emotional that could happen happened. But she wouldn't let up. All she said was "NO." They one day, very much toward the end of the quarter, I was so exhausted, mentally and emotionally, that I could barely speak. The only thing that I had gotten back, except the "No" was "Do it again." So I did it. Then she said, "Can you re-

member what you have just done?" She said, "I will give you an incomplete in this course, and then we can tackle Hamlet next quarter." Finally in the third quarter of that year, for which she did not charge the $35, I became proficient in reading Shakespeare. My experience with her had taught me this skill.[6]

Another unusual aspect of Maud's teaching was the use of light calisthenic exercises taught in conjunction with the oratorical classes. This method, known as Delsarte (after its inventor, Francois Delsarte, a nineteenth-century French teacher), was popular in 1885 when Maud was attending classes at the Philadelphia School of Oratory. She was exceedingly frail, almost to the point of being an invalid, and the gradual improvement in her health resulting from these exercises impressed Maud to further explore the uses of physical culture. She was eventually led to the Harvard Gymnasium at Harvard University, where she taught Delsarte and voice culture for two years (1890-92). Truly converted to the idea that "healthy spirits cannot attain full development in diseased, impure and deformed bodies," it became her mission to share this message with other women like herself.[7]

In the summer of 1891, Susa Young Gates, Brigham Young's daughter, went from Utah to Cambridge to take Maud's class, and the two women soon became close friends. Maud says of her fateful encounter with Susa,

She gave the most wonderful descriptions of the land among the mountains, the beauty of its scenery and the intelligence of its people. Above all, this charming woman spoke of the intense need of physical culture and elocution, and that one coming here now would be, as it were, a missionary or chief reaper in this field already white for the harvest.[8]

Susa knew how to appeal to Maud's enthusiasm, and the next year Maud accepted an offer from the University of Utah to teach there at a salary of five hundred dollars a year. At the same time she rejected an offer to supervise the Department of Physical Education and Oral Expression in the Bridgeport, Connecticut, schools for three times the salary.

This was a rather drastic step for a cultured lady from East Worcester, New York, someone who had trained at the best schools, who had taught in the homes of wealthy New York society, and who had never been further west than Niagara Falls. Her father called her his "runaway girl" who would go wherever anyone said "come." One of her former students, Ethel B. Callas, tried to imagine Maud's arrival in the West:

She had taught at Harvard, lived in the East, she had every kind of refinement and culture and beautiful clothes. She had never had a shoe that wasn't handmade. She came out here ... muddy roads, everything dirty ... imagine how it would be for

her with those beautiful handmade shoes going down in the mud.[9]

But Maud maintained, "I have never regretted my choice."[10] She intended to stay a year, but stayed for sixty-two instead.

Maud May Babcock was the second woman to be elected to the faculty of the University of Utah, where her methods found instant support. So great was the demand for her physical culture class that she was given a suite of rooms in the Constitution Building on campus where she could hold private lessons. She returned to Harvard University the next summer, "taking with her four of Utah's brightest girls, to prove to her Eastern friends that some good and grace does come out of Nazareth."[11] She returned to Utah in 1893, accompanied by her brother, Dr. William W. Babcock, a well-known specialist in spinal surgery, and $2,500 worth of gymnastic equipment purchased from Harvard. Together they opened a gymnasium in the remodeled Social Hall and began conducting a "physical education summer school, which featured outstanding visiting professionals in the field. The blending of oratory and physical culture developed into what is reputed to have been the first university theatre in the United States."[12]

The first public performance given by the Babcocks' students took place in the Salt Lake Theatre on May 23, 1893:

> While the production was largely a demonstration of drills with dumbells, wands, Indian clubs, and dances, it possessed dramatic elements of picturization, selection and climax. In 1895, "An Exhibition of Educational Gymnastics" combined drama and dance in a presentation based upon the Greek harvest festival of Eleusthenia, and by December 11, 1897, the newly organized University of Utah Dramatic Club offered the plays "The Happy Pair" and "A Box of Monkeys" in the 18th Ward amusement hall.[13]

It was not always smooth sailing for Maud's theatrical productions. In January 1903 ten students were suspended from the university for throwing vegetables at the Drama Club's presentation of "The Amazons":

> Personally, I had no grievance nor do the members of the club have any. On the contrary, I think they rather enjoyed the experience, particularly as they were victorious in the end—that is, they continued their performance to a triumphant conclusion.[14]

Even her students recognized certain flaws in her directing methods. According to Meacham:

> When she directed a play everybody in the play was a little Maud May Babcock. Some of us escaped from this, but she did have a habit of dominating any situation that she could dominate and she always dominated any direction of a play.

Maud tired of giving her productions in church cultural halls and rented theatres, and she determined to secure a little theatre and auditorium for the university campus. Her approach was typical Maud May Babcock, as Meacham recounts:

> I don't know how she did it, but she did it. She took President Thomas to task when she found there were not enough lofts to fly sets, and made him order a change in the design of the building so that she could have loft space. That was typical of her. She had been on sabbatical when construction began. She came back and found it was not to her specifications, and she went to the president of the university and got the change made. She had them make the ceiling fifty feet higher than they had built it. They had to tear down part of the structure to make the change. I did the set for the first play in the new theatre. The play was "The Bluebird."[15]

The production of *The Bluebird* took place on May 22, 1931. In that year, 1,896 students were enrolled in the Department of Speech, the highest per capita enrollment of any American university.[16] During this period Maud also found time to be a guest director for the Washington Square and Provincetown Players in New York, to write articles for professional journals, and to write numerous textbooks, including *Studies in Dialect, The Handbook for Teachers of Interpretation, Interpretative Selections for High School,* and *Interpretative Selections for College.* Her reputation as an innovative teacher and director reached international proportions. Because George Bernard Shaw, the famous English playwright and critic, had read her books and approved of her methods, he consented to meet with one of her students, Joseph F. Smith, when Smith visited England. Such tributes to Maud's success were not uncommon.

There was always time in Maud's life for volunteer service to the community. Her volunteer work was as varied as were her interests. In 1897 she became a member of the board for the Utah State School for the Deaf and Blind, and in 1905 she was elected president of the Board of Trustees for the school. She was the first woman to preside over a state coeducational institution; in all, she gave twenty years of service to the school. She was the first woman elected president of the National Association of Teachers of Speech, and for two years she was national president of Theta Alpha Phi, a dramatic fraternity. Because of her work in the field of physical education, she was the first of the only two honorary members of Pi Delta Pi, the national physical education fraternity.[16] In another first for a woman, Maud was named chaplain of the Utah State Senate in 1945, an honor given in recognition of her work in drama.[17]

These tributes were not unsought. Maud was an aggressive pioneer in obtaining recognition for women and was, throughout her life, a champion of women's rights. Her interest in physical education was to introduce it to women deprived of any specific physical training. She said,

Our women must and are freeing themselves from the false ideals of our grandmothers that little girls should "sit still, be quiet, fold their hands, and grow up little ladies."[18]

Nor was all Maud's service given as an executive or teacher. She was generous with her talents as an actress and interpretative reader. Throughout her life she gave readings to help various civic organizations raise funds, and even while she was on a year's sabbatical leave from the University of Utah in 1928-29 and was traveling around the world, she found time for philanthropy. While in London in 1929 she advertised that her services were available free for any worthy purpose, and she was immediately asked to give a reading of Shaw's *Caesar and Cleopatra* to London society, the proceeds from which went to building homes for disabled officers and men of World War I.[19]

The world tour mentioned above was one of many tours made during her life. She had a great passion for travel, particularly to the Orient (she visited China seven times and served as a guide there for numerous groups), and she had a magnificent collection of Chinese art, jade, ivory, robes, and dolls; the dolls are now part of a collection at the University of Utah. She was famous for her four Chinese chow dogs and for her Chinese cooking.

Maud's travels had an effect on her students, some of whom had never been farther than twenty miles from the spot where they were born. They relived Maud's travel experiences vicariously, often being used as guinea pigs for a food or a recipe she had just discovered. In fact, food was of major interest to Maud, but only as a source of health and vigor. One of her students, Ethel Baker Callas, recalls, "She always had interesting foods to eat. She taught us how to eat artichokes, avocados, Chinese food . . . things we'd never heard of."[20] She was always the purveyor of culture, in whatever form.

Many of Maud's students were allowed a more personal relationship with her than that of teacher-pupil. But even in a relaxed setting she continued to be the teacher, particularly of her theories of health and exercise. Meacham remembers:

During a period when I was ill and was living in her house—mentally ill, not phys-
ically ill, I'm quite sure—I was only nineteen. She took me up to her cottage in
Brighton. She kept me there for the whole summer. She made me walk hills, which I
didn't believe I could do. She had a regular routine. We had in the morning, for
breakfast, a lot of oatmeal cereal and a lot of raisins and dried prunes and dried
peaches, or whatever else she found to put into the kettle. We all had to eat this. At
noon, we usually had lunch, sometimes on the top of the hill, with bars of chocolate
and raisins in a bag. Sometimes we stayed at the house and then had some kind of
eggs for breakfast or lunch. She was very versatile about how she managed eggs. She
would do them customarily in a double boiler on top of the stove. She put on the eggs
first, whipped the eggs, put a little of the hot milk in the eggs, and they made a
kind of custard. Then she would give us vegetables and fruits of various sorts. Maud
May had a cabin right across from Emma Lucy Gates (Bowen). Emma Lucy was a
prima donna at the Staats opera in Berlin. We had a congenial group; I played the
piano and Madame Gates sang, still, very well. Summers at Brighton were always
reminiscent, I suppose, of their times in Europe . . . Miss Babcock was relatively per-
missive. When I was living at Brighton in the summers I used customarily to bathe
in the nude in the stream which came down over the hill behind her cottage. This
despite the fact that there was another man and another girl and Miss Babcock liv-
ing in the house. When I came back in, exhilarated of course by the cold water, she
would set up a set of exercises. This was part of her teaching—at least her teaching
to me. I don't know where she got this idea. We did pushups—not just the ordinary
ones but the Japanese pushups where you would bounce off your hands and come
down again before you started your pushups. There were other exercises which she
used, among them the ability to walk. We used to walk up Mount St. Caterine. And
she was indefatigable. The woman had energy that was hard to believe. She would
go up that hill leading all of us. It was a 3,000-foot climb. This was in 1930 or
so. Maud was sixty-three years old.[21]

The Mormon Church, which Maud joined four months after
coming to Utah, also found an active place in her life. Her family
was horrified by her conversion and believed that she had been
forced to join against her will and would be murdered if she left
the church. Maud lived her life to prove to them otherwise. In
1935, she told an interviewer from the *Deseret News* that her religion was the "keystone of her life" and that the two most valuable
things in her life were her inner sense of the true and of the beautiful, and the affection of her students.[22] She taught a Sunday
School class in the Eleventh Ward in Salt Lake City for many
years, did temple work, and presented special classes in the dramatic arts for the youth of the church. Upon her death in 1954,
she left her personal genealogical records and her real estate—valued at $10,000—to the Mormon Church.[23]

Maud May Babcock enjoyed a large degree of celebrity during
her lifetime, and she enjoyed the admiration and devotion of her
students throughout her career. There is, however, one dimension

to Maud May that has received little attention but that seems to be one of her major accomplishments as a woman: and that dimension is the fact that she never married. Maud's marital status is noteworthy both because of the often difficult position of the single woman in the Mormon culture and because Maud herself never seemed to view it as a difficulty.

In Mormon theology marriage and family form the foundation on which an individual's exaltation in the next life is built. Although church doctrine ultimately provides a means for the righteous single person to achieve salvation, the unmarried woman has often found herself in the uncomfortable position of being outside the mainstream of Mormon life. Education and careers for women are encouraged, but often with the idea that they are merely insurance policies; the most valued achievement is often considered to be marriage. Career successes are seen by many as a threat to the traditional roles of housewife and mother.

Maud May Babcock, a staunch Mormon woman, seemed to have coped well. First, she did not view singleness as a problem. Maud's life reflects this—her outlook was healthy, uncompromising, and genuinely content and happy. During an interview with one of the local newspapers it was intimated that she came to Utah seeking love. What other reason could a woman have for leaving her comfortable and cultured life in the East? Maud's simple reply was, "No, it wasn't a man. I missed that." No apologies, no explanations, no regrets. She was devoted to her career. She truly believed in the principles of physical education for women and in the importance of the dramatic arts as a way to better the lives of her students; teaching this was enough to make her life full.

The fact that her students continued to think of themselves as products of Maud May Babcock's techniques long after they had developed careers of their own attests to the strength of this woman's influence. Maud's travels, her work for the deaf and blind, and her contributions to her profession were never merely time-fillers. She attacked each activity with the zeal of a person who was happy with herself and happy with her life. Her contributions to society were made by a total human being, not by one who was waiting to be made whole.

Notes

1. *Deseret News,* May 23, 1946.

2. *Deseret News,* April 30, 1947.

3. Raye Price, "Utah's Leading Ladies of the Arts," *Utah Historical Quarterly,* 38(Winter 1970):81.

4. Transcribed by Bernell W. Meacham from a tape dictated by Malcolm R. Meacham in the fall of 1975. Mr. Meacham became ill shortly after this period of dictation and died two months later. I am indebted to his wife, Bernell Meacham, for her compilation and transcription of the tape during what must have been a difficult period for her.

5. Price, p. 81.

6. Meacham tape.

7. "Literary Department: Biographical Sketch of Maud May Babcock, B. E.," *The Young Woman's Journal, The Organ of the Y. L. M. I. Associations,* 5(June 1894):421.

8. Price, p. 78.

9. *Ibid.,* p. 79.

10. *Deseret News,* April 30, 1947.

11. *The Young Woman's Journal,* June 1894, p. 413.

12. Price, p. 79.

13. *Ibid.,* p. 80.

14. *Journal History of The Church of Jesus Christ of Latter-day Saints,* January 24, 1903, p. 15.

15. Meacham tape.

16. Whitney, Orson F., *History of Utah,* Salt Lake City, Utah: George Q. Cannon and Sons Publishers, 1898, Volume 2, pp. 215–217.

17. *Deseret News,* January 10, 1945.

18. Price, p. 77.

19. John L. Clark, "London District Spring Conference," *The Improvement Era* 32(July 1929):775-77.

20. Price, p. 81.

21. Meacham tape.

22. Eugene Middleton, "Personality Portraits of Prominent Utahns," *Deseret News,* March 15, 1935, p. 18.

23. *Salt Lake Tribune,* January 23, 1955.

Alice Louise Reynolds 1873–1938

*Reba L. Keele received her associate
of science degree at the College of
Eastern Utah, her bachelor of science
and master of arts at Brigham Young
University, and her doctor of
philosophy at Purdue University. At
BYU she was named Outstanding
Graduate Student, and she was both a
BYU and a Purdue Fellow.
Throughout her education, her
emphasis has centered on
communications—speech, rhetoric and
public address, and the psychology of
education. Now serving as director of
the Honors Program at BYU and
working as a coordinator for the
development and use of a new general
education system at BYU, she has in
the past worked and written
extensively about aspects of
individualized instruction programs
and tutoring in education. In addition
to her teaching on both the secondary
and college levels, Dr. Keele has
worked on developing programs for
the individual study of educational
psychology; modular instruction; and
workshop training and self concept,
communication, and tutoring. She is
associate director of the Consortium
for Utah Women in Higher
Education, and is a frequent speaker
and communications workshop director
in student and church groups. She has
written Relief Society lesson material
for The Church of Jesus Christ of
Latter-day Saints and served as a
Relief Society president on branch and
stake levels. She was named Utah's
outstanding Young Woman in 1975.*

Alice L. Reynolds

Reba L. Keele

At a time when twenty-five percent of the adult women in the Mormon Church are single (never married, widowed, or divorced),[1] the need to know women who have built rich lives, open friendships, and meaningful service while differing from the traditional model of family, home, and children, may be the greatest in our history. While it is important to recognize that the "mother in Israel" is a role given great emphasis in the gospel of the Mormon Church,[2] such emphasis should not obscure the recognition due those who provide examples of individual growth for the women of today.

A woman who was such an example of hundreds of students was Alice Louise Reynolds, "spinster," Relief Society member, professor, friend, and lover of learning. Her list of accomplishments include teaching at Brigham Young University for forty-four years, being the second woman in the state to be named a full professor, and establishing the first library collection at Brigham Young University. A single room in the new addition to the now million-volume library for which she laid the groundwork will display her picture and name, helping to undo the neglect she has received from an organization with which she first affiliated at the age of thirteen.

What are the strengths exhibited in the life of a single woman who ended her days saying, "I have lived the best I could, and I am sure no girl or woman ever had a more wonderful life, with more opportunities, more privileges, and more friends"[3]; and which of those strengths are instructive for young women in the 1970s and beyond? The qualities that emerge from interviews, biographies, and the meager journals Alice Louise Reynolds left for us may be classified under three headings: self-acceptance, self-development, and service. Though an examination of each will not result in a chronology of her life, perhaps it will expose enough about this remarkable woman to allow her to become real to a new generation.

1. *Alice accepted herself as a person of worth.*

Perhaps this life-long confidence came from an upbringing that
was unusual for her time—perhaps for any time. Her father,
George Reynolds, was the secretary to four Mormon prophets
(Brigham Young, John Taylor, Wilford Woodruff, and Joseph F.
Smith) and was the author of several books still in use today, including the *Concordance to the Book of Mormon.* He was chosen by the
Mormon Church as the defendant in the first test case of the constitutionality of the Antibigamy Act of 1862, and he served for two
years in prison when the law was upheld. Her mother, MaryAnn
Tuddenham, was an English woman of some education. The family was very close, with an unusual emphasis on education and
ideas. Alice Louise said of her father that "he loved knowledge
and it certainly was a dreadful thing in [his] eyes to be unneces-
sarily ignorant."[4] Her mother was a strong enough influence that
Alice could write on December 17, 1935, "It is 50 years ago today
since mother died. Few things that one can think of are so bad for
a family as the loss of mother . . . I was twelve. . . ."[5] (Alice was
born April 1, 1873.)

It is not likely that many children in that pioneer country had
the almost exclusive attention of a mother figure, but when Alice's
sister was born when Alice was only fifteen months old, an aunt
moved into the home and assumed care of Alice for the next ten
years.[6] An important part of Alice's care was intellectual stimulation, and she was enrolled in school for the first time at age
four.[7] There are other indications that the Reynolds home atmosphere offered Alice the freedom to develop. The freedom from
real want is indicated by her statement that she was wheeled to
her first school in "a baby buggy by my mother's maid."[8]

An indication of a second kind of freedom comes in her descriptions of the polygamous home in which three wives seemed to live
harmoniously with an unusual husband. Her father was extremely
considerate of each woman's feelings, being careful to remember
anniversaries, birthdays, and special occasions. (However, Alice
points out that any of his wives could best her father at laying carpet, putting up stoves, or hanging doors![9] The fact that this in no
way detracted from his masculinity in his family's eyes may help
us understand how she could be so different from the average
woman of her time and yet feel no loss of femininity.) Alice was
called "Princess Alice" by her family and by the neighborhood,
yet this title apparently was free of jealousy; it was descriptive, not
judgmental. The picture derived from her writings and from the
writings of others about her is of a happy home with stability and
love providing a foundation for a real emphasis on education and
intellectual achievement; but, most importantly, it is the picture of

freedom to grow in her own direction.

Even while she was alive the folklore about her began to grow, in part because of her extreme absent-mindedness. It is said that she carried her teakettle to school, thinking it to be her purse,[10] she wore a dress the wrong side out to a play,[11] she slid through a window to a classroom, bloomers first, and once she walked while reading a book through a herd of cows, absently swatting them with her purse.[12] Far from bothering her, she seemed to accept the stories as being accurate descriptions of one part of her, without drawing generalized conclusions about the rest of her abilities. This was indicated by her pointing out to students, with a twinkle in her eye, an old umbrella that she had carried to Europe three times and brought home, while no one else with her had made it through the whole trip with the same umbrella![13]

Algie Ballif, a former student, describes Alice as "absolutely free of any need to impress," and in describing the help that Alice gave her in an oratorical contest, adds that there was no false modesty or depreciation of her ability to help improve the speech.[14] She loved to entertain (which she believed Mormon women did not do often enough), but was not good at the details of hostessing, such as serving, so she prevailed upon relatives, friends, or students to serve for her during her soirees. On one occasion when the number of guests exceeded the supply of ginger ale, she handed a student a bottle of liquid, indicating that it was more ginger ale that could be used. The student did not tell Alice that the bottle contained vinegar, and it is doubtful that Alice Louise would have been chagrined had she known—it was not those concerns which were most important to her in entertaining.[15]

Dr. A. E. Winship of Boston said of her, " ... Miss Reynolds knows more about more things that I am interested in than any other woman I have ever met."[16] She seemed to have no hesitation about discussing these "things of interest" with either men or women, sharing her knowledge and gaining from theirs. Another student summarizes "Princess Alice's" confidence:

We all agreed that she was remarkably free from ego-centric hang-ups ... My superficial guess is that she was spontaneously in touch with her unconscious, and her own center ... Her rich interior life took some precedence over the mundane ... I have the feeling that she rang true almost from birth, and was consequently freer to do her own thing than most of us. Her environment touched her deeply, but could not distort. Perhaps this core integrity is part of what drew others to her. They sensed a life of purpose—books, learning, beauty, human rights—but lived out beneath an eternal canopy.[17]

She was a woman of confidence and self-respect, with no need to downgrade or denigrate her contribution or strengths.

2. *Alice seemed always to be conscious of the need to develop her own talents.* When she was thirteen and her sister was eleven, they were sent to Brigham Young Academy to study under Karl Maeser. Alice also attended schools in Salt Lake City and Logan, because of individual teachers, before graduating from BYU's Normal School in 1890.[18] Like her father, she was inept at doing handwork, and at performing certain household duties, but she seemingly accepted both that and the fact that she had a good mind and the responsibility to develop it, and that to do such was to be true to her gifts.

Even though she was too young to teach legally in the state, she accepted a teaching job when she was seventeen. When Benjamin Cluff, then president of Brigham Young Academy, approached her after she had taught for two years and suggested that she prepare herself through further schooling to teach at the Academy and establish a department of literature, she grasped the opportunity. Alice had seventy-five dollars she had saved, her father's offer of the railway fare, and access to a student loan fund, and that is all she needed.

She eagerly joined the small Mormon student community at the University of Michigan in 1892. Her previous skill as a student continued, and she thrived on the exposure to a broadened world of art, music, and literature. In the fall of 1894 at the age of twenty-one, she started teaching classes at Brigham Young Academy.

She had a seemingly insatiable need to know. She used her sabbaticals regularly to travel and to study, taking classes at the University of Chicago, Columbia, Queens College in London, Berkeley, and Cornell as well as the University of Michigan and BYU, always seeking the best teachers. She visited Britain, France, Switzerland, Italy, Austria, Germany, Belgium, the Netherlands, Scotland, Egypt, Palestine, Syria, Turkey, Greece, Denmark, Norway, Wales, and Ireland, some of them as many as three times. She had a passion for world fairs and expositions, and attended all that she could. And she read constantly and widely, with catholic taste and a search for quality as defined in her time. She could describe Thomas Hardy's work analytically,[19] she read Sandburg's *Lincoln*,[20] and she copied into her autobiographical notes feminist writings of her time,[21] famous and not famous, which expressed some of the issues important to her in the women's movement.

In short, she considered her mind a gift from God, and she set out to build upon that gift. She seemed to truly believe that which she wrote: "That which every seeker after knowledge knows to be true is that any information paves the way for adding to our information. Knowledge is a magnet that attracts knowledge."[22] That she rejected the stereotypes of the gifts women were to develop is indicated by her reactions at two different times to one of the prominent feminists of her day:

But the thing I delighted in above all else was hearing Carrie Chapman Catt for the first time. I still think her the most outstanding public woman I have ever known. She is such a marvelous combination of brains, industry, courage, and charm.[23]

And when Alice heard Catt again in 1919, she said:

Mrs. Catt was at her best. But the finest thing about Carrie Chapman Catt was her well-trained mind which made possible such distinguished accomplishments. The cause of suffrage was advancing.[24]

Her appreciation of gifts was not limited to the intellectual alone. She taught theology at the Brigham Young Academy, and she seemed to feel that she had the best of both worlds in her occupational choice:

There is one thing that is beautiful about religion and about art. To religion you can bring all the beauty and all the uplift there is in art. To art you can bring all the reverence, all the holiness and beauty there is in religion.[25]

She was a woman of high intellect, wide knowledge, and a great desire to learn—and she had no hesitations about learning because she was a woman or because it might hamper her chances of marriage.

3. *Alice's orientation was one of service to others.*

Like her contemporaries, Alice seemed not to have carried any bitterness or fears about her single state, but to have accepted and enjoyed her calling as a different one without ever communicating any negative attitudes toward marriage. In fact, she maintained a close relationship with all members in most families. Her political discussions with Earnest Partridge's father took no less time than did her intimate chats with his mother. Her love for the children of the family was evidenced by her arranging her theater schedule so as not to miss scheduled baby feedings.[26] Amy Brown Lyman, a friend of Alice's from their early years at BYA, explained that Alice spent many Christmas holidays and summer vacations with her family, and described their last summer together in 1937 in London. (Alice knew at this time of the cancer that killed her a year later. It is interesting that she filled her last summer with more learning experiences). Note the role Alice filled both for her friend and her friend's family:

Her proposed trip to Southern England was to visit the birthplace and home of

Thomas Hardy ... an opportunity she had not had before ... Miss Reynolds explained that ... Hardy is one of the titans of English literature ... and she briefed us on his life and writings ... My little granddaughter, Amy Kathryn, and I were Alice's guests on a trip to Stratford-on-Avon ... It was a very choice and valuable experience for Amy Kathryn and me.[27]

Many families of friends and students reported this loving, teaching relationship with "Aunt Alice."

At an Alice Louise Reynolds Club celebration of her birthday in 1932, she said, "To some of you the sweetest word in the English language is 'husband,' to some of you, 'child,' but to me the sweetest word in the English language is 'friend.' "[28] She built many meaningful relationships with all kinds of people, church and non-church, man, woman, and child.

However, her service was not limited to individual friends or students. Her activities were balanced among people, profession, country, and church. In the political arena, she was one of the first women to participate in a political convention, giving the seconding speech for the nomination of William McAdoo for president of the 1920 National Democratic Convention. She participated in the fight for women's suffrage, served as a leader in the Federation of Women's clubs, participated in the National Education Association (addressing national conventions), represented the Relief Society General Board[29] in the National Council of Women, served on the Relief Society General Board and as editor of the *Relief Society Magazine*, was a frequent speaker at funerals and other occasions (in February 1934 she recorded that since she had returned from New York, presumably for the beginning of the school year, she had given twelve "major addresses"—to audiences ranging from Unitarians, Founder's Day celebration and University Women to several sacrament meeting talks—and four "minor addresses").[30] She was the first woman to give a Founder's Day address at BYU—and she gave two at that.

She was respected by the men with whom she associated, both as students and as peers. One young male writer indicated that she showed the same care and concern for his excellence as she did for the young women whose rights she fought for:

My Dear Miss Reynolds:

... Your gentleness in reviewing me over the phone this a.m. is quite typical of you, Miss Reynolds. I don't think I ever knew you to be other than gentle. This is one reason—among many—why Glenn and I love you.[31]

Arthur

The speeches at her funeral and the lifetime tributes paid to her by prominent men demonstrate that she was respected and cared for by them. Yet, she was equally loved by her sisters. Amy Brown Lyman, then the General Relief Society President, said that Miss Reynolds was a "woman's woman,"[32] and both her service to the Relief Society (board member, magazine editor, and lesson writer) and her political and intellectual interests were focused toward helping women improve their contributions to the world and to the work of the Mormon Church. Part of that work was the struggle for suffrage, a concern for most Relief Society members of the time. Another part of that work was to help women recognize the gifts they had. Her women students talk of individual time Alice spent helping them with their writing, and of her support of those who edited harshly the works of others, feeling that tough criticism would help them to grow.[33] Perhaps indicative of her feelings for women was a long article written by Kathleen Norris that Alice copied into her journal sometime between 1935 and 1938, titled "What Every Woman Almost Knows." A short excerpt may give some glimpses into Alice's thinking:

[*There are no women geniuses*]. *Those who point out these facts tell us that the old plea of her subjection to male domination does not wholly account for woman's ineffectualness. But I think they underestimate the accumulating weight of injustices down through the ages. To be enslaved, ignored, punished, unrewarded, scorned, belittled even for a few days has a fearful effect even on a child. Thus treated, it may never rise to normal free development again. . . But as a matter of simple biological truth the women never have been the weaker sex: women never stayed out of wars, feuds, vendettas, crusades, and piracy and inquisitions because they had not strength to face them! They kept them away because they saw from the very beginning how stupid, wasteful, expensive, and ridiculous all these things were. . .* [34]

An important part of Alice's service was to help women rise above the place in which they found themselves in society. To that end she wrote widely for the church in the *Young Women's Journal,* the *Improvement Era,* the *Instructor,* and the *Relief Society Magazine.* In addition, she wrote lessons for the auxiliaries, including ten years of literary lessons for the Relief Society.[35]

Her admiration for the mind and effective use of the intellect was expressed partly by her love for books, a love which she gave to most of her students and which served to open new horizons for them. Her love of books became the foundation of tangible service. As early as 1922 the first *book shower* was held, in which women of the state honored her for her service by donating books to the Brigham Young University Library. Such spontaneous activities were replaced by the formation of the Alice Louise Reynolds Club on February 19, 1933. There were thirteen chapters of the club located in such diverse places as Provo, Springville, Salt Lake City, Hurricane, St. George, and New York City. Six of these literary clubs, concerned with giving women more study and development of the mind, still exist and are actively concerned with achieving some recognition of Alice Louise Reynolds on the campus where she served for so long. The club was described recently by a member and former student:

Members found in her a champion of their sex, a custodian of their cultural and spiritual values, and an exponent of friendship. They continued to send back books and money, and to sponsor an English student scholarship. Their meetings became spontaneous centers of continuing education.[36]

It is entirely possible that she was so busy using her talents in the service of those around her that she had not time to develop depressions and to pull into herself—at least none of her journals, interviews, or published materials discovered by the author record any such incidents. A delightful note: she was never too busy to notice beauty, wherever she found it, and to express it to those around her. Impishly she remarked in a 1933 Founder's Day Address, "Had I not seen a guide in Rome, in 1906, I should be tempted to say he [J. M. Tanner] was the most handsome man I have ever seen at 28 years of age."[37] (Absent-minded? Twenty-seven years later she remembered the guide, and more than that she remembered Tanner!) "Miss Reynolds," said a student, "managed a remarkable balance—her pleasure in good food, in pretty things, her humor, and her availability to persons and causes."[38]

On December 27, 1933, Miss Reynolds underwent surgery. That she had cancer was not generally known, and her treatment of the fact was such that very few ever suspected. Seemingly her activities were little hampered by the knowledge she had of her approaching death. On April 22, 1934, she records that she spoke at the funeral of Mary J. Allorton, the mother of a student (other speakers included Franklin S. Harris, president of Brigham Young University; Aldous Dixon, superintendent of Provo Schools; Hermese Peterson; and John Nuttal, superintendent of Salt Lake City Schools), and then records other recent funerals at which she had been a speaker. They numbered sixteen.[39] The summer of 1937 saw her visit Europe for the last time, and on December 6, 1938, she died at the LDS Hospital in Salt Lake City after another short illness. Her summary statement to her sister Polly has already been mentioned:

Well, I am not afraid to die. I have lived the best I could, and I am sure no girl or woman ever had a more wonderful life, with more opportunities, more privileges, and more friends. I have been most fortunate and for all these blessings, I am sincerely grateful.[40]

It is significant that this single, childless woman influenced as many lives (perhaps more) as she would have if she had married and had a large posterity. It is a little frustrating that, in studying a person of so legendary a character, little can be discovered that tells of her struggles or that helps one to discover the warts of personality inherent in human nature. At the same time, it is encouraging that so few around her focused on the fact that she was unmarried.

It was recognized that here was an uncommon woman—in strength, in mind, and in her combining of religion, art, and the intellect—and it was recognized that her contributions and gifts were accepted despite the fact that she was not a mother in Israel.

Though Christ is the only ultimate model for any of us, the qualities of self-acceptance, a striving to develop personal gifts, and to use those gifts in the service of others as shown by Alice Louise Reynolds are worthy of consideration in seeking models of those who hear a different drummer yet who exemplify the Christ-like life. There are far too few models for women at all in the church, and even fewer who demonstrate the full and abundant life of courage and peace while not in the traditional mold. Alice deserves further study, and there are many other women in our heritage who can help us through the maze of current issues. We need to find them, to study them, and see them as real people who can help us to solve real problems.

Notes

1. Dallin H. Oaks, August 27, 1975, speech at Brigham Young University reported in *The Y News*, September 2, 1975.

2. *Gospel* is a term used by Mormons to refer to the theology and doctrine as contained in the scriptures and preaching of Church leaders.

3. Amy Brown Lyman, *A Lighter of Lamps, The Life Story of Alice Louise Reynolds*, Provo, Utah, The Alice Louise Reynolds Club, 1947, p. 72.

4. Alice Louise Reynolds, "History of George Reynolds," manuscript, Brigham Young University, p. 35.

5. "Autobiographical Notes 1935-1938," Holograph, Archives, The Church of Jesus Christ of Latter-day Saints, Salt Lake City, December 17, 1935, entry.

6. Lyman, p. 7.

7. "Autobiography of Alice Louise Reynolds" typescript, Brigham Young University, pp. 1-2.

8. *Ibid.*, p. 2.

9. Reynolds, "History of George Reynolds," p. 33.

10. Interview with Helen Stark, Algie Ballif, and Naoma Earl at BYU on August 8, 1975.

11. Elsie C. Carroll, "Our Alice Louise," pamphlet published by Alice Louise Reynolds Clubs, March 1950.

12. Stark, Ballif, Earl interview.

13. *Ibid.*

14. *Ibid.*

15. *Ibid.*

16. "Supplement to Miss Reynolds Autobiography," typescript, BYU.

17. Helen C. Stark, Letter of August 11, 1975, in possession of author.

18. "Autobiography," pp. 3-9.

19. Amy Brown Lyman, Speech to Alice Louise Reynolds Clubs,

April 1, 1957, typescript, Harold B. Lee Library, pp. 2-3.

20. "Autobiographical Notes," 1934.

21. *Ibid.*, 1935-38.

22. Alice Louise Reynolds, "Music that Pays Dividends," *National Education Association Journal of Proceedings and Addresses,* University of Chicago Press, Chicago, Illinois, 1913, p. 610.

23. "Autobiography," p. 39.

24. *Ibid.*, p. 39.

25. Alice Louise Reynolds, "The Story of My Life," speech given to Alice Louise Reynolds Clubs, April 1, 1935, typescript, BYU, p. 11.

26. Telephone conversation, Earnest Partridge, September 28, 1976, by Sharon Christensen.

27. Lyman speech, p. 3.

28. Lyman, p. 60.

29. The Relief Society is the Women's Organization of the LDS Church. The *General Board* refers to the Church-wide leadership, which supervises individual stake (diocese) and ward (parish) boards.

30. "Autobiographical Notes."

31. Letters of Alice Louise Reynolds, Brigham Young University.

32. Alice Louise Reynolds' Journal, 1935-38.

33. Interview, August 8, 1975.

34. Alice Louise Reynolds' Journal, 1935-38.

35. Lyman speech.

36. Helen C. Stark, unpublished manuscript, in possession of author.

37. Alice Louise Reynolds, "Founders Day Address," 1933, typescript, BYU, p. 7.

38. Stark letter.

39. "Autobiographical Notes," February 18, 1934, to October 29, 1937.

40. Lyman, p. 72.

Stena Scorup 1888–1950

*As a citizen of Salina for the first
eighteen years of her life, the author,
Vicky Burgess-Olson, grew up
hearing the legends about Stena
Scorup. The two never met, since the
author was only five years old when
Stena died. Determined to learn more
than legend, Dr. Burgess-Olson spent
a number of years researching the life
of Stena Scorup. In the search she
produced not only this essay, but
developed an increased awareness of
herself as a woman, politician, and
an educator with foundations in a
small town in southern Utah.*

Stena Scorup

Vicky Burgess-Olson

It was 1922 in the little town of Salina, Utah, 150 miles south of Salt Lake City; national suffrage had been granted only two years previous. The *Weaker Sex* were still rarely taken seriously in exercising their ballot, though, and the mere thought that one of them might be trusted in an executive position of government was intolerable to many.

A woman walked to the polls to vote after a long day of being principal and English teacher at the local high school. A group of friends had urged her to become a candidate for mayor on the Citizen's Ticket; she had had no desire to take part in the campaign, but after considerable thought had decided to let her name be placed on the ticket—she thought it might add a little excitement to an otherwise uninteresting city election. Her opponent turned out to be her brother, P. C. Scorup, a prominent sheepman and Republican in the community.[1]

As she walked she thought, "I was surely a fool to let my name be used on that ticket. Won't I be embarrassed if I am the only person who votes for me? I'll see that I get at least one vote." When she went home for dinner, her brother Albert bet her five dollars that she'd be elected. She was sure she wouldn't be and sincerely *hoped* she wouldn't be but she wanted a few votes anyway. She was busy with school plans when the telephone rang. It was her opponent congratulating her on her victory in the election. Not believing him, she returned to her desk. The telephone rang again, and the chairman of the Citizen's Ticket notified her that she had been elected mayor.[2]

This was just one event in the life of Stena Scorup, a legend in the town of Salina, but it was a significant event and an event that demonstrates how she met most of the situations in her life: she wanted to run for public office, yet she had a pronounced (and understandable) fear of losing the election and failing as mayor.

Another example of this type of ambivalent behavior is found in the characteristic way she describes herself in her autobiographies as having been a large, awkward child with a big mouth and mouse-colored hair, who liked nice clothes and wore them whenever possible. She never hesitated to perform in plays, to sing, or to speak in public. Later her peers pictured her as tall, graceful, stately, personable, energetic, dynamic, and as having a very strong personality. It was frequently reported that she liked to have her hair done and that she enjoyed facials.[3]

Even her name represents some ambivalence. Her name was neither Stena nor Scorup, for she was christened Mary Christena—Mary for the great-aunt who had reared her father, Christena for her mother's dearest friend. Her mother called her *Stena* with the Danish accent, and Stena came to love her name and would never sign herself anything else. Her father's name was Christen Christensen, but after coming to Utah from Denmark he adopted the name Scorup to identify himself among the throng of Utah Christensens. *Scorup* was the *Gore* (or farm) on which he worked in Denmark.[4]

The Scorups experienced constant struggle. Stena was the seventh of eight children. Her father was an invalid who had suffered from a severe hernia for as long as Stena could remember. His suffering—fainting, crawling to the house on his hands and knees, being confined to his bed for more than half the day—was an indelible memory for Stena. The care of eight children was sufficient work for any mother with the poor conveniences at hand in those pioneer days, and her mother had to assume even greater responsibility. Stena's heart ached for her mother, and she tried to help by taking part of the responsibility of the household. Because of this, Stena became aware of the problems of adults at an early age. She often thought the world was unkind to her mother and Stena resented this, wondering how to lighten her mother's burdens, wanting to help and anxious to learn. Throughout her life Stena sought to give aid to her family, but she also sought and felt a sense of freedom and relief the few times in her life when she was able to leave her family for extended periods.[5]

The Scorup children were an interesting and varied lot. Peter Christian Scorup, known as *P.C.*, was the eldest. He became a prominent citizen in southern Utah with extensive dealings in livestock, particularly sheep, and in the mercantile business. He is listed in a book of *Utah's Distinguished Personalities*.

The next two sons left Salina as young men to make their fortune. James Halvor was slow-speaking and reserved, dominated by the more outgoing personality of his younger brother, James Albert. Their large holdings in land and cattle in San Juan County became a legend in southern Utah and are described in a book that Albert commissioned Stena to write in her later years (to keep her occupied and financed) entitled *J. A. Scorup, Utah Cattleman*. Both brothers helped finance schooling and missions for Stena and her sisters. Stena obviously adored Albert; her book is a one-sided tribute to his virtues, with nothing about the controversial aspects of his financial dealings. Albert apparently filled many masculine roles as one of the few adequate men in Stena's life. James died when he was a fairly young man, leaving orphan children; his wife had died in a flu epidemic nine months before James died.

Another brother, Victor, contracted either infantile paralysis or spinal meningitis (it is difficult to determine) at the age of nine months, which left him paralyzed on his left side and almost helpless. Stena describes his early life as a very unfortunate existence; he was teased constantly by neighborhood children and was subject to fits that had to be controlled. In spite of all this he was cheerful most of the time.[6]

Stena had three sisters, all of them cultured and refined by the standards of their time. In terms of Mormon theology, her older sister, Caroline Johanne, had a rather unusual ordinance performed posthumously. Johanne died unwed when she was twenty years old. Her parents were anxious to have her married to someone suitable because of the Mormon emphasis on marriage and its importance in the afterlife. A friend of the family had an unmarried son who also died when he was very young; though he was older than Johanne and they had never met, the parents of the two young people had a marriage ceremony performed in the Mormon temple by proxy, thus sealing them together for eternity.

Alvilda, Stena's next older sister and a near centenarian, is still living at this writing. The venerable woman is in many ways Salina's intellect-in-residence.

Little is known of Stena's early childhood. Stena remembered it as a time when she lived with her own thoughts and in her own closed world. Her mother had too much to do to dote on her, and she grew into school age "nearly free from the interference or attention of others."

Because of ill health, Stena did not begin school until she was eight. There, to her surprise, she found that she could be the best student in the class if she tried. Another surprise to her was that her teachers liked her. Where at first Stena had avoided school, she then encountered it and achieved continual success.

As a student Stena had no sorrows except that the other children pulled her hair frequently because they thought that she was the teacher's pet.

In 1899 when Stena was seventeen she attended one year at the

University of Utah with her sister. By "burning the midnight oil" Stena found that she and her sister had the ability "to out-class" the better trained Salt Lakers. Their brothers were paying the sisters' tuition, and there were not even pennies for clothes. Socially the girls were ostracized, but Stena, who thought of herself as "plain and awkward" anyway, found the price cheap for the privilege of studying with admirable and stimulating teachers who "taught students, not subjects," as she recorded in her autobiography. This was the last full year that Stena ever attended school; there were problems at home that needed her attention.[7]

The demands of Stena's family kept her in Salina for most of her life. At eighteen it was necessary for her to begin teaching school for eighteen dollars a month. Almost anyone in Salina over the age of forty-seven can remember being taught by Stena Scorup. As a classroom teacher Stena taught music, psychology, and English. She taught in the Utah schools of Redmond, Richfield, Elsinore, Heber City, and Park City, but most of the time she taught in Salina. She was a motivating teacher, yet she was not overbearing; she did something for the students besides just teach. She inspired her students, developing in each one thoroughness and determination by giving each a "relative ideal." For example, she told one boy that he reminded her of Matthew Arnold; after learning who Arnold was, the boy had both his teacher's praise and a goal. She was insistent. When she called roll each day, each student said "prepared" or "unprepared" for the daily assignment. When a student was unprepared, Stena looked over her glasses at him, and he went ahead and did his work.[8]

Venna Poulsen Johnson, now a teacher herself, reported:

I was not any great student, not a great whirlwind but if it had not been for Miss Scorup, I would have never gone on with my education. She called me into her office one day and said, "You have a fine mind." Now as I think about it I am sure she must have told this to many, but to me, it was a personal touch. At that age, I was so impressionable I thought, I do? Maybe there is hope for me after all. You know, this is something I do not think teachers do to kids anymore. You do not get the personal contact with them. You stand up in front of the school room and give them the devil, lay it on the line, tell them what they should think and what they should do. But she would very often call you in. I do not know how she got around to as many as she must have done.

Over the years Stena developed a philosophy that education should be experience-centered and full of activity and involvement. She implemented these ideas as principal of North Sevier High School, an office she held for nine years beginning in 1929. Along with intensive classroom work, her students were involved in

operas, concerts, plays, an elaborate annual carnival, beautiful formal dances, clubs, lyceums, assemblies, yearbooks, school newspapers, and bulletins.[9] The high school also became a community
center for student events and for an adult education program.
Stena worked night and day with the young students so that they
might enjoy the same opportunities as did the high school students
from larger and better financed schools.

In 1911, at the age of twenty-nine, Stena Scorup was called to
serve her church on a mission to the northern United States. She
had no money, her father was still ill and quite old and needed
her help, and her invalid brother also needed her. Yet she really
desired to go, and her father wanted her to go since his sons had
never filled missions. Her family came to her aid. One of her
brothers promised to finance the mission, and her youngest sister
made arrangements to care for the family. Stena was supremely
happy. She would have no financial worries, no family cares, and
no school anxieties.[10]

She became an unusual missionary, using her own individual
approach with never a loss of energy. Working in Michigan and
Chicago, she became a good public speaker—she even became good
at street speaking. She also liked tracting (knocking on front doors
seeking people to teach) in spite of the doors that were slammed
in her face. She had a method of calming people down when they
became excited and angry, and then initiating a good gospel conversation. She made a number of converts, and when her release
came she did not want to go home where people cared little for
religion.[11]

All her life Stena was a devout member of the Mormon Church.
She had started teaching Sunday School when she was twelve
years old, and had been in the MIA presidency since she was fourteen; she was also president of the Primary for awhile. When she
returned from her mission she became a very popular Sunday
School teacher, and people came from all over the state to hear
her "preach."

Stena had a number of accomplished, well-educated nieces who
became missionaries for the Mormon Church. She seemed to serve
as an example for them, and was much involved in the lives of
both her nieces and her nephews.

Stena had a continual drive for further learning. By attending
summer schools, Stena was able in 1928 to receive her bachelor of
science degree with honors at the age of forty-seven at what was
then Utah State Agricultural College; one of her professors had
tried to talk her out of going back to school because she was "too
old to learn." And at age fifty-one she received a master of science

degree in the Department of Philosophy of Education at Brigham Young University. Her excellent thesis was entitled *Character Education*.[13]

Just for variety, one summer instead of attending summer school Stena forsook her books and tackled the trials of ranch cooking on Indian Creek Cattle Ranch, one of the largest ranches in Utah, owned by W. G. Summerville and her brother, John Albert. Here her acquaintances ranged from cow punchers to oil magnates. She spent a delightful summer and learned that a bad cook made everything go wrong and a good cook made life pleasant. Although she enjoyed the change and the wonderful scenery, she preferred her schoolroom for a permanent place of occupation.[14]

The public reputation that led to Stena's election as mayor was preceded with much community involvement. As a popular speaker, Stena spoke frequently at state teacher conventions and at such civic functions as Memorial Day and Fourth of July celebrations.

The small community of Salina produced a number of plays and operettas, and Stena almost always was in the main cast. She particularly enjoyed comedy roles, but she directed and sang in concerts, cantatas, and operettas, some of which she wrote herself.

Stena joined important women's clubs and was a progressive in public movements in the communities in which she taught. As one of an influential group of citizens in Salina who established the Public Library, she became a member of the first library board and was later president of the board for a number of years. Her friends were many, both men and women, Mormons and non-Mormons, and she enjoyed an active social life.

Then in 1921 she became involved in the "snarls of local politics." Newspapers all over Utah reported that Stena Scorup had been elected mayor of Salina, running as an Independent against her "standpat" Republican, political boss brother. Prohibition was a big issue then, and Stena was opposed to drinking, while her brother thought that people should be allowed to do as they chose. The people knew Pete and they knew Stena, and they chose Stena.

Thus Stena Scorup became the second woman to be elected mayor in the state of Utah. She did her job well. During her term of office the main street in Salina was surfaced, power lines were moved from the middle to the sides of the streets, electric lights were installed along the main streets, the city was helped out of debt, and water conditions were improved.[15] Stena tried to stop bootlegging, but it was too powerful and complicated a problem for her office.[16]

As mayor of Salina she received so much publicity that it became embarrassing for her. At state municipal conventions she was the only woman delegate. She claims in her autobiography that the men expected a beautiful, sophisticated, aggressive woman of note while "I was merely a homely, humble school teacher. Still they fussed over me so much and insisted that I dance with all of them, that I make speeches at the meetings and toasts at the banquets and that I discuss with them my political philosophy."[17]

On New Year's Eve when Stena's term of office as mayor was over, she and her town council, all men, hosted a barbeque for the entire town. Beeves were roasted in large pits in the center of town, and there was dancing in all the public buildings that were large enough to hold dancers.[18]

Caring for an invalid brother, attempting to guide and care for her adolescent nieces and nephews, teaching a full course in English in a rural high school, and at the same time being the mayor of a city of 1,500 people so depleted Stena's seemingly inexhaustible energies that at the end of her term as mayor she had to consult a physician. Her heart had begun to "wobble."[19]

In 1944 she retired from school when her poor health finally made the decision for her. On November 28, 1945, "Stena Scorup Day" was declared in Salina. Cards, letters, and telegrams poured in from all around the United States. A program was held at the high school in her honor, and she was presented with a seventeen-jewel lapel pin. The tributes must have been joyful rather than ponderously sincere, for the superintendent of education in his summary tribute observed that "No one is dead and I am so happy this program is being carried out accordingly." With a joyful twinkle in her eye, Stena said, "No one is happier than I that no one is dead." At the reception following the program hundreds of guests greeted her, many of them former students.[20] Many remembered her as the teacher who had most influenced their lives.

Stena Scorup made a mark on the town of Salina and its people. She was not a flamboyant person, but she was always there. She was unpretentious. She never imposed herself; she was a natural leader.

Stena herself saw her life as an ordinary one, full of missed opportunities, and she saw herself as a school teacher, nothing more. As her life drew to a close and she reflected on its disappointments, she decided that a more traditional course might have made her happier:

To my nieces and nephews and to all the previous and younger generation whom I adore and in whom I am so much interested. Do not follow my example. Get married and make a home of your very own and have as many children as you can educate as they should be. Do not get so lost in your profession and work or allow home respon-

sibilities, however urgent and necessary, deprive you of having a family and making a real home of your own for them.[21]

In evaluating Stena's basic approach to life, there is a definite pattern. Psychotherapists would call this pattern approach-avoidance behavior. Most every life lived has its share of anxiety, and avoidance is the automatic reaction to this anxiety. Where a situation cannot be physically avoided or where responses lead to anxiety, avoidance occurs by repressing the situation and the response events.

All of us approach and avoid life in different aspects and degrees. Whether or not we reduce the tension produced by difficult situations in our lives by meeting them and mastering them, such as Stena did with formal education, or whether we avoid them, or whether to some degree we do both depends upon the degree of our mental strength at the time.

In Stena's case there seemed to be a pattern of approach-avoidance behavior beginning with her self concept. She described herself as ugly, yet she took every advantage to present herself and to present herself looking well. She even changed her name—the badge of life.

This woman sought public office when it was a unique thing for a woman to do, yet she was afraid of winning; she wanted to win, but did not think that she would. Thus she approached a situation, wanted to avoid it, and then took the challenge well.

Feeling a great responsibility for her parents and her siblings and her nieces and nephews, Stena still sought to leave them whenever she could justify it. Perhaps being single without the responsibility of her own husband and children caused her to feel more responsible for caring for her family of origin than do others, and the simple need for relief from this time- and energy-consuming job drove her to totally enjoy and seek out the few extended periods of time when she was relieved. But here again there was great ambivalence.

Though active in the Mormon Church, she had difficulty with one basic principle—"celestial marriage." She writes, "I am one member of our family who will never go to heaven. I am doomed, according to our faith, to be a servant in the next world for ever and ever."[22] In another autobiography, written in the third person, she is even more revealing about her ambivalence. "According to her religious faith, since she is doomed to continue a servant to others through eternity, she thinks it won't matter much anyway."[23] What won't matter—her life, eternity, being doomed? Does she believe or doesn't she? Total acceptance does not seem to exist, but externally she seemed to accept her interpretation of Mormon doctrine and to remain dedicated to her church her entire life.

Interesting comments as to why Stena remained single were obtained in oral interviews. "Stena admired the young men her age, but she was not congenial enough to them. She was too busy teaching. The things Stena did did not make up for her not having marriage and a family. It does for some women, but not Stena."

"No man would have her."

"She fell in love, but the man married someone else."

"Not much choice of men in Salina."[24]

There was a definite love-hate relationship between Stena Scorup and the town of Salina. It was in Salina where she both succeeded and failed. She felt the town as a whole did not appreciate the finer things of life, such as music and art and a firm commitment to religion. It was in Salina where the businessmen saw her carnivals as competition. Each year her school carnivals would take in a large sum of money for other school projects, thus taking business away from downtown. The business people joined forces to have her removed as principal of the high school. She felt held back by the town from accomplishment, but it was also there that she accomplished. The town thus became her scapegoat and her success.

Though this approach-avoidance sequence is apparent in many issues of her life, there was one major area where Stena Scorup made full commitment and effort—that of being an educator. After holding back from first attending school as a young child, she knew what she wanted to do and did it without hesitation. External events such as lack of money caused her to delay her education, but internally she was committed and sought that end. Teaching was the pure and applied science of her life. She could philosophize about it and work at it twelve hours a day, every day of the week. It filled her need for a satisfying self-concept, a significant relationship with Salina, a way to earn a living as a single woman, and an excuse not to marry. Stena Scorup was foremost an educator, and here there was no avoidance.

Notes

1. Scorup, Stena, *The Story of a School Teacher: An Autobiography of Stena,* unpublished, p. 26.

2. *Ibid.*

3. *Ibid.,* pp. 4-5.

4. *Ibid.,* p. 1.

5. *Ibid.,* p. 3.

6. *Ibid.,* pp. 2-3.

7. *Ibid.,* pp. 11-12.

8. Oral interview, L. A. Christensen.

9. Scorup, Stena, "A Critique of Current Educational Methods of Character Education," unpublished master's thesis, Brigham Young University, 1933.

10. Scorup, *The Story of a School Teacher,* pp. 19-21.

11. *Ibid.*

12. Oral interviews.

13. Scorup, *The Story of a School Teacher,* p. 24.

14. *Salina Sun,* September 3, 1926.

15. *Salt Lake Tribune,* "Woman Directs Salina Affairs," February 19, 1922.

16. Scorup, *The Story of a School Teacher,* pp. 27-28.

17. *Ibid.,* p. 29.

18. *Ibid.,* p. 30.

19. *Ibid.,* p. 31.

20. *Salina Sun,* December 7, 1945.

21. Scorup, Stena, *Mary Christinia Scorup: Stena, Aunt T and Miss Scorup,* unpublished autobiography in possession of Vicky Burgess-Olson, unpaginated.

22. *Ibid.*

23. Scorup, *The Story of a School Teacher,* p. 20.

24. Oral interviews.

Bibliography

Burgess-Olson, Vicky, "Stena Scorup: First Lady of Salina," *Ensign*, March 1976, pp. 29-30.

Freud, Sigmund, *General Introduction to Psychoanalysis,* Garden City Publishers, Garden City, New York, 1943.

Genealogical Society of The Church of Jesus Christ of Latter-day Saints, Salt Lake City, Utah, family group sheets, vital statistics of the Scorup families.

Oral Interviews, summer of 1969, Salina residents and former Salina residents: Alvilda Scorup Anderson, Oscar Allred, Stanley D Burgess, G. M. Burr, L. A. Christiansen, Edith Scorup Clinger, Verna Johnson, Annie Jorgensen, Edith MacDonald, Bell Sorensen

Judge Ferdinand Erickson, interviewed in the Sevier County Court House December 3, 1969. Sixth District Judge and formerly prosecuting officer in Sevier County in 1925.

Salina City Council Minutes, Roll Book 1922-1923.

Salina City Sexton Records.

Salina Sun 1911-1969.

Salt Lake Tribune, "Woman Directs Salina Affairs," February 19, 1922, pp. 1-2.

Scorup, Stena, *J. A. Scorup, Utah Cattleman,* privately published, 1944.

Scorup, Stena, "A Critique of Current Educational Methods of Character Education," unpublished master's thesis, Brigham Young University, 1933.

Scorup, Stena, *Mary Christinia Scorup: Stena, Aunt T and Miss Scorup.* unpublished autobiography in possession of Alvilda Scorup Anderson, Salina, Utah.

Scorup, Stena, *The Story of a School Teacher: An Autobiography of Stena Scorup,* unpublished autobiography in possession of Vicky Burgess-Olson.

The actual scenes set in this essay and the words of Stena Scorup were taken from those described in the sources above and are not an invention of the author.

Patty Bartlett Sessions 1795–1893

Susan Sessions Rugh is the great-great-great-granddaughter of Patty Bartlett Sessions. Susan was born in Provo, Utah, and her childhood was spent in such widely scattered locations as Salt Lake City, Utah; Cambridge, Massachusetts; Alhambra, California; Lima, Peru; and Palo Alto, California.

She attended Brigham Young University and majored in history with a Spanish minor. A member of the Honors Program and active in student government, she graduated in April 1974 magna cum laude.

She is married to Thomas F. Rugh and they have two sons. The Rughs recently returned from residence in Salzburg, Austria, where they were affiliated with the Brigham Young University Study Abroad Program.

Patty B. Sessions

Susan Sessions Rugh

Patty Sessions is now well known for her service as a pioneer midwife. Her legendary 3,977 deliveries earned her the title of "Mother of Mormon Midwifery."[1] However, Patty's accomplishments extended far beyond her role as midwife, even into the fields of horticulture and education. From an historical perspective perhaps her most significant contribution is her diary, which presents a fascinating account of the Mormon exodus from Nauvoo and the early settlement of the Salt Lake Valley.

Patty was born in Bethel, Maine, on February 4, 1795, to Enoch Bartlett, a shoemaker, and Anna Hall, a weaver. Patty's childhood was strongly influenced by her mother, who taught her the art of weaving and the value of hard work. Much against her parents' wishes, Patty married David Sessions of Newry, Maine, on June 28, 1812.[2] The young couple settled near the elder Sessionses in Ketcham, Maine, and David soon "bought land and made a farm built a log house and a large fraim barn."[3]

Shortly after their marriage Patty had her first encounter with midwifery:

They [the Sessions] lived ten miles in the woods and were not near any physician. One day a young woman was taken suddenly ill, and sent for Mother Sessions, who was in the habit of attending obstetrical cases in the vicinity; she was very feeble and had to be led, and before she had time to go any distance, another messenger came telling the young Mrs. Sessions to run as quickly as she possibly could. She hurried on with all speed and when she arrived it was thought the young woman was dying; Mrs. Sessions who was entirely unskilled in affairs of the kind, but had abundant nerve force and moral courage, took the child and put the mother in bed before Mother Sessions arrived; the old lady showed her how to dress the baby, which after doing she started homeward. A short time afterwards the doctor and some other help came, but all was over. The doctor examined the mother and child to see that all was right, and finding everything in a good condition, he was anxious to see the young and inexperienced woman who had so skillfully performed the work. The doctor called upon her and congratulated her upon her ability, and told her she must attend to that business, not to have any fear, for she would prosper in it, as it was a new country and there were many about to move in, it would be necessary to have more help of this kind.[4]

This experience marked the beginning of Patty's lifelong career as a midwife. Training from Mother Sessions and the near-daily event of delivering children enhanced Patty's natural skills.

The expansion of the farm to four hundred acres was paralleled by the growth of their family to eight children. Only three—Perrigrine, Sylvia, and David—survived the backwoods epidemics of cholera and typhoid fever.[5]

Patty was baptized into the Methodist Church in 1816, having read in the Bible that baptism was necessary. David, her husband, later professed the same faith and was baptized in January 1820. The family remained Methodist until Mormonism was introduced into the neighborhood in August 1833. As with Methodism, Patty became converted to the new religion before her husband did; she joined the Mormon Church in 1834, and he followed a year later.[6]

In a church conference held in August 1835 at which Brigham Young and other church officials were present, "the gathering of the Saints was taught and preparations began to be made to remove to Zion." On June 5, 1837, the Sessionses left their family and friends and traveled to Kirtland, Ohio.[7] From Kirtland the family journeyed to Missouri, "where they lost all they possessed when the Saints were driven from that state in 1838."[8] The Sessionses then made Nauvoo their home until the Mormon exodus of February 1846.

On February 10, 1846, Patty's diary begins in the "City of Joseph, Hancock Co., Ill." Patty and her husband "bade ... children and friends goodby and started for the West" two days later.[9] They traveled in a company of fifty that was captained by their eldest son, Perrigrine.[10] David Sessions was lame, so Patty generally walked at the yoke, traveling a total of 1,030 miles on foot.[11]

From the pages of her journal a clear picture of the pioneer journey emerges. It was often difficult to keep the wagons upright and the livestock near, and Patty and David were no exception. She had to keep a constant vigil over her possessions; after the group had been out for a month she wrote, "Yesterday felt bad. I was not well and I and our things were scatured on account of a heavy load and bad road and were in 9 different places. We are all together now but our cow."[12] These troubles caused her some delay in traveling, and she feared that she would be left behind.

The heavy rains in the initial months of the journey caused her some "anxiety of mind," but a sunny day brightened her attitude:

I rose this morning the sun shines with splendor which gladens our hearts. Our waggon cover is froze hard and mud and watter a little froze overshoes to the tent. The ground is so wet that many could not lie down without lying in the water.[13]

Despite the heavy seasonal rains, "Br Brigham came up with his company driving his team in the rain and mud to his knees as happy as a king."[14] His leadership was a calming and unifying force as the Saints traveled through the constant downpour.

Although the pioneers lived in primitive tents and wagons as they traveled, they did not forget the habits they had formed in a more civilized past. This juxtaposition of lifestyles is often startling, as in the July 18, 1847, entry: "Bake mince pies bread and meat over buffalo dung." Patty faithfully ironed clothes as they moved along.

Not all was housekeeping and drudgery in the pioneer camps. Patty portrays an atmosphere of mutual encouragement and unity in a common cause that led to many happy associations and enduring friendships. The Mormons achieved a special closeness in their Sabbath meetings. Patty described such a Sunday reunion:

Went to meeting. Dr. Richards at the close of the meeting spoke very feeling said it was two years this time that he came into Nauvoo with the bodies of the Prophets. How changed the scene. The people then were in tears howling and lamenting their loss. Now they were without a house in tents and waggons clothed with a spirit of rejoicing and a smile upon every face.[15]

The memory of the death of Joseph Smith and the problems of Nauvoo had been overshadowed by the rigors of their journey. Facing these new challenges together produced an initial cheerful tolerance in the pioneer camp.

At times the appearance of Indians lent excitement to a dull journey. On July 4, 1846, Patty recorded: "It being independence the Indians rode out in style. Came to our camp danced the war dance. Were painted dressed in their fashion." She recounted another friendly visit from the Indians more than a year later, talking of mutual celebration:

The Indians have come in sight this morning . . . 10 A.M. they began to come. We stay here today. Many squaws came today. They appear friendly. They sing dance and ride around. We dance and have music. Fire two cannons. Parley and Taylor feast and smoke with the Chief.[16]

The Mormons made great efforts to keep peace with the sometimes friendly, sometimes hostile tribes of plains Indians.

Patty served as a midwife to women in the camps. Her position was a fulltime occupation and demanded great energy, which Patty willingly devoted. As a midwife she was an expert in delivering the babies that proliferated among Mormon women. One day she "put three women to bed" with babies before noon![17]

Often she had to travel quite a distance at great inconvenience to herself to deliver a baby. Patty's uncomplaining acceptance of calls to duty is seen in her description of one particularly difficult task:

Went to bed and It soon began to thunder and lighten and the rain came faster than ever. About 2 o'clock in the morning I was called to go back two miles. It then snowed. I rode behind the man and through mud and water some of the way belly deep to the horse. I found the sister that I was caled to in an old log cabin. Her child was born before I got there. She had rode 13 miles after she was in travail. Crossed the creek on a log after dark. Her husband carried over such things as was necessary. Left his waggons and teams on the other side as water had carried of the bridge.[18]

Patty's knowledge of herbal remedies and first aid were also in demand. Her home remedy for jaundice was to take "one table spoonful of casteel soap shavings mixed with shugar three mornings then miss three untill it is taken nine mornings. Shure cure." Tea was often used to cure minor ailments, as here in the case of Brigham Young: "Br Brigham and wife came in. He said he was sick. I made some tea. He drank it said he felt better."[19]

Patty was also called to treat injuries as well as illnesses. After the pioneers had been traveling four days, she wrote: "Brother Taylor . . . Had one team that got frightened ran down hill upset the waggon. Hurt a lady and a boy some. I helped dress her wounds and made her tea." Again, tea was an indispensable medicine.

While in Winter Quarters Patty was asked to help an unmarried woman who was pregnant. Patty took compassion on her and arranged "to have a bedstead fixed up for her and to make her comfortable." She wrote of her feelings in her diary on January 26, 1847: "Although I thought she was a bad woman yet she lay on the ground and about to be confined and I pited [pitied] her."

Patty supplemented midwifery and herbal medicine with her own brand of medicine: spiritual healing. She often blessed the sick by the "laying on of hands."[20] Although presently Mormon Church convention is for male priesthood holders to perform such an ordinance, in Patty's day women, too, were healers. Patty and her sisters frequently blessed one another when they were ill. One such incident was described by Patty: "Sister Buel had the toothache bad. We laid hands on her."[21] Early in the journey across the plains Patty recorded, "Our horse was sick last night but they laid hands on him and he is better to day."[22]

David Sessions joined his wife at times in visiting and healing the sick. Patty wrote on April 1, 1847: "Mr. Sessions and I then visited the sick. Anointed and laid hands and [*illegible*] a blessing."

When there was no one to assist her, Patty went alone, laying on hands and anointing the sick.

Association between the sisters led to the organization of informal gatherings of women in the camp. The purpose of these meetings is unclear, but it seems that they were of both a spiritual and a social nature. There must have been a great need for close sisterhood to provide encouragement and spiritual relief in times of hardship and tedium on the prairies. The meetings were generally held at least once a week.

Patty was a proponent of these meetings. She called one on January 1, 1847: "I had a new years party. Eliza Snow, Eliza Beaman, Zina Jacobs etc were here. Enjoyed myself well. Opened and read the sixtyeth chapter of Isiah." A second meeting was also initiated by Patty: "Then in the evening collected Zina Jacobs, Eliza Snow, sister Mancum at sister Buels . . . we prayed sung in tongues spoke in tongues and had a good time."[23] Eliza R. Snow collaborated with Patty in arranging the reunions. Patty wrote on May 1, 1847: "Sylvia and I went to a meeting to Sister Leonards. None but females there. We had a good meeting. I presided. It was got up by E R Snow. They spoke in tongues. I interpreted some prophesied. It was a feast."

In addition to speaking in tongues and interpreting the tongues, the sisters gave one another prophetic blessings at these meetings. The blessings were a great comfort to the pioneer women and seemed to fill a spiritual void that was created by the demands of their temporal life. One blessing that was given to Patty at such a gathering is recorded in her diary on May 29, 1847:

Sisters Young and Whitney laid their hands upon my head and predicted many things that I should be blesed with that I should live to stand in a temple yet to be built and Joseph would be there. I should see him and there I should officiate for my labours should then be done in order and they should be great and I should be blesed and by many and there I should bless many and many should be brought unto me saying your hands were the first that handled me. Bless me and after I had blesed them their mothers would rise up and bless me for they would be brought to me by Joseph himself for he loved little children and he would bring my little ones to me and my heart was fild with joy and rejoiceing.

Patty continued to derive great solace and hope from this blessing. On one occasion, Eliza R. Snow sang a blessing to those present.[24]

Patty was also instrumental in developing the spiritual gifts of younger girls who felt intimidated by mature women in the regular gatherings. She held special meetings for the girls alone to help them overcome their reticence. Patty told of the first such meeting on June 27, 1847, in her diary:

I then came home had a little meeting in our waggon. It was good. My grand-daughter Martha Ann had the gift of toungues but through fear did not speak. After the sisters had gone she aked [asked] me to let her and Martha Van Cott have a litle meetting and wished me to attend. We went into our waggon. She Spoke in toungues and prayed. I gave the interpretation and then told them to spend their time in that way and they would be blessed. She is eleven years old.

Patty felt that the Lord was "pouring his spirit out on the youth,"[25] and so nurtured their gifts by sponsoring these gatherings.

A close friendship with Eliza R. Snow was an outgrowth of these frequent meetings of women. The prominent Mormon poetess and theologian spent a great deal of time with Patty, often staying overnight in Patty's wagon, visiting the sick and attending spiritual meetings with the midwife. On Patty's birthday on February 4, 1847, when Eliza came to take her to a party Patty asked Eliza to bless her. A month later Eliza made Patty a cap and composed a poem for her.[26] The style of Eliza R. Snow is unmistakable in its comforting and hope-filled lines addressed to Patty, her sister in the gospel. Eliza and Patty gave each other mutual encouragement and together led the female Saints in spiritual meetings.

The spiritual feasts of the prairies were not limited to the sisters. Often Patty and her husband visited their neighbors, speaking in tongues, interpreting, and prophesying. On one occasion David Sessions presided at a women's meeting he attended with his wife. Patty wrote on April 23, 1847: "Mr. Sessions presided and we had a good time. We prayed prophesied and spoke in tongues and interpreted and were refreshed." David and Patty also enjoyed spiritual experiences at parties, where they "feasted then blesed and was blesed."[27]

Although Patty and David attended such meetings and visited the sick together, their relationship deteriorated with the return of David's other wife. Rosilla Cowans was sealed to David (in essence, married) for time and eternity by Brigham Young in Nauvoo on October 3, 1845.[28] Rosilla did not accompany David and Patty when they left Nauvoo, but joined them on June 22, 1846, four months later. At that point Patty's lifelong trials with the Mormon institution of polygamy began. Patty's marriage to David was severely tested by the strain that was imposed by another wife.

After Rosilla's arrival and David's subsequent disappearance
from Patty's bed, Patty recorded her sadness on July 11, 1847: "I
eat my breakfast but I am so full of grief that there is no room for
food and I soon threw it up. I can only say I feel bad." Patty and
David became further estranged later in July, after which a severe
illness confined Patty to her bed for a month. She emerged from
her illness to her old problems, and wrote of her disappointment
on September 8, 1847:

*I feel bad again. He has been and talked to Rosilla and she fild his ears full and
when he came to my bed I was quite chled [chilled] he was gone so long and I was
so cold I had been crying, He began to talk hard to me before he got into bed and
thretens me very hard of leaving me.*

Later in the month Patty and her husband seemed to have come
to an understanding and he had long talks with Rosilla, advising
her to help Patty with the housework.

Rosilla refused to work, and harsh words passed between her
and Patty. On November 2, 1847, a confrontation between the two
wives occurred, as Patty describes:

*. . . before supper [she] gave me the lie many times and talked very saucy to me and
when I could bear it no longer I told her to hold her toungue and if she gave me the
lie again I would throug the tongs at her. She then talk very saucy to me. I told her
there was the tent door and she might walk out if she could not carry a better
toungue in her head. About a half hour after she got up and went into the waggon
then told Mr. Sessions I drove her out doors with the tongs. They all know to the
contrary.*

The feuding continued over the work, and the two wives refused
to speak to each other.

Patty was especially fearful about the prospects of David's leaving her. Rosilla was "trying to have him take her to Nauvoo and
then to Maine and leave me for good . . . I go to bed know [ing]
not what to do."[30] Patty's desperation and loneliness severely tried
her patience, but she was able to ride out the storm. After another
month of altercations and misunderstandings Rosilla left for
Nauvoo. This unfortunate experience with polygamy made it difficult for Patty to cope with similar trials later in her life.

Patty arrived in the Great Salt Lake Valley on September 24, 1847. She expressed her feelings on this long-awaited occasion in her diary: "Got into the valley. It is a beautiful place. My heart flows with gratitude to God that we have got home all safe lost nothing have been blesed with life and health. I rejoice all the time." Truly this was a time of rejoicing. She was reunited with friends she had not seen since their departure from Winter Quarters the previous spring.

Patty's talents as a midwife were required only two days after her entrance into the valley. She wrote of this event:

... then went put Lorenzo youngs wife Harriet to bed with a son the first male born in this valley. It was said to me more than 5 months ago that my hands should be the first to handle the first born son in the place of rest for the saints even in the city of our God. I have come more than one thousand miles to do it since it was spoken.

Patty continued to feel the weight of her calling as the fruitful Mormon mothers were delivered of their children. On August 24, 1848, after nearly a year in the valley, one good brother wrote:

Above all, they report that "Mother Sessions" has had a harvest of 248 little cherubs since living in the valley. Many cases of twins, in a row of seven houses joining each other, eight births in one week...[31]

In addition to the challenge of a large number of births, Patty also encountered some difficult deliveries with tragic complications. The midwives were more trusted than were the doctors who often lacked proper training. Patty's low opinion of doctors in general was well-known. "What greater sign of death, and loss of faith, can be supposed, than to see a physician's horse hitched before a sick one's door?"[32] The women in labor preferred the sympathetic care of the midwives to the sometimes brutal treatment of doctors. However, when complications set in, sympathy could not substitute for medical knowledge.

One such case caused wide repercussions in the community. Patty was an attendant midwife to the woman and was deeply impressed by the experience. She tells the story in her diary:

I was called to sister Roads. She was dangerously sick. Susanah was there. I soon found we could do nothing for her. We sent for Sister Shearer. She could do nothing for her. We then proposed to her to have a Dr. But she said she had been butchered once by Dr. Vaughn and she would not have a Dr.... the childs arm was born before I was sent for.. We all staid all night.[33]

The three midwives attending the mother felt incapable in such a serious situation. The following day passed uneventfully until late afternoon.

Eat her supper after 6 and commenced having pains. The childs arm still in the birth place could not be put back. About 9 we became alarmed. Sent for the Elders again and for a Dr. He was not at home. The Elders came. Br Woodruff staid by her. Br Willard could not come. Dr. Sprague was sick. Brigham was not to be found and we got no Dr. untill she was dead . . . The next day she was opened. Found that the child had made a rupture through the womb in her left side . . . The child was taken out she sewed up again. The child laid in her arms and . . . she was buried.[34]

This tragic death must have been appalling to the community, for "Br. Brigham preached a great discourse" on the following day and "told the people that he had searched into the whole of the affair and there was no blame to be laid on anyone and he did not wish to hear stories about it."[35] Patty felt that she had done her duty, recording "I know she would not have anything done for her that was not done neither would she take any medicine."[36]

However, this misfortune had a great impact on Patty. Not only was her reputation as a midwife threatened, but she personally experienced dark aftereffects. She did not put anyone to bed for several weeks because she feared they might die. Patty felt that the experience had evil implications, and the superstition and mystery that shrouded the unfortunate woman's death haunted her physically as well as emotionally.

Since sister Roads was opened I have done but litle work. I touched some of the clothes that was under her when she was opened got my fingers bloody on my right hand. They have been very sore ever since. One is not well yet. Those that opened her have had very bad hands and also the one that washed her. They seem to be mortification sores.[37]

It is evident that the detrimental consequences of the tragedy continued to plague both Patty and the community long after the event.

Patty served as a midwife until old age, delivering most of her grandchildren and some of her great-grandchildren. In connection with her obstetric work, she became a member of the Council of Health that was established by Dr. Willard Richards in 1848. Other members of the organization were Susannah Richards, Zina D. H. Young, Emmeline B. Wells, and Prescinda D. Kimball. Classes were held in which ladies received "practical instruction in midwifery, care of children, children's diseases, etc."[38]

Patty attended these meetings regularly, sharing her knowledge with other women by taking them through a "course of medicine." Patty became a leader in the organization dedicated to the promotion of good health. Apparently the women's mode of dress was of some concern to them, for at one meeting they "spoke much on the subject of taking care of our health to avoid tight laceing."[39]

At a later meeting it was decided that one of the projects of the council was to "form a fashion for the females that will be more conducive to health than the long tight waisted dress filed with whale bone and hickery that they ware now."[40] As a member of the council Patty dedicated much of her time to medical learning and instruction as well as to service.

Her associations with her sisters in women's meetings in the valley continued, as did her friendship with Eliza R. Snow. Shortly after arriving, Patty expressed her joy in reuniting with her friends: "In the evening visted E R Snow. She has just come in. This week has been a good time to me. My heart has been glad in seeing my sisters."

Throughout the next year the women united for spiritual sustenance. The frequency of these gatherings increased, reaching a high of five in the last week of November 1847. Patty attended and presided at many of these meetings when she was not delivering children.

In late December there was some concern expressed by the brethren of the valley regarding these meetings. On December 27, 1847, "the patriarch John Smith was caled with many of the sisters to Br Wilises that he might understand our order." However, as Patty wrote, "I presided had a good meeting." No more complaints were made until early in February of the following year. On February 4, 1848, she invited Father John Smith to her home to celebrate her fifty-third birthday. Apparently he was displeased with their meetings, for Patty wrote: "I invited Brother John Smith and wives but Father Abot told me that Father Smith told him that I was trying to take advantage of his weakness and get him here to one of my meetings." To smooth over any bad feelings, she and Eliza visited the aged patriarch, taking a cap and some fried cakes as a peace offering. The sisters' efforts achieved the desired results. Patty recorded: "He blessed me and said many good things to me and we left with good feelings."

Despite the "good feelings," more protests were made two days later by some slighted sisters:

Father Abot called again. Told me Sister Leonard said that there was as good sisters as I was and she could have a meeting without me or Sister Snow. He also said that Mary Pratt had been misrepreting [misrepresenting] some of our words that we said at sister Cotchners [Kartchner's] carying the idea that we thought we stopped very low to visit her. This we know was false.

Although these outside protests did not stop the meetings entirely, the meetings occurred less frequently as time went on. The exclusiveness of the meetings and the decreasing need for them in an expanding settlement were probable factors in the weakening of the group.

With the disintegration of the women's group, the friendship of Eliza and Patty waned. The length of time between visits from Eliza grew from weeks to months to years. Their deep friendship on the prairies and frequent associations when first in the valley dwindled to a cordial, but not close, relationship. This sisterhood suffered from the dispersal of the women's group.

However, Patty's spiritual experiences with her sisters did not stop with the disbanding of the organization. On her birthday, February 4, 1851, Patty wrote: "My birthday . . . sisters Brown, Loretta, Zina and Persis Richards were here on a visit. Loretta got the supper. Zina and Persis staid all night. We had a good visit. We prayed and blesed and was blesed spoke in toungues etc." In 1852 she began attending "female meetings" of a different sort in her ward. This group was organized on June 18, 1854, into a "benevolent society to clothe the Indian squas," with Patty as president. The bishop commended her efforts to aid the squaws, telling Patty that she had fulfilled her calling "firstrate."[41] The women were then given the task of caring for the poor "in each ward." She continued to work in this Benevolent Society until June 18, 1857, when, as Patty wrote, "female releif society organised."

As on the plains, spiritual "parties" were prevalent in the valley as social functions for both sexes. On February 19, 1855, Patty attended such a gathering and described it in her diary:

Went to Br Birches to the party . . . We had a good dance. A good spirit prevailed. Many speeches were spoke songs sung speaking in toungues interpretations and thus we spent the time good order and the spirit of God which caused peace governed the party and truly it was a good time.

These spiritual and social functions were vital to Patty, and they exemplify the sometimes curious mix of temporal and spiritual among the Saints.

This blend of temporal and spiritual is seen also in Patty's service as a midwife. She was frequently called to the sick and often with another sister she would lay hands on the distressed, just as she had done on the plains. Occasionally they would also wash and anoint the patient to insure healing. Patty felt this ordinance was efficacious, and requested it when she was afflicted. She wrote on September 15, 1862: "Went to sister Buels. She anointed my arm and laid hands on me. It was very lame." This ministration by the sisters did not replace the ordinances of the male priesthood members. When a case was grave, the elders of the priest-

hood were called in, and Patty's husband joined her in administering to the sick from time to time.

While Patty was busy delivering babies, she and her husband
began to part ways. David often traveled north to his son Perrigrine's settlement, where the family owned a farm. Although Patty was very self-sufficient, she resented having to perform chores
such as chopping wood for the stove and feeding the livestock.

Again polygamy saddened Patty's life. Unknown to her, David
had been courting another woman, Harriet Teeples. On November
24, 1849, "Mr. Sessions asked Brigham" for his consent. A week
later he told Patty of his "plans and contracts that he has made
with Hariet also what Brigham said about it." The protocol of
asking the first wife's consent had not been followed, and Patty
felt humiliated. However, she was determined to live the Lord's
law, and she prayed for sustenance. She wrote on December 30,
1849: "I wish to do right but I fear I shall fail through sorrow. Oh
Lord give me thy spirit to guide me safe in the right way." She
knew her duty as a Mormon wife, and she endeavored to look
upon this experience with a positive attitude.

After a month of bad feelings and loneliness for Patty, David
married Harriet on January 13, 1850.[42] A month later David asked
Patty for her consent to have Harriet move in with them. Patty
acquiesced, and the second wife came to live with Patty and David shortly thereafter.

Harriet and Patty seemed to get along well with one another,
because no altercations or complaints are recorded in Patty's diary.
In August of that same year David died of "numb palsey."[43] Harriet subsequently moved away, but Patty and her son Perrigrine
continued to support Harriet. Patty worked hard at maintaining
friendly relations, and delivered Harriet's child a few months after
David's death.

Patty was lonely without a husband and had difficulty maintaining her house and garden alone at the age of fifty-six. After a
hard week of cutting wood Patty entered the following in her diary on December 14, 1851: "I was married to John Parry and I feel
to thank the Lord that I have someone to cut my wood for me."
Her second husband was a Welsh immigrant who was the first
conductor of the Tabernacle Choir.[44] The marriage of convenience
lacked romantic love, but Patty was content with her new husband.

Her happiness was fleeting, for on March 28, 1854, "Mr. Parry
saw Brigham." Again, Patty's husband arranged to marry another
woman without first asking Patty's consent. Patty revealed her
wounded pride in her diary: "[Mr. Parry] told me what he [Brig-

ham Young] said. I felt bad that he did not tell me before. Oh
Lord help me to do right. He is to have a woman sealed to him
next Sunday and this is the first I knew about and he has known
it a long time but denied it to me." Harmony in polygamy was
not Patty's lot. She felt betrayed by her husband but resolved "to
do right."[45] Notwithstanding Patty's feelings, John was sealed to
Harriet Parry on August 2, 1854.[46] Harriet did not live with Patty,
but at John's house, much to Patty's dissatisfaction. She wrote on
February 9, 1856:

*Mr. Parry told me that Hariet had but little beside cornbread to eat. I told him not
to let her suffer. If she would come and live here she should fare [as] I did and if
she would not come here to carry some from here to her as what I have here I have
provided it myself. I told him I thought we had better live together . . . He made me
no reply.*

Patty felt that John was not supporting her properly, and that
much of her own earnings were being given to Harriet. On April
30, 1857, she bitterly recorded that her husband brought her ten
and a half pounds of flour and one pound of butter, "the first he
has brought me of his earnings for about to year."

Patty was again called to deliver a baby of her husband's wife.
In August 1855 Harriet experienced difficult labor, and after a
twelve-day vigil by Patty, the twins died.[47] A son was born in June
1860, delivered by Patty. Even though polygamy was a trial to
Patty, the trio continued to associate amicably until John's death
in 1868.

Patty's activities as a midwife and homemaker were demanding,
yet she found time to pursue her agricultural interests. Although
she was a middle-aged woman by the time she reached the valley
with her seedlings and fruit trees, she expended amazing amounts
of energy working in her garden and orchard, and selling her produce.

Each spring Patty spent weeks in her garden sowing seeds,
among them onions, beets, peas, and corn.[48] Throughout the summer she watered and hoed and watched for thieves who carried off
peas and melons. More than once she missed her Sunday meetings
to prevent her fruit from being stolen.[49] In the fall Patty and some
hired help harvested her crops. One October day she delivered a
baby at five in the morning and then dug eleven bushels of potatoes![50]

The fame of Patty's orchard spread, and she conducted a brisk
business selling her fruit. From her tithing calculations one can assume that she earned approximately $1,085 in 1857, $620 in 1859,
and $805 in 1862. Patty's pride in her garden and orchard can be

seen in the following diary entry on May 24, 1858: "He [William Smoot] went over my garden and orchard said he never saw such a beautiful sight in his life. So many trees so full of fruit so says everyone that has seen them." Especially prized were her plums, now known as the "Sessions plum"; the plums are still sold on the Utah market today.

In 1872 she moved to Bountiful to be near her son, selling her home in Salt Lake City to the railroad company.[51] She built a "fine brick home" in Bountiful and also had a large brick school-house constructed, which was known as the "Patty Sessions Academy." It was dedicated on December 20, 1883, at which time Patty "stated that she had been inspired to put some of her money into a free school, for the education of her posterity, and others whose parents were unable to pay for their schooling." After appointing a committee to "transact the business of the school" it was reported that she "stated that when herself and family came into the Valley, all the money she had was 5 cents, and now she had $16,000 invested in Z.C.M.I. [Zions Cooperative Mercantile Institution] at Salt Lake City."[52]

Patty died on December 14, 1892, at the age of ninety-seven years. Her obituary on the front page of the *Deseret Evening News* concluded with the following statements:

She was ever a true and faithful Latter-day Saint, diligent and persevering, her whole soul, and all she possessed being devoted to the Church and the welfare of mankind. She has gone to her grave ripe in years, loved and respected by all who knew her.[53]

The pioneer community had grown to love and admire a woman who had served them with all her energies for over half a century. Their high regard for her was well-deserved in light of her labors on their behalf.

Patty's contributions to the Saints' welfare were important ones. Her service as a midwife and efforts to improve the health of those in the Mormon Church were vitally important to those who experienced the physical rigors of crossing the plains and settling the frontier. In addition to caring for their physical well-being, Patty attended to the spiritual welfare of the Saints, especially to that of the sisters. Her horticultural pursuits also aided a community that was struggling to adapt crops from New England and Europe to a hardier clime.

The descendants of the pioneers continue to benefit from Patty Sessions' service. Naturally her accomplishments as a midwife, horticulturist, and philanthropist have endured. However, her service to us now is primarily one of helping us understand pioneer life.

Her account of crossing the plains and her record of life as a plural wife aid us greatly in our knowledge of pioneer times. Patty was a great woman not only in her own lifetime; her long-lasting contributions in many fields augment her historical stature today.

Notes

1. Noall, Claire, "Mormon Midwives," *Utah Historical Quarterly* 10:100.

2. *Woman's Exponent,* September 1, 1884, p. 51.

3. Sessions, Perrigrine, *The Diaries of Perrigrine Sessions,* Bountiful: Carr Printing Co., 1967, p. B4.

4. *Woman's Exponent,* September 1, 1884, p. 51.

5. Perrigrine Sessions, pp. B6-B7.

6. *Ibid.*

7. *Ibid.*

8. Carter, Kate B., *Our Pioneer Heritage,* 16 vols., Salt Lake City: Utah Printing Company, 1958-73, vol. 2, p. 58.

9. Sessions, Patty, Diary, February 12, 1846, holograph, Church Archives, Historical Department, The Church of Jesus Christ of Latter-day Saints, Salt Lake City, Utah, hereinafter cited as LDS Church Archives. Excerpts from the diary of Patty Sessions are quoted verbatim with original spelling retained. Minimal punctuation and bracketed words have been added in the interest of clarity. Patty and David had three children whom they left behind: Perrigrine, Sylvia, and David. All three joined them later in the journey.

10. Journal History of the Church, June 21, 1847, microfilm, LDS Church Archives.

11. Noall, "Mormon Midwives," p. 100.

12. Patty Sessions, March 9, 1846.

13. *Ibid.,* April 5, 1846.

14. *Ibid.,* April 6, 1846.

15. *Ibid.,* June 28, 1846.

16. *Ibid.,* July 23, 1847.

17. *Ibid.,* October 19, 1846.

18. *Ibid.,* April 6, 1846.

19. *Ibid.,* April 13, 1846.

20. Joseph Smith "remarked, there could be no evil in it, if God

gave his sanction by healing; that there could be no more sin in any female laying hands on and praying for the sick, than in wetting the face with water; it is no sin for anybody to administer that has faith, or if the sick have faith to be healed by their administration." From *Teachings of the Prophet Joseph Smith*, compiled by Joseph Fielding Smith, 1938, as quoted in *Priesthood and Church Government*, by John A. Widtsoe, Salt Lake City: Deseret Book Company, 1950, p. 357. The laying on of hands is generally accompanied by pouring a small amount of pure olive oil especially consecrated for this purpose on the crown of the head of the person that requests healing. This is known as "anointing."

21. Patty Sessions, May 11, 1847.

22. *Ibid.*, March 6, 1846.

23. *Ibid.*, February 14, 1847. Speaking in tongues is one of the lesser pentecostal manifestations of the influence of the Holy Ghost. Generally the person thus gifted speaks in a language unknown to him or her, and another present interprets what has been said for the benefit of the group.

24. *Ibid.*, June 4, 1847.

25. *Ibid.*, July 19, 1847.

26. *Ibid.*, March 15, 1847.

27. *Ibid.*, January 1, 1848.

28. *Ibid.*, June 16, 1860.

29. *Ibid.*, June 16, 1860.

30. *Ibid.*, November 4, 1846.

31. Noall, "Mormon Midwives," p. 102.

32. Taylor, Samuel W., *Nightfall at Nauvoo*, New York: The Macmillan Company, 1971, p. 175.

33. Patty Sessions, February 9, 1853.

34. *Ibid.*, February 10, 1853.

35. *Ibid.*, February 12, 1853.

36. *Ibid.*, February 12, 1853.

37. *Ibid.*, February 28, 1853.

38. Carter, 6:361.

39. Patty, Sessions, March 23, 1852.
40. *Ibid.*, April 24, 1852.
41. *Ibid.*, January 19, 1855.
42. *Ibid.*, January 13, 1850.
43. *Ibid.*, August 11, 1850.
44. Carter, 4:157.
45. Patty Sessions, April 1, 1854.
46. *Ibid.*, August 2, 1854.
47. *Ibid.*, August 10, 1854.
48. *Ibid.*, April 18, 19 and May 4, 5, 1849.
49. *Ibid.*, September 1, 1861, and August 1, 1862.
50. *Ibid.*, October 18, 1851.
51. *Deseret Evening News,* December 22, 1892.
52. *Deseret Evening News,* December 20, 1883.
53. *Deseret Evening News,* December 22, 1892.

Ellen Brooke Ferguson 1844–1920

Using the sparse amount of information available on the life of Dr. Ellen Brooke Ferguson, Ann Gardner Stone skillfully presents the life of this multi-talented woman. She has written other essays in this collection.

Ellen B. Ferguson

Ann Gardner Stone

There is a short story by Isaac Bashevis Singer entitled "Yentl the Yeshiva Boy," recently made into a play, which tells of a young Jewish girl who is secretly trained by her father in the study of the Torah and the Talmud. The law says, "He who teaches his daughter Talmud is corrupting her—a learned woman is a monstrosity!" This proves to be the case for Yentl in her repressive Hasidic village. First she tries to pass herself off as a boy in order to continue her studies, then she finally leaves the village after revealing her disguise to a man she fell in love with. The solution seems satisfactory to everyone except Yentl, who must give up her home and her love in order to remain true to her real self.[1]

Had circumstances been different for Ellen Brooke, she may have found herself in a dilemma similar to Yentl's. However, she was fortunate to have been born on April 10, 1844, into the more tolerant society of Cambridge University in England, to have married a man who seemed to view her accomplishments as compliments rather than as threats, and to have been able to use her talents in helping build *Zion* in Utah, where women were valued for more than their abilities to make chicken soup.

Like Yentl's father, Ellen's father, a prominent lawyer, saw that she received a proper education. He engaged private tutors and professors from the University of Cambridge to teach Ellen Latin, Greek, and mathematics, subjects he felt provided the strongest foundation for a good English education. He did not approve of the training in superficial "ladies accomplishments" that prevailed in the young ladies' schools and seminaries of the day.[2] Ellen's own training proved so comprehensive that she found she had an education equivalent to that of a university graduate. Unfortunately she also found that, as a woman, there were few practical avenues open to her for establishing a career.

Ellen then decided to begin the study of medicine. Just as today a doctor needed never fear unemployment, and Ellen felt that her sex might prove the least hindrance in this profession. She studied first under Dr. J. Taylor of Cambridge and subsequently studied under Dr. William Ferguson of Edinburgh. This same Dr. Ferguson became her husband in 1857, and together they emigrated to America in 1859.

Their first line of work after settling in America was to purchase the *Eaton Democrat,* a weekly newspaper published in Eaton, Ohio. They worked together on this project, and Ellen often furnished all the copy for the paper while William was involved with his physician's practice. When the Civil War broke out "nearly all the able bodied men of the town went into the army, and printers became scarce. For several months the editors and proprietors (the Fergusons) of the 'Democrat' were unable to obtain any help in the office. This state of affairs compelled Mrs. Ferguson to learn the printing trade, and frequently, in order to get the paper out on time, she was obliged not only to furnish all the copy, but to set up most of the type; being editor, compositor and 'printer's devil' all in one."[3]

A few years later, Ellen returned to England for health reasons, and when she returned to America in 1876 she found that her husband was preparing to move to Utah, having become acquainted with the Mormons through certain Mormon missionaries and through correspondence with Mormon Church President Brigham Young. There seems to have been no hesitation on Ellen's part to support her husband's decision to relocate, and she became completely involved in Utah society from the moment of her arrival in the Salt Lake Valley. A brief four years later William died and Ellen decided to return exclusively to the study and practice of medicine.

There seems to be some dispute as to whether Ellen ever actually received a medical degree. "No record has been found to substantiate the traditional view . . . that Ellen B. Ferguson was a certified practitioner, or that she ever graduated from a recognized medical institution. However, her husband was a doctor, and she had studied the profession in London in the 1850s; this seemed to give Ellen Ferguson the freedom to advertise herself as an M.D. in 1878."[4] According to Emmeline B. Wells, when Ellen arrived in the United States she matriculated at the United States College in New York, and she attended a full course at the Eclectic Medical College of Cincinnati. She also practiced medicine for eight years in Indiana and Illinois before coming to Utah in 1876.[5] Emmeline Wells doesn't mention a degree, but she does indicate that more went into Ellen's early training than marriage to a doctor. In the October 15, 1876, issue of the *Woman's Exponent* is an article that "introduces" Ellen to Salt Lake society; it mentions that she had practiced medicine in London and Paris for four years and had practiced for twelve years in the United States.[6]

During the next four years Ellen practiced medicine in Utah. There are intermittent advertisements in the *Woman's Exponent* explaining her specialties and announcing various medical classes available to women. For example, she announced the opening of a class for ladies on October 1, 1878, which would include anatomy, physiology, obstetrics, puerperal diseases, and diseases of children. It would also include instruction in the medicinal properties of herbs, plants, and their domestic uses. The article says, "fees can be paid in grain, dried fruit or produce."[7]

Ellen taught classes not only in medicine, but she also taught music, French, drawing, elocution, Latin, German, and drama. During a lecture tour of the territory, she spoke about ancient and modern Rome. Her singular qualification for teaching these courses was her early comprehensive education in England and a natural facility for anything she tried. All indications are that she was amply qualified for these pursuits. The *Woman's Exponent* quotes an eastern paper as describing Ellen with a "rare intellectual ability and literary culture," and says that she is "one having in large degrees those qualities of heart and mind that must always be the crowning glory of true and enlightened womanhood."[8]

Her first music classes were given in her Provo home in 1876. In 1878 she advertised in the *Woman's Exponent* classes in music, French, and drawing to be conducted in her home, and also announced her intention of "organizing a class of young ladies and gentlemen to learn elocution and dramatic reading."[9] In September of 1878 she began a "select morning class for Ladies for instruction in the higher branches of comprehensive English education," an apparent introduction to a basic liberal arts curriculum.[10] Later that year came the announcement that she, along with Mary Cook, was to establish a musical conservatory in the "European style," a school for both pupils and teachers. They called it the Utah Conservatory of Music, "and for over two years it was the leading music school of the Territory."[11]

It is not clear why Ellen maintained such a frenetic schedule—whether it was from desire or necessity. She obviously had the ability to teach any of these subjects, and perhaps she felt compelled to utilize her talents and training to the fullest. There is also the possibility of financial burdens after the death of her husband in 1880. Perhaps he had been incapacitated by an illness that made it mandatory for her to become the sole support of their four children (the youngest died in infancy, about the same time as William died). Whatever the reasons, these activities are witness to Ellen's rainbow of talents and her ability to make the most of them.

After William's death Ellen decided to travel to New York and attend clinics in gynecology, obstetrics, and minor surgery at Bellevue Hospital. There she spent the winter of 1881-82 visiting and examining the various hospitals, her goal being to become qualified to perform hospital work upon her return to Utah.[12] This seemed to have been a most rewarding experience for Ellen. In a letter written to the *Woman's Exponent* near the end of her stay in New York, she voiced her enthusiasm for the work she had been doing:

Though New York abounds with opportunities of culture in every department of art and science, and under other circumstances I should have deeply appreciated them, I determined that nothing should interfere with my entire devotion to the course of study I had marked out for myself before coming here. I feel grateful to acknowledge the hand of God in opening up my way and enabling me to accomplish even more than I had ever anticipated. During the first three months my time was almost entirely occupied at Belle Vue Hospital, attending the clinical lectures, and in Dispensary work in the out door department where I made a special study of diseases of the Nose, Throat, Lungs and heart, examining and treating from forty to fifty patients every week. The knowledge and experience that I have gained in this department alone would more than repay me for my visit. The remaining three months I have spent in the Woman's Hospital of the State of New York studying the diseases of women, under the most eminent gynecologists of the present day. In this department I have had large opportunities for practical work, as well as clinical instructions. . . .[13]

Before leaving Utah for New York Ellen had received a call, along with Zina Young, from the Mormon Church authorities to participate in an activity to which she was already committed—the advocacy of women's suffrage and the defense of the institution of polygamy. Her period of study in New York doubled as a lecture tour of the East in which she defended the principles of polygamy from the point of view of the Mormon woman. The *Deseret News* said, "[Mrs. Ferguson] is a woman of culture and intellectuality, a more recent convert to 'Mormonism,' but gifted with powers of mind and speech to enable her to ade [sic] her sister in defending its principles from pulpit or rostrum."[14]

Ellen and Zina arrived in New York in the fall of 1881, and from the accounts they sent back to the West, their lecture tour showed signs of becoming a concentrated missionary effort. Their main purpose was to preach the tenets of Mormonism wherever and whenever asked, and to try to dispel the myths and misinformation about the Mormons that abounded in the popular press of the day. In October Ellen was invited by an old friend, Isabella Beecher Hooker, to speak at a memorial service for President James Garfield, held in Hartford, Connecticut. Ellen writes,

Leaving Long Island, I went to Hartford, Conn., where I spent a week very pleas-
antly, doing all I could by social intercourse, answering questions and conversation, to
present a reasonable and correct view of our faith and practice. After delivering an
address in Unity Church, at the Memorial Services for President Garfield, several
persons asked me seriously if it was true that the Mormons had prayed for President
Garfield's death, as the papers said they did. This is the character of nearly all the
inquiries made of us—some question arising out of the falsehoods and misstatements of
the newspapers.[15]

While in Hartford, Ellen met Harriet Beecher Stowe and other
feminist leaders and received an invitation to attend the Woman's
Congress in Buffalo, New York, to be held a month later. It was
suggested that Ellen deliver a speech on the subject, "Can Woman
Organize?", and she thought that she could present the Relief Society, the YLMIA, and the organization of Utah's sericulture as
prime examples of woman's organizational abilities.[16] Zina Young
attended the Congress with Ellen.

The Congress was a gathering of women leaders in all fields.
Julia Ward Howe, then president of the Association for the Advancement of Women, was the best-known leader, and she made
the most favorable impression on the Mormon women. According
to Ellen, her "dignity and grace, aesthetic culture and enthusiastic
philanthropy have won for her the warmest admiration of all who
come within the scope of her influence."[17] Despite Ellen's earlier
invitation to speak, when the group learned that Ellen and Zina
were Mormons, she was denied the opportunity to address the
meeting. "They were afraid to give truth even a chance to be
heard, and while pleading for the ballot for woman, quietly ignored the presence and help of the only women citizens [Utah
women had been given the vote by the Utah territorial legislature]
in the whole assemblage—because they were Mormons."[18] The reason given for denying the Mormon women a voice was that the
Mormons were violating the law by practicing polygamy. Ellen's
answer to this charge was eloquent:

When I heard this [i.e., violating the law of the land], and looked upon the women
who sat before me, many of whom were crowned with the silver lilies of seven dec-
ades, memory involuntarily recalled the time, when these same women in their prime
proudly planted the banner of Freedom for the Negro on the neck of the violated
Fugitive Slave Law. Every advance step in the social, religious, and political progress
of our race has been taken over the debris of broken statutes and violated laws. Re-
sistance to and violation of unjust and oppressive enactments were the birth-pangs of
American Independence, and the problem of women's salvation and exaltation through
the principle of Celestial Marriage will be wrought out under similar conditions. The
higher law under which the old-time abolitionists achieved their greatest victories has

never been repealed—God's truth marches not backward, and the trumpet of His Gospel "shall never call retreat." The speeches and essays were good, some of them excellent . . . but for the brave daughters of the desert, the women of the New and Everlasting Covenant, "who make womanhood the synonym for wife" and crown motherhood with eternal honors, there was neither place nor voice.[19]

One of the speakers at the assembly pleaded for the poor unprotected Indian women and begged the audience "not to forget in their pitiful sympathy the down trodden women of Utah." This infuriated Ellen, who promptly cornered the unnamed speaker and asked her never again, from a public platform, to plead for pity for the Mormon women, who were God's daughters.

The convention was an exasperating experience for Ellen and Zina. Knowing that Utah women were enjoying the benefits of the franchise and were being denied the right to speak of these benefits to a group that was most vocal in its appeal for the same privileges, caused Ellen and Zina feelings of bitterness. However, they maintained their dignity, and their demeanor at the convention spoke in their favor; they continued to speak for Mormon women and for suffrage in general. In February 1882, Ellen attended the Woman's Suffrage Convention for the State of New York, accompanied by Zina Young and Dr. Romania B. Pratt. This convention proved to be less hostile to the Mormon delegation, although they were still not allowed to address the entire group. They met with Susan B. Anthony and established a friendship with her that lasted throughout the women's suffrage movement. She explained to them that the Mormon issue was so volatile that the suffrage movement had to guard their cause by shunning even the appearance of "evil." She said that she could never accept the principle of plural marriage, but that she fully supported the Mormon woman's work for suffrage. The three Utah women seemed content to argue their cause personally among the delegates rather than from the speaker's platform.

In a report of the convention written to the *Woman's Exponent,* Romania Pratt insisted that despite the barriers, it was important to continue sending effective representatives to these gatherings to advocate the Mormon woman's situation. In the same letter she related a story that indicates the treatment the Utah women often received:

One little experience of Sister Zina D. H. Young shows the actual power of the saying, "Seeing is believing." As she was standing waiting to sign the memorial to send to the legislature, asking for the franchise for the women of New York State, a lady close by her thus addressed her: "I believe you are Mrs. Young." Sister Young said, "I am." And thereupon the lady withdrew herself a pace, and while Aunt Zina stood there in her sealskin sacque and velvet robe, but above all with the light of truth beaming forth from every feature of her face, she took a scrutinizing survey of her from top to toe, and said, in accents of supreme surprise, "Why you do not look very degraded!" The woman seemed totally oblivious to the burning insult her every word, act, and look implied, but seemed wholly swallowed up with her discovery. And I dare say dear, good Aunt Zina bore this with a smile, but it has proven that you can smile when you are maddest. . . .[20]

The paradox operating in these events is evident. No women anywhere were enjoying the blessings of freedom as were the Mormon women of this time, yet prejudice and ignorance denied them their rightful roles as leaders in the national movement. Perhaps it is just as well, because Ellen was ready to return to Zion at the completion of her studies at Bellevue, and Zion was ready to receive her.

Upon her return to Salt Lake in 1882 Ellen began to draw up plans for a Mormon community hospital in Salt Lake. The plan provided for a full staff of physicians, surgeons, nurses, and assistants. When presented to Mormon Church President John Taylor and his counselors, it was approved by them, and Ellen was promised whatever help she needed in implementing the plan.[21] Funds were raised by the Relief Society and the YLMIA, and the general church funds were also provided. In May it was announced that Ellen was to be the resident physician and surgeon of the new Deseret Hospital; the *Deseret News* said, "The recent thorough training which the resident physician, Dr. E. B. Ferguson, has lately undergone in the eastern medical institutions amply qualifies her for the responsible position she has been selected to fill."[22] The hospital was dedicated, and Ellen was given a special blessing as the resident physician and surgeon by President John Taylor. For three months Ellen was in sole charge of the institution. When it seemed that the hospital was to be a success, Ellen's attention was diverted toward other pursuits. She was replaced as head of the hospital by Martha Hughes (later Cannon), and although she was still associated with the hospital as a visiting doctor, she went back to her private practice. There were new vistas to be charted and explored.

Besides her intense involvement in medicine and women's suffrage while she was in New York, Ellen also got a taste of politics, and liked it. Because of her eloquence, her education, and her experience in defending the faith, Ellen was sent to Washington, D.C., in 1886, along with some other Mormon women, to present a protest to President Grover Cleveland against enforcement of the Edmunds Law, which had been passed by Congress in 1882. The Edmunds Law provided for punishment of polygamists by fines and prison sentences as well as by revocation of their political rights; Utah women's suffrage was taken away because such suffrage was considered a means to increase Mormon power: it was believed that the women were being told how to vote by their "harem masters." Over 12,000 persons were deprived of their vote by the Edmunds Law.[23] Persecutions, imprisonments, and indignities continued to be heaped upon the struggling Mormons, and it was these things that Ellen argued against in Washington. It was hoped that because Ellen was a monogamist and a woman, her perspectives might be looked upon as less biased as she argued against the unconstitutionality of denying so many people the vote.

The entreaties were in vain. In 1887 the Edmunds-Tucker Bill was enacted by Congress. The bill, among other things, created stiffer penalties for those convicted of polygamy, dissolved all corporations of the Mormon Church, and disenfranchised all the women of Utah, not just the polygamists. This latter tenet of the bill is perhaps a testament to the effectiveness of women like Ellen, whose independence made men like the lawmakers a bit uneasy.

Ellen was not discouraged by these unsuccessful forays into politics. When the territory of Utah began preparing for statehood, she joined the Democratic Party in order to work more closely in the movement toward statehood. She, along with other women, worked hard to have the new state constitution reestablish the vote for women. Ellen campaigned and gave prosuffrage speeches throughout the territory. She engaged in a debate for women's suffrage in the Salt Lake Theatre against Dr. Ellen Gage, and the *Woman's Exponent* noted that she "acquitted herself most favorably, her discourse being logical and clear, her language excellent and her manner dignified." Such tactics brought success—equal voting and equal voting clauses were incorporated in the new state constitution.

Success did not lessen Ellen's interest in politics, and she continued to be very active in the state Democratic Party. In 1896 the National Democratic Party was undergoing some internal strife as various factions vied for control; the major split occurred between the established eastern politicos and a rising group of western delegations representing the agrarian elements of the country. Ellen was, of course, in the latter's camp, and was given the honor of being the only woman chosen to occupy a seat at the National Democratic Convention held in Chicago in July 1896. It was a raucous affair as the hostile factions battled to control the nomination. When William Jennings Bryan gave his famous "Cross of Gold" speech, the delegates gave him a thirty-minute ovation, and awarded him the party's nomination for president of the United States. The eastern press labeled the convention a "political debauch" and "an orgy," but the people had a new hero and a new cause.[24]

One might wonder how the dignified and elegant lady from Utah felt attending a "political debauch" and "an orgy," but the outcome must have been to her liking, because she subsequently spoke at "hundreds of meetings for Democracy, Bryan and Free Silver."[25] She too had a new hero. When the campaign was over, Ellen went on to organize the Woman's Democratic Club of Salt Lake City and she served as its president for two years. The club was a major force in keeping the Democratic Party alive in Utah after the resounding defeat Bryan received in the election. Besides activity in party politics it is noted that Ellen served in public office as well, being the first woman deputy sheriff in the United States.[26] The cultivated lady from Cambridge, England, had truly been Americanized.

Throughout her career in Utah Ellen gave continual support and service to the Mormon Church. Not only was she a spokeswoman for the church's political causes, but she served in the Primary organization and in leadership roles in the Relief Society. Her activity is often noted in terms of speeches she delivered, a duty for which her education, experience, and eloquence suited her well. Her topics were varied—the evils of personal adornment, prostitution (she said that men were equally to blame as the woman), home industry, and caring for the poor and destitute. The following excerpt from a speech given at the stake Relief Society conference signals a common theme:

I hope we will not get careless and indifferent concerning that which is for good. I have read with surprise the letter which has been referred to, written by a lady in the United States declining public work because she was a wife and mother. We, who are in this kingdom feel that it is because we are wives and mothers that our hearts and sympathies go out to all humanity and we seek to bless and benefit others beside those of our own households.[27]

She defended the Mormon Church against the barbs and inaccuracies clarioned by the eastern press and the intellectual community in which she had often moved so comfortably. In an interview given to the *Washington Post* during Ellen's 1886 trip there, she strongly defended the Mormons, their stand on polygamy, and their loyalty to the government. Her defense was always reasoned and intelligent. In a letter to the *Woman's Exponent* written from New York in 1882, she says, "My association with the people of the world made me feel more than ever thankful that I am a Latter-day Saint, and I pray to be kept humble and faithful to the end."[28]

All of this somehow doesn't prepare us for the change that Ellen's sentiments were to undergo around 1896 or 1897. During this
period she became involved with a movement known as Theosophy, a system whose teachings "involve belief in a Universal
Spirit, reincarnation as part of an evolutionary process, ideas of
various planes of reality, and existence of a hierarchy of perfected
beings who supervise processes of the world."[29] She severed her relations with the Mormon Church, and in a sacrament meeting
held in the Salt Lake Eighteenth Ward on March 6, 1898,

*Bishop (Orson) Whitney said he had an unpleasant duty to perform and explained
that means had been taken to show Sister Ellen B. Ferguson the error of her ways in
embracing and advocating theosophy openly and was now the President and lecturer
for that society—and said my counselors Robert Patrick and William Barton had visited her but to no avail. Special teachers J. A. Clawson and John Eraus had also
visited her.—A Bishop's trial had been had on Friday, March 4, 1898, and from
evidence produced she was excommunicated from the Church, which action was sustained by the meeting.*[30]

Little is known about Ellen after this period. The Utah papers
note that she and her two daughters later moved to New York,
where she died on March 17, 1920, in her seventy-sixth year.

What conclusions can be drawn from the life of Ellen Ferguson?
For a woman who achieved success as a newspaper editor, a medical doctor, a hospital administrator, a musician and music teacher,
a politician, a woman's suffragist, a scholar, and a lecturer, there
are numerous epithets that might apply. Little if any mention is
made of Ellen's role as a wife and mother, although that is perhaps a good sign. Unhappiness and failure are more often chron-
icled than is success, and so we must assume that her familial relationships were happy ones. But where were the children when
Ellen took her eastern trips, went on lecture tours, and practiced
medicine, and what were her husband's feelings about her activities outside the home? There is also the mystery of her changed religious sentiments. Does this diminish her previous accomplishments? Is there some clue in her actions that could explain
the metamorphosis? And what of her accomplishments in terms of
a woman today? Is there room in the modern Mormon society for
a woman so obviously and aggressively talented?

The Ferguson marriage appears to have been a marriage of the
minds as well as of the hearts. As already indicated, Ellen studied
medicine under the tutelage of her husband, and she soon joined
his practice. Thus, from the beginning William was aware of Ellen's talents, and he obviously nurtured them. Publishing of the
Eaton Democrat was very much a joint project, with responsibilities

shared equally by husband and wife. Ellen's competence appears to have been no threat to William, but was rather a complement to a true partnership.

Ellen was always very vocal in stating her belief in the sanctity of the home and family. Most of her professional activities were planned so as not to interfere with her domestic activities. The classes she taught were held in her home, as was indicated in the advertisements. This would have enabled her to maintain her household and tend her children at the same time as maintaining a profession. How she had her children cared for when she went back East is not known, but her eagerness to return to Utah after one year in New York was in large part an eagerness to return to her family.

Reasons for Ellen's advocacy of Theosophy after such staunch defense of the Mormon Church are not so easy to postulate. One can never be sure of motivations for such behavior, particularly when the one involved left no personal explanation. There was, at this time, a very strong spiritualist movement in Utah and throughout the West, and Theosophy had certain spiritualistic and occult tenets. Perhaps Ellen was swept away by the fervor of this movement, although there is nothing in her previous actions that would indicate any such tendencies to do so. She had always been in the vanguard of advocating unpopular and sometimes unusual causes—Mormonism, woman's suffrage, polygamy, William Jennings Bryan, and Utah statehood. When polygamy was outlawed and statehood was accomplished, Mormonism took a step toward becoming more socially acceptable. The women of Utah also had the vote. Perhaps Ellen was in need of a new cause to espouse, and Theosophy offered itself to her. However, Ellen's motivations for leaving the Mormon Church are secondary in importance to the years of faithful service she gave to it. She was invaluable to the church leadership as an outstanding spokeswoman and representative of the church's beliefs. Perhaps the return of her ashes to be buried in Salt Lake in 1923 indicates an earlier desire on her part to reestablish contact with a society she had loved and served for so many years.

Notes

1. Pogrebin, Letty Cottin, " 'Yentl': Better a Fool Than a Woman," *MS. Magazine,* 4(February 1976): 37-39.

2. Whitney, Orson F., "Ellen Brooke Ferguson," *History of Utah,* Salt Lake City: George Q. Cannon and Sons, 1904, 4:602.

3. *Ibid.*

4. Terry, Keith C., "The Contribution of Medical Women During the First 50 Years in Utah" unpublished masters thesis, Brigham Young University, 1964, pp.39–40.

5. Wells, Emmeline B., "Ellen Ferguson." *Charities and Philanthropies: Woman's Work in Utah,* Salt Lake City: George Q. Cannon and Sons, 1893, p. 87.

6. *Woman's Exponent* 5(October 15, 1876): 77.

7. *Woman's Exponent* 7(September 1, 1878): 52.

8. *Woman's Exponent* 5(October 15, 1876): 77.

9. *Woman's Exponent* 6(May 15, 1878): 188.

10. *Woman's Exponent* 7(September 15, 1878): 61.

11. Whitney, p. 602.

12. *Ibid.,* p. 603.

13. Ferguson, Ellen B., "New York Letter," *Woman's Exponent* 10(April 1, 1882): 165.

14. *Journal History of the Church,* 30 July 1881, manuscript, Church Archives.

15. "Dr. Ferguson's Letter," *Woman's Exponent* 10(November 15, 1881): 90.

16. *Journal History of the Church,* October 13, 1881.

17. "Dr. Ferguson's Letter," p. 90.

18. *Journal History of the Church,* October 22, 1881.

19. "Dr. Ferguson's Letter," p. 90.

20. Pratt, Romania B., "Woman's Suffrage Convention," *Woman's Exponent* 10(March 4, 1882): 146.

21. Whitney, p. 603.

22. *Journal History of the Church,* June 23, 1882, p. 3.

23. Oberholtzer, Ellis P., *A History of the U.S. Since the Civil War,* IV, New York; Macmillan Co., 1931, p. 669.

24. Josephson, Matthew, *The Politicos-1865-1896,* New York: Harcourt, Brace and Co., 1938, pp. 678-679.

25. Whitney, P. 603.

26. "Ellen B. Ferguson," *Utah Historical Quarterly* 10(1942): 30.

27. *Woman's Exponent* 4(July 15, 1881): 30.

28. *Woman's Exponent* 10(April 1, 1882): 165.

29. Brandon, S.G.F., ed., *Dictionary of Comparative Religion,* New York, Charles Scribner's Sons, 1970, pp. 610-611.

30. Minutes of Fast Meeting of Eighteenth Ward, Salt Lake City, Utah, March 6, 1898, Church Archives.

Romania Bunnell Pratt Penrose 1839–1932

*Chris Croft Waters is an historian
with a bachelor's and master's degree
in history. She is from Centerville,
Utah, and is presently living in Salt
Lake City, where she is active in
The Church of Jesus Christ of
Latter-day Saints. She and her
husband, Michael Bryce Waters, are
the parents of two daughters.*

Romania P. Penrose

Christine Croft Waters

When Romania Pratt returned from obtaining her medical degree in 1877 she was welcomed into Utah society with open arms. She had been supported both morally and monetarily by President Brigham Young and by the sisters of the Relief Society, for the church leaders realized the great lack of medical knowledge, especially in obstetrics and child care, along its members.

This supportive attitude had not always prevailed, for the Prophet Joseph Smith had taught the people in 1830 to depend on the principle of healing by faith and the laying on of hands by the elders of the church.[1] He had also taught them the Word of Wisdom, whereby they were commanded not to use strong drinks and tobacco but to partake of herbs, which he said were ordained for the use of man.[2] Because of this admonition and because medicine was in its infant stages of development in the mid-nineteenth century, the Latter-day Saints turned to the elders, not to those who had studied physics, in times of sickness. They depended upon the midwives who had been set apart by church leaders, and they sought remedies from the herbal doctors who lived among them.

Upon the Saints' arrival in the Great Basin, Brigham Young stressed the building of *Zion*. Most of the thirteen physicians who came into the valley during the 1840s and 1850s set aside medicine, because workers were needed to settle, plant, and irrigate and to make habitable the kingdom of God on earth.

Three women physicians came into the valley in the 1850s. All were European converts, and all had obtained their medical degrees from noted European hospitals and medical schools. Netta Anna Cardon emigrated from Switzerland, and upon her arrival in the Salt Lake Valley she received a blessing at the hands of Brigham Young in which he blessed her to practice medicine and to not charge for her services. For many years she solitarily rode her horse between Ogden and the small settlements in Cache Valley delivering babies, setting broken bones, and dispensing medicine. Vigdis Holt, an emigrant from Iceland, was the first practicing physician in Spanish Fork. Janet Downing Hardie was graduated from Edinburgh Medical School in Scotland, then the center of medical erudition in Europe. Her medical activities in Salt Lake City are obscure.

In the 1860s only one woman physician, Sophie Ruesch from Switzerland, came into the valley. She was a plural wife, and she moved with her husband to St. George. As time passed, her medical practice lessened until she no longer practiced.

In 1869 when the railroad ended isolationism for the Saints, Brigham Young knew that transportation and the mines would bring gentile merchants, gentile families, and gentile influences. He therefore urged the people to become proficient in all fields and to become independent of the gentiles. In 1873 he urged women to study physics and nursing, for he believed women should be treated by other women.

When Romania Pratt heard this plea she responded with enthusiasm and determination. She had been preparing herself for many years spiritually, educationally, and mentally for this decision.

Romania was reared on a farm in Indiana where she was born on August 8, 1839, to Esther and Luther Bunnell. Both parents embraced the Gospel by the time Romania was six, and when she was seven they moved her to Nauvoo, Illinois, to gather with the rest of the Saints. Romania remembers "investigating with childish wonder and eagerness the mysteries of the Nauvoo Temple from the white marble font on the backs of white marble oxen in the basement to the wondrous bell in the belfry."[3] However, 1846 was not a good year in Nauvoo; persecutions drove the Saints across the Mississippi River, and Brigham Young was forced to lead his people into Iowa, where the majority settled in Winter Quarters. Further hardships awaited them there, for as the Saints prepared for the journey across the Rocky Mountains, word came that a battalion of Mormon soldiers was needed to fight in the Mexican War. Romania remembers

being present when the martial band was marching round, and the call was made for the "Mormon Battalion," for Mexico. Although too young to appreciate the severe ordeal our devoted and persecuted people were subject to, I can never forget the feeling of grief which oppressed my little heart, as one after one the brave-hearted men fell into ranks.[4]

As preparations continued for the journey west, Romania's father prepared to return to Indiana. Esther's health was delicate, since she had recently given birth to a second daughter, Josephine, and Luther thought it wise to postpone the journey west until more adequate preparations could be made. So the Bunnells separated from the body of the church, journeyed east, and purchased a farm.

In 1849 news of gold in California reached the Bunnell farm, and Luther enthusiastically banded together with a number of others to journey to California in hopes of acquiring enough gold to take his family to Zion. He was successful in the mines, but he contracted typhoid fever and died. Only a portion of his gold was recovered, because he died before he could tell his nephew where he had hidden it.

Luther's death must not have caused undue financial stress on the family, for Romania continued her regular attendance at the Female Seminary in Crawfordsville, Indiana, where she studied German and music, among other things. She recalled that she would have

obtained a very finished education; but my blooming womanhood began to draw around me admirers which warned mother to flee from Babylon before I became fastened by Gentile bonds.[5]

So in 1855 Esther Bunnell sold the farm and took Romania, Josephine, and her two sons, Luther and Isaac, to Omaha, where they joined Captain John Hindley's wagon train of fifty. Romania recounts that

The journey across the plains with ox teams was a summer full of pleasure to me; the early morning walks gathering wild flowers, climbing the rugged and oftimes forbidding hills—the pleasant evening gatherings of the young folks by the bright camp fire while sweet songs floated forth on the evening air to gladden the wild and savage ear of the red men or wild beasts as well as our own young hearts.[6]

On September 3, 1855, the wagon train arrived in the sight of the Salt Lake Valley. Romania remembered climbing Little Mountain

with fleet footsteps and anxious heart to get the first peep at the great city of the saints. With lightening glances I rapidly swept the whole valley north and south but no city could I find; my disappointment was extreme. I looked for bristling spires and flashing metallic cupolas which I had been accustomed to see when first coming into sight of other cities. After a long but fruitless search for the city some one came to my relief and called my attention to a small collection of black spots indicating houses.[7]

The wagon train camped on Union Square, which later became the University of Deseret, and they soon learned that the Saints were in the midst of a grasshopper famine. Romania said that "for the first time in life did I face its [famine's] stern realities." Though the Bunnells had arrived in the valley with little, they had an inheritance back in Indiana in the hands of a guardian, who would not release the money so that the family could "come among the Mormons."[8] However, Esther was thrifty and industrious and soon began taking in laundry and doing miscellaneous tasks for neighbors. Romania earned money by teaching in Brigham Young's school.[9]

In 1857 word came that the family could receive money from the Bunnell estate, so Esther left Romania in charge of the family and journeyed back to Indiana to collect the inheritance and buy a piano for Romania. She returned to Utah and bought a small home for the family. Romania had a great love for music, and the piano soon became a most cherished possession when General Albert Johnston and the United States Army marched toward Utah the next year and the Mormons determined to burn their homes and flee rather than to surrender, Romania prepared her piano to be burned in the "event of our enemies taking possession." But "God did not permit the burning of our homes, for our enemy was harassed and their efforts anticipated until they made a treaty to pass quietly through the city and form a camp called Camp Floyd."[10]

In her twentieth year Romania married a "son of promise," Parley P. Pratt, Jr., eldest son of Apostle Parley P. Pratt. Romania's husband had been born under unusual circumstances: his mother, Thankful, had been childless for the first nine years of her marriage. When his father, Parley, was called on a mission to Canada, Thankful's illness and their heavy indebtedness had filled their minds with doubts. A visit was paid them by Apostle Heber C. Kimball, who gave Thankful a blessing, promising that if Parley would go on his mission, the way would be opened for him to pay his debts and to do a great work in Canada, which work would later spread to England. He also promised Thankful that within a year she would bear a son and call his name Parley. The fulfillment of the promised birth came in Kirtland on March 25, 1837, when Thankful gave birth to Parley, Jr. She died soon afterward.[11]

Parley, Jr. fulfilled two missions for the Mormon Church. Two years after his marriage to Romania he was called to labor in the Eastern States Mission. A short time after his return he was called to England and was gone for four difficult years, leaving Romania to support herself and two-year-old Parley, Jr. as best she could while expecting another child in December. The baby was born and he lived only three days; Romania sadly buried Luther, named for her father, in the Salt Lake Cemetery.

Upon Parley's return, the Pratts added five children to their family. An only daughter, Corinne, died when she was less than two years old and caused her mother a lingering sorrow that Romania would recall many years afterward. In 1873 when her last

child was born, Romania heard President Brigham Young's plea
for women to study medicine. It appealed to her for several reasons. First, she had once watched a close friend die:

*I saw her lying on her bed, her life slowly ebbing away, and no one near knew how
to ease her pain or prevent her death; it was a natural enough case, and a little
knowledge might have saved her. Oh, how I longed to know something to do, and at
that moment I solemnly vowed to myself never to be found in such a position again,
and it was my aim ever afterward to arrange my life work that I might study the
science which would relief suffering, appease pain, prevent death.*[12]

Besides her desire to relieve suffering, Romania had an intense
desire to further her education. She had always been a "digger,"
as her Spanish and French teacher called her—a seeker after
knowledge—and much fulfillment came to her through her educational pursuits.[13] She also desired to help build Zion, and Brigham
Young's request was the incentive she needed to make the necessary sacrifices.

Romania sold her piano and her home and left Parley, Jr., age
fourteen; Louis, age eight; Mark, age four; Irwin, age two; and
baby Roy, less than a year, in the care of her mother.[14] She boarded the train in December of 1873 and left for New York City,
where she met her husband; together they spent six weeks editing
and proofreading his father's autobiography. When this work was
completed in late winter, Romania began medical school at the
Women's Medical College in New York. Since the semester was
nearing its completion, Romania mostly observed.[15] However, she
recalled that she would

*not soon forget my extreme confusion on being asked a question during a quiz by a
professor who for the moment forgot I was a new studentмnor the mischievous smiles
of the students, but my revenge was more than complete at the beginning of the next
term in witnessing their astonishment because of my advancement. During the summer
vacation while they were recreating, sea bathing and visiting with friends, I daily
plodded studiously up the rugged hill of knowledge; reciting as a private student every
day to the professor of physiology. I also took lessons in opthalmology of Dr. Wm
Little . . . also a courage under Dr. P. A. Callan and finally by special permission I
joined a class taught by Prof. H. D. Noyes in Bellevue College. Dr. Little said I
was the first woman ever admitted to Bellevue.*

Bellevue College was a part of Bellevue Hospital, and it coupled
practical clinical experience with medical theory. Bellevue was
well known as one of the outstanding medical college in the
United States in the last half of the nineteenth century; through
the private tutelage she received during the summer and her class
at Bellevue, Romania distinguished herself as a leader in the freshman class. She especially excelled at dissection, which was one of

the most formidable challenges for most women students. Said one medical student, "the sight of eight stark, staring bodies, every age and color, stretched upon as many tables, was not reassuring to say the least."[17] Many students asked Romania to demonstrate dissection, and she was told that one professor would call his class to him after she had left and show them the manner and style of her dissection, using it as a model. He often said it was the neatest work he had seen done.[18] The cost of dissecting a cadaver was forty dollars, which was split by a "club" of four girls—two juniors and two freshmen—who worked as a team.[19]

The cost of medical school was prohibitive to Romania, who lived in a small, cramped room for which she paid one dollar per week. Such housing was necessary, however, if she was to pay matriculation and lab fees as well as the one dollar per hour fee for medical instruction.[20]

Spring came, and with her freshman year over, Romania returned to the Salt Lake Valley, where she "had the joy of the society of my children and the Saints."[21] Her finances had been depleted, however, and in desperation she called on President Brigham Young for assistance. He in turn called Eliza R. Snow to him and said regarding Romania:

She must continue her studies in the east. We need her here, and her talents will be of great use to this people. Take this upon yourself, Sister Eliza, to see to it that the Relief Societies furnish Sister Pratt with the necessary money to complete her studies. Let them get up parties and thus provide the means.[22]

With her finances secured, Romania turned her energies to her family and to her new calling as president of the Young Ladies Retrenchment Association in the Salt Lake Twelfth Ward. Organized throughout Zion, the Retrenchment Association was formed, said Romania, "to draw the attention of the young girls to the principles of the gospel and to suppress the growing evil of vanity and extravagance of dress which was rapidly on the increase, as the fashions of babylon were more and more brought into our midst."[23]

In the fall Romania returned east to complete her final two years of medical school, this time at the Women's Medical College in Philadelphia. Rooming with her for a time was Ellis Shipp, the second woman to go east to obtain her medical degree. Romania later recalled the difficulty of the days of study at medical school. She said that all days "seemed so much alike that it was as one long day."[24] Her long day included five or six one-hour lectures five days a week; after class, there were hours of studying ahead. One woman medical student said the evenings would find the student

skull in hand, striving manfully to trace out numerous almost invisible lines and marks, each with a Latin name as long again as itself. . . . When tired nature will no longer be denied, he retires to his couch but not always to rest. Long lists of those interminable Latin names, interspersed with bones of every description, or the latest experiment tried in the chemical laboratory, flit before him in kaleidoscopic procession and he awakes in the morning feeling as though he had continued his labor during the whole twenty-four hours.[25]

In her two years Romania took courses in obstetrics and diseases of women, anatomy, chemistry and toxicology, principles and practice of medicine, surgery, materia medica, physiology and hygiene, microscopy and histology, and dentistry.[26]

The summer following her junior year, Romania was offered a position at the New England Hospital for women and children in Boston. She recalled that her

earnestness and diligence won the esteem of all the physicians who were all women, both resident and attending, insomuch that they held a counsel as to the propriety of sending me to Europe after my graduation. I believe that the fact of my being a Mormon decided the case against me.[27]

As a senior Romania returned to a "winter full of work," but completed her courses of study and wrote a thesis entitled "Puerperal Hemmorrhage, Its Cause and Cure." She successfully passed all of her examinations and defended her thesis both before her professors and before the studentbody, making it possible for her to graduate on March 15, 1877. She was thirty-eight. She recalls it as

one of the most eventful days of my life . . . . Dressed in black and with throbbing hearts we repaired to Association Hall—the house was crowded full of interested friends and spectators, but alas! Few were mine. A stranger in a strange land, besides being almost a "hiss and a by word" on account of my religion. Nevertheless after we had received our diplomas and a present of the code of Medical Ethics, I received two beautiful bouquets and a book from friends.[28]

After graduation Romania remained in Philadelphia to continue her studies of the eye and ear; for the entire sixteen months that she had been in New York she had attended the Eye and Ear Infirmary. Additional courses on the eye and ear in Philadelphia after graduation gave her the distinction of being one of the earliest physicians to specialize.

After finishing these courses, Romania went to the Elmira Water Cure for a month at the request of Brigham Young's son, John, to observe the methods used.[29] Water cures were popular in the nineteenth century, and as she journeyed to Bloomington, Indiana, to take care of her sister, Josephine, she visited the noted water cures along the way. Josephine was expecting a baby, and Romania had promised to deliver the baby and care for Josephine in return for train fare to Salt Lake. However, her stay necessarily lengthened into two months. When she was finally able to leave Bloomington she was very anxious, and she recalled that the "journey [home] was long and wearisome though of only a few days." When she finally arrived home September 18, 1877, she recalled her home was

still, quiet, and empty, but hearing voices in the orchard I wandered back and found my dear faithful mother and two youngest children gathering fruit. My heart was pierced with sorrow when my little ones opened wide their eyes in wonder and with no token of recognition of their mother. I wept bitterly that I had been forgotten by my babes. Very soon all my dear children were gathered around me and we soon renewed old acquaintances and affections.[30]

Parley was now seventeen but Roy was only four, so began Romania's difficult task of balancing motherhood with the establishment of a medical practice. Romania's husband was in poor health, and the year of her return he had taken Brighamine Nealson as a plural wife. Romania said,

the principle of plural marriage seemed a most rational and eternal truth. I never opposed the principle when practiced with singleness of heart as commanded. Were it lived according to the great and grand aim of its author, though it be a fiery furnace at some period of our life, it will prove the one thing needful to cleanse and purify our inmost soul of selfishness, jealousy, and other mundane attributes which seem to lie closest to the citadel of life ... Plural marriage is the platform upon which is built endless kingdoms and lives and no other or all combined principles revealed can be substituted as a compensation.[31]

Romania soon became a busy medical practitioner, and in the spring following her return, announcements of classes she would teach in anatomy, physiology, and obstetrics began to dot the pages of the *Woman's Exponent:*

Mrs. Romania B. Pratt, M.D., continues her interesting and instructive free lectures to the Ladies Medical Class, every Friday afternoon, as usual, at this office [the Exponent office].... All ladies desirous of obtaining knowledge of the laws of life, and how to preserve their health, and rear children, how to determine the cases of illness, should improve these opportunities and not fail in punctuality.[32]

Romania's articles on hygiene also became a regular feature in the *Exponent,* as they later did in the *Young Woman's Journal.*

Another absorbing interest in Romania's life was women's suffrage. She wrote in the *Exponent* in 1879 that it was a woman's "duty and privilege to do whatever she can that will promote the advancement and elevation of her own sex."[33] She spoke to a large audience in Ogden City Hall and told them that "Knowledge feeds and fattens on itself ... it is good to become self-sustaining and have a complete knowledge of some branch of work.... [A woman] must work her way up to the position she desires to fill in life [keeping in mind that] her mission as a mother is a sacred one."[34] Romania later wrote in the *Young Woman's Journal*, "why not let capacity and ability be the test of eligibility and not sex?" She continued:

In a nutshell our duties as suffragists are to inform ourselves and instruct each other in the science of government, to interest all our friends in the movement, and convert our fathers, brothers and husbands to the fact that we can understand and wield an intelligent power in politics, and still preside wisely and gracefully at home.[35]

In 1880 Romania asked *Exponent* readers:

Is law a protection or a guide, or is it a vicious weathercock set up on the cross roads, pointing the road just as the wind may blow? ... It is high time women set a high price on all her works and abilities, and see which bill foots up the highest.[36]

Romania did set a "high price on all her works and abilities." She did not allow circumstances to hold her back. She was a real-ist who acted without hesitation when the situation demanded; in 1881 she concluded that she and Parley should be divorced. It is difficult to ascertain the reasons for this decision. Parley had never been able to support the family because of his delicate health and his frequent absence, and Brighamine now had children that needed any support Parley could give. The years of separation in early marriage while Parley was on his missions and later as Ro-mania attended medical school had likely alienated the Pratts and had probably added to Romania's decision for a final separation.[37]

Romania seems not to have suffered condemnation because of her divorce. That same year she was called to be the treasurer of the Young Ladies Mutual Improvement Association of the Salt Lake Stake. She was also given a blessing by President Joseph F. Smith, in which he asked God to bless her

with the light, wisdom and power of His Holy Spirit in your occupation as a doctor, as a midwife, as a teacher of obstetrics and of medicine and of all things connected therewith.[38]

In the following year Romania was chosen to accompany Zina D. H. Young, a prominent Relief Society member, and Ellen B. Ferguson, another Mormon physician and later president of the Women's Suffrage Association of Salt Lake City, back to New

York to attend the Woman's Suffrage Convention. Romania also attended lectures at the Eye and Ear Infirmary. In a letter to the *Exponent*, Romania reported on the convention and on Susan B. Anthony:

Everybody who is not as mean and green with prejudice and jealousy, as a tomato worm, cannot help admiring and liking Miss Anthony. If she is terse and decided, and hits the nail a peeling clip square on the top of the head, is not that the way to do, when we are in dead earnest to accomplish anything.[39]

However, Romania also revealed that her

attendance at the convention was quite a digression on my part from my daily attendance at the Eye and Ear Infirmary. Rain, snow, storm or sleet are mere feathers before my all-devouring interest in their field of study ... I know that I have gained a more comprehensive grasp of the vast subject, and dipped deeper into the minutiae of it, during these three months, than I possibly could have done in years alone. I only regret that I cannot stay longer; but the home notes sound loud in my heart, and I must return at latest by the middle of May.

I will not indulge in any platitudes of how I long to be at home ... for just as true as twice one is two, any true Latter-day Saint woman, when she turns back upon Zion, has to possess more will force than the wife of Lot had to keep her from looking back all the time.[40]

Six months in New York had prepared Romania to open an office on Main Street in Salt Lake City, equipped with the newest instruments available for surgical operations on the eye and ear. Because of her pioneering work on the eye and because of her modern equipment, it is thought that she performed the first cataract operation in Utah.[41]

Romania's hope for the establishment of a Mormon hospital became a reality in 1882 when the Catholic sisters decided to vacate St. Mary's Hospital and the Mormon Church First Presidency granted the Relief Society sisters permission to move into the vacated building. Using donations to obtain operating funds, the Relief Society soon equipped the hospital with the necessary supplies to begin operation. The Deseret Hospital Association was organized, allowing every woman in good church standing to belong by paying one dollar annually. Eliza R. Snow was appointed president of the association with Zina D. H. Young as vice-president, Emmeline B. Wells as secretary, and Romania Pratt as visiting physician. Romania later became a resident physician.[42] The dedication services for the Deseret Hospital were held on July 16, 1882.

The facility soon became a leading hospital in the territory, with a capacity of between forty and fifty patients. In the beginning each patient was charged three dollars per week for board, room, and nursing, but the fees were later raised to six dollars per week.[43] In 1893 a pamphlet distributed at the World's Fair extolled the accomplishments of the Deseret Hospital:

Over four hundred operations, including some of the major operations, have been performed and have been attended with unusual success. The school of obstetrics and training of nurses was opened in June, 1887, and has been in successful operation since that time. About thirty have received certificates and have gone to distant parts of the country to fulfill important positions.[44]

Lack of financial income closed the Deseret Hospital after eleven years of service.[45]

Romania was outspoken on issues that needed emphasis. In 1882 Congress passed the Edmunds Bill, making plural marriage illegal and punishable by a five hundred dollar fine or five years imprisonment. Romania wrote a defense of polygamy in the *Exponent* in 1886 stating that every woman should have the "undeniable right to be an honorable wife and mother—of fulfilling the end of her creation, and do not the circumstances of life and statistics prove this to be impossible under the monogamic system."[46]

Romania was in a good position to defend plural marriage, for on March 11, 1886, she had become the third wife of Charles W. Penrose. Charles had been born in England in 1832 and had become converted to Mormonism at the age of eighteen; he served a seven-year mission after his conversion, and upon its completion began writing for the *Millennial Star*. He continued his work on the *Star* until 1861 when he emigrated to Utah, teaching school in the winters and farming in the summers. Charles eventually returned to England to serve three additional missions. In 1886 when he married Romania he had two other wives and was working as the editor of the *Deseret News;* he went on to become assistant church historian, a member of the Council of the Twelve Apostles, and a second counselor in the First Presidency of the Mormon Church to both Joseph F. Smith and Heber J. Grant.[47]

During the busy years after their marriage when Romania had a heavy medical practice in addition to her writing and teaching and when Charles was required to spend many hours on church business, they still managed time together. Charles was a story teller and mimic; people were quickly made to feel at ease in his presence and soon joined in the laughter of a joke. Romania's temperament was sober, and she would often merely smile as others joined Charles in a hearty laugh.[48] Their difference in temperament, however, did not prevent them from enjoying each other's company; their personalities complemented each other. They loved

to attend the theater and travel together. They always treated
each other with respect and fondness. After twelve years of marriage to Romania, Charles wrote the following poem:

> *No words of mine can ever tell*
> *The feelings of a loving heart*
> *Which, rising like a fountain, swell*
> *And with the richest joys impart.*
>
> *As years march on with rapid stride*
> *And weakness comes to limb and brain*
> *Sweet love has Time's attack defied*
> *And stamped his fiercest efforts vain.*
>
> *Dear "M" your charms of mind and soul*
> *Will bloom afresh, though wrinkles come*
> *Their fragrance still hold sweet control*
> *And shed perfume around our home.*
>
> *. . .*
>
> *Peace be to thee, and lengthened life*
> *Eternal bliss and glory given.*
> *A loved and loving honored wife*
> *Thou shalt be crowned, in earth and heaven!*[49]

Romania was well suited to be the wife of an apostle. Besides
being in excellent health and being well respected for her work in
medicine and suffrage, she was also a spiritual leader. She served
as general secretary of the Relief Society, and her memoirs tell
about the spiritual feasts she often enjoyed:

*One was held in an upper room of the house of Mrs. Emeline B. Wells, Editor of
the Exponent. The ladies present were as follows: Eliza R. Snow Smith, Elizabeth
Ann Whitney, Mrs. M. I. Horne, Mrs. Zina D. Young, Mrs. Bathsheba Smith,
Mrs. Sarah M. Kimball, Mrs. Hannah Z. King, Mrs. S. M. Heywood, Mrs.
Elizabeth Howard, Mrs. Emeline B. Wells, Mrs. Lydia Wells, Mrs. Hannah Pid-
wek and myself. I never witnessed such a rich flow of the spirit of God as was
manifested on that occasion. Sister Snow Smith spoke in tongues and gave each one
present a rich blessing. Sister Whitney sang a song of Zion in the pure language.
Sister M. I. Horne also sang in tongues. Sister Zina Young gave the interpretations
of all. Each lady present spoke (not in tongues) by the power and spirit of the Holy
Ghost and we truly had a time of feasting the soul and rejoicing.*[50]

Susa Young Gates, a long-time friend, described Romania in
1891 as a

*wonderful woman. Not because she has done anything impossible to be done by other
women, but because in becoming a doctor able to sever a limb, or take out an eye,
now delivering a woman, then attending with gentlest care the sick bed of some poor
old man at the hospital, yet with it all she has a home on another street where she*

keeps a corner warm and cozy for mother and her unmarried boys; also is she a wom-
an with religious duties devolving upon her shoulders, and with it all she is the same
sweet, quiet-voiced, gentle lady that my childish memory so vividly produces.

If you should ever have the honor of being her guest, you will discover that with all
her many gifts she has one rare and beautiful one, that of a perfect hostess; her guest
is apparently her only care—she who is weighed down with a thousand burdens. She
is honored and loved by all who have the pleasure of her acquaintance and their name
is legion.[51]

On August 8, 1889, Romania was given a surprise party to celebrate her jubilee year. Held in a room of the Deseret Hospital gar-
nished with flowers and vines, Romania was congratulated "on
having reached the half century so active, bouyant, fresh, and
blooming a matron." Speeches were given and a large photograph
album was presented. Dr. Ellis Shipp paid tribute to her:

In you we recognize many gifts and graces that glorify the character of women. We
admire your talents, we honor your undaunted courage and perseverance in toiling
alone up the rugged hill of science, opening the path to a higher and broader field of
usefulness for your sex. . . . It was said of Napoleon that he could win battles but
Josephine had achieved the greater success for she could win hearts; the presence of so
many appreciative friends assembled here tonight to honor your Jubilee proves that you
have learned the art known to the charming. . . .[53]

Romania also found time to join two literary clubs founded by
her friend, Emmeline B. Wells: the Press Club and the Reapers'
Club. Both sought to train writers for publication and newspaper
work. Founded in 1891 in the parlor of the *Exponent* office, the
Press Club chose Emmeline B. Wells as president, Susa Young
Gates and Lula Greene Richards as vice-presidents and Romania
Pratt Penrose as auditor. Meetings were held regularly on the last
day of the month; members read and listened to compositions
from their midst, enjoying "a feast of reason and a flow of soul."[54]
The membership in Salt Lake City was about thirty, but the idea
spread throughout the territory, and other clubs were soon estab-
lished. The Press Club was formally dissolved by Susa Young
Gates in 1928.[55]

In January 1907 Romania and Charles left Salt Lake City to
preside over the European Mission; Romania organized branches
of the Relief Society while traveling through Europe with Charles.
She wrote to the *Exponent,* delighting in her travel down the
"Rhine, the beautiful Rhine"; she described the "broad, deep,
placid, blue river of romance" where the shores on either side "are
dotted with towns and villages and castles, many old and ruined,
built in times of long ago, having each a legend weird, romantic
and mysterious." She described the castles and grape vineyards,

and took *Exponent* readers around every bend of the river peeking into towers, "gray and ice-covered, full of mystery."[56]

While in Europe, Romania was appointed by Utah Governor John Cutler to attend the Woman's International Suffrage Alliance held at Amsterdam on June 15, 1908, where representatives were in attendance from all the civilized countries of the world. Romania addressed the convention and spoke about suffrage in the west, and her comments were favorably received.[57] In May of the following year she was again asked to participate in the International Alliance representing the western states.

But as their stay in Europe lengthened, Romania longed to return home to Utah. Writing to Emmeline and the *Exponent,* she reported with enthusiasm that there were now forty Relief Societies in Europe in good condition, where previously there had been only three.[58] But she added with melancholy:

[I] feel that I shall almost walk the streets of Salt Lake as a stranger when I get home. I approach a new newspaper with some dread for fear of reading the death of some one I have known, and yet with that fear upon me I look the first thing to see who had died, and if I am a stranger to them I say to myself some one else is sad. . . .

I cannot tell you how much I long to have a heart to heart talk with you again. Do take care of yourself and not expose your health by being out late the coming cold winter nights. When I think of what you do at your time of life I feel ashamed of what little I can do, yet I am busy all the time and feel almost I have not time to read the papers because I need to do so many things.

I have been making warm bonnets for the poor in our branch. I have made four and have two more and a cap to make. We have a milliner belonging to our branch Relief Society and she taught me how.[59]

In June 1910 the Penroses were finally released from the mission. Romania wrote a farewell message to the Relief Societies, advising each society "not to take pride in hoarding a large sum in the treasury, but rather to look about and see where good can be done and someone helped and comforted." Leaving friends in England was difficult, but Charles was now seventy-eight and Romania was seventy-one, and they longed to reunite with friends and family in Utah.

Upon their return, Romania and Charles moved into their home at 1175 South Ninth East in Salt Lake City. Though advanced in years, they hosted many family gatherings, attended the Salt Lake Theater often, and traveled to Saltair, the Chicago World's Fair, and California.

In her later years Romania's granddaughters describe her as being a little bit heavy, but loving to dress up:

*She always had fancy hats with a lot of flowers and things on her hats. She wore
... elaborate blouses ... and she had a lot of what they used to call pesimentary and
sequins and beads, and she would sew the beads all over and she wore high collars
and then she wore a chocker around her neck to hold her chin in.*[60]

Though Romania returned to her medical practice for a short
time, she found she was too busy to continue her practice, and she
retired in 1912 after thirty-five years as a practicing physician.[61]
Charles continued vigorously in his work as counselor in the Mormon Church First Presidency until his death on May 16, 1925. After Charles's death, Romania's final years revolved around her
family, her work in Relief Society, and her reading. Toward the
end of her life, she became blind and finally died on November 9,
1932, at the age of ninety-three.[62] Romania was survived by four
sons, ten grandchildren, and eight great-grandchildren.

Five years before her death, Emmeline B. Wells wrote a tribute
to Romania:

> *A wondrous gift thou hast, I know thy power,*
> *To help the sick, to comfort in distress;*
> *Greater than riches is the potent dower,*
> *The magic touch that charms like a caress.*
>
> *Tis good to do such deeds of usefulness,*
> *To be so calm, so wise, such skill to lend;*
> *To brave the world with such deep earnestness*
> *One cannot prize too highly such a friend.*[63]

Notes

1. Doctrine and Covenants, section 35, verse 9. (The book of scripture is published by The Church of Jesus Christ of Latter-day Saints in many editions.)

2. *Ibid.*, section 89.

3. "Memoir of Romania B. Pratt, M.D.," uncatalogued manuscript, The Church of Jesus Christ of Latter-day Saints, Historical Department (hereinafter cited as Church Archives), p. 1.

4. *Dedication and Naming of 22 Buildings,* Brigham Young University, 1954, p. 36.

5. "Memoir of Romania B. Pratt, M.D.," p. 2.

6. *Ibid.*

7. *Ibid.*

8. *Ibid.*, p. 3.

9. Edna Sutherland and Phyllis Pratt Hoppie oral interview, in possession of Edna P. Sutherland, Salt Lake City. Photocopy

10. "Memoir of Romania B. Pratt, M.D.," p. 4.

11. *Deseret News,* March 27, 1937, p. 11.

12. Kate B. Carter, comp., *Our Pioneer Heritage,* 17 vols., Salt Lake City, Utah: Daughters of the Utah Pioneers, 1958-1974, vol. 6, p. 366.

13. Sutherland and Hoppie interview, p. 10.

14. Records of Romania Bunnell Pratt, manuscript, original in possession of Edna P. Sutherland, Salt Lake City. Xerox copy available in Church Archives.

15. "Memoir of Romania B. Pratt, M.D.," p. 5: *Woman's Exponent* 17(September 1, 1888): 48.

16. "Memoir of Romania B. Pratt, M.D.," pp. 5-6.

17. *Young Woman's Journal* 2(September 1891): 533.

18. *Ibid.*, p. 534.

19. *Ibid.*, p. 533.

20. *Ibid.*

21. "Memoir of Romania B. Pratt, M.D.," p. 6.

22. *Young Woman's Journal* 2(September 1891): 534.

23. "Memoir of Romania B. Pratt, M.D.," p. 6.

24. *Ibid.*, p. 7.

25. *Young Woman's Journal* 1(September 1890): 473-73.

26. Romania Pratt Papers, uncatalogued manuscript, Church Archives.

27. "Memoir of Romania B. Pratt, M.D.," p. 7.

28. *Ibid.*, pp. 7-8.

29. *Ibid.*, p. 8.

30. *Woman's Exponent* 6(November 15, 1877): 92.

31. "Memoir of Romania B. Pratt, M.D.," p. 3.

32. *Woman's Exponent* 6(July 15, 1877): 30.

33. *Ibid.*, 7(April 1, 1879): 217.

34. *Ibid.*, 9(June 1, 1879):5.

35. *Ibid.*, 18(August 15, 1890):331.

36. *Ibid.*, 9(October 1, 1880):65.

37. Sutherland and Hoppie interview, pp. 4, 11.

38. "Blessing pronounced upon the head of Sister Romania B. Pratt. . . ." Romania Pratt Papers, uncatalogued manuscript, Church Archives.

39. *Woman's Exponent* 10(March 1, 1882):146.

40. *Ibid.*, 15(March 15, 1886):158.

41. *Ibid.*, 9(July 15, 1882):28.

42. Carter, *Our Pioneer Heritage,* 6:412-13; *Woman's Exponent* 9(August 1882):36.

43. *Ibid.*, pp. 7-8.

44. *Ibid.*, p. 367.

45. *Ibid.*, p. 415.

46. *Woman's Exponent* 14(March 1, 1882):158.

47. Edward W. Tullidge, *The History of Salt Lake City and Its*

Founders, Salt Lake City, 1886, pp. 140-43.

48. Sutherland and Hoppie interview, p. 12.

49. Charles W. Penrose Papers, uncatalogued manuscript, Church Archives. In the third stanza, "M" is an abbreviation for a name of endearment.

50. "Memoirs of Romania B. Pratt, M.D.," pp. 10-11.

51. *Young Woman's Journal* 2(September 1891):535.

52. *Woman's Exponent* 18(August 15, 1889):45.

53. *Ibid.,* 18(August 15, 1889); 45.

54. Kate B. Carter, comp., *Heart Throbs of the West,* 12 vols., Salt Lake City, Utah: Daughters of the Utah Pioneers, 1939-1950, vol. 5, p. 165.

55. *Ibid.,* p. 231.

56. *Woman's Exponent* 36(October 1908):53.

57. *Ibid.,* 37(August 1908):14-15.

58. *Ibid.,* 38(January 1910):42.

59. *Millennial Star,* Liverpool, England, 1840-1970, 72(9 June 1910):858-59.

60. Sutherland and Hoppie interview, p. 7.

61. Keith Terry, *The Contribution of Medical Women During the First Fifty Years in Utah,* master's thesis, Brigham Young University, 1964, p. 48.

62. *Ibid.*

63. *Relief Society Magazine,* Salt Lake City, 1914-1970, 19(December, 1932):720.

Ellis Reynolds Shipp 1847-1939

Gail Farr Casterline was raised in the midwest and holds degrees in history from Northwestern and Utah State universities. She has served on the editorial staff of the Western Historical Quarterly *and is the author of several works on nineteenth-century social and intellectual life. She has taught and written women's history, sustaining an interest in the Latter-day Saints through the Utah State Historical Society and the Mormon History Association. She is currently on the staff of the Chicago Historical Society. She is married to Jeff Casterline.*

Ellis R. Shipp

Gail Farr Casterline

In April 1885 six women gathered in an office at Number 18 Main Street in Salt Lake City for a small ceremony. One spoke. "I trust the principles that have been inculcated in your minds may remain with you and serve you faithfully in case of every emergency," she said. "And I would suggest that you keep your minds bright and active by continued research—study the latest and best works, and keep posted in the medical literature of the day."[1]

The speaker was Ellis Reynolds Shipp, M.D.; the occasion was the commencement of the School of Obstetrics and Nursing that she had founded in 1878, and in which she was the teacher.

There are still people alive today who remember Ellis Reynolds Shipp and who say of her, "What a wonderful woman!" Her career has almost the dimensions of folklore; historians have pointed to her as an eminent example of the instrumental role many women played in early Utah medicine.[2] She traveled east to secure the best medical training available to women in the United States. She trained a phalanx of midwives and nurses. She helped transform Utah's medical arts, particularly obstetrics, from the application of age-old home remedies to the more scientific approach of modern medicine.

The nineteenth-century Church of Jesus Christ of Latter-day Saints could claim many capable and dedicated professional women, a surprising number of whom were polygamous wives and mothers.[3] Why did Mormon women wield such a strong force in a field such as medicine, which stoutly resisted female intrusion in other parts of the country? What were the motivations that led these women to seek independent lives outside the home, perhaps earlier and more zealously than did their non-Mormon contemporaries? How and why did Mormonism foster career-mindedness among women? What was the role of polygamy?

As scholars probe for explanations of the various roles women have assumed in American life, some answers may be found in a discussion of Ellis Shipp's life.

Ellis Shipp's autobiography and personal papers tell of her moving struggle to live a life equal to her abilities.[4] Her diary, spanning the years between 1871 and 1878, traces the striking metamorphosis from young mother with vague yearnings for wider horizons to medical doctor and teacher. Through it all the significance of her achievement is broadened by the story of moral support and practical assistance rendered by other Mormon women, including her sister-wives.

Daughter of William Fletcher and Anna Hawley Reynolds, Ellis was born in southeastern Iowa on January 20, 1847. Soon thereafter the Reynolds family was converted to Mormonism; in 1852 they joined a wagon train bound for Utah, the new-claimed Zion of their faith, where William Reynolds acquired a farm in Pleasant Grove.

By her own account, Ellis was an active, fanciful child who read everything she could find. She grew up knowing the strains of pioneering, especially on women. Her own mother died young when Ellis was but fourteen. Upon the loss of her mother Ellis assumed adult cares, looking after the household and her four brothers and sisters.

Life offered its bright moments to the young ladies of rural Utah, where books, social organizations, and at times even local musical and dramatic performances teased one's imagination. As a teenager, Ellis made occasional visits to Salt Lake City and at some point met Zina D. Young, the cultivated wife of the prophet Brigham Young. Ellis must have made a memorable impression, for in 1865 Brigham Young himself invited her to live at the Beehive House in Salt Lake and to attend school with his own children. She accepted, and spent ten months there. Whether Brigham Young sought to prepare Ellis for some special mission or whether he was merely exercising paternalistic good will is not known. It seems that her desire for learning was not as keen as it would later become. In May 1866, she prevailed against Brigham's admonitions and became the wife of Milford Bard Shipp.

Eleven years Ellis' senior, Milford Shipp may have impressed Brigham Young as something of a drifter. Raised a Methodist, Milford attended DePauw University in Indiana before he embraced Mormonism and moved to Utah in 1856. Then he reportedly studied law and helped start a canning factory. A mission to England followed. He had been married twice before: one wife had died and the other had divorced him, as Ellis heard, for his "unkindness." When he married Ellis, Milford was helping his father manage a hat and shoe store in Salt Lake.[5]

Why Ellis so adored him—and continued to do so from then on—is best expressed in her own words: "He was to me all that the enlivened fancy of girlhood or the matured judgment of woman could picture in her imagination. So kind and affectionate, so faithful to the cause of Mormonism .... He was ambitious, ardent and energetic in all that was noble and laudable. Enthusiastic and spirited in conversation. In truth, I never saw a person who could so enchant and fascinate by the power of language."[6]

Ellis clearly hoped that theirs would be a marriage of intellectual vigor. Practical matters intervened, and homemaking, babies, and settling in Fillmore—where Milford's father opened a branch store—consumed their first years together. Of lonely days in Fillmore she later recalled, "it was then I began to realize most fully the blessings of work and mental activity more than I ever had before."[7] After the Fillmore business floundered, the Shipps returned to Salt Lake City, and Milford soon embarked on other missions for the Church. In rapid succession he took three other wives: Margaret Curtis in 1868; Elizabeth Hilstead in 1871; and, finally, Mary Smith.

By nature introspective, Ellis began to brood over her lot. Her melancholy deepened with the deaths of an infant son in 1868 and a young daughter in 1873. Her diary records her brave acceptance of these events and the spiritual faith which helped her to cope with them. Four years after her marriage she was convinced that her life was to be one of self-sacrifice: "And thus began my creed, the pattern of a weak and unsophisticated life as yet to meet the crucial tests whereby we gain and thus, alas, may lose."[8]

In Salt Lake City again Ellis was mustered into service with other Mormon women to carry out Relief Society programs aimed at insulating the Mormon economy then threatened by the completion of the transcontinental railroad in 1869. Association with other church women through various retrenchment programs encouraged Ellis to better her lot. She determined to fill in the gaps left by an irregular education by mapping out her own plan of self-improvement: a reading regimen followed daily between 4:00 and 7:00 a.m. Meanwhile the Shipps grappled with financial problems, since Milford could not support his ever-growing polygamous family. For a time Ellis, "with two children and a cow to milk," taught at the ward school so "that we might comfortably provide for ourselves without the need of charity."[9]

A growing confidence in her own abilities combined with nagging economic need to challenge her yet further. In November 1872 she reflected, "I know that I am tired of this life of uselessness and unaccomplished desires, only so far as cooking, washing dishes and doing general housework goes. I believe that woman's life should not consist wholly and solely of routine duties." By

June of 1873, at the age of twenty-six she triumphantly declared, "I think my desires for health and long life were never so strong, for my earthly work is but just begun."[10]

The work to which she alluded had already begun to manifest itself as the care of the sick. She knew full well the heartache of infant death and the perils of childbirth; here, it seemed, lay the great purpose for which she was meant. On January 5, 1872, she told of studying privately with a Dr. Gunn, "as I deem it the duty of every mother to understand perfectly the laws of health." Two years later she vowed to acquire the knowledge needed to help other women as well.[11]

Such statements were quite daring when voiced in a society that possessed a deep-seated distrust of physicians. Since Joseph Smith's time, Mormon leaders had recommended the laying-on of hands for the cure of all earthly ailments; even as late as 1869 Brigham Young preached: "Doctors and their medicines I regard as a deadly bane to any community."[12] Loyal Saints relied upon the home remedies proffered by church-sanctioned botanic doctors. These Thomsonian doctors prescribed cures made from the plant lobelia to induce vomiting, and they believed they were ridding the body of its "poison." Educated physicians deplored such practices, but they were nonetheless common and not unique to the Mormons, who, like other frontiersmen, occasionally resorted to the lancet to release "bad blood." Other self-taught healers administered herbal teas and poultices.[13]

The results of these measures were obviously disappointing, and when gentile physicians brought the latest techniques to the territory and began to establish hospitals in the seventies, church leaders feared that Mormons might seek their help. Eager to keep pace by providing his followers with better care by those of their own faith, Brigham Young soon called several young men to become physicians and dispatched them to eastern medical schools. Ellis' desire to make her services available to those of her own sex could not have been more timely, for prejudice and excessive modesty excluded all but midwives in obstetrical cases. These midwives became skilled through experience, but they were not equipped to handle all the possible complications of childbirth.[14]

Ellis Shipp's career reflects the influence of Eliza R. Snow, one of the leading women of the Mormon Church, who had meanwhile spearheaded a crusade to familiarize the sisters with the principles of health. A course in basic physiology taught by Sarah Kimball got under way in July 1872 under the aegis of the Cooperative Retrenchment Association.[15] Since Ellis belonged to this organization, she may well have attended some of the classes. Chris

Rigby Arrington points out that Brigham Young had suggested the training of women obstetricians by July 1873, when the ladies of the retrenchment society met to discuss his recommendations for organizing a special school for this purpose. On this occasion Eliza Snow argued in favor of women becoming full-fledged doctors as a sure means of keeping men out of the delivery room. According to Arrington, Brigham Young conceded, and in October 1873 he gave a sermon in which he said, "The time has come for women to come forth as doctors in these valleys of the mountains."[16]

Although no printed account of Brigham Young's sermon survives, this seems to be a plausible explanation of the circumstances that soon prompted a number of women to step forward to become physicians. The first Mormon woman to do so was Romania Pratt, who entered the Woman's Medical College of Pennsylvania in Philadelphia in the fall of 1874. Ellis was no doubt inspired by her example, but her sister-wife "Maggie" Curtis Shipp acted sooner by enrolling in the same Pennsylvania institution in October 1875. A month later a homesick Maggie returned to Salt Lake City. On November 10 Ellis' diary contains this startling interjection: "What a strange fatality! This morning I start for Philadelphia to attend the Medical College." That this came as such a surprise suggests that arrangements for Maggie's tuition had already been made and that the Shipps were financially obligated to the college.

Ellis' goal of obtaining a thorough understanding of the body was now fortuitously within reach, but she felt unprepared. Beset with doubt and anxiety, she left her three small children in the care of her sister-wives and boarded a train heading east.

Once matriculated she took heart, for "soon my interest was awakened and I began to feel my desires for knowledge increase as I began to see and realize how little I knew."[17] The thought of how much she could do for her community as a bonafide medical doctor sustained her.

But a letter from Maggie to Ellis in January 1876 reveals other motivations as well. Wrote Maggie,

You know too well what our home is; noble hearts inhabit the rooms but our circumstances are so unfavorable. Are you not anxious to better your situation, think of your boys, *what* poor advantages *they have, what could you do for them if you were* here. *You have tried for* eight long years. *Think of how your heart* ached, ached, ached, *day after day, and I tell you, as time as the sun shines . . .* it would be no better *if you were* here again. *No, we must get out of this, our children must have a beautiful home, splendid advantages, or they will be as they have been.*[18]

Thus is Ellis' dilemma painfully conveyed: in polygamy the wives and children learned to fend for themselves. As this letter demonstrates, plural wives sometimes found their greatest solace in each other, sharing household duties and childrearing so that one or another could acquire the skills needed for self-support. Polygamy thus offered practical advantages that ambitious Mormon women could well make use of. And while one might think that polygamous households were fraught with jealousies, Maggie's statements show how some plural wives banded together in providing for all of the children's futures.

Ellis had every reason to believe that the Woman's Medical College would equip her for a significant and gainful career. Founded in 1850, this institution was the oldest and most prominent offering the M.D. degree to women. It was one of the few places where women could get such training, for in this era of prudery most schools opposed mixed classes. Under the direction of such eminent physicians as Emmeline Horton Cleveland, expert on ovarian tumors, and Dean Rachel Bodley, noted chemist and botanist, Ellis's three-year course combined intense study with a rigorous practicum that taught the newest diagnostic and surgical procedures as well as the principles of hygiene and anaesthesia. During this time the college set exceptionally high standards; Harvard Medical College, for instance, had not required a three-year course until 1871.[19]

Exposure to all branches of medicine failed to lure Ellis from her interest in obstetrics and diseases of women. Since her class consisted of less than twenty students, a sense of kinship developed. Romania Pratt was a favorite companion. Even so, Ellis's emotional and financial distress was evident. "You always appear so sad, as though you were grieving over something," an acquaintance rightly intuited.[20]

Each day Ellis longed for letters from home. Those from Maggie and the other sister-wives were frequent and cheering, but Milford's letters sometimes unleashed a turmoil in Ellis that she vented in her diary. In January 1876 she observed, "I think he does not realize how almost harsh some of his letters seem, and did I not know him so well and understand his great desires for my success I should feel hurt, at times. His words, though bitter and sharp, have a good tonic effect and urge me ever onward." Ever willing to forgive him, she added a month later, "I cannot say that I had the best letter I ever had from my dear Bard but I think there could not be a better."[21]

Yet however stressful separations may be for any marriage, polygamy did not seem to make matters worse in this instance. In fact, Ellis often expressed relief that her husband was surrounded by an affectionate family circle in her absence. Harder to bear was the separation from her children. Of them she asked rhetorically, "Will you ere know the depth of love that fills my heart for you? I feel no sacrifice too great to make for your interest, not even the deprivation of your precious society."[22]

Anxiety and overwork resulted in illness, and in June 1876 Ellis's professors advised her to go home and rest for the summer. "September days of 1876 brought many hours of conflicting emotions," she remembered;[23] to the surprise of her friends and family, she departed that month to resume her studies. The future looked more uncertain than ever, since she knew that she was pregnant.

This condition did little to prevent her successful study, but money became an urgent concern as the months wore on. Milford informed her that he had none to send, so Ellis took up dressmaking to help meet her expenses. Interestingly enough, many a tuition bill was paid with money orders sent by Shipp's other wives. With all too little to spare themselves, their role in ensuring Ellis's professional advancement stands as a moving testimony to the close relationships possible among Mormon plural wives. Ellis made many appreciative references to Milford's "wise counsel," but it was the sister-wives who offered sympathy and practical wherewithal. "How pure and heavenly is the relationship of sisters in the holy order of polygamy," Ellis wrote. "How beautiful to contemplate the picture of a family where each one works for the interest, advancement, and well-being of all. *Unity is strength.*"[24]

She forged ahead on her thesis, "The Function of Generation." All the while she could reexamine her theories firsthand, for in May 1877 she gave birth to her sixth child, a baby girl. The following summer Ellis served residency at the hospital affiliated with the Woman's Medical College while a landlady looked after her infant. In August Ellis attempted to make some money at dressmaking in rural New Jersey. Toddler in one arm and dress patterns in the other, she hiked from one farmhouse to the next until she earned enough to return to school. Despite the additional burdens of motherhood, Ellis rejoiced in her young daughter: "it is to me the crowning joy of a woman's life to be a mother."[25] Less lonely now, she completed her course and completed her degree in March 1878.

Ellis felt deeply indebted to Maggie, who reentered the Woman's Medical College and earned an M.D. in 1883.[26] Then, as if reluctant to be outdone by his accomplished wives, Milford, too, announced his own aspirations to become a physician, and he completed his studies at the Jefferson Medical College of Philadelphia the same year as Maggie finished her studies. Ellis confessed,

I was not really anxious to engage in a busy medical practice immediately for I had all these years been longing for the joys of home companionship. Yet there truly existed a burning need of financial help, and how gladly I came to the rescue of those dear ones who had done their very best for me. . . .[27]

She bought a horse and buggy and advertised herself in local papers as a "Physician and Surgeon; Special attention given to Obstetrics, diseases of women and minor surgery."[28]

The unofficial church vehicle, the *Deseret News,* was receptive. On April 5 its editors announced, "We are pleased to see ladies belonging to the community of Latter-day Saints adopting the medical profession" for "they are better adapted for several branches of it than the sterner sex." On June 3 this paper again called attention to Dr. Ellis Shipp, urging "that the competent and educated doctors of our community . . . be patronized when necessary, by those of their own sex and faith, in preference to others. This is one of the occupations in which qualified women can act to advantage, and is a feature of the woman's rights question we can endorse and support." The Mormon Church itself publicly endorsed the medical women in August 1878 when Ellis Shipp, Margaret Curtis Shipp, Romania Pratt, and Martha Paul were set apart by the Mormon elders to practice medicine among the Saints.[29]

Ellis Shipp herself gave birth to a total of ten children, five of whom died in infancy. Once she understood how such tragedies could be avoided, she was restless to spread the word. Women of her day were expected to rear large families; this was especially true of the Mormons, who interpreted this as a responsibility of their faith. Many mothers and their babies suffered needlessly from lack of proper attention and from sheer ignorance. Realizing that the good she could do in private practice was limited, Ellis set forth to raise up an army of midwives to give lay service in every community.

To accomplish this, she announced the opening of her School of Obstetrics and Nursing in Salt Lake City in the fall of 1878 "with the object of qualifying women for the important offices of nurse and accoucheur."[30] The course of study she proposed took six months, and there were to be two sessions each year. She invited students from the entire region to attend the school at a nominal fee.

Her course gave women a basic understanding of physiology, obstetrical procedures, and the principles of health and nursing. Ellis phrased her rules for longevity in homespun words that all could comprehend: "peaceful mind, pure air, good food, clean body; cheerfulness, regular habits, sufficient sleep, relaxation, religion, and self-respect."[31] Women of the territory immediately began to take advantage of this opportunity to learn about the human body from an authoritative member of their own sex. All told, Ellis gave over 1,000 lectures during the first four years of the school's lifetime. Students from far-flung communities throughout Utah, Idaho, and Arizona enrolled in her course. Some of them came on scholarships set aside by local Relief Societies; railroad officials cooperated by letting them ride for half fare. By 1893 one hundred graduates had been certified for obstetrical work by a committee of examining physicians. The Utah State Board of Registration licensed a total of 467 midwives between 1893 and 1906 alone, leaving no doubt as to the thriving demand for their services.[32]

All the while Ellis saw many patients herself, reportedly attending to 1,543 obstetrical and 2,350 gynecological cases by 1893, when she completed a year of study at the University of Michigan Medical School.[33] Eager to keep abreast of news emanating from Europe, where researchers had only recently proven with certainty that bacteria caused disease, Ellis also did postgraduate work at hospitals in New York and Philadelphia in 1887 and 1888. This training made Ellis one of Utah's most well-educated physicians, and male colleagues often consulted her on nonobstetrical cases. Nevertheless, Ellis preferred her chosen field, explaining, rather poignantly, "Let men care for their own sex and do the major operations. I never had an ambition to take such responsibilities, for even men have fatal cases and, if a woman should have them, [she] would always be condemned because she was a woman!"[34]

As an obstetrician Ellis continued to expand her influence in innovative ways. One can well imagine the grand ideas volleyed about at the Shipp family dinner table where Milford, Ellis, and Maggie, all M.D.s, gathered with the two other sister-wives, both graduates of Ellis's course. They formed an extraordinary group. Among other things, these conversations gave birth to one of Utah's first medical journals, the *Salt Lake Sanitarian,* which appeared in April 1888 with Milford, Ellis, and Maggie as editors. Ellis contributed a regular column called "Mother's Methods" as well as articles denouncing alcohol and tobacco. Other pages discussed the findings of Louis Pasteur and applied them to life in Utah. Polluted water supplies, impure milk, lack of sanitation, and ill-kept domestic animals headed the Shipps' list of health menaces, and surely their warnings were well aimed, since infantile diarrhea, typhoid fever, and diphtheria were leading causes of death in Utah before 1900.[35] But the *Sanitarian* lasted only three years. Feuds between Maggie and Milford, who were eventually divorced, may have been the cause of its demise.

Ellis and Milford then hit upon collaborative lectures as another means of disseminating their ideas. Their first "private lecture to the ladies" evokes vivid images of the era when children were born at home. Asking their listeners to sympathize with the plight of the new babe, "just got quieted down serenely from the terrible ordeal of 'being born'," the Shipps urged "placarding the 'lying in' apartment something after this fashion: 'No admittance on any pretext whatever'" to prevent contamination by curious neighbors and relatives. They also warned against the prevalent assumption "that it is an unavoidable circumstance that children must go through the seige of measles, diphtheria, scarlet fever, etc." Inoculations for these diseases were still in the experimental stage, but the Shipps had their own prescription: a "simple, unexciting childhood life" that allowed maturation to proceed at its own rate. Condemning late hours, rich foods, and an endless social whirl, the Shipps advised mothers to "keep your child a child as long as possible."[36]

From the 1890s to the outbreak of World War I, Ellis Shipp made innumerable trips to teach in outlying districts of Mormon colonization. Scraps in a record book place her in Blackfoot and Pocatello, Idaho, in 1899; in Oregon and in Rexburg, Idaho, in 1901; in Colonia Juarez, Mexico, in 1902; in Vernal, Utah, in 1903-04; in Idaho again in 1916; and in Canada in 1916-17.[37] This extension program touched thousands of lives, for students used and passed along their training wherever they went.

Many graduates let Ellis know of their lasting appreciation and affection. A former student in Mexico informed her that "my companion in the class had no knowledge whatever of those subjects before, and now does all the obstetrical work for the whole Colony." Another from Driggs, Idaho, wrote, "To me you have been an inspiration for all these many years. I still am able to remember and apply, in my home and in the homes of friends, many of the interesting and useful things you taught. Not last, not least, many of the beautiful attributes of your character have helped me."[38]

Sarah Young Vance of Mesa City, Arizona, who studied under Ellis in Salt Lake, went on to practice for forty-five years and claimed to have delivered 1,500 babies. In her autobiography she added that Dr. Ellis Shipp organized a class in Mesa City in the early 1900s but "not one of these women worked at it or made a success of it."[39] Remote outposts of Mormonism resisted medical professionalism long after it was accepted in the larger cities and towns.

Midwives proved invaluable when no trained physician could be had. Neighbors summoned them at all hours to set bones, treat accident victims, and advise on troublesome aches and pains. On the other hand, some of them clung to homemade remedies that infuriated the regular physicians who settled in Utah in growing numbers after the turn of the century. Dr. Ezra Rich, who established a practice in Farmington in the 1890s, complained that the midwives in this community were so suspicious of his treatment of a case of puerperal sepsis that "had the patient not recovered, I would probably have been practicing in some other locality."[40]

Graduates of the Shipp school lacked the training necessary to diagnose and treat all the illnesses they encountered, but they possessed enough awareness of the fundamentals of health to ward off the skepticism of male M.D.s. To the extent that these women preached cleanliness, sanitation, and a balanced diet, they joined the battle in uprooting the very causes of disease. They were prepared to give patients a simple explanation of how the body functioned, replacing superstition with sound principle. And because the Shipp course included guest lectures by male physicians, to whom students were advised to turn when the need arose, its founder advanced the idea that women should forego modesty when their health was at stake. By 1900, when male physicians far outnumbered the female physicians in Utah, Ellis and her followers had already paved the way in convincing the public, especially women, that better care was needed.

But it was some time before trained midwives became obsolete, and Ellis received enough queries to warrant the teaching of her obstetrical course through the 1930s. She continued to publicize it, stressing the need for all young women to have a means of supporting themselves. A circular issued in 1927 indicates that the school shifted its emphasis to nursing, a reflection of advancing medical professionalism in Utah, which has since almost squeezed midwives out of the picture. But many communities, especially in rural Utah, did indeed have a crying need for nurses well into the thirties. "So many girls and women are wondering what they can do," wrote Dr. Ellis Shipp. Go into nursing, she proclaimed, for "This is the Golden Age of Opportunity."[41]

But she was disturbed that few young Utah women showed an interest in becoming physicians, and she chided them in the *Salt Lake Tribune* of February 22, 1938: "In a land renowned for its equal opportunities for women, it's simply amazing such a few follow a profession so befitting them." Feisty at ninety-one, she protested the chronically high maternity rate, "still a reproach to the nation." In her opinion, cars, clothes, new homes, and other comforts had distracted women from challenging undertakings.

Ellis' own life had been one of constant motion. She served on the staff of the Deseret Hospital, served on the general board of the Relief Society between 1898 and 1907, and officiated in two women's cultural societies, the Reaper's Club and the Utah Woman's Press Club. She even published a volume of poetry, *Life Lines,* which dealt with such themes as nature, friendship, and the family. In recognition of her work, the Woman's Medical College awarded her an honorary degree in 1935. Her home state honored her with membership in the Utah Hall of Fame. After she died on January 31, 1939, it was estimated that she had personally delivered more than 5,000 babies; that number did not include the many more her students had brought into the world. According to Ellis' daughter, graduates of the School of Obstetrics and Nursing totaled about five hundred.[42]

Was there, as she had intimated, a fundamental change in Mormon women that made conventional roles preferable to the broad spheres she and other early sisters had explored? The hardships of making new homes in the west taxed women to their fullest and commanded them to make resourceful use of their energies. This was especially true in the Mormon west, where settlement went hand in hand with religious faith and a communitarian outlook that asked the contributions of both men and women. The stark circumstances of frontier life were evident each day as disease and death struck family and friends. Ellis Shipp's own sorrows of losing a mother and five babies merged with religious commitment in fueling her seemingly inexhaustible fund of energy.

The passage of the frontier as well as the church's abandonment of polygamy after 1890 certainly changed the economic circumstances that pressed upon women like Ellis Shipp. As we have seen from her example, polygamy made it advantageous, if not utterly necessary, for women to have their own source of income. In turn, polygamy made this possible. The sharing of household and maternal duties presented women with options that could and did lead to their achievement of economic autonomy, a crucial first step toward personal autonomy. In this sense, polygamy was liberating.

That there were emotional costs is unquestionable. Ever modest about her accomplishments, Ellis Shipp looked back in old age to make this touching appraisal: "During the long years of continued effort, of unbounding will, of unwavering purpose, there were frequent disappointments. Often a wanderer, a homeless laborer, the great object was ever in the limelight of my consciousness."[43] Often in her travels she yearned for the comforts of home and family.

Throughout the years she had managed to create a loving home. Her loyalty to Milford remained unbending until his death in 1918. She helped each of her five surviving children through college so they could reach out for the great destinies she had long envisioned for them. One son became a physician, the other a lawyer. Of the daughters, one studied music at the University of Michigan, another received a master's degree from Columbia University, and a third graduated from the University of Utah. Perhaps even more important than this was her belief that all of her children possessed a firm character and shared her own religious faith. To Ellis, their accomplishments seemed a due reward for her efforts.

Eulogies delivered at Ellis Shipp's funeral praised her as a dutiful public servant. They also made it plain that her life had been hard.[44] Those closest to her recalled her devotion to her children, who were always uppermost in her mind and the subject of her final semiconscious murmurings: "I am so glad to see them. I haven't been with them for a long time...."[45] How often has a mother's love been considered as a moving force in history? We need only turn to a poem Ellis Shipp wrote for her children one Christmas to get a sense of why she struggled as she did:

> I twined a wreath while others slept.
> An ivy wreath. I worked and wept.
> It was not for the bonny bride,
> This verdant wreath at Christmas tide.
> It was not for the somber bier,
> This Ivy wreath and briny tear.
> It was for love, devotion true,
> Beloved ones, I twined for you.[46]

Ivy, a traditional symbol of academe....

Her ivy wreath deserves a special place in our memories.

Notes

1. *Woman's Exponent,* May 1, 1885.

2. Particularly Chris Rigby Arrington, "Pioneer Midwives" in *Mormon Sisters,* edited by Claudia L. Bushman, Cambridge, Mass.: Emmeline Press Limited, 1976, pp. 43-65, and Keith Calvin Terry, "The Contributions of Medical Women during the First Fifty Years in Utah," master's thesis, Brigham Young University, 1964. Claire Noall's *Guardians of the Hearth,* Bountiful, Utah: Horizon Publishers, 1974, and "Pioneer Women Doctors" in *Our Pioneer Heritage,* compiled by Kate B. Carter, 17 vols., Salt Lake City: Daughters of the Utah Pioneers, 1958-74, VI, pp. 361-424, both discuss Dr. Ellis Shipp at length. Ellis Shipp Musser's "Tribute to Dr. Ellis Reynolds Shipp" in *Hospitals of Utah,* compiled by Kate B. Carter, Salt Lake City: Daughters of the Utah Pioneers, 1938, gives a daughter's perspective.

3. Numerous examples are found in Bushman, ed., *Mormon Sisters.*

4. This study is based primarily on the Ellis Shipp Papers at the Utah State Historical Society, Salt Lake City, herein after cited as Shipp Papers. This collection includes holograph portions of the autobiography, personal correspondence, poetry, and materials concerning the School of Obstetrics and Nursing. Quotes from the diary and autobiography have been taken from *The Early Autobiography and Diary of Ellis Reynolds Shipp,* Salt Lake City: Deseret News Press, 1962, compiled and edited by her daughter, Ellis Shipp Musser. Segments of the autobiography are undated; dates have been included in references whenever possible.

   In addition, the William Fletcher Reynolds and Milford Bard Shipp family group sheets at the Genealogical Archives, The Church of Jesus Christ of Latter-day Saints, Salt Lake City, have supplied background data.

5. Shipp, *Autobiography, p. 30. See also Bardella Shipp Curtis, "Dr. Milford Bard Shipp," typescript manuscript, n.d., Shipp Papers; Deseret Evening News,* March 15, 1918; and American Medical Association, *American Medical Association Press, 1909,* p. 1163.

6. Shipp, *Autobiography,* p. 37.

7. *Ibid.*, p. 54.

8. *Ibid.*, p. 57.

9. *Ibid.*, p. 63.

10. *Ibid.*, pp. 110, 127.

11. *Ibid.*, January 20, 1874, pp. 150–51.

12. *Journal of Discourses,* XIV:109.

13. Studies of early Mormon attitudes toward doctors and various folk remedies include Robert T. Divett, "Medicine and the Mormons," Bulletin of the Medical Library Association, 51 (January 1963), pp. 1-15; Ward B. Studt, Jerold G. Sorenson, and Beverly Burge, *Medicine in the Intermountain West,* Salt Lake City; Olympus Publishing Company, 1976, pp. 22–31; Joseph R. Morrell, "Medicine of the Pioneer Period in Utah," *Utah Historical Quarterly,* 23 (April 1955), pp. 127–44; Claire Noall, "Medicine Among the Mormons," *Western Folklore Quarterly,* 18 (April 1959), pp. 157–164; and "Pioneer Medicine: in *Heart Throbs of the West,* compiled by Kate B. Carter, 12 vols., Salt Lake City; Daughters of the Utah Pioneers, 1939–51, VII, pp. 189–228.

14. Terry, "Contributions," pp. 24–25, cites various examples.

15. *Woman's Exponent,* August 1, 1872.

16. Arrington, pp. 57–58; see also Terry, pp. 35–38.

17. Shipp, *Autobiography,* p. 177.

18. Margaret Shipp to Ellis Shipp, January 2, 1876, Shipp Papers.

19. Gulielma Fell Alsop, *History of the Woman's Medical College, Philadelphia, 1850-1950,* Philadelphia; J. B. Lippincott, 1950; Bertha L. Selmon, "The Woman's Medical College of Pennsylvania," *Woman's Medical Journal* (July 1945), pp. 48–55.

20. Shipp, *Autobiography,* January 11, 1876, pp. 179–80.

21. Shipp, *Autobiography,* pp. 186, 193.

22. *Ibid.*, May 5, 1876, p. 214.

23. *Ibid.*, p. 238.

24. *Ibid.*, April 14, 1877, pp. 252–53.

25. *Ibid.*, August 19, 1877, p. 264.

26. Dates of Maggie's and Ellis's graduations confirmed by The Medical College.

27. Shipp, *Autobiography*, p. 280.

28. *Woman's Exponent*, May 15, 1878.

29. "Journal History of the Church," August 13, 1878, Church Archives, Historical Department, The Church of Jesus Christ of Latter-day Saints, Salt Lake City, hereinafter cited as LDS Archives.

30. *Woman's Exponent*, September 1, 1878.

31. "Longevity," manuscript, n.d., one of a number of hand-written lectures available in the Shipp Papers.

32. Regular announcements of the curriculum, names of students, and general progress of the school appear in the *Woman's Exponent*, while statistical information on its work is found in Emmeline B. Wells, ed., *Charities and Philanthropies: Woman's Work in Utah*, Salt Lake City: George Q. Cannon and Sons, Company, 1893, pp. 86–87, and Eugene Wood, "History of the Practice of Obstetrics in Utah," *Rocky Mountain Medical Journal*, 64 (April 1967), p. 69.

33. Wells, *Charities and Philanthropies*, pp. 86–87.

34. Ellis Shipp, "No. 20," manuscript, n.d., Shipp Papers.

35. Ralph T. Richards, *Of Medicine, Hospitals, and Doctors*, Salt Lake City: University of Utah Press, 1953, pp. 20, 140–53, 190–93.

36. Ellis Shipp and Milford Bard Shipp, *Infancy and Childhood: The First of a Series of Private Lectures to the Ladies* Salt Lake City: Salt Lake Sanitarian, [ca. 1890].

37. Transcript of record book, 1898-1917, Shipp Papers.

38. Rhoda J. Merrill to Ellis Shipp, May 10, 1908; Letter to Ellis Shipp [signature obscured], January 20, 1936, both in Shipp Papers.

39. Sarah E. Young Vance, "The Story of My Life," typescript manuscript, n.d., p. 29, LDS Archives.

40. Ezra Rich, "Early Practice of Medicine and Surgery in Ogden," *Rocky Mountain Medical Journal*, 50(January 1953), p. 26.

41. Typed circular, June 9, 1927, Shipp Papers.

42. *Salt Lake Telegram*, February 2, 1939; Musser, "Tribute," p. 22.

43. Shipp, *Autobiography*, p. 290.

44. "Funeral Service," Yale Ward Chapel, February 5, 1939, typescript manuscript, Shipp Papers.

45. As transcribed by a granddaughter. Typescript manuscript, Shipp Papers.

46. From "For Love" in Ellis Reynolds Shipp, *Life Lines*, Salt Lake City: Skelton Publishing Company, 1910, p. 103. In the *Autobiography* Ellis Shipp Musser indicates that this poem was written in the 1880s.

Martha Hughes Cannon 1854–1934

Jean Bickmore White was reared in Paradise, Cache County, Utah, and gained her early education there. She has a doctor of philosophy degree in political science from the University of Utah. Professionally she has worked as a reporter and feature writer for the Deseret News *and the* Salt Lake Tribune, *and she has also worked in advertising. Currently she is a professor of political science at Weber State College, where she has a full schedule of teaching duties and is also involved with an associate in a two-year Environmental Protection Agency grant to design a management program. Dr. White has been married for twenty-five years to Dr. John Stephen White. The couple have two children.*

Martha H. Cannon

Jean Bickmore White

It was a night to remember in Utah politics.

The night was November 3, 1896, and it ended the first election since Utah had become a state and it climaxed an emotion-filled, sometimes bitter campaign. The major local issue was silver, and within the new state the sentiment rather clearly favored the colorful William Jennings Bryan and his free-silver presidential platform.

But the eyes of Utahns were not turned solely to the presidential race. There was intense interest in the races for the state legislature, not only because control of the state's policymaking body was at stake, but because at that time the United States senators were elected by state legislatures.

Utah's 1896 election had several unique aspects. A black man ran for the legislature in Salt Lake County and picked up a respectable share of the vote—although he did not win. Two women won seats in the Utah House of Representatives, matching the accomplishment of two Colorado women who had been elected to their House of Representatives in 1894.

But the victory most often recalled from that turbulent campaign was that of another woman—Dr. Martha Hughes Cannon. She became renowned and gained widespread publicity not only because she was the first American woman elected to a state senate, she was a prominent suffragist, and she was a medical doctor, but because she won her seat in a race in which her husband was also a candidate.[1]

Actually, the two were not running directly opposed to each other for the same senate seat, as is so often implied. Martha was one of the five Democrats running at large for the five seats in the Sixth Senatorial District in Salt Lake County. Her husband, Angus M. Cannon, Sr., was one of five Republicans running on the Republican ticket for the same five seats. Voters could select any five candidates from the ten that were running on the two tickets. So both Cannons could have won seats, or both could have lost. The winners were the five who received the most votes, and the five top vote-getters—all Democrats—included Martha Hughes Cannon. Although the vote could have been attributed to the strong silver sentiment favoring the Democrats, it was still a sweet triumph for Martha, and undoubtedly was something of a blow to the pride of her husband.

Martha had become the first woman state senator in the United States in a dramatic fashion, and the stage was set for a brief but fruitful career in public life. She had dreamed and worked for the opportunity to advance the cause of public health—and now she had her chance.

Martha Cannon's success in politics could not have surprised anyone who had followed her life up to that point. She had shown an amazing capacity for self-discipline and hard work as a young woman and had proved that she could attain a goal most women in her time would have considered far beyond their reach. Without her exceptional energy and ambition, she never would have become a physician. But become one she did, joining that hardy band of Utah women doctors who enjoyed considerable prominence in the new state.

But her independent course of action in the legislature probably did come as a surprise to many. In the debates on giving Utah women the vote, it was suggested that any women who were elected to office would merely be pawns of their husbands, meekly following their husbands' wishes. This certainly did not happen in the case of Martha Cannon.

Martha—or Mattie, as she later was generally known—was born July 1, 1857, at Llandudno in northern Wales, the second child of Peter Hughes, a cabinet maker, and Elizabeth Evans Hughes. Her parents were converted to The Church of Jesus Christ of Latter-day Saints while Martha was just an infant.[2] They emigrated to America when Martha was less than a year old, but they stayed in New York for nearly two years because of the poor health of Peter Hughes. Finally their trip to join the Saints in the west was arranged by Erastus Snow, and they were on their way to Utah. From Florence, Nebraska, the family's journey was by covered wagon; Martha's mother walked by the side of the wagon so that the sick husband and little girls could ride. Along the way a baby girl, Annie, who had been born in New York, died and was buried beside the trail.

As if Annie's death were not enough tragedy for the family, Peter Hughes died three days after the family's arrival in Salt Lake City, and his young widow was faced with the problem of supporting herself and her two daughters. Then she met a Scottish carpenter, James Patton Paul, a widower with four children of his own, and they were married. They soon set about building an adobe home—one which is still standing—on Ninth East in Salt Lake. Both the husband and wife worked on this home, which soon was filled not only with the six children of their first marriages, but with five more sons and daughters from their own marriage.

This sizeable family survived the same way other families did in this period. A daughter of Martha Cannon has recalled:

The family picked the native currants that grew along the creeks. They planted fruit pits and seeds they had brought with them across the plains. The children gleaned in the grain fields to feed the pigs. Their lunch was bread spread with sorghum.

The girls braided hats of straw and steeped wild sage for a hair tonic. They dressed for parties by "witch lights"—a rag tied around a button which sputtered in a pan of grease.[3]

Obviously their means were modest. But Mattie's ambitions were not. She dreamed of becoming a physician and of finding ways to educate the public so they would promote the health of the community. During her childhood she witnessed many babies and mothers die; Martha was deeply disturbed by this.

With apparently little education, she began to teach school. She became discouraged with this, however, when she found at age fourteen that some of her pupils were bigger than she was and were becoming hard to handle.

At this time she was called by Mormon Church leaders to learn to set type for the *Deseret News* and the *Woman's Exponent*. For the next seven years she held this job, for it was a means to her goal of becoming a doctor. She learned to set Scandinavian type, although she knew not a word of the language, because the pay was better. In 1876, while keeping her job, she enrolled in the premedical department of the University of Deseret (now the University of Utah). She was determined to gain entry to the University of Michigan, which had opened its medical school to women in 1870. She was encouraged in this ambition by Eliza R. Snow and by her stepfather, who offered to lend her money.

Her daughter has written of Martha's struggle to make this dream come true:

In order to add to her savings she was economical with clothes but decided no one should be cleaner. She took a cold bath every morning. In winter she had to break the ice in the tub. She practiced deep breathing exercises. In advocating more air and less food she was again ahead of her time.

She cut out social affairs and concentrated on increasing her savings. Money was secreted in an old umbrella cover that lay flat in a small wooden trunk her devoted

*father had made for his favorite step-child. Later, when she went east to study medi-
cine, this was less than half full of her books and clothes.*[4]

Finally, in the fall of 1878, she was blessed and set apart by
Mormon Church President John Taylor, and Martha was on her
way to Michigan. To help with her expenses she washed dishes
and made beds at a boarding house the first year; the second year
she acted as secretary to a wealthy woman. She graduated with
her medical degree on her twenty-third birthday, July 1, 1880. She
felt that she needed still more education, so in the autumn of that
year she went to Philadelphia, where she entered the auxiliary department of medicine at the University of Pennsylvania. She also
enrolled at the National School of Elocution and Oratory to improve her speaking skills so that she might become a lecturer in
public health. In 1882 she received a bachelor of science degree
from the university, the only woman in a class of seventy-five. She
also received a bachelor of oratory degree from the elocution
school.

Some years later the extent of her medical ability was ques-
tioned by the noted British socialist author, Beatrice Webb. But
she apparently was considered a skillful doctor after her graduation. A Michigan newspaper reported that Martha had performed
"a very skillful surgical operation" in Algonac, Michigan, in 1881,
and that she had graduated from the Medical Department of
Michigan University "with a reputation for superior scholarship. . . ." The newspaper also reported that she was assisted by
two prominent male physicians, but that she took the principal
part in the work "and thus demonstrated by actual experience
that some of her sex at least are capable of performing the most
difficult and complicated operations in medical practice."[5]

On her return to Salt Lake City, she opened a private practice,
but soon was called to be a resident physician of the Deseret Hospital. Here she met her future husband, Angus Cannon, who was
a member of the hospital board and was president of the Salt
Lake Stake. He was twenty-three years her senior and was already
married to three wives. He was described by a daughter as "handsome, magnetic, with a gift of language," and was characterized
by great spirituality.[6] She married him secretly on October 6,
1884, in the Endowment House in Salt Lake City.

Then began a life that was marked by periods when she attempted to build a medical practice and that was punctuated by
periods of exile following the birth of each of her three children.[7]

The first child, Elizabeth, was born on September 13, 1885,
while Martha was living with the Samuel Woolley family in

Grantsville, Utah. To keep her husband from having to go to prison, Mattie went into exile in England during 1886 and 1887. In many ways this was not a bad experience, for it greatly broadened her views of the world. She was able to visit several European countries and enjoy a glimpse of a world far different from late nineteenth-century Utah.

On her return to Utah she established a school for nurses and attempted to reestablish her medical practice. This was interrupted again by the impending birth of her son, James, and this time she went to San Francisco for her exile. She remained there for about a year and a half, returned to Utah in 1891, and again attempted to establish a medical practice.

At this time she began the career in public life that meant so much to her. She became actively involved in the women's suffrage movement. In 1893 she went to Chicago with a group of prominent Utah women and spoke at the Columbian Exposition. Her picture and an account of her address were carried in the *Chicago Daily Tribune*.[8] Though she could ill afford it, she bought a beautiful dress for that occasion because she thought the Utah women looked a little "dowdy."[9]

Another important event in her career as a suffragist was a trip to Washington, D.C., in 1898 to speak at a convention marking the fiftieth anniversary of the Seneca Falls declaration of women's rights. While there she also spoke to a Congressional committee urging the national lawmakers to give women the vote.

By that time she had become nationally known for her election to the Utah State Senate and for her championship of public health measures. She had also become locally known for her independence from her husband's views.

This was shown most dramatically by her votes for United States senator in 1897 and 1899. Her daughter reported that in 1897 Angus M. Cannon was upset because Martha had voted for the excommunicated Mormon apostle, Moses Thatcher, for senator against Angus's wishes and in the face of strong opposition from Mormon Church leaders.[10] Angus's annoyance may have been compounded by the publicity Martha received when she switched her vote to Thatcher and made a stirring speech in his behalf. The *Salt Lake Tribune* reported on February 2 that "Senator Cannon prefaced her vote with an address so eloquent that despite parliamentary decorum and the rigid rules against demonstrations she was cheered and cheered again at its conclusion."

Again in 1899 Martha Cannon defied her husband's wishes by failing to support his nephew, Republican Frank J. Cannon, for the United States Senate. Among her reasons was her feeling that it would be improper, since she had been elected as a Democrat. Martha Cannon controlled her own vote in the legislature, and everyone knew it.[11]

Martha undoubtedly would prefer to be known as a legislator for the public health acts she sponsored. In the first month of her senate term she introduced three bills: "An Act to Protect the Health of Women and Girl Employees" (S.B. 31); "An Act Providing for the Compulsory Education of Deaf, Dumb, and Blind Children" (S.B.22); and "An Act Creating a State Board of Health and Defining its Duties" (S.B.27). The first bill made it mandatory for employers to provide "chairs, stools, or other contrivances where women or girls employed as clerks might rest when not working."[12] Today protective legislation is considered a mixed blessing for women in their struggle for equality of treatment by employers; in 1897 it was considered progressive legislation.

Dr. Martha Cannon was most vitally involved in the third measure, since her interest in sanitation and public health had been a motivating force for her study of medicine and her entry into politics. This act became part of the revised statutes that were compiled by a special commission, and it provided the basis for a statewide attack on problems of sanitation and contagious disease.[13] It established a seven-member State Board of Health to stimulate and encourage establishment of local boards of health and to carry out a number of other functions designed to improve sanitary conditions, water supply, and disease control.

Martha was one of the first members appointed by Utah Governor Heber Wells to the Board of Health, giving her the privilege of going through the first few frustrating years of the new board. It was the mission of the board to try to get apathetic local officials to organize local boards of health and to get public support for enforcement of a law prohibiting school attendance of children who had contagious diseases.[14] Because of the difficulty in enforcing the new health regulations, Martha introduced an act during the second half of her four-year term providing more teeth for enforcement. This act provided for the suppression of nuisances and contagious diseases, provided for protection of water supplies, and established rules for inspection of school buildings and the exclusion of persons with contagious or infectious diseases from schools.[15]

She was interested in the Utah State School for the Deaf and Dumb, serving as a member of its board, and she introduced the bill authorizing the erection of a hospital building at the school.

Another bill she introduced in 1899 to provide for the teaching in the public schools of the effects of alcoholic drinks and narcotics (S.B.37) was passed by the senate but was defeated in the house.

Apparently alcoholism and drug addiction were not matters of pressing concern to the legislature at that time.

In public, Martha Cannon strongly defended careers for women outside the home and she defended the institution of plural marriage. When she was interviewed by a writer for the *San Francisco Examiner* a few days after her election, she maintained that a plural wife was not as much a slave as was a single woman. She asserted (perhaps facetiously): "If her husband has four wives, she has three weeks of freedom every month." And she firmly defended women working outside the home: "You give me a woman who thinks about something besides cook stoves and wash tubs and baby flannels, and I'll show you, nine times out of ten, a successful mother."[16]

Because of her unique position as a physician, state senator, and wife of a prominent Mormon leader, Martha Cannon was the subject of an interview by the noted English socialist, Beatrice Webb, who described her as "a self-respectful vigorous pure-minded little soul: sensitive yet unself-conscious, indiscreet yet loyal."[17]

In a long discussion of the theological and practical reasons for polygamy, Martha Cannon told Beatrice Webb that it was an enormous advantage for a woman to be able to select a really good man as father to her children instead of putting up with any miserable fellow who might be left over by other women. She said she believed polygamy was based on fundamental physiological and psychological truths and she felt that "if the law had been honestly practiced according to the doctrine of the church and maintained by the law of the State, then we should have become a splendid race and converted the world to our creed." She added that she felt plural marriage ultimately would have given women who chose it an independent life, for "they were not completely absorbed as one wife is in her husband."[18]

Although Martha Cannon was loyal to the institution with which she had cast her lot, and although it seems clear that she truly believed that celestial plural marriage was necessary for her eternal salvation and exaltation, it was the cause of much difficulty and unhappiness for her. It is evident in her letters that she found it hard to share her husband's affections with other women, to accept the hardships of exile, and to face the difficulties this created for her in building her career as a physician.

In her letters written while in exile in Europe she often expressed strong feelings of love and concern for her husband. She also began to see how different her marriage was from that of monogamous husbands and wives. In a letter to her husband on February 3, 1888, she observed that the trials of plural marriage would be great without "a thorough knowledge from God, that the *principle* for which we are battling and striving to maintain in purity upon the earth is ordained by Him, and that we are chosen instruments in His hands to engage in so great a calling." She continued: "Even with this assurance grounded in one's heart, we do not escape trials and temptations, grievous at times in their nature."

She recalled that she had become well acquainted with several families not involved in plural marriage, where the marriage relationship was "a joy and comfort to witness, where the wife and Mother is proud and happy in the devotion of a noble husband, while he in turn is equally contented and happy in the possession of the partner he has chosen for life; while at *home* in each other's association, is where their greatest joys are centered."

She noted that her own wedded experience up to that time had consisted of "a few stolen interviews thoroughly tinctured with the *dread of discovery*. . . ." Without the belief that celestial marriage was divinely ordained and that those who lived it would "associate in the eternities as only those who have passed this ordeal successfully will be permitted to associate," she wrote, she probably would have given the plural marriage system "a wide berth," except perhaps as "first wife."

In the same letter she said she realized that her husband was probably more oppressed by the difficulties of living plural marriage in violation of civil law than she was, and she assured him that "I would rather spend one hour in your society, than a whole lifetime with any other man I know of. I suppose after all, things with me are just as they should be for I should certainly be *too happy* for this testing scene of earth were I permitted to be near you *always*."[19]

Despite her often-expressed affection for her husband, the strain of separation and exile and the insecurity of her situation made her marriage relationship difficult. Because she was often in poor health and was constantly interrupting her life with the absences to bear children, she found it hard to establish a remunerative medical practice. Consequently, she was frequently asking Angus for money that he could not always provide. In 1891, when she was in California after the birth of her son, James, she wrote to her husband of her unhappiness:

Oh for a home! A husband of my own because he is my own. A father for my children whom they know by association. And all the little auxiliaries that makes life worth the living. Will they ever be enjoyed by this storm-tossed exile. Or must life thus drift on and one more victim swell the ranks of the great unsatisfied![20]

Perhaps this was a low point in her life, before she had tasted the satisfaction and fame of public life. But the sense of insecurity and loneliness in her marriage returned at the turn of the century, after her legislative service had ended. By that time she had three children to support: Elizabeth, born in 1885; James, born in 1890; and Gwendolyn, born in 1899.

Angus Cannon's letters and journal show that he tried in many ways to meet Martha's needs and that he was deeply saddened by the increasing estrangement and strain in their relationship. But the difficulties continued, and Martha decided it would be best for her to move permanently to California, where her health might improve.

She spent the last decades of her life near her daughters and son in Los Angeles, where she worked at the Graves Clinic and in the orthopedic department of the General Hospital. Her oldest daughter, Elizabeth, was a writer, and her son founded Cannon Electric Company (now a division of International Telephone and Telegraph). Her youngest daughter, Gwendolyn, was gifted with artistic and musical talent and had a close relationship with her mother. Gwendolyn's death in 1928 at the age of twenty-nine was a blow from which Martha Cannon never quite recovered. Martha died in Los Angeles on July 10, 1932, following an operation, at the age of seventy-five. She was eulogized at funeral services in Los Angeles and in Salt Lake City, where she was buried. Among other tributes, she was praised in a *Deseret News* editorial as "a woman of unusual intellect and ability."[21]

During her life Martha Cannon knew both distinction and despair. By nature she was both a romantic and a practical woman. She was able to work hard and sacrifice for her goals and her beliefs, but at the same time she longed for romantic love and the security of a "normal" home.

When she visited Paris during her first exile in 1887, she was overwhelmed by her glimpses into the grandeur of the past. She wrote to her husband:

Wherever the eye rests in this great centre can be seen the impress of intellect. To wander through this collection of art—its palaces of departed monarchs, its halls of pleasure or drive through its gardens and boulevards . . . has been a period of enchantment such as I never thought to experience on this mundane sphere. . . .

Do not think I am becoming intoxicated with the allurements of Babylon—not so. I look upon this treat as an oasis in the dreary desert I have trod for the past two years—an oasis sent from God, to chase away the shadows that have enthralled me. Wedded, yet experiencing none of the elements of true wedded life—looked upon with suspicion by those who see me tarry here—but I must not complain as I am happier now than ever before. . . .[22]

During her stay in California after the birth of her son, she wrote to a friend from her medical school days of the need to replace the romantic with the mundane:

'Tis now nearly seven years since I launched forth on the great sea of matrimony, and I feel that I have not learned the ABC of the great volumes, have scarcely culled from my sentimental nature those romantic dreams which are a delusion and a snare to young or old married life. And the sooner they are rooted out and supplanted by the practical facts and conditions of the mundane, the sooner will attain those tranquil shallows of contentment, far removed from those surging billows of life's ocean that causes us to "sound the heights and depths of human emotions."[23]

She continued this letter by remarking that soaring in the heights is just a transient condition, and to expect it to last is torment. What she sought was an ultimate condition of happiness and serenity, one she found difficult to achieve.

Early in her life Martha was instilled with faith in the gospel of The Church of Jesus Christ of Latter-day Saints, and it was the mainstay of her life. She accepted various calls from the church leaders, and would not have dreamed of entering medical studies without their blessing. Although she found the plural marriage calling difficult, she accepted it and tried to forget how different her marriage could have been. She garnered favorable publicity for the church at a time when Mormon women were thought to be downtrodden and dominated by men. Throughout her life she was loyal to the church and its leaders.

As she lived out her life in California, Martha Cannon seemed to mellow, and the disappointments of her past life faded. She was a strong woman with great expectations of life; she was married to a strong man under conditions in which her dreams could not be realized.

It seems that she was caught in conflicts between the romantic side of her nature and the hard realities of her life. She appears to have suffered some of the conflicts faced by women today, wanting to be loved and protected in the classic role of women and yet to express herself in a life and career of her own. She could not be content with just being part of Angus M. Cannon's life; she wanted her own personal fulfillment. Although her public life brought much satisfaction, she could not escape the feeling that she should have had more peace, contentment, and fulfillment in her marriage.

In 1970 a number of Utah medical and public health groups joined in erecting a monument and plaque on the corner of South Temple and Second West, near where her little home and office stood long ago.

Time and a renewed attention to the needs and accomplishments of women has restored her fame and brought deserved attention to the sprightly, ambitious young doctor who won a seat in the Utah State Senate in 1896. The inscription points to her achievements as "pioneer doctor—first woman state senator in U.S.—Author of Utah sanitation laws—member of first state board of health."

There are not many monuments to women in Utah. This one honors the memory of an idealistic, ambitious, proud, and independent-spirited woman who could not grasp all of her life's dreams, but who gave a great deal to others in the course of her own personal struggle.

Notes

1. For a complete account of the 1896 election in Utah see Jean Bickmore White, "Utah State Elections: 1895-1899," Ph.D. dissertation, University of Utah, 1968, pp. 110-179.

2. Several biographical articles on Dr. Martha Cannon have been published. Information herein generally is from an unpublished manuscript by her daughter, Mrs. Elizabeth C. McCrimmon, in the Utah State Historical Society Library, and from Andrew Jenson, *Latter-day Saint Biographical Encyclopedia*, 4 vols., Salt Lake City: Andrew Jenson History Company, 1901-1936, vol. 4, 86-88.

3. McCrimmon manuscript, pp. 3-4.

4. *Ibid.*, p. 6.

5. *Marine City Reporter*, as reprinted in *Woman's Exponent* 10 (August 1, 1881):33.

6. McCrimmon manuscript, p. 8.

7. It was necessary for many women who were not the first wives of husbands living the Mormon doctrine of plural marriage (polygamy) to go into hiding so that their husbands would not be prosecuted by the United States government for unlawful cohabitation. Angus M. Cannon was arrested and tried in 1885, was fined three hundred dollars, and was imprisoned for six months. To avoid further prosecution, it was agreed that Martha must leave her medical practice in Salt Lake City whenever her pregnancies became noticeable. For Angus M. Cannon's experience with the law see Beatrice Cannon Evans, "Angus M. Cannon," in *Cannon Family Historical Treasury*, Beatrice Cannon Evans and Janath Russell Cannon, eds., Salt Lake City: George Cannon Family Association, 1967, pp. 210-11.

8. May 20, 1893.

9. Interview by the author with Mrs. Elizabeth C. McCrimmon, August 4, 1969, in Alhambra, California.

10. McCrimmon interview, op. cit.

11. *Ibid.*

12. Utah, *Laws of Utah*, 1897, Ch. XI, 24-25.

13. Utah, *Revised Statutes,* 1898, Title 24, 315-18.

14. See Utah, *Public Documents,* 1897-98, Sec. 22, "Report of the Board of Health."

15. See Utah, *Public Documents,* 1899-1900, Sec. 22, "Report of the State Board of Health."

16. Interview published in the *San Francisco Examiner,* November 8, 1896, reprinted in the *Salt Lake Herald,* November 11, 1896.

17. *Beatrice Webb's American Diary,* 1898, ed. By David A. Shannon, Madison, Wisconsin: University of Wisconsin Press, 1963, pp. 134-5.

18. *Ibid.,* pp. 133-4.

19. Letters in Angus M. Cannon Collection. Historical Department, The Church of Jesus Christ of Latter-day Saints. The author is greatly indebted to Miss Constance Thorpe of the Church Archives for her assistance with the letter collection and to Mr. Richard L. Jensen for his assistance with other research sources.

20. Letter of December 30, 1891, from Heraldsburg, California.

21. *Deseret News,* July 14, 1932.

22. Letter of September 16, 1887, from Paris, France.

23. Letter to Barbara Replagle Atkinson, June 6, 1891, from San Francisco. Letter in possession of granddaughters, Mrs. Martha Monti and Mrs. Mary Ober, Alhambra, California. The author is grateful to Mrs. Monti and Mrs. Ober for their comments and insights, particularly on Dr. Martha Cannon's later years, obtained in interviews in 1969 and 1975.

Margaret Ann Freece 1872–1957

*Hearing tales as a child of a woman
medical doctor in her community,
where women did not seem to be
doing very interesting kinds of things,
Vicky Burgess-Olson became interested
in studying the life of Margaret Ann
Freece. But the medical aspect of
Margaret's life proved to be only one
dimension. Historically, Dr. Margaret
Freece's life intertwined with many
and varied monumental events and
interesting people. Dr. Burgess-Olson
was introduced as author of another
essay.*

Margaret Ann Freece

Vicky Burgess-Olson

Margaret Ann Freece is a unique woman in Mormon history. Her Mormonism was in her roots only—her early family life—but these roots were major forces in her future. That family life and her educational opportunities led her along unusual paths and toward diverse goals, but in a lifetime perspective, Dr. Margaret Freece's contributions to her community, state, and nation were similar to those of the other women in this collection. Although she was the product of a financially impoverished polygamous family, Margaret died a wealthy woman. As an entrepreneur she accumulated property, but her medical work was a humanitarian donation to society.

Nestled in a valley west and north of Salina, Utah, is the isolated town of Scipio, consisting of six hundred people, a Mormon chapel, a service station, and a mercantile store. Over one hundred years ago there came to this rural village a twenty-four-year-old Danish immigrant concert to Mormonism, Margaret Sorenson. She was taken into the home of some other Danes, Peter Friss Rasmussen and his wife, Ann Margaret Jensen. After looking over the marriageable men of the community (which included both married men and bachelors, since polygamy was practiced at this time), Margaret Sorenson, upon the invitation of the couple, became the second wife of Peter Friss Rasmussen.

In his diary, Peter Freece (who dropped the name *Rasmussen* because it was such a common name in the area and who changed the *Friss* to *Freece*) reported: "We had now lived in unlawful and cruel polygamy until we was tired of it and especially the women, the good souls meant well and had only one fight wherein one has pushed the other over on the bed."

Their difficulty in living polygamy was only one of the things that made the Freece family the most colorful family in Scipio history. As the Freeces struggled with polygamy, a new challenge was placed in their path—the United Order was established in Scipio. Here is Peter's reaction:

Despite their misgivings, the Freece family entered into the order. Peter was appointed as "storekeeper" and was responsible for distributing the goods. But he became disillusioned when some of the prominent people of the community quarreled over the supplies. Peter reports that Brigham Young later returned to Scipio and instructed the people to give up the United Order. Apparently there was much bitterness over the subsequent redistribution of the goods.

Religion for Peter Freece aroused his deepest concern; he tried against all odds to conform to the beliefs and practices of Mormonism. He left his homeland and struggled to cross the plains to Utah, pulling a handcart with his first wife. He married another woman as a polygamous wife, a family organization that was foreign to his background, and he tried to make his family life peaceful. He gave up his few material possessions to the cause—he saw his cattle branded with the Mormon Church brand—and he attempted to make the United Order successful. Then the church members were instructed to abandon the United Order. Peter's need for religion to provide security was not met, so rather than putting the blame on God as he might have done, he blamed God's representative, Brigham Young. Peter began receiving his own revelations. He organized a group of people who had also become disillusioned with the Mormon Church structure; opposed by the local church authorities, they all moved into an area just outside of Scipio, where the foundations of the homes they built still stand today.

Records show that on March 10, 1878, Peter Freece Rasmussen of the Scipio Ward, Millard Stake, was excommunicated from the Mormon Church for apostasy.[3] Peter never did deny that Joseph Smith was a prophet—his problems were with the policies instituted under Brigham Young.

Peter Freece and his family of two wives and twelve children (seven by the first wife and five by the second) moved out of the

Scipio area. His first wife and children went to Richfield, Utah. He divorced his first wife and legally married his second wife, with the result that his children from the second wife became legitimate under the law. He settled with his second wife and children in Salina, where he obtained a small farm and where his wife opened a small "Vest Pocket Store" in their home.[4]

In a vision, Peter Freece said he was told never to cut his hair because long hair would give him faith in God. As he grew older, this white-haired and bearded man would occasionally preach his philosophy in Salina and in surrounding towns. He never opposed polygamy, and he even liberalized it. He claimed in his diary:

> In the beginning of the Bible people were not restricted by marriage laws and customs that we have today, but they had not yet become so corrupt that a man that was loved of one woman could also therefore love another and a woman that liketh one man could therefore also love another. Else, what would become of the love one another idea?[5]

Peter Freece died an old man with many idiosyncracies, still trying to cope with religion and life in his own way. His daughter Margaret was the attending physician at his death.

Margaret Ann Freece was born in 1871—seven years before her father's excommunication—the first child from the second marriage. Throughout their lives, most of the children from both families remained congenial, although those with the same mother had a closer relationship, especially after they moved to different towns. After some of the children had left southern Utah, when they returned for visits they would go to the homes of all their siblings, no matter from which marriage. Few, if any, of the children remained active members of the Mormon Church.

Hans Peter Freece, one of Margaret's three younger brothers born one year after his father's excommunication, became the most vocal against the Mormons and southern Utah. He became a lawyer and had an interesting career lecturing in the United States and Europe and writing against Mormons. Some of the titles of his works speak for themselves: *How Mormons Recruit Abroad, Letters of an Apostate Mormon to His Son,* and *Are You That Damn Presbyterian Devil?*

In 1908 *The Richfield Reaper,* a newspaper in southern Utah, replied to Hans Peter Freece's tirades. He was denounced as a "mendacious liar" and accused of gross exaggeration. The article said that Peter Freece's first wife still lived in Richfield; that one of Hans Peter's brothers, Eiler, was the principal of the high school in Salina; that his sister was a doctor in Salina; and that all these people were accepted and appreciated by their communities.

The article ended with a statement from Dr. Freece:

An article published in one of the State papers which is a synopsis of a lecture given in New York by H. P. Freece came to my notice, and I want to say to the community that I do not approve of the article. I want to say that in no community could the people have been more considerate. I have been given a square deal by the people, as a whole, since the day I landed in Salina. I can also speak for my brothers and father and they feel that they owe an apology to the people for the article that appeared in the paper, which was uttered without our knowledge or sanction and that we are none of us responsible for anything that comes from that quarter.

Yours truly,
Margaret A. Freece[6]

Of all the Freece children, Hans Peter Freece appears to have been the most embittered toward the church. He claimed to have had his father's support in his actions. Working for the Presbyterian Mission, an organization which supported missionaries and schools in Utah, he was trying to get financial support for them on his lecture tours. Just how did the Freeces get involved with the Presbyterians in the remote Mormon village of Scipio?

The Protestant School System in Utah was a missionary effort. Beginning in 1869, the schools were used to combat polygamy and encourage conversion. Forty-nine schools were built in Utah prior to 1888, although they were all not in operation at the same time. Although fifty thousand pupils passed through these schools, the number of conversions was very low. One major effect of the Protestant system was that it stimulated the Mormon Church to establish twenty-two academies in Mormon settlements from Mexico to Canada. Later, public education came to Utah, permanent Presbyterian churches were established in a number of Utah towns, and Utah gave up polygamy officially just prior to gaining statehood. So ended the Protestant School System.[7]

Many members of the Freece family became converts to Presbyterianism through this missionary and school effort. Margaret Ann Freece was billed as a product of the Presbyterian School System in later advertisements for funds that claimed she was one of the first children of Mormon parents to enroll in these schools. She attended the Presbyterian School in Scipio and the Wasatch Academy in Mount Pleasant, Utah (still in existence today). This Presbyterian school, founded in 1875, included a high school curriculum, and later a two-year college course was added. Here Margaret worked for her schooling as an assistant matron over the younger girls; she also received funding from a scholarship donated by a family from the east. At Wasatch Academy, Margaret became an official member of the Presbyterian Church, and she remained a faithful member of this church all her life.[8]

After graduation this determined young woman went to Salt Lake City and was graduated from yet another Presbyterian school, which was then called the Collegiate Institute of Salt Lake City: Westminster College. Later in her life Margaret donated scholarship and property for bulding sites to Westminster College, indiating an appreciation for her experience there.[9]

Other members of the Freece family also obtained higher education through the Protestant School System. Through the opportunities provided by these schools, they were well-educated people for their time and culture. Hans Peter and James Serenas became lawyers, and other siblings attended Oberlin College in Ohio and Park College in Missouri, both Presbyterian schools.

Margaret Ann Freece became involved in another historically interesting educational institution when, diplomas in hand from the Utah Protestant School System, she was accepted at Northwestern University Woman's Medical College.

The Woman's Medical College was founded in Chicago in 1870 out of a need to train women as medical doctors. Previously women had been admitted to Chicago Medical College through a sympathetic faculty member, Dr. William H. Byford, but male members of the class claimed that "certain clinical materials and observations have been omitted because of the presence of women," and the college reversed its decision, forcing the women students to leave. Under Dr. Byford's suggestion to Mary Harris Thompson, M.D. (the first woman to perform major surgery in Chicago), a separate institution for women was formed. When Margaret Ann Freece attended this school, it had become a department of Northwestern University as the Northwestern University Women's Medical School (1891).[10]

The Woman's Medical College, after a period of struggling for existence, was at last an impressive institution. All students were required to pursue their medical studies for four years. The 1894–95 Northwestern University Catalogue included:

Freshman Year
Anatomy
Chemistry
Histology
Materia Medica
Histological Laboratory
Anatomical Laboratory

Chemical Laboratory

Sophomore Year
Anatomy
Physiology
Pathology
Pharmacology
Therapeutics
Organic Chemistry
Physical Diagnosis
Chemical Laboratory
Hygiene
Clinical Microscopy Laboratory
Toxicology
Laboratory Work in Pathology
College Clinics and Practical Pharmacy

Junior Year
Practice of Medicine
Special Pathology
Diseases of the Chest & Throat
Renal Diseases
Nervous Diseases
Surgery
Dermatology
Obstetrics
Gynecology
Diseases of Children

Clinics
Medicine
Surgery
Diseases of the Chest & Throat
Nervous Diseases
Gynecology
Dermatology

Senior Year
Medicine
Gynecology
Obstetrics
Surgery
Nervous Diseases

Renal Diseases
Ophthalmology
Otology
Medical Jurisprudence
Dental Pathology
Clinics as in Junior Year

Board and room was from three to six dollars a week, and various fees for schooling added up to a hundred and thirty-five dollars a year.[11]

In 1897, Dr. Margaret A. Freece graduated from the Woman's Medical College in this yet pioneering educational effort. Some years later when the property of the college was absorbed into the Northwestern Medical School and was sold, a trustee and former president made a public statement in which he assigned the abandonment of the school to the fact that "It is impossible to make a doctor out of a woman. Women cannot grasp the chemical and pharmaceutical laboratory work, the intricacies of surgery, or the minute work of anatomy." Alumnae among the 475 graduates, including Margaret, enraged at this calumny and at the suppression of the real reason for closing, challenged this statement and demanded his dismissal.[12]

After graduation, Margaret obtained medical experience in Chicago. She served as "house surgeon" at the Mary Harris Thompson Hospital, and also enjoyed the privilege of working with Jane Addams at Hull House. Next she went to Iowa and served as house physician at the Iowa Industrial School for girls.[13]

In 1898, a letter written by Margaret to Dr. R. G. McNiece, a pastor associated with The Collegiate Institute of Salt Lake City (Westminster), indicated her plans: she asked the pastor to write a recommendation for her to the Board of Foreign Missions of the Presbyterian Church. She wanted to serve as a medical missionary in China.

The next year, when Botilda Kathrina, a sister living in Salina, became ill, Margaret returned to Salina to assist in Botilda's care. She never left the town again for anything other than vacations and business trips.

Margaret opened up an office in her home, where her mother still had a small store. Half of her office consisted of a pharmacy lined with bottles, where she made out her own prescriptions since there was no pharmacy when she came to town. The other half of her office was lined with books (including medical journals), a desk where she kept track of her medical and financial affairs, and a large swivel chair similar to the ones dentists use today.

Her transportation mainly consisted of the finest bicycle in town. She had her medical bag strapped to it on a custom-made stand. One little boy in town said he wanted to be a doctor (and became one) so he could have a bike just like Margaret's. When she left town she rode a horse and buggy; toward the end of her career she owned a car, but she seldom used it.[14]

Her territory included Wayne County on the south, Sanpete County on the north, and her own town of Scipio on the west. To keep warm on winter buggy trips, she put heated rocks at her feet and bundled herself in a buffalo robe.

But in an emergency, any transportation would do. Once on a ranch at Gooseberry, near Salina, a boy had a pitchfork thrown into his stomach. His parents came to town in the only available vehicle to look for Margaret; driving very swiftly along Main Street, they took her back to their ranch in the manure spreader.[16]

In southern Utah, Margaret won wide patronage of her medical practice which, though there were other doctors in the area, constantly increased. She was recognized not only by the laity but by representatives of her profession. She was a member of the American Medical Association, the Women's National Medical Council, and was the first woman vice-president of the Utah Medical Association. As a member of the Medical Women's Hospital Association, she organized her county alone, and during World War I she raised nearly half of the state's quota for the American Medical Women's Hospital in Europe.[17]

The following are comments made after her death by members of the community:[18]

"Doctor Freece was a good woman and a good doctor."

"We did not think it was strange to have a woman doctor, we were just grateful for her."

"It did not seem unusual to have Margaret Freece as a doctor because there were so many midwives in town. She fit right in to the community."

"She was more careful about spreading germs than another doctor in town. He let blood stay on his clothes as he went from patient to patient. He probably caused the spread of smallpox throughout the town because he let the blood of smallpox victim stay on his clothes. She kept things more sanitary."

"Dr. Freece was very good with children and she could get them to do anything that she wanted them to do. Each year she would give all the school children in Salina free physical examinations."

"In Dr. Freece's days you were purt near dead before they called the doctor."

"Dr. Margaret A. Freece was one of the well known physicians in Utah who by

professional ability and force of character is a credit to the calling that she represents and an honor to her sex."

It was not only as a physician that Margaret A. Freece made an enviable record, but through her other services to the community as well. She was a member of the school board for nine years, and she worked untiringly to help erect a beautiful new school building, now North Sevier High School. As treasurer of the board at one period, she was instrumental in having interest paid on school bonds for the first time. She also gave scholarships to high school students. She was a founder of the *L'Progresso Club* in Salina, a club which promoted many cultural and progressive projects in the community. It was she, for instance, who had the club petition the State of Utah that Maple Grove be preserved as a recreation area for the public.

In newspaper accounts of the various social functions of Salina, Margaret was frequently mentioned as a member of prominent social circles.

Public speaking was also a pastime for Margaret; notes from her speeches reveal her to have been progressive in some of her attitudes and archaic in others, as measured by today's standards. She was constantly advocating that more women be appointed to public office: "A woman has not necessarily had the opportunity for experience yet so that does not mean that you should not appoint her," she wrote. "It takes ability; nevertheless, the assumption that the woman does not have the ability to make a department head is always present until the contrary is proven. How can it be proven without opportunity to prove it by trial?" In speeches on public health, Margaret spoke about the importance of sex education for children: "Lessons on reproduction should begin at about ten years old beginning with plant reproduction and the union of cells. Then frogs and fish up to the higher animals. The child should learn physiology and anatomy of the human body."[19]

Other speeches inveighed against corsets, liquor, and venereal disease. She claimed that she had seen a child develop epilepsy at six months of age due to a "drunken conception." As for corsets: "It is marvelous that the monstrosities of fashion have completely overshadowed the natural bodily form and figure. Is the garment fitted to the woman, or the woman fitted to the garment? Who shall say that woman is so inferior to the lower animals in form and figure that she must take in some places and out in others?"[20]

An intelligent woman, Margaret appeared to be interested in everything around her, from coal mining to fishing.

One characteristic of many members of the Freece family that appeared to be a result of childhood poverty was the love of money. There were standing jokes in the community about this characteristic. One such joke claimed that Margaret would boil a rock to get the grease out of it rather than buy a soup bone. Margaret admitted to loving money, and she was happy owning things. The more she owned, the happier she was; she vowed that she would never again experience the poverty of the past. Very careful with her money, she was a good financier, and her account books were meticulous.

Margaret owned the property and building where the Community Church in Salina now stands. She was financially involved in the coal mining industry in southern Utah as the director of the Sevier Valley Coal Company. She was one of the early directors of the First State Bank of Salina and was secretary, treasurer, and largest stockholder in the Salina Grain and Milling Company.[21]

On July 1, 1925, in Manti, Utah, at age fifty-four, Margaret A. Freece married John Arneson, age sixty-seven.[22] It was an unusual couple they made, the scholarly doctor and the craftsman, John Arneson, a Norwegian with a distinct Norwegian accent. They did both belong to the same political party and to Masonic orders, since he was a Mason and she was an Eastern Star. They were also both large stockholders in the Salina Coal Mine, and from various written and oral descriptions they enjoyed one another's company. In 1927 John Arneson sold his successful lumber business for a large sum of money, and three months later he died. According to newspaper accounts, John Arneson sold his business because he had been in poor health for the "past year or more,"[23] so perhaps he was already ill when Margaret married him.

Although Dr. Margaret Ann Freece arose from rather complicated beginnings with scars and motivations from her past so involved with Mormonism that marked her future, her life generally seemed full. Her emotional life appeared to be lacking, although she had many acquaintances. Money was a strong motivation in her life, and she geared many of her activities around it; when she died, her brothers fought over her wealth. She contributed greatly to the people of her community through her medical knowledge.

From a variety of sources she is portrayed as being very straightforward; people knew where they stood with her. It is indicated that she was a stern person, and that is understandable considering her background.

This woman emerged from a background of discord with the Mormon Church and she supported non-Mormon institutions, yet she lived among the Mormons most of her life and did not seem antagonistic. When asked a few years ago if she would write her philosophy of living, she said, "There would not be a lot to write, but I think that to be a true Christian and to follow the teachings of Christ is my philosophy. And now that I am old, I would like most to keep a kind sweet spirit and never become bitter or disagreeable."

In retrospect, Margaret wrote the following: "When circumstances called me to Salina to care for my beloved invalid sister, which lasted five years, the people here were wonderful to me and welcomed me with opened arms. You can't know how I appreciate you all. I hope I shall always keep a kind and sweet spirit with me. I love you all in the Savior's name and admire your religious fervor. May God bless us and keep us till we meet above. This is written poorly, I can not see to follow the lines. I want you to know how we had to struggle. Thank you for everything.

Dr. Freece."[24]

Notes

1. Freece, Peter, *Diary of Peter Freece,* Special Collections Library, Brigham Young University, Provo, Utah, p. 15.

2. *Ibid.,* p. 14.

3. Letter from The Genealogical Society of The Church of Jesus Christ of Latter-day Saints, dated December 29, 1969, to author.

4. Peter Freece Diary, p. 20.

5. *Ibid.,* p. 23.

6. "Light from the Home Paper of Hans Peter Freece," *Richfield Reaper,* May 26, 1908.

7. Clark, James R., "Church and State Relationships in Education in Utah," unpublished doctoral dissertation, Utah State University, 1958, pp. 360–362.

   Lyon T. Edgar, *Evangelical Protestant Missionary Activities in Mormon Dominated Areas: 1865-1900,* unpublished doctoral dissertation, University of Utah, 1962, pp. 128, 131, and 133.

8. Letter from Hans Peter Freece printed with a picture of Dr. Margaret Freece and used for financial promotion drives for Westminster College; in possession of Westminster College.

9. *Ibid.*

10. Wilde, Arthur Herbert, *Northwestern University—A History 1855-1905,* University Publishing Society, New York, 1905, vol. 4, pp. 367-371.

11. Northwestern University Catalogue 1894-1895, pp. 196-206.

12. Arey, Leslie B., *Northwestern University Medical School 1859-1959,* Northwestern University Press, Evanston and Chicago, 1959, p. 122.

13. Noble, Warrum, ed., *Utah Since Statehood: Historical and Biographical,* S. J. Clarke Publishing Company, Chicago—Salt Lake City, Utah, 1920, vol. 4, pp. 84-87.

14. Oral interviews of Salina residents by Stanley D. Burgess.

15. *Ibid.,* Edith MacDonald.

16. *Ibid.,* Bell Allred Sorenson.

17. Noble, *Utah Since Statehood,* p. 87.

18. Oral interviews: Alvilda Scorup Anderson, Edith Scorup Clinger, Stanley D. Burgess, Ada Freece Neilsen, and Bell Allred Sorenson.

19. Freece, Margaret Ann, *Diaries and Notebooks,* Special Collections Library, Brigham Young University, Provo, Utah, unpaginated.

20. *Ibid.*

21. Simons, Ralph B., ed., *Utah's Distinguished Personalities,* p. 47.

22. *Salina Sun,* September 2, 1927.

23. *Ibid.*

24. Margaret Freece Papers, Brigham Young University.

Sarah Elizabeth Carmichael 1838–1901

*Miriam Brinton Murphy attended the
University of California at Berkeley,
and was graduated from the
University of Utah in 1956 with a
bachelor's degree in English. During
her senior year there, she was editor
of the student newspaper,* The Daily
Utah Chronicle. *Pursuing a career
in advertising, public relations, and
editing, she worked in New York and
San Francisco. She is currently
assistant editor of the* Utah
Historical Quarterly *in Salt Lake
City. She is the mother of a son,
Bill. Her interests include travel,
painting, and writing; she is active in
the Episcopal Church.*

Sarah E. Carmichael

Miriam Brinton Murphy

The poetry of pioneer Utah lies for the most part forgotten in the periodicals of the day and in a few slim volumes of verse that are preserved in local libraries. While a surprising number of early Utahns wrote poetry, only a handful of their poems survive—most notably in hymns such as the familiar "Come, Come Ye Saints" by William Clayton. The neglect of pioneer verse is readily explained by a reading of the poems. Many of them reflect the sentimentality and didacticism that sometimes marred nineteenth-century poetry; additionally, these Mormon poets tended to explore religious themes with a dogmatic zeal that no longer appeals to most readers. Sarah Elizabeth Carmichael—Lizzie, as she was called—overcame these faults to produce poems of genuine literary merit. Regrettably, her work has been obscured in the general eclipse of pioneer poetry.

Two facts about Lizzie Carmichael emerge: she displayed a poetic brilliance that was admired by her peers both in Utah and elsewhere, and she lived with a tragic heritage that darkened her life during what should have been its crowning years. While brief sketches of her life have appeared from time to time in various local Utah publications, research has uncovered additional material on both the poet and her husband, Jonathan M. Williamson, that will flesh out her story and correct some of the misconceptions.[1]

Lizzie was born in 1838 at Setauket, Long Island, New York, a daughter of William and Mary Ann Carmichael. Her destiny was shaped in large measure by the family's flawed heredity. Her parents were double cousins, and of a reported seven children born to them, only Lizzie with her superior mind and a sister of below normal intelligence survived infancy. Just when and where the Carmichaels were converted to Mormonism is not known. However, in October 1842 the family joined the Mormons at Nauvoo, where Lizzie's father worked as a carpenter on the Nauvoo Temple. By the spring of 1847 the family was living at Winter Quarters, Nebraska; and in 1850 they made their final move to Salt Lake Valley, settling in the city's Eighth Ward. Lizzie was then twelve years old.[2]

The earliest plat of Salt Lake City shows William Carmichael as owner of a lot on the northwestern corner of State Street and Fifth South. This location opposite the Eighth Ward Square gave Lizzie an ever-changing view of incoming settlers who camped there prior to establishing permanent residence elsewhere. In 1851 an adobe school where Lizzie may have attended classes was built on the north side of Fourth South near State Street. She may also have used the facilities of the fledgling territorial library housed in the Council Hall. Despite the limited educational and cultural resources of Zion, the "pretty, big-eyed retiring girl" began her solitary, self-taught career as a writer.[3]

That the tender bud flowered, given its environment, indicates a personal persistence and a commitment that ran very deep. Edward W. Tullidge called Lizzie's birth "in the severest sense untimely; she was reared in these valleys of Rocky Mountain isolation, when the poet, the musician and the painter were told to go to the canyons with ox teams for wood and earn their daily bread."[4] On the Mormon frontier the struggle for survival made the arts expendable. If, as some have suggested, her home life was characterized by misunderstanding or even resentment, the fact would not be difficult to understand.[5] Artistic genius and domestic order are fitful companions at best. Nevertheless, some communion—fostered perhaps by parental pride—did exist. A charming picture of Lizzie's father describes him

with his dinner pail in one hand and the manuscript of a poem written by his gifted daughter in the other, he might have been seen almost any day going to work and stopping at the newspaper office to leave the manuscript.

Beginning in 1858, more than fifty poems by Miss Carmichael were published in the *Deseret News* over a period of eight years. Her first offering was apparently so well done that it cast doubt upon her authorship. The poet sought the help of "a high church official," who assured the editor of the girl's genuineness, and Lizzie thereafter became a frequent contributor.[7] The first poem to carry her name was "Truth," which appeared in the March 10, 1858, issue. Then a young woman of twenty, Lizzie found her work readily acknowledged by the pioneer intelligentsia, and in 1859 the powerful Eliza R. Snow made her approval public:

Make room for the rising minstrel—
List, list to her minstrelsy;
Its numbers are rich and truthful,
And pure is its melody.[8]

As Lizzie's genius continued to unfold, it brought her a measure of fame, but at the same time it exposed areas of tension between the artist and her family and church.

Lizzie's early published poems are remarkable for their lack of distinctively Mormon subject matter. Often homiletic in character, the verses treat friendship, love, personal integrity, writing, Indian pride, and similar topics from a humanistic, nonsectarian point of view. Even in the poem "Pharaoh," where man's contending with God is explored, she avoided heavy-handed parallels between the exodus of the Israelites and that of the Mormons.[9] And in a rare poem on a Mormon subject—Brigham Young—Lizzie retained control over her topic, refusing to be overawed by his power. The result is a poem that praises but does not cloy:

> We do not call thee chieftain,
>   We do not name thee king,
> We wreath no brilliants for thy brow,
>   No ermine round thee fling[10]

The verse continues, expanding the theme of the Mormon leader as a beloved man who belongs to the people: He is "ours." By contrast, there is the remoteness in these lines by Eliza R. Snow:

> Servant of God, most honor'd—most belov'd:
> By Him appointed and of Him approv'd.
> Prophet and Seer—You stand as Moses stood,
> Between the people and the living God.[11]

A recently uncovered document asserts that Lizzie "often sought the society and literary counsel of Sister Eliza." Sometime after the 1856 publication of Eliza's first volume of poetry, the two visited Brigham Young, seeking help for "a similar recognition of the youthful aspirant for literary honors." The church president advised the girl to "use your gifts to build up truth and righteousness in the earth and your gift will be preserved as long as you shall live. If you prostitute your powers to gain fame or gold, your light will go out in darkness." This should not be construed as indicating antagonism on Brigham Young's part toward Lizzie and her work.[12] The practical man of affairs probably knew far better than the two women that the world honors poets with laurel wreaths and love but seldom with money. Then, too, he may have recognized that despite a close bond of sympathy, the young poet would never emulate the older woman's preferred zeal. One cannot imagine Lizzie penning lines such as these:

> O God, bless Brigham Young;
> Bless him, and all that bless him;
> Waste them away, O God, we pray,

Who, rising to oppose him,
Contend with Thee.[13]

The times generally favored zeal over art.

From her earliest years, Lizzie must have longed for the benefits of a broader education. Her facile mind absorbed what it could from the limited resources that were available in Salt Lake City, but it craved more. John R. Young remembered meeting Lizzie, probably sometime in 1858, when he attended a school taught by Sister Pratt, and here became acquainted with Miss Lizzie Carmichael, "one of Utah's most gifted daughters."[14] Far from desiring merely "fame or gold," Lizzie may have wanted, even at this early date, to earn money from her poetry only to pay for further education in the east.

While little is known of Lizzie's personal life in the early 1860s, the "rising minstrel" mixed with prominent members of local society, winning their admiration and acceptance. An elaborate program of speeches and music celebrating Independence Day 1862 included her poem "Life and Liberty," read by John T. Caine. A few weeks later, similar activities commemorating Pioneer Day brought from her pen not a poem but a brief address to the pioneers read by William Clayton.[15] She had entered the most productive, challenging, and ultimately tragic decade of her life. National recognition, marriage, and travel lay ahead of her, but by the end of the 1860s, her life—the life of the mind—was essentially over.

Edward W. Tullidge may have been the most perceptive of Lizzie's contemporaries. He saw her as a genius whose powers of improvisation carried her to the heights, but the patient shaping and reworking of a master such as Keats "cannot, we fear, be justly accredited among her higher poetic gifts and graces."[16] While she appears to have "lisped in numbers" as naturally as Pope, many have lamented along with Tullidge that "the poet was born out of due season."[17] Had her intellectual environment been more challenging and critical, her powers might have matured more fully despite the brevity of her creative years.

Nevertheless, the poet did grow. She began to see her subjects in dramatic terms, using conflict, contrast, and irony in an increasingly sophisticated way. "The Daughter of Herodias," "Esau's Petition," "The Stolen Sunbeam," and the "Feast of Lucrezia Borgia" reveal a growing command of her art. A few lines from the latter poem will illustrate how the muse was maturing:

Wine! wine! it flowed in a crimson stream
Through the crystal cups, till its ruby gleam

> *Shadowed a blush on the soft white hand*
> *That raised the glass from the marble stand.*

As the bacchanal progresses and the wine takes effect, the guests become fearful:

> *They spurn the wine with a frenzied ire,—*
> *Their hands are ice, and their lips are fire.*
> *There's a mantle of blackness above them spread*
> *They hear a chant for the dying and dead;*
> *They see priests moving; wan tapers gleam;*
> *But each life-pulse stands like a torpid stream;*
> *And they gaze with a stupor of brain and heart*
> *As the gorgeous curtains are torn apart,*
> *And a form in velvet of sable dye,*
> *With the forehead bound by a jeweled tie,*
> *Stood looking upon them with eyes severe,*
> *And they shuddering whisper: "Lucrezia's here."*

But the poisoner's triumph over the nobles is brief; Lucrezia's son is one of the victims.[18]

Lizzie's advancing skill eventually brought her recognition outside of Zion. William Cullen Bryant published "The Stolen Sunbeam" in his two-volume collection, *A Family Library of Poetry and Song*. Retitled by Bryant "The Origin of Gold," the poem has been justly acclaimed for its fine conceit depicting heaven's fallen one tearing a plume from the setting sun and burying it in the earth where it becomes gold. Another anthologizer, May Wentworth, selected two Carmichael poems, "A Christmas Rhyme" and "Sorrow," for her volume *Poetry of the Pacific* in 1867. In addition to the anthologies, some have claimed that Lizzie's poems were often reprinted without credit by the eastern press. In any event, ample evidence exists that the Utah poet was recognized and respected in the literary circles of mid-nineteenth-century America.[19]

Like many other writers of the period, Lizzie was profoundly moved by the Civil War. The conflict that set brother against brother captured her imagination and brought from her pen vivid, dramatic poems such as "Ashes to Ashes." The war indirectly affected her personal life as well. Miles from Zion a call to arms led Jonathan M. Williamson, a surgeon, to enlist with the California Volunteers in San Francisco on September 27, 1861. A year later the doctor entered Salt Lake City with troops under the command of Colonel Patrick E. Connor. Lizzie may have caught a first glimpse of her future husband at that time as the soldiers marched up State Street past her home.[20]

Jonathan Williamson surfaced in the local news early in 1863,

following the Battle of Bear River, when he traveled fifty miles
north with another physician to meet the wounded. One can only
speculate on Jonathan's activities during the following year and a
half. In the summer of 1864 the post newspaper reported his return from California, where he had been "for some time past." A
few months later the surgeon was mustered out of the service, his
three-year enlistment having expired. Wanting to take a more active part in the Civil War, Jonathan signed on as a surgeon with
the artillery brigade, 16th Army Corps, under General A. J.
Smith, and he saw action in the "great campaign of 1864-65." In
August 1866 he returned to Zion "in his own conveyance," reportedly making one of the quickest trips on record.[21]

One uncertainty remains: when and where did the bright poet
and the army surgeon meet? Evidence suggests the couple became
acquainted during the doctor's stay at Camp Douglas during the
year and a half between the Battle of Bear River and Jonathan's
trip to California in 1864. This assumption better explains references—many of which are highly overdrawn—to Lizzie's conflict
with church and parental authority.

Beyond question feelings ran high when Connor and his men
marched into Salt Lake City. The Mormons felt harassed, and
they viewed the troops with suspicion. Many of the soldiers saw
the Saints as traitorous lawbreakers, and the troops enjoyed poking
fun at Mormon beliefs and leaders. Despite the atmosphere of mutual distrust, social contacts must have been made. Jonathan evidently read the poems Lizzie was then writing with some frequency for the *Deseret News*. Perhaps the dazzling "Feast of Lucrezia
Borgia" charmed him as it did so many others.[22] If he actively
sought her acquaintance at this time, he probably found his status
as a physician rather than an ordinary soldier an asset. While he
was both a gentile and an army man, Jonathan posed no personal
threat to the populace. Indeed, his interest in the poet may have
been welcomed by some of the city's social leaders as a sign that
bridges between the two hostile camps could be built.

In 1863-64 Lizzie was in her middle twenties and unmarried in
a society that had little place for that kind of nonconformity. Her
wide acquaintance with the city's influential families makes it difficult to believe that no one had proposed marriage to her. As a
plural wife Lizzie would have added distinction to a family, and
any artistic temperament she displayed could have been easily ac-
commodated by a husband who need not share her company except when he wished. A refusal to marry into a local family and
her subsequent alliance with a gentile probably would have exasperated her family. Reports by J. H. Beadle and others that her

actions nettled Brigham Young sufficiently to ban her works or that they moved Mormons generally to dissociate themselves from her are questionable. Evidence abounds that Lizzie remained a loved and admired figure locally despite her feelings about polygamy—feelings that were shared by at least one other notable woman poet of the period.[23]

While Lizzie may have encountered some closed doors and cold shoulders, her poetry never fell out of favor. Indeed, Utahns were eager to claim her as their own. For example, Mormon historian Brigham H. Roberts heaped praise on Lizzie's "President Lincoln's Funeral," asserting that it "is not anywhere surpassed in the literature—prose or poetry—that the sad event produced; no, not even Walt Whitman's 'O Captain! My Captain.' " The poem did attract national recognition following its publication in the *San Francisco Golden Era*. The famous actress Julia Dean Hayne, who frequently appeared at the Salt Lake Theatre, came on stage during one performance "in appropriate mourning dress, and read the poem with a pure pathos and perfect elocution, considering the immense capacity and imperfect acoustics of the room. It requires genius to read as well as write good poetry." The elegy merits acclaim. Its expression of grief achieves a solemn dignity in lines such as these:

> Bands of mourning draped the homestead,
>   And the sacred house of prayer;
> Mourning folds lay black and heavy
>   On true bosoms everywhere:
> Yet there were no tear-drops streaming
>   From the deep and solemn eye
> Of the hour that mutely waited
>   Till the funeral train went by.
> Oh! there is a woe that crushes
>   All expression with its weight!
> There is pain that numbs and hushes
>   Feelings's sense, it is so great.[24]

If Lizzie were out of favor with Mormon leaders over polygamy or, as some have suggested, her espousal of the Union cause, they were strangely unsuccessful at keeping her poems from the public. During only one extended period of time, from late 1864 to early 1866, did the poet fail to publish with some frequency in the *Deseret News*. Most likely the anti-Mormon press seized upon Lizzie's distaste for polygamy and her failure to interest Brigham Young in publishing her poetry to blow the incident out of all reasonable proportion. J. H. Beadle, for example, had Lizzie leaving Utah under the safety of a military escort to marry Dr. Jonathan Williamson. And as recently as 1969 Stanley P. Hirshson uncritically asserted that Brigham Young banned her works until they were so well recognized that he "finally offered to help her, but the proud girl refused." From many sources it appears that Lizzie's home life was marred by a lack of understanding. Evidence also supports the notion that she rebelled against her parents and the establishment. Far from being a sign of yet another malevolent Mormon plot, Lizzie's conflict with authority seems *de rigueur* for a poet of any intellectual pretension.[25]

The publication of Lizzie's only book of poetry sometime in mid 1886 ushered in a series of events that greatly altered her life. The slender volume, entitled simply *Poems*, was

published with the consent—somewhat reluctantly given—of the authoress, by a devoted circle of her friends and admirers, who design thus to preserve an early momento of her talents and genius as a writer; and by its circulation among kindred spirits, who as yet are strangers to her muse, secure for her poems a more extended acquaintance and recognition.

Included among the twenty-six poems selected for publication were the frequently praised "April Flowers," "President Lincoln's Funeral," "The Stolen Sunbeam," and "Moonrise on the Wasatch," which is among her best descriptive poems as its opening section illustrates:

> The stars seemed far, yet darkness was not deep;
> Like baby-eyes, the rays yet strove with sleep;
> The giant hills stood in the distance proud—
> Of each white brow a dusky fold of cloud;
> Some coldly gray, some of an amber hue,
> Some with dark purple fading into blue;
> And one that blushed with a faint crimson jet—
> A sunset memory, tinged with cloud-regret.
> Close to my feet the soft leaf shadows stirred;
> I listened vainly, for they moved unheard—
> Trembled unconsciously; and languid air
> Crept to the rose's lip, and perished there.
> It was an hour of such repose as steals
> Into the heart when it most deeply feels;
> When feeling covers every shred of speech
> With one emotion language cannot reach.
> And Nature held her breath and waited there.
> An awed enthusiast at the shrine of prayer;
> Like a pale devotee, whose reverent lips
> Stifle the breath that burns her finger-tips.[26]

Much of the book's story can be traced in the columns of the *Daily Union Vedette*. On August 6, 1866, the Camp Douglas newspaper carried a review of *Poems* by Carrie Carlton, originally published in the San Francisco *New Age*. Praising both book and poet, the reviewer noted that "True to a refined and heavenly instinct she stands up bravely to resist all example, all entreaty, all parental authority." According to the reviewer, Lizzie hoped to be able to enter Vassar College. The following day the *Vedette* reported that Aaron Stein, who evidently handled the book's sale, had sent Lizzie $581.15, proceeds from subscriptions to her volume of poetry. Stein said that he had another "gentleman" who had been responsible for promoting the book, and they felt rewarded for their efforts and pleased by the "flattering reception given it by a critical press."[27]

The *Vedette* continued to take an interest in Lizzie's poetry, publishing several of her poems during September and October. On November 20 the newspaper was pleased to report that *Poems* had been well received in Boston by a "high authority in matters of letters," who believed the poet was destined to achieve greater prominence in the field of literature.[28] The future must have looked bright to the poet, who had every reason to believe at age twenty-eight that she had many years left to develop her art to its full potential. Jonathan must have felt pleased with Lizzie's modest success, and hopeful that as her prospective husband he might help her sustain it. The dream was not to be.

Not long after his return from the east, Jonathan became embroiled in a controversial claim-jumping case. Albert Brown, a former captain in the cavalry, and Jonathan had claimed an unoccupied piece of land west of the Jordan River. Late one night they were surrounded by forty men and forced down the bank of the river. When Albert Brown was recognized by one of the men as having treated him kindly while on provost guard in the city, the would-be-settlers were helped from the water on their promise to immediately leave the country. This potentially tragic event must have discouraged any plans Jonathan had for settling in the area at that time.[29]

In late October a probable obstacle to Jonathan's marriage to Lizzie was removed: Mary Ann Carmichael, mother of "our distinguished poetess," died of a heart attack at age fifty-eight.[30] On November 4, Jonathan and Lizzie were married at Fort Bridger by the well-known Judge W. A. Carter. The *Vedette* gave its blessing to the occasion:

The happy couple are both well and favorably known in this community, the gay Benedict as the late Surgeon of the Second Cavalry C. V., and worthy bride as the sweet poetess of Utah. May their path through life be strewn with flowers, and every step a fountain of friendship gush forth to water them.[31]

Nearly a year later, the *Vedette* reported that the Williamsons were living in Ohio, the doctor's native state. The newspaper reprinted a letter, "evidently from the pen of the accomplished Mrs. J. M. Williamson," originally published in the Cincinnati *Commercial*, denouncing polygamy and claiming that Lizzie had bearded the Lion of the Lord in his den:

> *I am no Hagar wandering desolate from the tent of a Mormon Abraham, but one of the few women who have grown up in the shadow of Brigham Young's despotism, and dared to defy him in the presence chamber of his power . . .*[32]

Reportedly, Jonathan wanted his wife to write a history of the Mormons, a project that never got beyond the planning stage, as most sources agree that Lizzie went into a severe mental decline about a year after her marriage. The Williamsons showed up next in Pioche, Nevada, a booming mining town, the naming of which has been credited by several authorities to Lizzie.[33] Then, some time after 1870, the couple returned to Salt Lake City, where they lived out the remainder of their lives. Jonathan continued his medical practice and cared for his wife and sister-in-law, Mary Carmichael.[34]

Whatever the nature of her mental debility, Lizzie apparently enjoyed periods of lucidity. In 1874 Mary Jane Mount Tanner, a childhood friend, visited the invalid and described her manner:

> *She is better now but not well enough to take her place in Society. Poor Lizzie! It made my heart ache to see her. She was so changed. The light of intelligence had gone from her eyes, and her voice had a strange sound like some one speaking in the distance, but she talked intelligently and wanted me to come again. She has a beautiful home nicely furnished. Her husband's mother and sister lives [sic] there to take care of her. It made me feel very nervous to see her, and my health is so poor I do not think I can go again.*[35]

In 1880 the doctor's mother, Abigail Williamson, died, and two years later death came to him. J. R. Walker and Boyd Park were executors of his "considerable property." When home care for Lizzie became too difficult, she was sent to the state mental hospital at Provo, where she had "special privileges and attendants." Ellen L. Jakeman saw her there in the 1890s, "a slender figure in a close fitting black dress, with a white crepe shawl over her shoulders, at Sabbath services—with them, but not of them." Finally, after more than thirty years of mental instability, Lizzie died at her Salt Lake City home on November, 10, 1901.[36]

With no family to mourn her, the city's newspapers provided generous eulogies and recalled for their readers the achievements of her youth. The *Deseret News* praised "the once brilliant poetess whose literary gifts placed her name among those of the best writers of the nation." The *Salt Lake Herald* called her "a literary genius and born poetess, who at one time was ranked the peer of American writers, and whose work has been characterized as the spontaneous outbursts of a poetry-filled soul." The *Tribune* opined that "had she retained the brilliant mind of her youth she would have found a place in the foremost ranks of American literature."[37]

The headstone on her forgotten grave in Salt Lake City Cemetery has disappeared, and the poetry that brought a heightened sensitivity to the crude frontier eludes all but the persistent seeker. Lizzie penned her own best epitaph in these haunting lines that foreshadow her mental collapse and the obscuring hand of time:

> Pale, blighted flowers, the summer time
> Will smile on brighter leaves;
> They will not wither in their prime,
> Like a young heart that grieves;
> But the impulsive buds that dare
> The chill of April showers,
> Breathe woman-love's low martyr prayer—
> I kiss your leaves, pale flowers.[38]

Despite changing literary fashion, Lizzie's best poems break the bonds of time and place to speak with a voice that readers of today can appreciate. Certainly the genius of nineteenth-century Utah literature merits a permanent place in the state's pantheon.

Notes

1. Brief accounts of Lizzie's life are found in Ellen L. Jakeman, "Sarah Elizabeth Carmichael Williamson," *Relief Society Magazine* 15(September 1928):478-90; Mary M. Root, "Pioneer Poet of Utah: Study of the Life and Work of Sarah Carmichael, One of the State's First Literary Producers," *Salt Lake Tribune,* February 16 and March 8, 1936; Edward W. Tullidge, "Carmichael," *Western Galaxy* 1(May 1888): 334–40; Catherine Hazel Selby, "Sarah Elizabeth Carmichael," master's thesis, University of Utah, 1921.

2. Jakeman, "Sarah," 478-79, 489; *Deseret News,* November 21, 1866, and November 11, 1901; *Salt Lake Herald,* November 11, 1901; Brigham H. Roberts, ed., *History of the Church of Jesus Christ of Latter-day Saints,* 7 vols., Salt Lake City, 1902-32, 6:175, 7:326, 463; Kate B. Carter, comp., *Heart Throbs of the West,* 12 vols., Salt Lake City, 1939-51, 11:404; Francis W. Kirkham and Harold Lundstrom, eds., *Tales of a Triumphant People: A History of Salt Lake County, Utah, 1847-1900,* Salt Lake City, 1947, p. 24. See also United States National Archives, 1850 Census Schedules, Utah, microfilm of holograph, #A143, Utah State Historical Society, Salt Lake City. The census shows the Carmichaels as Eighth Ward residents and lists the four family members: William, joiner, 46; Mary Ann, 42; Mary, 15; Sarah, 13.

3. Kirkham and Lundstrom, *Tales,* 25; Andrew Jenson, *Encyclopedic History of The Church of Jesus Christ of Latter-day Saints,* Salt Lake City, 1941, p. 746; Kate B. Carter, comp., *Our Pioneer Heritage,* 14 vols., Salt Lake City, 1958-71, 2:18.

4. Tullidge, "Carmichael," 335.

5. Jakeman, "Sarah," 489; Root, "Pioneer Poet."

6. *Salt Lake Herald,* November 11, 1901.

7. Jakeman, "Sarah," 480-81; Carter, *Our Pioneer Heritage,* 2:18.

8. "To Miss Carmichael, G. S. L. City—" Deseret News, April 13, 1859. Eliza R. Snow copied the poem on some unused pages in her Journal and Notebook (1842-44) now in the Archives Division, Historical Department, The Church of Jesus Christ of Latter-day Saints, Salt Lake City.

9. Lizzie's poetry was signed Sarah E. Carmichael, Miss S. E.

Carmichael, or S. E. Carmichael. The latter usage led one childhood admirer to assume the writer was a man. See Louisa L. Greene Richards, "Memories of Miss Carmichael's Writings," *Young Woman's Journal* 13(January 1903):23-25. Under the editorship of Albert Carrington, the *Deseret News* published many of her poems following her debut with "Truth." Titles and dates of publication through 1859 are: "Perseverance," May 19, 1858; "The World's Wisdom," February 2, 1859; "Pharaoh," March 30, 1859; "Wine," May 18, 1859; "What Is There Worth Living For?" June 22, 1859; "The Father's Legacy," August 3, 1859; "Time," September 14, 1859; "Willie's Dream," September 21, 1859; "The Chieftain's Reply," October 26, 1859; "Thy Mother's Love," November 2, 1859; "History, Romance, and Poetry,"November 23, 1859; "Armaund," December 14, 1859.

10. "Brigham Young," *Deseret News*, October 17, 1860.

11. *Poems, Religious, Historical, and Political,* vol. 2, Salt Lake City, 1877, p. 1.

12. The handwritten document, undated and untitled, is found in the Susa Young Gates collection, Miscellaneous Box 8, Utah State Historical Society. The writings look like Susa's; however, since she was not born until 1856, she likely would not have been an eyewitness to the encounter. The document claims that although Lizzie's husband was kind to her, he wanted to commercialize her work. When that failed, the writer continues, he hoped to reap quick profit from an exposé of the Mormon people and their religion that he urged his wife to write. Since Lizzie never wrote a history of the Mormons, one cannot pass judgment on its contents. It is doubtful, nevertheless, that her writing would have fallen into the lurid, exposé class.

13. Eliza R. Snow, "Anthem," *Deseret News*, March 12, 1862.

14. John R. Young, *Memories of John R. Young, Utah Pioneer*, 1847, Salt Lake City, 1920, p. 117. Prior to Young's mission to the Sandwich Islands in 1864, Lizzie wrote "A Parting Word to My friend John R. Young," p. 127-28. It is not clear whether Lizzie was a teacher or a student at the school. One source indicates that she was a "reticent and sensitive public school teacher." See Root, "Pioneer Poet."

15. "Programme for the Celebration of the 86th Anniversary of Our National Independence," Utah State Historical Society;

Deseret News, July 9 and July 30, 1862. The poem and the address are printed in full in the *News.*

16. Tullidge, "Carmichael," p. 338.

17. *Ibid.,* p. 335.

18. "Lucrezia Borgia's Feast," *Deseret News,* May 6, 1863. "The Daughter of Herodias" and "Esau's Petition" appeared in the *News* on October 22, 1862, and March 11, 1863, respectively. "The Stolen Sunbeam" may be found in Sarah E. Carmichael, *Poems* (San Francisco, 1866), pp. 25–27.

19. William Cullen Bryant, ed., *A Family Library of Poetry and Song* ... 2 vols., New York, 1878, pp. 654–55; May Wentworth, *Poetry of the Pacific: Selections and Original Poems from the Poets of the Pacific States,* San Francisco, 1867, pp. 326-29; Jakeman, "Sarah," p. 484.

21. Fred B. Rogers, *Soldiers of the Overland,* San Francisco, 1938, 75; *Daily Union Vedette,* July 4, 1864, and August 12, 1866.

22. One writer says the doctor read Lizzie's story of the "Lily of the Valley" and sought her acquaintance. *Salt Lake Herald,* November 11, 1901.

23. Ina Coolbrith, poet laureate of California and a niece of Joseph Smith, Jr., vigorously opposed polygamy. Nevertheless, Joseph Fielding Smith said his father regularly corresponded with the Oakland Librarian and mentor of Jack London. See Kate Thomas, "Ina Coolbrith," *Relief Society Magazine* 15(November 1928):580-85.

24. Brigham H. Roberts, *A Comprehensive History of The Church of Jesus Christ of Latter-day Saints,* Century 1, 6 vols., Salt Lake City, 1930, 5:72-75; *Daily Union Vedette,* October 14, 1865; *Deseret News,* October 19, 1865. The complete poem is reprinted by Roberts and may also be found in Tullidge, "Carmichael," pp. 337-38, and in Carmichael, *Poems,* pp. 21-24.

25. J. H. Beadle, *Polygamy; Or, The Mysteries and Crimes of Mormonism* ... Philadelphia, 1882, pp. 320-21; Stanley P. Hirshson, *The Lion of the Lord: A Biography of Brigham Young,* New York, 1969, p. 293. Hirshson's reference is the New York *World,* October 2, 1870. See also Albert D. Richardson, *Beyond the Mississippi* ... Hartford, Conn., 1867, pp. 470-72. Richardson accompanied Schuyler Colfax on his visit to Salt Lake City and the West in 1865.

26. Carmichael, Poems, p. v and pp. 28-29.

27. *Daily Union Vedette*, August 6, 7, and 12. Stein was cashier for Wells, Fargo and Co.'s Overland Express and lived near the Salt Lake Theatre on First South. E. L. Sloan, comp., *The Salt Lake City Directory and Business Guide for 1869*, Salt Lake City, 1869, p. 140.

28. *Daily Union Vedette*, November 20, 1866.

29. Accounts of the incident are found in Roberts, *Comprehensive History*, 5:201-2; T. B. H. Stenhouse, The Rocky Mountain Saints . . . , Salt Lake City, 1904, p. 618; R. N. Baskin, *Reminiscences of Early Utah*, Salt Lake City, 1914, pp. 166-67; and *Daily Union Vedette*, September 26, 1866.

30. *Daily Union Vedette*, October 26, 1866.

31. *Ibid.*, November 6, 1866.

32. *Ibid.*, October 18, 1867.

33. Hubert Howe Bancroft, *History of Nevada, Colorado, and Wyoming, 1540-1888*, San Francisco, 1890, p. 272; Walter R. Averett, *Directory of Southern Nevada Place Names*, rev. ed., Las Vegas, 1962, p. 109.

34. Evidently Mary Carmichael boarded with the Thomas Gamble family. The 1870 Census lists her as an "idiot," age thirty-two, living in the Gamble household between Main and State streets on Fifth South, around the corner from the old Carmichael home on State Street. See 1870 Census Schedules, Bear-Weber Counties, Utah #A145 and Sloan, Salt Lake City Directory ... 1869, p. 107. When the Williamsons returned to Salt Lake City, they resumed care of Lizzie's sister. See 1880 Census Schedules, Utah: Salt Lake-Sanpete Counties, #A148. In 1880 the household consisted of Williamson, physician, 52; Lizzie, 42; Mary 44, Eliza Julia Elliott, housekeeper, 24; and Richard Whitmore or Whitman, stable man, 17.

35. Mary Jane Mount Tanner, Journal, May 17, 1874, p. 147, microfilm of holograph, LDS Archives.

36. *Salt Lake Tribune*, March 31, 1880; Jakeman, "Sarah," 490.

37. *Deseret News*, November 11, 1901; *Salt Lake Herald*, November 11, 1901; *Salt Lake Tribune*, November 11, 1901.

38. Carmichael, "April Flowers," Poems, pp. 7-8.

Louisa Lula Greene Richards 1849–1944

Carol Cornwall Madsen holds a degree in English literature from the University of Utah and a master of arts degree in American history from that same institution. She is a member of Phi Beta Kappa and of Phi Kappa Phi.

Professionally, Madsen has taught English on a college level and is presently employed by the Historical Department of The Church of Jesus Christ of Latter-day Saints. She is a member of the Utah State Historical Society and the Mormon History Association.

Living in Salt Lake City, Carol and her husband, Gordon A. Madsen, are the parents of six children.

Louisa G. Richards

Carol Cornwall Madsen

On May 16, 1849, the *Frontier Guardian,* weekly newspaper of Kanesville, Iowa, announced that cholera was raging along the river from Pittsburgh to Kanesville. It reported that this "malignant and fatal disease had made its appearance at Council Point," five miles from Kanesville, attacking four people.[1] Just two weeks later, of thirty-seven internments reported to the city register in Kanesville in one day, twenty-seven had resulted from cholera.[2] Later, as the disease continued to plague the county, the *Guardian* issued a plea to the women of Kanesville to refrain from going house to house in mourning. It suggested that the best remedy was to "keep the spirits high and cultivate cheerfulness." A postscript added that "since writing the above, there have four more deaths occurred by cholera."[3]

The gloom that hung heavy over the usually active community temporarily dissipated in the Evan and Susan Greene household. Easter Sunday, April 8, 1849, brought the Greene family a healthy new baby girl.[4] Yet even with such a hopeful beginning, the odds against her surviving her first year were formidable. Kanesville was at the beginning of a long siege of cholera, and as a frontier outpost it experienced the high mortality rate prevalent in pioneer communities. Two other Greene children had already succumbed as infants, and others were yet to follow them. But Louisa Greene, the new child, defied the odds and lived ninety-five years.

As a typical pioneer child, Louisa was subject to the difficulties of frontier life, but as a young woman she became another kind of pioneer. All of her youthful experiences converged in time to fashion the woman who was to be an able advocate of the rights and beliefs of the women of her church and the rights of women everywhere. As one of the earliest spokeswomen for the women of Utah (most of whom were Mormons) through an established "voice," the *Woman's Exponent,* Louisa Greene Richards is memorialized in Utah annals as Utah's first woman journalist.

Louisa's parents were first cousins, their mothers being sisters of Brigham Young. Her father, Evan Molbourne Greene, was teach-

ing school in the western frontier communities of his native New
York by the age of fifteen. An early convert to the Mormon
Church at age eighteen, he followed the movements of the main
body of the church, moving first to Kirtland, Ohio, where he lived
for a short while at the home of the Prophet Joseph Smith. He
performed missionary work for a short period, but eventually returned to New York to accept a teaching position, where he
boarded with his aunt and uncle, who were recent converts to the
church. While there he met his cousin, Susan Kent. In time the
two married and returned to Kirtland to live. Evan continued to
teach school, numbering Joseph Smith among his students. During
his sojourn in Kirtland, Evan learned to speak Hebrew fluently,
and he continued his own studies in the School of the Prophets.
He was primarily a scholar throughout his life, and he introduced
his children to a love of learning.[5]

Following the westward course of the church, the Greenes left
Kirtland, settled in Nauvoo (where they remained for six years),
and then moved with the general Mormon exodus to Kanesville,
Iowa, on the banks of the Missouri River. From 1848 to 1852,
Kanesville was one of the major outfitting posts for westward trav-
ellers as well as for Mormon immigrants. It was named for
Thomas L. Kane, a non-Mormon friend of Brigham Young.[6]

In Kanesville, Evan Greene served as United States postmaster
as well as recorder and treasurer of Pottawattamie County. He
continued teaching in a small school which he had established.[7]
Land was productive, goods were accessible, and life was profitable
for the Mormons in Kanesville under the leadership of Orson
Hyde, presiding authority of that branch of the Mormon Church.
Though many families remained for only a season in Kanesville,
the Greenes and other Mormon residents of Pottawattamie County
did not make preparations to leave until the injunction from Salt
Lake City came in unmistakable terms: "We wish you to evacuate
Pottawattamie County and the States. . . . Come to this place; *and
fail not.*"[8] Evan and his family followed counsel.

The Greenes left Kanesville on July 16, 1852, with the Allen
Weeks company. Louisa's recollections of that trek are sketchy because she was only in her fourth year, but two events remained
with her, and she often recounted them in later years because she
felt they demonstrated some of the perils to which children were
subjected during those arduous western migrations. She recalls
crossing the Missouri River at the outset of their journey and falling off the ferryboat when no one was near. Miraculously, in the
fall over the side, her dress became entangled on some nails jut-
ting from the side of the boat, but she was submerged in the wa-

ter. Fortunately, within minutes, an old Welsh neighbor, Brother Edwards, spotted the piece of clothing and saw the apparently lifeless form hanging from it. Summoning help, he reached down and rescued the little girl, who always remembered afterwards what it was like to be "buried in water."[9]

Later on, when their wagon company had crossed another river near the end of the journey, Louisa and her older sister, Nancy, age eleven, were alone in the wagon as the oxen pulled it up a steep embankment rising from the narrow edge of the water. Nearing the top of the bluff, one of the oxen slipped, and the wagon careened backwards. Clinging to each other, the two girls feared for their lives; at the bottom of the incline, however, the hind wheels swerved, and the wagon hit a stump, coming to a jolting stop without overturning. The girls, the oxen, and the supplies were saved.[10]

Louisa also remembered the unselfish spirit of her mother during that long journey west; her mother refused to ride in the wagon in order to spare the strength of the oxen. Not until she had walked to the fainting point did she consent to ride. Louisa never forgot the courage and strength of those early pioneer women, and her admiration for them initiated the attitudes she developed toward the capabilities and opportunities of women that were to find full expression later.

The Weeks company arrived in Salt Lake Valley on November 1, 1852.[11] The Greenes did not tarry long in Salt Lake, however; they learned within days that Brigham Young desired them to settle in Provo, where Evan was to establish an academy or high school. Again following counsel, Evan and Susan Greene travelled to Provo and selected some choice property for their home and for the school. The school was soon organized with Evan as schoolmaster and his oldest daughter, Rhoda, as assistant. Evan was elected mayor soon afterwards and was also elected representative to the territorial legislature.[12]

After four weeks in Provo, Evan Greene was asked to give up his property to the church for the establishment of the Brigham Young Academy. He moved his family to a ranch near the point of the mountain north of Provo. From there he travelled to Draper to teach during the next two years. The coming of Johnston's Army prompted him to return to Provo for three months until the threat of war was over.[13]

Another move in 1858 took the family to Grantsville, Tooele County, where Evan Greene was elected to serve two more terms in the legislature.[14] Years later, in 1869, when she was twenty, Louisa composed a poem, "By the Great Salt Lake Shore," a reminiscence of the period she spent in Grantsville near the shore of that great lake.[15]

Once more the family moved, this time in answer to a call to preside over a branch of the Mormon Church in Bennington, Bear Lake Valley. They endured much hardship in that northern settlement, including the death of Louisa's ten-year-old brother, Admanzah, and the death in childbirth of her older sister, Rhoda, who, with her husband and four children, had moved with the Greenes to Bennington. As soon as Evan was released from his responsibilities in Bennington, the Greenes bought a farm in Smithfield, Cache County, which was to be Louisa's last childhood home.[16]

From the time she was born in Kanesville through all the moves her family had made, many of which had been prompted by obedience to various church calls, Louisa was greatly affected by the spiritual and educational tenor of her family life. These influences remained strong with her, and her devotion to her parents and her family bracketed the public role she was to assume and the divergent activities which that role and the other involvements of her later life demanded.

In the fall of 1865, when the Greenes arrived in Smithfield, they found a small, struggling settlement that was recovering from recent Indian disturbances. The land was good for farming, and grass and grain grew well. A new rock meetinghouse was just being erected to answer the spiritual needs of the settlers, and a schoolhouse had already been built to meet their educational needs. A cooperative store had commenced operation, and within two years after the Greenes' arrival, the city was incorporated with a mayor, five counselors, two justices of the peace, and a recorder—Evan Greene.[17]

This was the home Louisa knew best and that she returned to often with her children. She and her family quickly became an integral part of the community. An account of the Smithfield celebration of the ninety-second anniversary of Independence Day, published in the *Deseret News,* July 6, 1868, reported that a long procession of city officials and school children and the usual band commenced early in the morning to parade through the main street, concluding at the "bowery," where a program was held. Among the participants on the program was "Louisa Greene, who gave a recitation."

For two years, Louisa Greene kept a personal journal. Her first entry, on April 8, 1867, exclaimed:

Eighteen years old today! Bright and beautiful the day has been. Nothing of note has transpired that I know of. But I have been so happy! ... Eighteen years old with hopeful, happy heart undisturbed.[18]

It is a journal of youthful enthusiasm and yearnings for the education that would make her more proficient as a teacher and writer and more worthwhile as a person. On May 5, 1867, she wrote that she and her sister, Lissa, opened a small school. From that time until the end of their school project in the fall, Louisa fretted about her lack of patience with the children and especially about her lack of formal education, which prevented her from being properly trained to handle them. "I want to be a very good School teacher," she wrote, "and do not know how. I feel that I am not competent as yet to do justice in this respect and so am not satisfied with what I do." Later she again wrote of the education she longed to have: "I do so wish I could attend a good school ... And oh, how I would study! and how much I could learn, and what lots of things I'd write about."[19]

Louisa's wish to attend school was realized in January 1869 when her father took her to Salt Lake City to begin a term at the Rogers and Tripp School. At the end of her first day, she opined that she enjoyed school even more than she had anticipated. At the conclusion of the term she recorded: "Today the school of Mssrs. Roger [sic] and Tripp closes ... I do not care anything about Mr. R...; but Mr. Tripp merits my sincere respect and kind remembrance and has it."[20] She then enrolled at the University of Deseret, a member of the first class conducted by John R. Park. Her diary concludes:

March 6. Professor Park commenced his school today ... think I shall be very well satisfied with it.

March 27. Three weeks' trial of the new school convinces me that it and I can agree very well. In fact I like it much. Neither of the teachers are like Mr. Tripp but then I did not expect they would be; few men are.... How my prayers with regard to school have been answered![21]

Louisa's interests and efforts in writing began to focus at this time, and her initial contributions for publication met with success. The *Salt Lake Herald* and the *Deseret News* accepted her poetic efforts, and "Lula," her preferred professional name, was seen with regularity in the newspapers.

Returning to Smithfield when school was over, Louisa rejoined the affairs of that community while continuing her writing. Before leaving for school in Salt Lake she had been appointed the first secretary of the Female Relief Society in Smithfield, and when she returned she was asked as well to be a teacher in the Sunday

School. While acting in the latter position, she founded and edited the *Smithfield Sunday School Gazette* in the fall of 1869. Sunday School newspapers were not uncommon in early Utah communities; generally handwritten in two columns of legal-sized pages, they contained stories, poetry, and faith-promoting messages.[22] The *Smithfield Gazette,* issued weekly, carried on its masthead: "Remember Thy Creator in The Days of Thy Youth." The themes of Louisa's first newspaper were "Attend Sunday School and preserve order," or sometimes "Attend Sabbath School and pay attention."[23]

Now twenty, Louisa was beginning to consider the direction of her life. Even though she was devoted to family, she yet felt stirrings that sometimes seemed to set her apart from them. A poem that she wrote at this time reflects not so much her poetic talents as her frame of mind:

> *Did I stay too long in the school room*
> *After lessons were through*
> *Leaving my mother and sisters*
> *With all the work to do?*
> *And has it vexed you, mother*
> *My mother, so patient and true?*
>
> *Forgive me, my mother and sisters,*
> *Smile kindly and gently speak;*
> *I'll try to do better tomorrow*
> *And all the rest of the week.*
> *If my wayward mind and feelings*
> *Do not play me another freak.*
>
> *For I have been writing something*
> *Which will likely enough be read*
> *By our children's children*
> *After we all are dead;*
> *And must I think I should have been*
> *Washing dishes instead?*[24]

By 1871 Louisa had established a correspondence with her "aunt," Eliza R. Snow. Since Brigham Young was her great-uncle, she claimed a kinship with Eliza, Brigham's wife, which the great lady of Mormondom chose to honor.

Evidently Louisa either had prospects of immediate marriage or had come to some other crossroad in her life and indicated in a letter to "Aunt" Eliza that she was uncertain of the course she should follow. Eliza's response, written in the spring of 1871, is the only clue to the content of Louisa's letter:

> *I am just as well satisfied with your present position as I would have been with*

the contemplated one. There is a great deal to be done, and if we are disposed we can do good in whatever position we may be placed. I never thought it necessary, neither do I consider it wisdom to rush ahead, or to take a step until we are satisfied with the direction. I think it the sacred duty and right of each individual to wait until satisfied. . . . To be sure, while unmarried, one cannot be fulfilling the requisition of maternity, but let me ask Is it not as important that those already born, should be cultivated and prepared for use in the kingdom of God; as that others should be born? If left to me to decide, I should say, that of the two, the cultivation is of the most consequence.[25]

Evidently following Eliza's advice, Louisa travelled to Salt Lake City the following October to attend the general conference of the Mormon Church and to enter one of the popular schools there as an instructor, by which means she intended to pay her way as a student in some of the higher courses. After completing arrangements for her schooling, she visited "Aunt" Eliza, and in their conversation Louisa asked about the possibility of publishing a second volume of Eliza's poems "for the comfort and good of the Church." She was informed that cost was the obstacle. As secretary of the Smithfield Branch of the Relief Society, Louisa was convinced that her fellow Relief Society sisters, not only in Smithfield but throughout the church, would be eager to subscribe to such a venture, and she fervently expressed this idea to Eliza and asked permission to draw up a circular announcing the intended project. Eliza gave consent, and with the help of Sarah M. Kimball, the venture was launched.[26] But Eliza cautioned later in a letter to Louisa:

Be particular with the sisters who receive subscriptions that the name of each subscriber and the amt. each subscribes be sent to you, so that in case anything shall prevent the publication, the money shall be refunded to each individual.[27]

Funds were raised for the publication, and Louisa's name was "introduced favorably among some of the leading sisters at headquarters"[28] because of her initiative and industry in that undertaking.

Just before Louisa was to enter school that fall, she received an urgent letter from home informing her of a serious illness requiring her presence. Without the necessary $7.50 railroad fare in hand, she was obliged to earn it as fast as possible, and so she spent an entire night writing a small collection of poems. In a cover letter she explained her situation, expressed admiration for the *Salt Lake Herald,* to whom she was submitting the poems, and requested an immediate reply. Early the next morning she took the envelope of poems to the *Herald* office, promising to return later. When she returned, she was handed a letter indicating a favorable response to her poems and containing the requested $7.50.[29]

Some time later at her home in Smithfield, she received a letter from Edward L. Sloan, editor of the *Salt Lake Herald,* indicating that a woman's paper was to be established in Salt Lake and that she had been selected as editor. Complimented but feeling unqualified, she declined the offer. Again Sloan wrote, informing her that it was her work that had inspired him with the idea of such a paper, and that if she further declined, the idea of a woman's paper would be abandoned. This time Louisa replied that if Eliza R. Snow approved the project and that if Brigham Young would call her to this assignment as a mission, she would accept it. With the whole-hearted endorsement of both, the *Woman's Exponent* was born, and Louisa Greene became Utah's first woman journalist.[30]

Years later in 1893 in response to a letter from Zina S. Whitney in behalf of her husband, Orson F. Whitney, who was then writing his prodigious four-volume *History of Utah,* Louisa indicated that after she had worked on the *Exponent* for a short time, she learned that the propriety of starting a woman's newspaper or "ladies' " magazine had been spoken of by some women in Salt Lake:

Sister Wilmarth East was one who told me that she herself had made reference to such an undertaking. . . . But Brother Edward L. Sloan first suggested the idea to me and his thoughts upon the subject were first awakened through my furnishing some little poems for the Salt Lake Herald. . . . *He first contemplated giving me work on the* Herald *but another member of the* Herald *Company did not agree with the plans he proposed. He then conceived the idea of starting a woman's paper, and favoring me with an opportunity of becoming its editor.*[31]

Louisa's only prior experience in editorial work was her work on the *Smithfield Gazette;* bringing that brief exposure to the demands and unrelenting deadlines of periodical journalism as her only stock-in-trade, Louisa, at age twenty-three, joined a select group of other women journalists then publishing in this country. Though most other avenues of employment were closed to women in the nineteenth century, the literary field, including journalism, embraced many talented and often courageous women. Considering the little preparation most women of that century had for such ventures, as well as the prejudices and disadvantages many of them had to contend with, their achievements were substantial.

By 1872, numerous women had already made names for themselves as writers and journalists in the east, but the exigencies of frontier life delayed such activities for western women. Thus it was that when the *Woman's Exponent* appeared in 1872, only two known newspapers edited by women were already publishing in the west: the *Pioneer* of San Francisco, edited by Mrs. E. P. Stevens, and the *New Northwest* of Portland, Oregon, edited by Abigail Scott Dunniway. Both newspapers, like the *Woman's Exponent*, were advocates of women's rights.

The *Woman's Exponent* first came into being in a small room in the home of Lorenzo D. Young, a great-uncle of Louisa's with whom she lived in Salt Lake City. Office equipment consisted of a table with writing materials, a few books, some magazines, and several chairs.[32] Louisa Greene comprised its editorial staff. She worked primarily alone until October 1873, when a consulting or executive committee was appointed. The October 15 issue of the *Exponent* for that year announced the appointment of Cornelia H. Horne as business manager and Mrs. Minnie Horne as secretary of the *Exponent* consulting committee. The November 27, 1875, issue dropped Cornelia Horne's name as business manager, and reported the name of Emmeline B. Wells as associate editor. Later that first year, the *Exponent* moved to its own quarters on "West Temple Street opposite the City Market, upstairs in the building being erected for the purpose."[33] It changed locations several times during its forty-two-year existence. The paper was an eight-page quarto size with three columns on each page and nine-inch by twelve-inch reading material. It was first printed by the Herald Publishing Company and was issued semimonthly at a subscription price of two dollars per year.[34]

In April 1872, preceding its first issue, a prospectus was circulated among the Relief Societies in the territory stating the purposes, intentions, and autonomy of the new periodical:

> *The women of Utah today occupy a position which attracts the attention of intelligent thinking men and women everywhere. . . . They have been grossly misrepresented through the press, by active enemies who permit no opportunity to pass of maligning and slandering them, and with but limited opportunity of appealing to the intelligence and candor of their fellow country men and country women in reply.*
>
> *Who are so well able to speak for the women of Utah as the women of Utah themselves? "It is better to represent ourselves than to be misrepresented by others!"*
>
> *For these reasons, and that women may help each other by the diffusion of knowledge and information possessed by many and suitable to all, the publication of the* Woman's Exponent, *a journal owned by, controlled by, and edited by Utah ladies has been commenced.*[35]

As an endorsement certain to win the support of the most traditional of its potential readers, the following paragraph concludes the prospectus:

> *Miss Eliza R. Snow, President of the entire Female Relief Societies, cordially approves of the journal, and will be a contributor to it as she has leisure from her numerous duties.*[36]

Louisa Greene's first editorial, entitled "Our Position," clearly stated her view of the paper's mission at the outset:

A woman's journal has come to be viewed as exclusively a medium through which woman's rights and woman's privileges must be discussed and strenuously advocated, in contradistinction to the rights and privileges of men. That is not our mission. We have no special need to advocate woman suffrage in Utah, for it is enjoyed by the women of the Territory. We have no particular wrongs to contend against, inflicted upon us by our husbands, fathers, brothers, or the male portion of the community; and no special claim to champion, throwing down the gauntlet against all comers. . . . We have no rivalry with any, no war to wage, no contest to provoke; yet we will endeavor, at all times, to speak freely on every topic of current interest, and on every subject as it arises in which the women of Utah, and the great sisterhood the world over, are specially interested.[37]

In the five years of her editorship, Louisa was more faithful to the promise of the latter half of "Our Position" than to the former. For suffrage *was* an issue of interest to the women of Utah. At least four allusions to women and politics appeared on the first page of the first issue of the *Exponent*, and thereafter it dealt consistently with this volatile subject, serving as a strong advocate for equal suffrage. The women of Utah had been enfranchised by their territorial legislature in 1870, which made suffrage a moot question for them; but, possessing that inherent right of citizenship themselves, Utah women were dedicated to the cause of extending it to all women.

Louisa Greene devoted twenty-one editorials to the subject of woman's suffrage while she was editor of the *Exponent*, and she continued to write numerous articles about it as a contributor to the paper in later years. She believed that the "fact that the motives of women are purer, their sentiments more refined and elevated than those of men, should be sufficient testimony that the right of suffrage ought to be conceded to them . . . that they may exert their more beneficient and chaste influences in endeavoring to purify the social atmosphere."[38] She also editorialized that if the rest of the world's men treated women as did the Mormon men, "gentlemanly and obliging in every true sense of the word," then there would be no necessity for woman's suffrage meetings being held all over the world. "Instead of spending time to establish the great truth that woman's voice as well as man's should be heard in all matters of public interest. . . ," she wrote, "these women might be employed . . . in any other good and useful pursuit."[39]

The young editor piloted her new journal into the mainstream of the woman's movement of her day, bringing notice and response to her paper beyond the perimeters of Mormondom. It enjoyed a lively exchange with most of the leading women's journals of that time, and it echoed the arguments of nationally prominent feminists in urging woman's right to vote as well as her right to equal employment and educational opportunities. The paper noted advancements of women in nontraditional careers and achievements, and it supported the "right of a woman to earn her living in any honorable career for which she has capacity."[40] As editor, Louisa declared to all who might have judged otherwise that "President Young proves himself to be the most genuine, impartial and practical 'Woman's Rights man' upon the American continent, as he has ever done; his counsel, instructions and advice to women being always directed toward their progress and advancement in usefulness and the possession of valuable knowledge."[41] Louisa's stance on these issues was continually reinforced by the contributors to her paper, and while it may not have reflected at all times the views of all Mormon women, or indeed of all women in general, she met no reproof for her position. She never, however, relinquished her perspective on priorities in the fervor of pleading "woman's cause." She wrote in 1872:

"With the right to vote, and the right to earn honest money by honest industry in pursuits from which women have been debarred is claimed the privilege to set natural laws and sound social regulations at defiance. It is demanded [by some] that the sacred bonds of marriage shall be disregarded whenever fleeting fancy desires change."[42]

To the latter sentiment, of course, she could not and did not subscribe, and she and other Mormon feminists made clear distinctions between temporal rights and eternal values.

While looking outward at the movements of her time that affected the status of women, Louisa also responded to the concerns and interests of women at home. Their involvement through the Relief Society in Brigham Young's far-reaching home industry program, for example, was extensive, and the value of this economic program was explained to *Exponent* readers in an editorial:

The community that chops its wood with imported axes, churns its butter in imported churns, clothes itself with materials brought from other countries or other parts of a country, imports its school books and its school teachers or sends its children abroad to be educated; and manages all its affairs in like manner, can never thrive and become wealthy like one which develops its own resources and is able to export instead of being obliged to import the common requirements which belong to civilized life.[43]

Louisa continually urged support of this program and called upon every branch of the Relief Society to "lay hold of the subject of home industry with a will and to take active part in bringing about the perfect organization of a self-sustaining people."[44]

Although Louisa did not enter the practice of plural marriage until some years after she resigned as editor of the *Exponent,* she was an ardent and articulate advocate in its behalf. In the first year of publication, she wrote eight strong editorials defending the practice of polygamy. One of her last editorials, written in May 1877, exemplifies the arguments that she and the many contributors to her paper advanced in support of this belief:

> The Mormon women trust in God, they have implicit faith in His promises; they are sincere and earnest in living practical lives, they are capable of great self-sacrifice; they believe God has spoken, and, true to the divinity of their natures, they are ready to honor Him and obey His commandments.
>
> How mistaken the world are, when they represent Mormon women in bondage to men. There is no greater freedom than the Gospel gives to woman. And it is this that makes Mormon women conscious of their power. They have suffered and become strong; experience has matured them, and given them a higher order of attainment than a mere mental education.[45]

Louisa had had an opportunity earlier to express her views on polygamy on a more personal basis. On June 16, 1873, she had married Levi W. Richards. A Chicago woman's paper, the *Balance,* which exchanged with the *Exponent,* reported that "the editor of the Salt Lake *Exponent* was married on the 16th ult. We are not informed whether she is Mrs. No. 1 or No. 12. If it is a matter of congratulation, we congratulate her." The new Mrs. Richards responded:

> We are pleased with this opportunity for stating that had our number, in entering upon the matrimonial stage, been Mrs. 2nd, 3rd, or 12th, we should have been as proud and happy in acknowledging the same as we are now in acquainting our Chicago friend with the fact that our position happens to be that of Mrs. No. 1—just the next thing to 0. But we are satisfied—there must be No. 1's, and there must be 0's too, but—poor things! We hope that does not touch any of our Chicago sister contemporaries, but are not informed. Now, we suppose "it" is "a matter of congratulation," and that we may accept the compliment.[46]

On June 16, 1884, eleven years from the date of her own wedding, Louisa welcomed into the family her husband's second wife, Persis Louisa Young. Persis was not new to the family; the daughter of Nancy Greene, Louisa's sister, and Franklin Wheeler Young, she had lived with the Richardses since she was fourteen, assisting her Aunt Louisa in the care of her children and household. Persis bore one son who died shortly after birth, and, unable to have more children of her own, she devoted her time to helping care for Louisa's children. Often while Louisa wrote and attended to her many church activities, Persis took care of the practical matters of the household as well. When their husband died in 1914, Persis and Louisa remained together in the family home for another thirty years. Persis often remarked that she felt it her duty to look after her Aunt "Lula." Though Persis was severely stricken with arthritis in her later years, she yet felt this responsibility and remained a companion, albeit a helpless one, to her sister-wife and aunt. Louisa lived to be ninety-five, dying in 1944. Persis died a few weeks after Louisa at the age of eighty-two.[47]

Two years before her husband's second marriage, Louisa wrote an article for the *Exponent* in which she described her conversion to the principle of plural marriage. She had experienced many doubts about it until adolescence:

> When I was fifteen years old, I began to realize the inconsistency of my being a staunch advocate of "Mormonism" in the main, while one of the vital principles, I could not say I understood or believed. One thing I acknowledged to myself, I had not striven diligently to find out for a certainty whether or not "Polygamy" was right. Instead of studying into it, I had simply looked at it, concluded it was a doubtful problem, and unheroically let it alone. I wanted to know about it for myself now, and began to pray earnestly for greater faith and light.... The Lord was merciful unto me, He heard my prayers, and the light came. Not suddenly, as it comes to some, but gradually and unmistakably. Not without many efforts on my part to grasp a ray when it was presented to me, to hold and nourish a gleam of truth when I got it, I learned to understand the principles of "Polygamy" very much as we learn to understand principles in mathematics or chemistry, and it seems as clear to me now as that two and two make four....[48]

Though the larger issues of woman's rights, polygamy, home industry, and other church affairs commanded most of the editorial attention of the *Exponent,* Louisa did not neglect other interests of her readers. She wrote frequently on domestic matters, particularly concerning the health and education of children, and she generously offered advice to parents, youth, and newlyweds (when she was hardly more than one herself). She had a special word for husbands:

> Husbands ... if you enjoy life at home better when your wife is sweet tempered and wears a smiling face than you do under the influence of fretful words or a cloudy countenance, don't be afraid to speak to her in a pleasant way and even to address her with endearing words.[49]

Speaking against "foolish" customs of her time and hoping to influence her readers toward self-improvement, she told them to "muster courage" under difficulties and to strive always for "sublimity of mind." She reminded them that "the first object of dress should be health, and next to that convenience," and not to imitate the fashionable ladies of the day with their "puffs and paniers, their beads and bawbles, false hair, disfigured forms, cramped feet, paint-spoiled complexions and general bogus appearance."[50] Louisa herself always dressed simply and modestly, wearing dresses nearly to her ankles, even though in the later years of her life fashion had moved the hemline considerably nearer the knee. She warned against reading "trash" (novels) as it "perverted the taste and hindered the advancement and development of the intellectual powers of the mind."[51] She consistently maintained that "self-reliance and self labor were the only true methods by which one could become intelligent or rich in any sense."[52] And unlike many women of her time, she sought to promote compassion and understanding toward her "fallen" sisters:

> *Women are at a decided disadvantage in regard to shortcomings. Faults which are excused in men become crimes when committed by women. . . . If women would look with a little more complaisancy upon all grades of her own sex, the yoke of injustice would not wound quite so deep or frequently as now.*[53]

Always a pressing need while Louisa was editor of the *Exponent* was obtaining sufficient copy for her journal. Enlisting the support of her family, Louisa wrote to her sister Lissie:

> *. . . I wish you would look about you a little more and try to jot down something every time that you think might be of public interest. Any little ideas no matter how commonplace coming from outer settlements give life to my paper and you know it is my business to keep it alive and nourish and brighten it up all the while. It is doing much good at home and some abroad, and if we can continue to make it grow, its mission will be a great one yet . . . remember when Sister Snow and I were there last summer, you promised to do something for the* Exponent. *It may be you will say, why does not Libie tell me of herself and not about that old paper. I'll tell you why. I want to see my sisters interested as well as other women in that which greatly concerns every true woman in Israel. When I get letters of congratulations and encouragement from poor, illiterate sisters who cannot write half so well as my own mother and her daughters and find they take an active interest in our paper I cannot sometimes help feeling grieved that with all the women in my father's family, not one exerts herself to aid my labors. I am jealous for my father's house. I think now you will write for the* Exponent.[54]

The August 1, 1877, editorial was the last one written by Louisa Greene Richards as editor of the *Woman's Exponent*. She had matured during her five years as editor, as had her paper, and she had established a solid base on which the *Exponent* would continue to meet its imperative for thirty-seven more years. She had written with the assurance and strength of deep-rooted convictions. She had tackled two of the broadest issues of her time concerning women—polygamy and suffrage. She had articulated the position of her people forthrightly and without equivocation. She clearly endorsed many of the basic issues of the nineteenth-century woman's movement, which struggled to obtain not only equal political rights for women but equal educational, economic, employment, and social opportunities. She demonstrated a knowledgeable grasp of the events of her day that affected Mormon women, and would probably have joined the ranks of the later nationally prominent spokeswomen of her faith had she not chosen a different direction for her life. Her "Valedictory" editorial ably defined that direction:

In announcing my exit from the editorial department of the Woman's Exponent *I do not feel that I am bidding its patrons and readers "a long and sad farewell;" but hope, as a contributor, to still communicate with them occasionally.*
. . . My general health is good, but my head and eyes need recruiting, and I have decided to humor them. I have also decided that during the years of my life which may be properly devoted to the rearing of a family I will give my special attention to that most important branch of "Home Industry." Not that my interest in the public weal is diminishing, or that I think the best season of a woman's life should be completely absorbed in her domestic duties. But every reflecting mother, and every true philanthropist can see the happy medium between being selfishly home bound, and foolishly public spirited.[55]

Perhaps the brief notice following that editorial gives the greatest insight into her motive for leaving the *Exponent* at that time.

A second little daughter was born to me on the 24th of June of this year. We named her Mabel Greene. I was blest with her sweet, happy presence only three weeks and three days. Although to all appearance strong and healthy from the first, she left us on the 18th of July, after a few hours' suffering, to join her sister and other blessed associates in the spirit world.[56]

In addition to serving in all of the church auxiliaries as well as being a member of the Primary General Board for twenty-five years, Louisa Greene Richards assisted Eliza R. Snow in organizing Primary associations throughout the church, and she travelled extensively as a representative to its various women's and children's organizations from Canada to Mexico. After the completion of the Salt Lake Temple, she was appointed to serve as a temple worker, serving in that position for forty-one years.

Louisa Richards continued an active literary life after leaving the *Woman's Exponent*, contributing hundreds of poems and stories to the *Exponent*, the *Deseret News*, the *Improvement Era*, the *Young Woman's Journal*, the *Children's Friend*, the *Relief Society Magazine*, and the *Juvenile Instructor*, whose department for "little folks" she edited for many years. She also contributed to other newspapers and periodicals throughout the intermountain region.[57]

In 1904 she published a collection of her poetry, *Branches That Run Over the Wall*. The next year, which was the centennial anniversary of the birth of the Prophet Joseph Smith, the Deseret Sunday School Union offered three prizes for the best poems written to celebrate that event. Louisa Richards won all three prizes. Many of her poems, including her first-prize poem in the Sunday School contest, were set to music, and they appeared in the church hymn book as well as in the Primary and Sunday School song books.

Louisa and Levi Richards were the parents of seven children, three girls and four boys. All of the girls died as infants. Levi (Lee) Greene Richards, their eldest son, became one of Utah's outstanding painters; Willard participated in the settlement of southern Alberta, Canada; Evan became a dentist; and Heber was a professor of English at the University of Utah.

A passage from a Centennial editorial that she wrote for the *Exponent* in 1876 well expresses the dictum of Louisa Richards' own life:

Let women shine by the intelligence of their own minds and not by that reflected from man. Let woman be qualified to stand alone, if necessar,, and then if she become a wife or mother, she can act with wisdom and judgment; and if her path be in smooth and quiet places, she is none the less womanly because of her innate powers. But should her lot be cast in rough and thorny paths, how great her need of strength from within and without to endure. Remember there are many lonely walks in life, and it is necessary to be well armed with courage and fortitude.[58]

Louisa Greene Richards' life knew both smooth and thorny paths, but she had armed herself well to meet them both. Her role as a "woman's exponent," though brief, displayed a vigorous determination to play it well. She is worthy to be remembered as Utah's first woman journalist.

Notes

1. The *Frontier Guardian* 1(May 16, 1849):8.

2. *Ibid.* 1(June 13, 1849):10.

3. *Ibid.* 2(August 21, 1850):15.

4. Louisa L. Greene Richards Papers, Daughters of Utah Pioneers Museum, Salt Lake City, Utah.

5. Helen R. Gardner, *Life of Levi Richards, 1799-1876, Some of His Ancestors and Descendants,* Logan, Utah: Unique Printing, 1973, p. 10.

6. Belle Palmer, "The Sojourn of the Mormons at Kanesville, Pottawattamie County, Iowa, 1846-1852," master's thesis, Colorado State College of Education, 1936, p. 8.

7. Gardner, p. 11.

8. Palmer, p. 66.

9. Louisa L. Greene Richards Papers, Daughters of Utah Pioneers Museum.

10. *Ibid.*

11. *Ibid.*

12. Gardner, p. 11.

13. Gordon Kay Greene, *Daniel Kent Greene, His Life and Times, 1858-1921,* Edmonton, 1960, p. 7.

14. *Ibid.*

15. Louisa L. Greene Richards Papers, LDS Church Archives, Salt Lake City, Utah.

16. Gordon Greene, p. 8.

17. Andrew Jenson, Manuscript History of Smithfield, Cache County, Utah, LDS Church Archives, Salt Lake City, Utah.

18. Louisa Greene Richards, Journal, April 8, 1867, Louisa Greene Richards Papers, LDS Church Archives, Salt Lake City, Utah.

19. *Ibid.,* June 20, 1867.

20. *Ibid.,* March 2, 1869.

21. *Ibid.*, March 6, 27, 1869.

22. Leonard Arrington, "Louisa Lula Greene Richards: Woman Journalist of the Early West," *Improvement Era* 72(May 1969):28-29.

23. Richards Papers, LDS Church Archives.

24. Gardner, pp. 25-26.

25. Eliza R. Snow to Louisa L. Greene, April 23, 1871, Louisa L. Greene Richards Papers, LDS Church Archives, Salt Lake City, Utah.

26. Lula Greene Richards, "How the Exponent Was Started," address delivered at Relief Society Conference October 6, 1927, in Salt Lake City, Utah, quoted in the *Relief Society Magazine* 14(December 1928):605-606.

27. Eliza R. Snow to Louisa L. Greene, November 16, 1871, Louisa L. Greene Richards Papers, LDS Church Archives, Salt Lake City, Utah.

28. Richards, "How the Exponent Was Started," p. 606.

29. *Ibid.*, p. 606-607.

30. *Ibid.*, p. 607.

31. Richards Papers, LDS Church Archives.

32. Richards, "How the Exponent Was Started," p. 607.

33. *Woman's Exponent* 1(October 1, 1872):69.

34. Andrew Jenson, "A Brief History of the Woman's Exponent," *Deseret News,* May 7, 1932.

35. *Woman's Exponent* 1(June 1, 1872):8.

36. *Ibid.*

37. *Ibid.*, p. 4.

38. *Ibid.* 1(August 1, 1972):36.

39. *Ibid.* 3(January 15, 1874):124.

40. *Ibid.* 1(October 1, 1872):68.

41. *Ibid.* 1(April 15, 1873):172.

42. *Ibid.* 1(June 15, 1872):12.

43. *Ibid.* 2(September 1, 1873):52.

44. *Ibid.* 3(March 15, 1875):156.

45. *Ibid.* 5(May 1, 1877):180.

46. *Ibid.* 2(August 1, 1873):33.

47. Gardner, pp. 140-142.

48. *Woman's Exponent* 11(November 15, 1882):94.

49. *Ibid.* 3(August 1, 1874):36.

50. *Ibid.* 1(July 1, 1872):22.

51. *Ibid.* 1(October 1, 1872):68.

52. *Ibid.* 1(December 15, 1872):108.

53. *Ibid.* 2(October 15, 1873):76.

54. Louisa Greene Richards to her sister Lissie, March 21, 1874, Louisa Greene Richards Papers, LDS Church Archives, Salt Lake City, Utah.

55. *Woman's Exponent* 6(August 1, 1877):36.

56. *Ibid.*

57. *Ibid.* 5(July 1, 1876):20.

Emmeline Blanche Woodward Wells 1828–1921

*For Judith Rasmussen Dushku and
Patricia Rasmussen Eaton-Gadsby,
sisters and authors, Emmeline B.
Wells has become a symbol and a
guide because of the latter's
beautifully combined submission to the
teachings of the Mormon Church at
the same time as her participation in
a rich variety of life's activities and
as her display of a strong,
independent, warm feminist spirit.
Judith Rasmussen Dushku is a
graduate of Brigham Young
University. She holds a master's
degree from Fletcher School of Law
and Diplomacy, and she completed the
classwork for her doctor of philosophy
degree at that institution in 1966.
She is a professor of political science
at Suffolk University in downtown
Boston. She has been a member of the*
Exponent II *staff from its
beginning, and it was through this
pursuit that she first came to
investigate Emmeline B. Wells. The
mother of three children, the author is
married to Philip Dushku.
Patricia Rasmussen Eaton-Gadsby is
introduced in their essay about
Augusta Joyce Crocheron.*

Emmeline B. Wells

Patricia Rasmussen Eaton-Gadsby and Judith Rasmussen Dushku

I feel very sad indeed my husband's affairs are very complicated indeed and we are obliged to practice the most rigid economy. I am determined to train my girls to habits of independence so that they never need to trust blindly but understand for themselves and have sufficient energy of purpose to carry out plans for their own wel-welfare and happiness.[1]

This quote from Emmeline B. Wells' diary of January 7, 1878, is characteristic of the philosophy of one of the Great Basin's most compelling and moving heroines. Most historians would look elsewhere than Salt Lake City in the nineteenth century for the glimmerings of feminism. But Emmeline B. Wells was one of the first and most persistent champions of her sex. Her own strong will and independence earned for her reverence from some and animosity from others. She was not universally loved, but she *was* universally respected. Yet her willfulness and instinct for self-preservation co-existed, almost incongruously, with a profound and sustaining faith in her God and a trust in her church and its leaders.

Emmeline was before all else a Mormon; and within this context, her contradictions become less incompatible. She endured ostracism and ridicule to be baptized, endured the persecutions of the Mormon stay in the midwest, and completed the trek west with all of its attendant hardships. She accepted many church responsibilities and was the devoted polygamous wife of two church leaders, Newell K. Whitney and Daniel H. Wells. She raised five daughters and suffered through the loss of her only son. She was a spokeswoman for her religion and a defender of polygamy to the entire world; and this ardent defense of the entire Mormon system committed her more and more totally to that system and increased her devotion and obedience to it.

History has often measured greatness by accomplishments, and using this scale Emmeline might well earn the title of greatness. But more fascinating and humanly rewarding is a knowledge of the woman herself. To know her is to be moved by her humanity and to be puzzled by her inconsistencies. She is one of those wonderful enigmas.

Emmeline believed that life had a purpose and that one had a kind of obligation to consummate that purpose. Mormonism revolves around several futuristic doctrines of predestination and salvation through works. Her Mormonism certainly validated her beliefs, but did not necessarily generate them. Her sense of purpose seemed to have been almost innate, and it seemed to have endowed her with a feeling of personal destiny that made her determined and indomitable and that left her with an unceasing desire to realize her potential and to succeed.

Emmeline frequently refers to others' "missions." In her eulogy of Susan B. Anthony, she wrote:

> *There are men and women born into the world at certain periods of time for distinctive purposes, with a mission to fulfill for their fellowmen* ...[2]

and she said of Eliza R. Snow, her good friend and the church's best-known female leader,

> *... let me say, although it may be looked upon with superstition, that I believe the Lord held in reserve certain women to practice the holy order of marriage and in my mind there is no doubt but that Sister Eliza was one of these chosen few.*[3]

Emmeline says that Eliza was aware of her "holy mission,"[4] and it appears that Emmeline was aware of hers. Her sense of purpose and destiny is apparent in her personal diaries and in her approach to her responsibilities. She writes frequently of her calling and the things she "must" do.

Early in her life and before the Mormon Church touched her, the very decision to become a Mormon was resolutely made amid the angry criticism of her conventional, God-fearing, New England community—a community into which she had fitted comfortably and by which she had been accepted and loved. Emmeline's mother embraced Mormonism while Emmeline was at boarding school. In 1842, at the age of fourteen, Emmeline returned home for a visit, and she too became converted and baptized. The baptism was attended by hecklers, many of whom had been her close friends, and she was totally ostracized by her schoolmates when she returned to school.[5] However, she remained adamant about her conversion, and she finished school with a teaching certificate but without a friend.

Her life was characterized by strong affiliations with causes and by the energetic pursuit of solutions to social and political ills. Her involvements were total and longlasting; Emmeline was not faddish in her interests or fickle in her commitments. She was always more able to demand for a group than for herself, yet her belief in her worth is evidenced in the letter written in 1852 to Daniel Wells that is virtually a marriage proposal. She had been recently widowed by Newell K. Whitney, a close friend of Daniel Wells, and Emmeline was in need of a husband and a means of support. While the letter is humble and self-effacing, that she should have written the letter at all is an example of her unique, determined spirit, for Daniel Wells was older and very influential and she had known him only casually. She calls the letter "A Letter from a True Friend," and in it she asks Daniel to "consider the lonely state" of his friend's widow. She asks him to remember his friendship with Newell Whitney and with her, and requests that he "return to her a description of his feelings for her." She implies this belief in her destiny when she says she has often seen herself "united with a being noble as thyself."[6] The marriage came to pass, although her relationship with Daniel Wells as his sixth polygamous wife was a bitter disappointment for her.

Em accepted many church and community responsibilities. Regardless of how much confidence Emmeline actually had in herself, she had respect for her pursuits. In fact, she may have *lacked* confidence in herself as a person, but she felt that her responsibilities transcended her self—that she had been called or destined to accomplish certain things for God and for people. For this reason, she felt her ideas were justified, her opinions were legitimized, and her actions were sanctioned.

As she became disillusioned with her personal life for various reasons, she became more self-sufficient, and she determined to accomplish great things and to create for herself happiness and satisfaction. Em's personal commitment sometimes became a need to control projects to the exclusion of others' participations. This was at least true of her editorship of the newspaper, the *Woman's Exponent,* a position that she held for nearly forty years. At one point an ambitious young woman, Susa Young Gates, was very anxious to participate in the publishing of the paper, or at least to write for it. When Emmeline did not respond to Susa's offer in a positive way, Susa inquired of Em's contemporary, Dr. Romania (Pratt) Penrose, how to become part of the *Exponent.* Romania suggested that Susa would have a better chance of publishing if she started her own paper. She said that the *Exponent* had initially been edited by a board, but

when the editorship passed on to Sister Emmeline's hands, she would never give any report of it to the committee and gradually the Board ceased to ask for one, and she now virtually owns the whole thing, and I presume would resent it as an impertinence for anyone to ask her the questions you propose.[7]

When Emmeline first began to write for the paper in 1873, she had wanted desperately to please the board, and her diaries express trepidation about presenting the board with her material. After she became editor she wanted just as desperately for the paper to be a success, and she apparently thought she could best achieve that by her own efforts. Her diaries almost daily describe how hard she is working and what an enormous and time-consuming task it is. As a result of her hard work, the paper did flourish. It was published bimonthly and often contained sixteen to twenty three-column pages. She became editor in 1877, and soon after that she became the publisher. *Woman's Exponent* was one of the first women's papers west of the Mississippi, but under Em's direction it became more than just a regional or religious paper. It included fiction and news from around the world, and contained discussions of political and sociological issues as well as commentaries on art, music, history, and medicine. It had an international circulation that included many non-Mormons. As time went on Em wrote more and more of the paper by herself, although she continued to accept articles from others both in and out of Utah.

Towards the end of her life a struggle developed over control of the paper, and there is some evidence that Emmeline wanted her daughter Annie to inherit the position, but many others objected to this.[8] Susa Young Gates still had literary ambitions, and she also had the advantage of the support of Joseph F. Smith, the president of the church. The problem was resolved when Susa was asked by Smith to edit the *Relief Society Magazine*, which simply replaced the *Exponent*, and Emmeline was therefore conveniently deposed. Many hard feelings resulted, but Susa's admiration is evident in the obituary she wrote years later for Emmeline:

> The dominant characteristic of Mrs. Wells' life was her supreme will. That she turned the current of this forceful will into peaceful channels of the Gospel of Jesus Christ made for righteousness and the building up of many good causes ... She might differ in methods or be widely separated from her associates in matters of procedure, for her ambitions were high, her purposes lofty; but through them all ran the thread of truth of her testimony which preserved her, which made of her a light set upon a hill.[9]

Many factors and combinations of circumstances contributed to the development of Emmeline's character. One of those factors was her family background. Emmeline was the seventh of ten children and the fifth of seven daughters. She was descended from a long line of successful New England landowners of comfortable means. She was born in 1828 in the little central Massachusetts town of Petersham, and though the town and Emmeline's family were

Congregational, Em calls her upbringing "Puritan."[10] (Emmeline must have meant puritan in values and style rather than in religious philosophy and practice.)

Emmeline's father, David Woodward, died in an accident when Em was only four, so she was raised by her mother, Diadema Hare Woodward, to whom Em refers as "a proponent of women's rights."[11] Just what she meant by this is unclear, but Diadema certainly encouraged Emmeline to educate herself and to make use of her opportunities. Emmeline started school when she was only three years old; she walked with her older brothers and sisters and spent part of each day napping underneath the teacher's desk.[12]

In later years she frequently recalled her childhood with fondness and nostalgia, and her daughters visited New England as adults to experience those places their mother remembered so lovingly.[13] Em's life as a child seems to have been carefree and secure. She remembers waking early and crying from the cold when she was very young, and an older brother leaving a treat for her on the mantle each morning to entertain and quiet her.[14] In a story published in the *Exponent* in 1888 she recalls an afternoon spent boating on a lake without parental consent. The story leaves the reader with feelings of quietude and contentment that one associates with lazy childhood summers. However, the puritan side of Em's upbringing balances the story and it ends with a near crisis that allows her to moralize:

Remember, discretion is the greater part of valor, and keep the propensity for romance always under the dictation of common sense . . . Our strongest and wildest passions beautify our life, but they require skill in their management and discipline and restraint, which is only to be obtained by carefully contrasting them with the stern realism of every day experience.[15]

Augusta Joyce Crocheron, a Mormon writer and biographer, wrote a sketch of Emmeline's life before Em died. Crocheron knew Em well, and apparently got much of her material firsthand from Em herself. Crocheron says, "There was a special destiny for her, undefined but nevertheless felt as something grand and great. So hovered the spirit of her mission around her through her childhood."[16]

Emmeline was an apt student and she was expected to accomplish and succeed. To encourage this gifted child, her mother took her to hear Daniel Webster speak and, when Em began to compose verses, took her with her poetry to visit John Greenleaf Whittier, who accepted her graciously and even praised her poems.[17]

Emmeline attended "a select school for girls" in New Salem, Massachusetts, and boarded with a married sister. She continued to do well, and she graduated when she was fourteen with a teaching certificate. This was the year of her traumatic conversion to Mormonism.

On July 29, 1843, at the age of fifteen, Emmeline married James Harvey Harris. Some sources say the marriage was arranged by Em's mother because James was the son of a presiding Mormon elder of comfortable circumstances.[18] However, Emmeline's diaries indicate that it was a marriage of love, and in later years she reflects frequently on James and their marriage, referring to him as her "dear husband" and commenting on their deep love and her "excited feelings" for him. It is the only one of her three marriages that she calls a "love-match"[19]; this may be because James, too, was young.

In 1844 they travelled to Nauvoo, Illinois, with James' parents and other Mormons to avoid persecution. The trip took about a month, and Emmeline's own account of the trip is positive and optimistic.[20] They arrived in time to meet the Mormon prophet, Joseph Smith, before he was assassinated in June 1844. Soon after their arrival in Nauvoo, the elder Harrises left Illinois and the church, and although they encouraged James and Emmeline to come with them, the young couple remained true to their faith. In September 1844, a baby boy, Eugene Henri, was born to them. Within a month this baby had died, and Emmeline had become very ill and almost died. Soon after, James did leave the church and Emmeline to seek his fortune in New Orleans.

Emmeline was devastated. When she recalled the incident in later years she told of the days of waiting for his return and how desolate, discouraged, and hopeless she felt. The diaries chronicle one miserable day after another, and her life seems to her like a nightmare. She cannot believe she has lost her child and her husband, and she continually watches for her husband's return. On one occasion she mistakes another man for James:

Last night there came a steam boat up the river. O how my youthful heart fluttered with hope. With anxiety my limbs were affected . . . not all that has yet been said can shake my confidence in the only man I ever loved . . . I watched the boat and looked out at the door. I walked a few steps out of the yard . . . I saw a person approaching. My heart beat with fond anticipation. It walked like James. It came nearer and just as I was about to speak his name, he spoke and I found I was deceived by the darkness. . . .[21]

Emmeline accepted an offer to live with a maiden lady, Olive Bishop, and she resumed writing poetry and teaching; she increased her involvement in the church. In later years she still remembered James fondly and blamed their youth and inexperience, rather than him, for his desertion. Her diary entry for September 1, 1874, includes many reflections about this period of her life, and she describes James as being

so young, and altogether unused to the world, we two so unsophisticated . . . having no idea of the stern realities of life . . .[22]

By 1845, Mormon Church leaders were admitting that polygamy was being practiced as a part of the doctrine of *Celestial Marriage.* This doctrine emphasized the importance of marriage, and held that, through specific ceremonies, marriages could become eternal, or *Celestial,* and that only through such ceremonies could one be assured of achieving eternal life. Of course, the most unique aspect of this new law was its encouragement of plural marriage—that is, that worthy men should take more than one wife at a time. The new doctrine caused considerable dissension among the members of the church.

Among the first to learn of the new doctrine were Newell K. Whitney and his wife, Elizabeth Ann. The Whitneys had been Mormons for about fifteen years, and Whitney was the presiding bishop of the church. The Whitneys had been intimate friends of Joseph Smith, and Whitney had given his eldest daughter, Sarah Ann, to Smith as a plural wife in 1843. Emmeline had become very close to this older couple and their children, and had probably even moved into the Whitney household.

During the winter of 1844 and 1845, the Whitneys taught Emmeline the principle of plural marriage, and in February 1845 Brigham Young performed the marriage ceremony between Newell and Emmeline, with Elizabeth Whitney as the only witness. Newell was fifty years old, Elizabeth was forty-five, and Emmeline was sixteen.

Emmeline's consent to this marriage resulted as much from her admiration for Elizabeth as from her love for Newell.[23] All available evidence indicates that the Whitneys were fine people; they are both praised and eulogized throughout Mormon literature for their admirable personal qualities as much as for their accomplishments. At this time Newell Whitney was inordinately busy with the government of the church and the financial arrangements for the trip west, and consequently Elizabeth spent much time with Em. They depended upon each other and became perhaps closer than Emmeline had ever been to anyone before. Everyone called Elizabeth "Mother Whitney"; Emmeline called her "Mother," and they remained the most faithful friends throughout their lives. It is not surprising that Elizabeth's eightieth birthday was spent at a party given by Emmeline and reported by the *Ex-*

ponent.[24] Em's diaries mention Elizabeth frequently, and even after Emmeline's marriage to Daniel H. Wells, she and Elizabeth travelled and dined together often and spent important family days with one another.

Newell K. Whitney had great confidence in Emmeline and had great respect for her intellect and abilities. On their marriage day he gave her a special blessing, in which he articulated his feeling that she was capable of assuming leadership responsibilities and that she would have tremendous influence in the building of the "kingdom" in the west.[25] This blessing confirmed Em's own belief in her calling.

The Whitneys, including Emmeline, began the trip west with the Heber C. Kimball Company in February 1846. Emmeline's first diary entries of the trek are cheerful and optimistic. She rather romanticized their lot by portraying them as "Eastern nomads," and her descriptions of the terrain and countryside are idyllic. She also enjoyed the conviviality of her fellow travelers; even the first nights spent in the rain were manageable and were valued as part of a great experience with nature.[26]

They arrived in Winter Quarters, Nebraska, during the summer of 1846, accompanied by Em's own mother. The summer remained bearable, but as the cold set in, spirits began to wane, and life became increasingly difficult. Em's diary entries stop. She was apparently teaching school as best she could, but most of the group's energies were devoted to survival. The cold was far more severe than they had anticipated, and there were serious food shortages. Many people died, including Em's mother.

They remained at Winter Quarters for two very long years, finally leaving with their number and spirits sorely depleted. It took five months to travel to the valley of the Great Salt Lake, and the trip was unexpectedly brutal. They arrived in October 1848. The fertile valley promised by Brigham Young was barren and dry. Indeed, the Salt Lake Valley in 1848 was a desert. Emmeline gave birth to Isabel Modelena Whitney soon after her arrival and remembers it thus:

*Nov. 2, 1874*M*This is Belle's birthday, she is twenty-six. What a contrast to the day when she was born, then the weather was severely cold and the wind blew fiercely, the snow, hail and sleet drove against our poor wagon and tents—the only homes we had.*[27]

The Saints went about settling the valley, Em took care of her baby, and taught both school and Sunday School. In August 1850, Melvina Caroline was born, and one month later Newell died suddenly, probably of pleurisy. His death shocked the community.

Elizabeth was left with nine children at home, and Emmeline was left with her two daughters. Emmeline was twenty-two years old.

Throughout her life Emmeline remembered Newell K. Whitney with tenderness and affection. From her diaries, in which she is often critical of others, Newell emerges as a fine man who encouraged her and treated her with sensitivity and concern. It is to Newell that she was sealed in a celestial marriage ceremony, and her plural marriage experience with the Whitneys left her with a life-long commitment to that institution.

Emmeline continued to teach, and she took medical courses at a nearby fort. It is not clear exactly when she met Daniel H. Wells or how well she knew him. He had been a friend of Newell's, but it is conceivable that Daniel and Emmeline were barely acquainted. He was an active, vital man who was respected for his leadership. He was a lawyer and landowner, and because of his land holdings he was called "Squire Wells" and "Justice of Peace" most of his life. He held many church and civic positions. After arriving in Salt Lake with Brigham Young in 1848, he had played decisive roles in establishing civil government in Utah, serving as Superintendent of Public Works for the Territory of Deseret under the governorship of Young, and also as Young's second counselor in the Mormon Church First Presidency. He organized the settlers' defense against the Indians, was Lieutenant General of the Nauvoo Legions (the Mormon militia), and was a brilliant military leader.[28]

Daniel had married before he joined the Mormons in Nauvoo, and his first wife left him after ten years of marriage when she learned of his intention to practice polygamy. She took their only son to Michigan and never saw Daniel again. Letters to Brigham Young from Daniel indicate that this was a tragic loss for him.[29] Though Daniel was a dashing figure and attractive to women, it appears that his ensuing marriages occurred more out of a sense of duty than out of love or passion. By the time Emmeline wrote to him her indirect letter of proposal, he had five other polygamous wives.

It is difficult to analyze this man's relationships with his wives, or even to describe the living arrangements accurately, since they changed from time to time. However, it seems that the wives lived alone in separate dwellings until 1862, when the luxurious and immense Wells Mansion was built in downtown Salt Lake City. Into the big house moved Louisa Free (the first plural wife), Martha Harris (the second), Hannah Free (the third wife and Louisa's sister), and Susan and Lydia Ann Alley (the fourth and fifth wives).[30] The Free sisters did not get along particularly well, and although

Louisa held a revered position as first wife, Hannah and Martha were more compatible with each other; they were more social, conventional, and at home with the management responsibilities that an influential family demanded. Hannah and Martha later moved into elegant dwellings of their own; the Alley sisters, less socially distinguished but good homemakers, later moved into their own home, leaving the big house temporarily to Louisa.[31] Emmeline is the only Wells wife who never lived in the mansion; instead she lived with her two Whitney daughters and the three daughters she had by Daniel: Emmeline Blanche Whitney Wells (Emmie), Elizabeth Ann Wells (Annie), and Louisa Martha Wells (Lou or Louie).

How much time Wells actually spent in Salt Lake City and how he divided his time and attentions among his many wives and children is not recorded. He did not, however, spend much time with Emmeline, and it is fairly clear that Daniel and Emmeline entered into their marriage for different reasons. For Daniel it was primarily a social and spiritual obligation, and he did fulfill his obligation to support Em and her children. For Emmeline, though, it was to have been her first real marriage. She had been deserted and widowed, but at the age of twenty-four she still had hopes of having a deep, mutually gratifying relationship with a man who loved her both spiritually and romantically. Just how she expected this man with five other families to play this role in her life is not clear, and Daniel should perhaps not be faulted for failing to meet the expectations of this woman he hardly knew. But fail her he did. And although Emmeline's mature years were busy and productive intellectually and politically, they were a personal disaster.

Emmeline's marriage to Daniel was a significant watermark. Her early background and her most unusual life of hardship, along with her Mormon belief in the eternal progression of the human spirit and the potential godhood of all people, had produced an independent, aggressive, and very nearly indomitable woman. It is for her strength of character, energy, self-sufficiency, and consequent accomplishments that she is honored. However, these later years too demanded enormous personal strength as she became reconciled to the fact that she would always be alone in a very personal sense and that she would always be dependent upon herself for emotional sustenance.

In her diaries of 1874 and 1875 she is frequently heavy-hearted, grief-stricken, and even, in her own words, "tortured" from lack of human understanding and lack of her husband's love and attention. On September 30, 1874, she says:

... O if my husband could only love me even a little and not seem to be perfectly indifferent to any sensation of that kind, he cannot know the craving of my nature, he is surrounded with love on every side, and I am cast out ... O my poor aching heart when shall it rest its burden only on the Lord, only to Him can I look ... every other avenue seems closed against me. ...[32]

On the anniversary of their marriage in 1874 she writes:

... Anniversary of my marriage with Pres. Wells, O how happy I was then how much pleasure I anticipated and how changed alas are all things since that time, how few thoughts I had then have ever been realized, and how much sorrow I have known in place of the joy I looked forward to. ...[33]

In her diary she dwells on her loneliness, searches for reasons, searches for answers, and longs for emotional support. This woman whom others saw as assertive and even as too outspoken sees herself as frail and needy. On the anniversary of her dead son's birth she writes:

The anniversary of Eugene's birth; he would have been thirty today ... it seems almost like a dream when I consider and reflect upon it; if he were here how much happiness he might bring to me: What a rock to lean upon What a shelter and protection his strong arm might be for his nervous and delicate mother.[34]

Emmeline often visited the big house hoping for a brief glance of this man whom she loved, and she usually came away disappointed. She saw him one evening at the theater, but he did not notice her and they did not even speak, though they were husband and wife. He did spend an evening with her now and then, but their meetings seem to have been characterized by a respect and friendship that remained distant. However, even the most brief encounter is recorded in her diary. Despite the frequent references in her diaries to her loneliness, she apparently never confronted Daniel with her unhappiness. A diary entry during 1879 reads:

Today it is 29 years since my last marriage. It calls up many tender remembrances of bygone days. My husband seemed to love me then. How is it today. Never has any unpleasant scene taken place between us, in all these years. Through trials that would pierce the inmost recesses of the human heart I have risen triumphant.[35]

This self-imposed burden of silence was all the more difficult because Daniel apparently had a more normal and rewarding relationship with Hannah. He lived at the mansion with Hannah, Martha, and Louisa, went out socially most frequently with Hannah, and it was she that he took to live with him in England when he was president of the British Mission and in Manti, Utah, when he became president of the Manti Temple.

Em's predicament totally frustrated her. In September of 1874 she wrote:

> ... *This evening I fully expected my husband here but was again disappointed. If he only knew how much good it would do me and what pleasure and happiness it brings to my subsequent days, he would not be so chary of his attentions, I suppose it is rather an exertion for him to come, he is not in want of me for a companion or in any sense, he doesn't need me at all, there are plenty ready and willing to administer to every wish caprice or whim of his indeed they anticipate them, they are near him always, while I am shut out of his life, and out of sight out of mind, it is impossible for me to make myself useful to him in any way while I am held at such a distance.*[36]

In addition to the rejection Emmeline felt from Daniel, she did not receive the support and companionship she expected from his other wives. Her experience with Elizabeth had been so good that it is safe to assume that she expected something similar from some, if not all, of Daniel's wives. When she was first married, she spoke of them with much fondness and deference in her diaries, and wrote many letters to them. She also sent Daniel messages through them and told them that she loved them and needed them and hoped to become a part of the "new relationship" existing between them and their husband.[37] They did not respond in kind and, in fact, there is some evidence that they were occasionally unkind to her. Abbie Wells, the daughter of Hannah's oldest son, Junius, and a grand old woman who still lives in Salt Lake City, has first-hand memories of the entire Wells clan. She recalls Hannah and Martha poking fun at the love poems Em wrote to Daniel.

Abbie Wells says Hannah and Martha considered Em "peculiar" and different from themselves. She was not an efficient homemaker, and she preferred to spend her time reading rather than housekeeping. She was not interested in high society, but she loved close friends and conversation that lasted until the wee hours. If these traits were not viewed by Hannah and Martha as actual faults, they were at least incompatibilities, and they estranged the other wives from her. She was also different in her appearance and in her attire.[38] Abbie remembers:

> *Aunt Em always wore long skirts (always in pale pastel shades) and always with long flowing scarves around her neck. She always wore rings and one on the first finger (the engagement finger in early days) the other on the third finger.*[39]

Emmeline was small and attractive, and in later years she often refused to conform to certain dress habits that were associated with women of her age. She would not wear dark colors, but preferred pastels, and would not wear violets because they were not youthful. She also refused to wear a veil over her face when other women her age did so. Even if the other wives did not actively dislike her, it is easy to imagine that this small, energetic, unconventional woman full of controversial ideas could have had an unsettling impact on any household.

In her diary Emmeline does mention lunching with Lydia Ann and Susan and occasionally with Louisa. But her social contacts with Hannah and Martha usually occurred only on official occasions, such as holidays and Wells family birthdays. During the Utah War there was an exodus south of hundreds of polygamous Saints, and Em moved to Provo, where she was lonesome and miserable. She wrote frequently to Daniel, complaining of her boredom and pleading for letters and visitors. She also wrote very affectionate letters to all five wives, but Hannah and Martha were the recipients of her greatest praise and her most numerous requests for attention. The returns from these requests were infrequent and unsatisfying.[40]

All of her disappointments, whether altogether real or partly imagined, threw Emmeline into frequent depressions and ultimately forced her to seek other means of fulfillment. Her most obvious outlets were her church and her political and literary activities both inside and outside the church. All of these activities were strongly influenced, motivated, and characterized by her philosophical beliefs.

Em was a Christian and a Mormon, a humanist and a feminist. Em's Mormon Christianity intensified her desires to serve her fellowman. Her Mormon belief in the worth of the human being and in each person's special calling and potential godhood legitimized her political support for human rights causes. She supported a fairly radical school of thought within the Mormon Church at that time that held that the true role of women—one of strength and purpose—was one of the eternal truths that was restored with the restoration of the gospel through Mormonism. With other Mormons who subscribed to this theory, Em regarded the coterminous emergence of the true gospel and the women's rights movement as no coincidence.

In many ways Em's Mormonism complicated her taking an active role in the national suffrage movement. In the first place, most non-Mormon feminists regarded Mormonism as inherently anti-female. They viewed polygamy, understandably, as an institution that subjugated women and relegated them to the inferior position of chattel. Many even thought that most Mormon women lived as prisoners who were forced into their marital arrangements and who were unable to escape. In fact, the feminist movement undertook for a long time to liberate the women of Utah by working to outlaw polygamy. However, the women who lived under the polygamous system and who were committed to it regarded polygamy itself as a liberating institution. They entered into polygamous marriages by choice, and they found that polygamy offered them more time for the outside pursuit of the companionship of other women and help with household duties. It also gave them a greater choice of worthy husbands, and gave every woman the opportunity to have children.

Secondly, the franchise was taken away from Mormon women in 1887 by the passage of the Edmunds-Tucker Act. The women of Utah had voted since 1870, when the territorial legislature had granted them the franchise. The Edmunds-Tucker Act was passed to discourage the practice of polygamy; however, it disenfranchised all women, not just polygamous women, and it did *not* disenfranchise the polygamous men. Mormon women were infuriated by this hypocritical act, which discriminated against the very women it purported to protect. For Em and other Mormon women this act encouraged commitment not only to suffrage but also to statehood for the Utah Territory, for only through statehood could the populace of Utah be responsible for passing their own suffrage acts.

As Em was philosophically a humanist and Christian, temperamentally she was an organizer, an orator, and a journalist. She combined these talents to further all of "her causes." Her primary literary outlet remained the *Exponent*. On its pages she commented intelligently on presidential elections, statehood, European diplomacy, slavery, and Congressional reform. Her editorials from 1877 to the 1890s confront all kinds of questions regarding women, from discrimination in penal codes and tax levies to inferior athletic training for girls. She wrote a great deal about securing rights for polygamous wives and their children, and she encouraged the women of Utah to increase their involvement in women's causes. However, her scope transcended the boundaries of the Great Basin, she frequently reproduced papers and speeches of women from around the world, and for over twenty years the masthead of the *Woman's Exponent* carried the motto: "For the Rights of the Women of Zion and All Nations."

Through her editorials she gained a podium from which she was free to expound on her favorite topics, and as she became more in control of the paper, she became correspondingly at liberty to speak out frankly. Her editorials are full of exhortations to women to stand up and proclaim their rights, to join organized movements, and to enrich their private lives by creating for themselves more stimulating and self-reliant roles.

She also wrote for other publications and for herself. Two of her papers, "Western Women in Journalism" and "Charities and Philanthropies," were published in the Chicago World's Fair Paper in 1893. In 1895 at the National Council in Washington, D.C., she delivered a lengthy paper entitled "Forty Years in the Valley of the Great Salt Lake."[41] She wrote poetry, much of it private and now lost, but she did publish one book of poetry, *Musings and Memories.* Many of her poems were sentimental treacle of the type that inundated the nineteenth century, but many of them were immensely personal and emotional and must have been one of the few ways in which this highly controlled woman gave vent to her most personal feelings.

As an organizer and orator, Em worked first within the church's Relief Society and later both within and without the church. She made speeches and tried to rally the women of Utah behind their own cause. She organized chapters of the Utah Women's Suffrage Association in local wards, and she participated in national organizations and conventions. The church leaders who were embarrassed by the widespread notion that Mormon women were subjugated and powerless encouraged Emmeline and women like her to represent them nationally. In 1879 church leaders asked Em and Brigham Young's daughter, Zina Young Williams, to go to Washington, D.C., for a meeting of the National Women's Suffrage Association. They presented a memorium to Congress asking that the children of polygamous marriages be considered legitimate, and in 1882 Em and Young's wife, Zina D. H. Young, travelled to an Omaha convention of the NWSA where Em delivered an exhaustive paper on Mormon life in Utah.

For the ten years that the Edmunds-Tucker Act was in effect, Em worked for its repeal and for the statehood that would allow Utah to pass its own suffrage laws. She participated in several drafting conventions for the new state constitution and she led the delegates who favored including a women's plank in that constitution. When statehood was finally granted in 1896, it was a victory for the church for several reasons, but it was also a victory for women, and Em was considered a prime contributor to that victory. For this reason Susan B. Anthony attended celebrations honoring Utah's statehood, and she publicly embraced and congratulated Emmeline B. Wells.[42] The relationship of Mormon women with other feminists was still tenuous. However, partly because of the mutual respect and affection that developed between Emmeline and Susan B. Anthony, Anthony and Elizabeth Cady Stanton prevailed upon their constituents in the important women's suffrage convention in 1890 and convinced them to accept Mormons once and for all into their ranks.[43]

Em's political pursuits had had some successes and some failures. She experienced first-hand the discrimination against women in 1879 when she was denied the office of Salt Lake City treasurer because of her sex, despite the unanimous endorsement of the county convention. In 1896, when she was nominated for the Utah legislature, she was forced to withdraw because it was not clear from the state constitution that women were eligible to run.

Despite these reverses, Emmeline had by that time established for herself an impressive reputation. In 1899 she went abroad for the first time to London for the Women's International Council and Congress where she was entertained by Queen Victoria, and she attended President William McKinley's inauguration in 1901. She was the chairman of the Utah Women's Republican League for a number of years, and in 1902 she was back in Washington, D.C., for the National Women's Suffrage Committee and Triennial of the Women's National Council, for which she was the first representative elected from a western state.

Emmeline's church callings were as time-consuming as were her outside activities. She was a leader of the Relief Society, the women's auxiliary organization in the Mormon Church, responsible for the welfare of every woman in the church. In a frontier state such as Utah, its task was enormous; the Relief Society provided guidance and instruction for women in every conceivable facet of their lives, and provided relief for any individual or family in the church. It was an efficient association and its standards were high. It exacted a prodigious amount of work from all who were involved, and Em had been involved since her Nauvoo days when Mother Whitney had been a first counselor to its first president, Emma Smith.

When the Relief Society was reorganized in Utah in 1866, Em was one of ten women called to lead it. In 1888, she was made a member of the general board—the executive body—and she helped organize two equally ambitious organizations, the YLMIA, a young women's organization, and the Primary Association, which undertook the instruction and development of children. In 1892, the Relief Society incorporated with 50,000 members, and Emmeline became the general secretary. She held this position until 1910, when she became president. Under her leadership, a department to provide burial clothes for all Mormons was added, as was an extensive Welfare Department. The Welfare Department had the huge responsibility of feeding and clothing all needy Mormons—a task that required most efficient leadership.

She had also been called upon in 1876 to head a grain-saving project. This project was conceived by Brigham Young as a food storage endeavor that at first focused on the needs of Utah, or at least western Mormons. Em accepted full responsibility for the success of this organization; its success was such that in 1918 President Woodrow Wilson called upon Em and her committee to provide Europe with grain during the final stages of World War I. The organization's grain was donated to Europe, and Em was rewarded with a private audience with Wilson just before his death and hers.[44]

Considering the vastness of Emmeline's undertakings, it is difficult to conceive of her having time for personal relationships of great depth. However, despite the disappointments of her associations with the Wells family, she had many lasting friendships and was unusually close to her daughters. In her diaries, hardly a day goes by but that several friends "come calling" and visit for long afternoons or evenings or entire days. It was not unusual for her to stay up until two in the morning talking with friends, and she often went visiting simply to boost her low spirits. Because her marriage to Daniel was not personally rewarding, her friendships with others were even more important. She counted among her friends most of Utah's most influential female leaders. Eliza R. Snow and Zina D. H. Young were particularly close to her, as was Mother Whitney until her death in 1882.

Em and her friends met to carry out various service-related church obligations and also to consciously lift one another's spirits and to "bear testimony to the Gospel." Mother Whitney spoke in tongues, and such special occasions were often seen as cures for spiritual ills. The women also ministered to each other's physical ills.

Em's diaries do not indicate the extent to which she unburdened her personal frustrations to her friends, but she does mention discussing polygamy. In one entry she describes visiting a young woman who has just entered into a polygamous marriage, and she has many questions to ask Em and some of the older women. Em despairs at her naivete, implying that the girl is too inexperienced for the older women even to be able to prepare her for the marital realities she will soon face.[45]

Em loved and appreciated her friends for themselves—for their individuality. Abby Wells recalls that Em regarded herself as unique, and that she consequently encouraged or at least accepted peculiarity in others. Abby's mother, Helena Fobes, was an "orphan girl" from Boston who was not yet a Mormon. Hannah Wells thought Helena was beneath her son Junius, and never fully accepted her even after Helena joined the church. Em, on the other hand, not only welcomed but befriended Helena, and when

Helena and Junius separated for several years and Helena returned to Boston with Abby, it was primarily Em who kept in
touch with them.

Abby herself had mixed feelings about Em's uniqueness. She re-
calls in a recent letter one visit that Em made in the east when
Abby and her mother were there. Abby was invited to accompany
Em to an important meeting, and says:

> *I was rather a snob and felt a little embarrassed when I was told I was to take
> Aunt Em to, I believe the Plaza (Hotel in New York City). It was near Central
> Park.*
> *I remember a large room and a lot of women. Before that meeting was over Aunt
> Em was the figure of attention (that small tiny oddly attired person) she was the
> one who knew all the Rules of Order and the proper procedure.*[46]

Abby remembers Em gratefully, however, as the aunt who always brought her books and took the time to talk with her about
the important things, such as world events.

The three Wells daughters lived with Em but visited their father
frequently. Belle and Mellie Whitney appear to have accepted
them as full sisters; they were close in age and lived together in
the same household for several years before the older Whitney girls
married. Em was close to her daughters, and they were rewarding
children who returned her love and esteem. Every diary entry
makes some mention of some of the girls' activities, and Em expresses many worries over their pursuits, social life, loves, and illnesses.

She seems to have been as sensitive to the differences in each
child as she was to the individuality of her friends. She admired
Belle's abilities to manage her young family, and called her "a superior woman for her age."[47] Mellie was strong-willed, but not
strong in her commitment to Mormonism. Em prayed about Mel's
lack of faith, but did not forbid her to follow her own path outside the guidelines of the church. Emmie Wells was the object of
Emmeline's adoration, and was frequently described by Emmeline
as "sweet," "precious," and "devoted." Emmeline loved the evenings Emmie and the younger girls spent at home entertaining
friends with their singing and playing. Emmie's accidental death
at the age of twenty-four was another tragic loss for Emmeline.
Annie Wells was always described as being most like her mother.
She read many books and was a participant in literary clubs and
intellectual organizations. Em's youngest girl, Louie, was a most
beautiful and talented woman, and she studied music and art in
the east. She also died early at the age of twenty-five, only two
years after Emmie's death.

Emmeline's life yielded enormous rewards: her successes, her reputation, her position in and out of the church, her friends, and the love of and for her daughters. Despite these rewards, it is apparent from her diaries that life for her was a continual struggle. She frequently fought off depression, or what she referred to variously as "not feeling well in my mind," "low-spiritedness," "being haunted by dreams," and "nervous attacks." She expressed often the feeling of being unable to endure any longer her loneliness and despair. Her private suffering is evident. However, to present her as maudlin and self-pitying would be both unfair and inaccurate; most descriptions of her note her optimism and enthusiasm. It would be equally unfair to represent her as entirely satisfied and confident; this diminishes her depth and denies her humanity.

Perhaps it is fair to say that whatever Em experienced, she experienced with totality. She greeted each day, each project, each feeling with an intensity that gave that day or project or feeling a quality of immediacy. She used her experiences to *create* a satisfying life for herself—to become responsible for her own goals and her own happiness. A most unusual quality that emerges from her diaries is her almost total refusal to assign blame or her own disappointments to individuals or even institutions. She simply recognized the disappointment and resigned herself to more hard work. She capitalized upon both defeat and success, and compensated for failure with yet more achievement.

Most unusual for a woman of her time and place, her devotion to Mormonism never impeded or undermined her inherent humanism. Emmeline *was* a humanist—not only a believer in the human spirit, but also a believer in the human being. She developed through her tragedies and joys a world view of the human condition that transcended her parochial environment. This view helped create for her a unique and important place in the vast design of history, and also in the hearts of each unknown woman whom her life touched.

Notes

1. Diary of Emmeline B. Wells, January 7, 1978, Emmeline B. Wells papers, Harold B. Lee Library, Brigham Young University, Provo, Utah.

2. Emmeline B. Wells, *Young Woman's Journal*, 1907, quoted in Ida Husted Harper, *The Life and Work of Susan B. Anthony*, vol. III, Appendix, The Hollenbeck Press, Indianapolis, 1908, p. 1582.

3. Emmeline B. Wells, "Pen Sketch of an Illustrious Woman," *Woman's Exponent* 9(Sept. 1, 1880):50.

4. *Ibid.* (August 1, 1880):33.

5. Augusta Joyce Crocheron, *Representative Women of Deseret*, J. C. Graham and Co., Salt Lake City, 1884, p. 64. Also, Mario S. DePillis, "Emmeline B. Wells", in *Notable American Women*, Edward T. James and Janet Wilson James, eds., Harvard University Press, Cambridge, 1971, p. 561.

6. Emmeline B. Whitney (later Wells) to Daniel Wells, March 4, 1852, Emmeline B. Wells papers, LDS Church Historical Department Archives, Salt Lake City.

7. Dr. Romania B. (Pratt) Penrose to Susa Young Gates, June 26, 1888, Joseph F. Smith Collection, LDS Historical Department Archives, Salt Lake City. (See also Susa Young Gates to E. B. Wells, May 5, 1888, Jos. F. Smith Collection.)

8. Minutes of the Relief Society General Board, April 3, 1914, September 24, 1914; vol. 5, 1914, p. 13. (LDS Historical Department Archives).

9. Susa Young Gates, *Improvement Era* 24(June 1921):719.

10. Crocheron, p. 63.

11. *Ibid.*, p. 67.

12. Jane Cannon King, "Daughters of Utah Pioneers History of Emmeline B. Wells", unpublished manuscript, LDS Historical Department, Salt Lake City, p. 11.

13. Melvina Caroline B. Whitney, "Letter from Mel", *Woman's Exponent* 9(Aug. 15, 1880):46.

14. King, p. 11.

15. E. B. Wells, "When We Went Gypsying", *Woman's Exponent* 9(June 1, 1880):7.

16. Crocheron, pp. 62-63.

17. Susa Young Gates, pp. 718-21.

18. King, p. 1.

19. E. B. Wells Diaries; see especially February 28, 1845; September 1, 1874; and September 4, 1874, Harold B. Lee Library, Brigham Young University, Provo.

20. *Ibid.*, May 1844.

21. *Ibid.*, February 28, 1845.

22. *Ibid.*, September 1, 1874.

23. Crocheron, pp. 65-67; also see E. B. Wells diaries, February 23, 1874; February 14, 1875.

24. Andrew Jensen, *Latter-Day Saint Biographical Encyclopedia,* vol. II, Andrew Jensen History Co., Salt Lake City, 1901-1936, pp. 563-64.

25. Crocheron, pp. 65-67.

26. E. B. Wells diaries, February 27, 1846, to May 4, 1846.

27. *Ibid.*, November 2, 1874.

28. Letter from Emmeline Y. Wells, August 15, 1937. (From personal papers in possession of Jeanne Kimball Hill).

29. Daniel H. Wells papers, LDS Historical Department, Salt Lake City.

30. See Annie Wells Cannon, chapter 18, "Home and Family Life," in Bryant S. Hinkley, *Daniel Hanmer Wells and Events of His Time,* Deseret News Press, Salt Lake City, 1942, pp. 337-362.

31. Abbie H. Wells, interview with Judith R. Dushku, August 1975, Salt Lake City.

32. E. B. Wells diaries, September 30, 1874.

33. *Ibid.*, October 10, 1874.

34. *Ibid.*, September 1, 1874.

35. *Ibid.*, October 10, 1881.

36. *Ibid.*, September 13, 1874.

37. Letters from E. B. Wells to Hannah Wells, also Martha, Louisa, Lydia Ann Wells et al., May 1858, E. B. Wells papers, LDS Historical Department, Salt Lake City.

38. Abbie H. Wells, interview with Judith R. Dushku, August 1975, Salt Lake City.

39. Abbie H. Wells to Judith R. Dushku, March 27, 1975.

40. E. B. Wells papers, LDS Historical Department, Salt Lake City.

41. DePillia, pp. 562-63.

42. For Emmeline B. Wells' own account of the suffrage activities in Utah and her role in them, see Susan B. Anthony and Ida Husted Harper, eds., *The History of Woman Suffrage,* Rochester, N.Y., Susan B. Anthony, 1902, vol. IV, pp. 936-956.

43. Alma Lutz, *Created Equal: A Biography of Elizabeth Cady Stanton,* The John Day Co., New York City, 1940, pp. 270-71, 281-82.

44. Olga W. Snell, "Emmeline B. Wells and the Relief Society", unpublished manuscript taken from a personal account by Annie Wells Cannon, and from the *Relief Society Magazine,* October 1940, pp. 613-51, and the *Improvement Era,* (March 1941).

45. E. B. Wells diaries, September 5, 1874.

46. Abbie H. Wells to Judith R. Dushku, March 27, 1975.

47. E. B. Wells diaries, March 23, 1875.

Augusta Joyce Crocheron 1844–1915

*Patricia Rasmussen Eaton-Gadsby
was born in Rexburg, Idaho, from
Mormon pioneer stock. She graduated
from Western Michigan University in
secondary education with an English
major. She is married to Sandy
Gadsby, and their combined family
consists of three children. Presently
the author is a housewife/mother;
previous to this she was employed by
a variety of OEO offices, including
Job Corps and Headstart. She has
also worked for Model Cities in
Boston. She has discovered a new
exhilarating interest in Mormon
women of the early frontier era:
"Considering the relative ease of my
own life, I am in awe of their
difficult lives and their strong survival
sense. I am intrigued by their
humanity and the complexity of their
relationships with their husbands and
with each other. I am excited by their
political activity and their connection
with the feminist movement of the
latter part of the nineteenth century."
Her sister, Judith Rasmussen
Dushku, coauthored this essay; she is
introduced in another essay that the
two sisters wrote.*

Augusta J. Crocheron

Judith Rasmussen Dushku and Patricia Rasmussen Eaton-Gadsby

Augusta Joyce Crocheron was one of the few female writers to emerge from the Great Basin Kingdom of Mormon Utah during the nineteenth century. That century was not known for its plethora of successful women writers, so despite the fact that Crocheron was not a great writer, she is interesting in an historical sense for several reasons.

First of all, she deserves some recognition for herself as an individual; she had her own history and her own life with its attendant triumphs and tragedies that make her interesting as a pioneer woman. Secondly, she is interesting as a reflector of her time and culture and as a product of it. Thirdly, she is important not only for her reflections of an era but for the contributions she made to literature, history, and Mormon culture.

Little biographical material is available about Augusta. The most complete biography is included in her own book, *Representative Women of Deseret,* a collection of biographical sketches of her contemporaries. She included herself in the collection only at the insistence of Emmeline B. Wells, and it is interesting that the better part of that autobiography consists of material about her mother and other ancestors and little about Augusta herself.

She was born on October 9, 1844, in Boston, the daughter of John Joyce and Caroline A. Perkins Joyce. It appears that she knew little about her father's background except that his parents were English and came via New Brunswick. However, Augusta often mentions her mother's ancestors, and she uses them in her writings. Her maternal great-grandfather was John Harriman, who was a companion of Lorenzo Dow, a well-known traveling preacher of the day. According to Augusta, Harriman at the age of twenty-one received a visit from a personage who gave him "a new doctrine to teach to the children of men."[2] He started the New Light Christian Baptist Church and traveled a circuit, building a large following.

The Harrimans' son, also John Harriman, became a preacher like his father, but their daughter Caroline, Augusta's grandmother, had a "more worldly spirit" and turned away from religious pursuits. She eloped with a handsome sea captain when she was only sixteen. She was bright and vivacious and loved to dance, but she was also very industrious (she had spun all her own bed and table linen by the time she eloped). She was also a politician—her home was used by many young men of the day as a meeting place for political discussion, and Caroline's opinions were an indispensable component of those meetings. Caroline was also a patriot: she wrote political articles; she composed and sang patriotic and campaign songs; and she willingly sent eight sons off to serve in the Armed Forces. She was an "Andrew Jackson Democrat," and she even named one son Andrew Jackson. She was strong-willed and direct—"no circumlocution about *her!*" says Augusta.[3]

The eldest daughter, also named Caroline, was Augusta's mother. When she converted to Mormonism as a young woman, her parents sent her to live with relatives, hoping she would come to her senses. A voice told her that if she remained true to her conversion and abandoned her parents she would have eternal life. Despite the remorse she felt for causing her parents such unhappiness, she remained a Mormon. She married John Joyce, also a Mormon, and together they sold all of their possessions, traveled to New York, and set sail for California with the Samuel Brannan expedition in 1846. Augusta was almost two when they began this voyage that evolved into a miserable, hot, disease-ridden nightmare lasting almost six months. It ended in Yerba Buena, or what is now San Francisco, a dreary, barren land that was embroiled in the turmoil of the war with Mexico. There are some discrepancies between Augusta's account of the dates of the trip and the history of the Brannan expedition,[4] but Augusta was about two years old when the family arrived in California. Her only sister, Helen, was born there on August 1, 1847.

Conditions on the ship had been unlivable, and Yerba Buena afforded little relief. Life was unexpectedly grim. The settlers lived in abject and unanticipated poverty and in terror of the surrounding Mexicans. The sixteen Mormon families moved into an old adobe building and partitioned it by hanging quilts. They rarely had enough to eat and were frequently sick, and communications with the outside world were poor. Augusta's short stories that refer to this period portray the settlers as a discouraged and isolated group, set off from their civilized homeland in alien and threatening surroundings.[5] These desperate conditions probably contributed to the apostasy of many of the Mormon settlers, including Samuel Brannan.

In 1849, however, gold was discovered, and some enterprising Mormons capitalized on the discovery and many became wealthy. This wealth, together with the worldliness and materialism that often accompany it, was seen by Augusta as another reason why many more Saints left the church. Among these was her father, who then became an alcoholic and dissolute rake.[6] He and her mother soon separated.

Augusta's mother remained devout in the Mormon faith and married Colonel Alden A. M. Jackson, a convert to Mormonism. He was an honest and considerate man and became a kindly father to the Joyce girls.[7] It is probably to him that Augusta's poem, "To My Father," is written. In it she says:

> And thou art gone! If thou hadst lived
> This book of mine to read
> Hadst thou approved and kissed my cheek
> I had been blessed indeed.[8]

Much harassment was visited upon Jackson and his family during the period of the Utah War in the late 1850s, and this prompted him to move his family to Utah, where they settled permanently in 1867.

Little is known about Augusta's personal life. She was an active participant in church activities and held many leadership positions. She married George Crocheron as a second plural wife in 1870, and they settled in St. George, Utah, where her parents had lived. She mothered three sons and two daughters. Her most consuming interest outside of her family and church was her writing. She wrote extensively for Mormon journals, winning medals two years in a row for short stories published in the Contributor.[9] Her publications consisted of an 1881 book of poetry, Wild Flowers of Deseret,[10] Representative Women of Deseret (1884), and a book of children's stories and poems, The Children's Book (1890).[11] She did not publish for the nearly two decades preceding her death in 1915.

As a poet, Augusta was not a great literary figure. However, she was typical of many poets of her time—no better, but certainly no worse than many Victorians who received more acclaim. The nineteenth century spawned much overdone, overblown, over-sad poetry, abounding with mixed metaphors, trite similes, and forced rhymes and meters. Indeed, it seems that every farm, village, shop, and rectory yielded its own poet, and it is difficult to arrive at any criteria for what was considered good or bad writing.

Augusta's poetry certainly fell into or out of that Victorian mold. It is very similar to the work of Lydia Sigourney and more specifically to that of Lucy Larcom, another Massachusetts woman with very strong religious convictions. In fact, Augusta's *Wild Flowers of Deseret* was published just two years after Larcom's book, *Wild Roses of Cape Ann*.[12] Augusta forced her rhythms and dressed up lines by using such words as *adown* for *down* and *aborne* forborne. She forced her rhymes with the constant inversion of noun and adjective, leaving too many lines with endings like "pathways rude," "volumes new," or "visage saintly." She possessed that Victorian urge to personify almost everything—inanimate objects, emotions, qualities, life, and what-have-you. Her poems have many of these ecstatic bursts of emotion that present themselves as "O! Life!" or "O Death!" She used the dialogue as a poetic vehicle, as many of her contemporaries did, leaving us with dramatic debates between such things as Truth and Reason, Heart and Head. She was responsible for her share of trite similes—poems are like flowers, some are sweet and some have briars, and:

> Truths like berries oft are borne
> On vines that show full many a thorn.[13]

However, in all of these ways she was representative of most of the minor poets, both male and female, of that period.

Her subject matter also reflects what was acceptable during that era. In their book *The Stuffed Owl*, D. B. Wyndham Lewis and Charles Lee say of the Sweet Singer of Michigan, Julia Moore, a contemporary of Augusta:

> ... her verse is concerned to a large extent with total abstinence and violent death—the great Chicago fire, the railway disaster of Ashtabula, the Civil War, the yellow fever epidemic in the South. She sings of death by drowning, by smallpox, by fits, accident by lightning stroke and sleigh. She also greatly relishes infant mortality, especially in cases where the little victim possesses blue eyes and curling golden hair.[14]

Augusta's propensity for the maudlin does not begin to compete with Moore's; however, her bent for pathos is there, and her subject matter is often similar to that of Moore and the other sentimental Victorians. She wrote of tragedy, especially tragedy in which children or young wives figure. Both her stories and poems are full of memories and nostalgia and lessons to be learned from life's woes. She longs for loved ones who are gone, for her childhood, and for carefree times and lost loves. She agonizes over life's difficulties and wonders at the meaning of it all.

However, Augusta made certain valiant strides. Though some of her descriptions are trite, she has some lovely moments, such as:

> The dying day sank faintly down
> Her golden light spun out in threads.

and,

> Then trooped the living colors back
> To heaven from whence their light had strayed.[15]

She also made successful attempts at blank verse. The results were quite good, and certainly indicate her progressive spirit. She was not totally devoid of a sense of humor as were many Victorians. She was most often serious, but her poem, "Trophies Taken in Love's Warfare," hints at the presence of humor and presents an almost modern view of ex-lovers:

> Ah, might every woman true,
> Love's warfare done, in peace discover
> Honor in every victory
> And a life-long friend in every lover.[16]

Augusta gained more popular success as a prose writer. She published two books and many short stories in journals. The stories in her *Children's Book* are undistinguished and are unfortunate testimony to her kinship with the Sweet Singer of Michigan. They are, for the most part, highly sentimental and moralistic narratives of personal tragedy. All characters who do not display righteous emotion and follow with righteous action are doomed to a tragic recompense. However, in Augusta's defense, her *Children's Book* does not differ from dozens of other children's books of the time—books designed to teach morality to children by example and by striking the fear of God into them.

Representative Women of Deseret is a collection of eulogies quite lacking in objectivity, which is intended to acquaint the many who are strangers to Mormon women with their labors and their virtues, to convince others by their noble lives that God was with them, and to teach young people to appreciate and honor their parents.[17] Mormons, and particularly Mormon women, were much maligned at this time because of society's view of polygamy as a heinous system that encouraged lustful and unfaithful husbands and jealous wives. Anti-Mormon literature portrayed Mormon women as weak and crude, oppressed and ignorant. And Mormons in general were condemned as unpatriotic for not upholding the law of the land and unchristian for violating the laws of God. That Augusta should write a strong defense of the virtues of her contemporaries was both timely and courageous.

In discussing *Representative Women*, it is also appropriate to consider one of Augusta's more popular and significant short stories, "Angela,"[18] which predates *Representative Women* and which was named by the *Contributor* as the best story of 1884. The Angela of the title is Augusta's mother, Caroline, and the story is a highly romantic, biographical account of this near-perfect woman. It begins:

You say you want a heroine, young, beautiful, gifted and yet with a cross to bear, a life shadowed and burdened by sorrow and trial . . .[19]

Caroline Joyce did indeed suffer many hardships and survive admirably. She bore up under the cruise from New York to California, the poverty and fear of the early California days, and the desertion of a profligate husband. The story "Angela" and the sizable portion of Augusta's autobiographical sketch in *Representative Women* devoted to her mother evidence a respect for her mother that approached a compulsion to immortalize.

It is interesting that Augusta often cites the same qualities that her mother possessed as the most admirable traits of the subjects of *Representative Women*. In "Angela" she frequently mentions her mother's generosity and selflessness. Under the most extreme circumstances her mother shared all she had with others—friends, strangers, and even enemies. She communicated and shared with the Mexicans even when it was dangerous to do so. She extended her hospitality to the Donner Party and to other travelers and missionaries whom she did not know. She cared untiringly for the orphans of the cholera epidemic, and eventually started an orphanage that she administered for several years.[20] This praise of selflessness is echoed throughout *Representative Women*.

Augusta also admired women of strength—strength of character, strength of purpose, strength of conviction, strength to endure. Most of the women in her book were contemporaries of her mother and had come to Utah under most difficult circumstances, many trudging behind handcarts. That they tolerated such a journey was a credit to their stamina and will, as was Augusta's mother's survival of her trip. They had to endure many personal losses and tragedies as a consequence of their devotion to a scorned and vilified church. The women in *Representative Women* have one and all an instinct for survival that sustains them without compromising their beliefs or character.

Despite this "salt of the earth" ability to conquer the wilderness, aesthetic sensibility and an affinity for refinement were important to Augusta. She frequently mentioned her mother's sweet voice and the fact that she was the first woman in San Francisco to teach melodion lessons.[21] Augusta commented on artistic and musical talents with the same enthusiasm that she allotted to kindness and strength.

Augusta also valued the ability to integrate a variety of political, cultural, and religious activities into the roles of wife and mother. Motherhood was deemed a divine and sanctified calling, and the family was viewed as an eternal unit, perfect in its organization and as inviolable and necessary for an individual's salvation. The domestic demands of the frontier were great, yet most of the women in the book found time for civic and church involvement as well. The church was particularly important to Augusta, for it was the common bond that made the women of *Representative Women* a cohesive group. Religious conviction, a strong testimony of Christ, and the courage to remain steadfast in time of persecution were necessary to earn a chapter in Augusta's book. However, the church was also an institution of activities, meetings, and organizations, and each of the women held many positions of leadership and participated in the organized activities of the church as well as carrying on many personal labors, inspired by conscience, for the sick and needy. The women also shared among them many contributions to community projects and to cultural and political affairs. Augusta specifically praised those who fought for suffrage and statehood and for the rights of the oppressed.[22]

That the women who appear in *Representative Women* deserved a place in the history of the frontier is unquestionable. Augusta's romantic style depicts them as saints, but even without her words, the exemplary life of each woman bears adequate testimony to her strength, integrity, and goodness. Augusta's descriptions are no more overdone than are other biographical essays of that time.

Nevertheless, there are certain aspects of the book and of Augusta's other writings that are unique. Augusta was something of a women's advocate; her literature had a feminine orientation. Her most honorable characters were women, and she endowed her heroines with various meritorious qualities. Though her fiction contains some women who were used up by circumstances, these characters were more than balanced by women of strength. Mormon women were not perceived by the general public as being worthy of much praise. That Augusta immortalized the women of *Representative Women* makes apparent her commitment to women and her desire to have them recognized for their merits. When the *Deseret News* reported in 1883 that Flora Hill was the first Mormon woman to undertake musical composition, Augusta's sense of justice flared and she wrote a detailed letter to the editor enumerating her own musical compositions, which had predated Hill's by some twenty years.[23]

It seems safe to assume that Augusta was more influenced by the women in her life than she was by the men. The men in her life receive comparatively short shrift: her real father is barely mentioned; her stepfather is afforded a complimentary but short paragraph; and her husband figures in only a few sentences. Augusta's interest in women might well be explained in psychological terms had we adequate information about her, but regardless of motivation, her need to honor women put her ahead of her time.

It is also to Augusta's credit that, despite her devotion to Mormonism, her themes involve universal Christian values and convey lessons that could apply to all. Her stories (particularly her children's stories), though highly moralistic, are not Mormonistic. There is much reference to God, but he is the Christian god of most nineteenth-century Americans, not a narrowly-defined deity with whom only Mormons could identify. That she eventually won some acclaim from non-Mormon sources and was published in non-sectarian journals evidences a broader appeal than one might expect.

One aspect of her writing that distinguishes her from most of her peers is her relatively liberal attitude toward nonwhites. *Manifest Destiny* and its inherent white chauvinism and paternalism was the credo of the day—nonwhites were considered inferior, and whites had a mission to civilize them according to white standards. Even the concession of some to the image of the *noble savage* was racist in its denial of the savage's human feelings and motivations. Augusta does not speak out adamantly against bigotry, but there is a seemingly unconscious undercurrent of humanism and a lack of prejudice in her writing.

The story of "Undrea"[24] is one example of this humanism. "Undrea" is a heart-rending account of a love triangle composed of a young, upstanding white man, his intended, and the lovely Indian maiden Undrea, with whom he unwittingly falls in love. Although the young man is the main character, Undrea receives as sympathetic a treatment and as much depth of character development as her white counterpart. Augusta avoids portraying Undrea as the symbol of passion and beauty only; at one point in the story this conversation takes place:

> *"Is there no hope of civilizing the savage?"*
> *"No, the influence of our Christian civilization acts corrosively on them, blighting rather than brightening their natures. If their rights rather than our own selfishness were studied it would be to their advantage ... We are the usurper of their possessions, destroyers of their rights, and barriers to their progress."*[25]

Augusta also uses examples from her mother's life to illustrate tolerance and understanding of other races.

Finally, Augusta does manage to achieve moments of objectivity and frankness, some humor, and even some comfortable skepticism. In her poem, "Earth Weary," her master asks, "What have you brought me?" and her first reaction is:

> *A broken heart all earth-defiled*
> *Whence faith in human kind is fled.*[26]

She is not unquestioning, and sometimes sheds her romantic vision to revile the difficulties God and life have visited upon her and others, and to wonder if enduring the struggle is worth the meager rewards.

In her paean to Mormon women, Augusta addresses the most controversial issue of polygamy with more equanimity than most other Mormon writers of that period, many of whom glossed over the issue with a light layer of celestial paint or ignored it entirely. Augusta never argues with the belief that polygamy was commanded by God himself; however, she is willing to point out that the introduction of polygamy into a previously monogamous Christian culture that had its roots in Puritanism was difficult for even the most righteous to accept. She recounts an incident in Sarah Kimball's life when the Prophet Joseph Smith told Sarah that he had been commanded to instruct her in the principle of eternal marriage. Sarah tells the prophet in no uncertain terms to go teach it to someone else![27]

More to the point is Augusta's inclusion in her chapter on Helen Mar Whitney of Helen Whitney's account of her long and debilitating struggle against the hardships polygamy had thrust upon her. Whereas most of the women in *Representative Women* possessed that never-give-up quality that causes privation to breed new strength and blessings to spring from injury, Helen frequently neared her limit and wanted very much to give up or escape, even through death. Helen, in an autobiographical statement that Augusta quotes, explained the defeat of her will to live as resulting from Satan's influence. Her spiritual ailment might today be diagnosed as depression: she passed an entire season in a tormented state; she lost her speech; she forgot the names of everyone and everything and was "living in another sphere." She had suffered through the western trek, but most of all, she admittedly hated polygamy deep in her heart. She eventually recovered, but it is evident that for her polygamy was anathema at the outset and remained an excruciating problem for her for some time.[28]

Whether Helen suffered from depression or from Satan's power is irrelevant to our consideration of Augusta, but the fact that the event is included in *Representative Women* is relevant. Many women must have anguished over their negative feelings about polygamy, but because it was considered a divine law and because of the intimate nature of the marriage relationship, there was much hesitation among Mormon women to admit their inability to live that law or to discuss openly their most personal problems involved in such an arrangement. Many women must have felt indebted to Augusta for including in her writing as a role model a woman who blamed polygamy for her unhappiness. The inclusion of such a woman must have made it easier for others to discuss their difficulties with this church doctrine and thereby probably afforded many women an enormous sense of relief.

Augusta did not view herself as an unusual woman or as a writer of great stature. The preface of her book of poetry is self-effacing and apologetic. She acknowledges that she would never have published it without the "kind encouragement of friends,"[29] and justifies her volume not for its "literary excellence" but as "a memento to those literary friends who will value the book for the sake of the author." She continues, "With this explanation, I hope the reader with whom I am unacquainted will overlook its defects."[30] The dedication is to Emmeline B. Wells, the editor of the Mormon women's newspaper, the *Woman's Exponent*, a woman who had given Augusta great moral support. Augusta writes of Emmeline:

> But for whose untiring encouragement and friendship my efforts would have remained in the obscurity of my desk, this volume is dedicated, wishing it were a more worthy tribute, and that it may prove an acceptable surprise.[31]

By present literary standards, Augusta was probably right—she was not a gifted writer. However, she was an important example for Mormon women and for other women as well. She valued her instinct to write enough to pursue that instinct, and she was often able to transcend the confines of a small, narrowly-defined society and to write for the world. She created for women a place in frontier history by hailing their contributions to the creation of western culture. She courageously defended her faith, and particularly the women of that faith, to the rest of the world. And she included in her writing an undercurrent of a humanistic and unprejudiced philosophy of the worth of human life, the fundamental quality of men and women, and the obligation individuals have to one another and to humanity.

Notes

1. Augusta Joyce Crocheron, *Representative Women of Deseret,* Salt Lake City: J. C. Graham Co., 1884.

2. *Ibid.*, p. 98.

3. *Ibid.*, pp. 98-101.

4. Crocheron says 1845; see also *Journal History,* February 4, 1846, for dates February 4, 1846, to July 31, 1846; see also Andrew Jenson, ed., *The Historical Record,* vol. 5, Andrew Jenson, Salt Lake City, 1886, for dates February 4, 1846, to July 31, 1846, pp. 875-76.

5. See especially, "California Memories", *Contributor* 7(1886):19, 23.

6. See especially, "Angela: A Christmas Story", *Contributor* 5 (1884):124 ff.

7. Augusta Joyce Crocheron, *Representative Women of Deseret,* pp. 106-7.

8. Augusta Joyce Crocheron, "To My Father" in *Wild Flowers of Deseret: A Collection of Efforts in Verse,* Salt Lake City: Juvenile Instructor Office, 1881, p. 238.

9. See *Contributor* 5 (1884):124 ff; 8(1887):112 ff.; also see *The Improvement Era,* May, 1915, p. 656.

10. Augusta Joyce Crocheron, *Wild Flowers of Deseret: A Collection of Efforts in Verse,* Salt Lake City, Juvenile Instructor Office, 1881.

11. Augusta Joyce Crocheron, *The Children's Book: A Mormon Book for Mormon Children,* Bountiful: A. J. Crocheron, 1890.

12. Lucy Larcum, *Wild Flowers of Cape Ann,* Boston: Houghton, Mifflin, and Co., 1881/1880.

13. Crocheron, "Wild Flowers" in *Wild Flowers of Deseret,* p. 3.

14. D. B. Wyndham Lewis and Charles Lee, *The Stuffed Owl,* New York: Capricorn Books, 1962, p. 234.

15. Crocheron, "Sunset" in *Wild Flowers,* p. 15.

16. Crocheron, "Trophies Taken in Love's Warfare" in *Wild Flowers,* p. 70.

17. Crocheron, "Introductory" from *Representative Women of Deseret.*

18. Crocheron, "Angela," p. 124.

19. *Ibid.*

20. Crocheron, *Representative Women of Deseret,* pp. 103-5.

21. *Ibid.,* p. 105.

22. See especially, "Zina D. H. Young, p. 16; "Sarah M. Kimball," p. 28; "Louie Felt," pp. 57-59; Emmeline B. Wells," pp. 62-71, in *Representative Women of Deseret.*

23. Augusta Joyce Crocheron, "Undrea, A Story of Real Life," *Contributor* 9(1888):68.

24. *Ibid.,* p. 68.

25. Crocheron, "Earth Weary" in *Wild Flowers,* p. 32.

26. Crocheron, *Representative Women of Deseret,* p. 26.

27. *Ibid.,* pp. 109-115.

28. Crocheron, "Preface" in *Wild Flowers of Deseret.*

29. Crocheron, Dedication in *Wild Flowers of Deseret.*

30. *Ibid.*

31. Augusta Joyce Crocheron, letter to editor, *Deseret News Weekly* 34(September 16, 1885):351.